SECULAR SENSIBILITIES

WHERE RELIGION LIVES
Kristy Nabhan-Warren, editor

Where Religion Lives publishes ethnographies of religious life. The series features the methods of religious studies along with anthropological approaches to lived religion. The religious studies perspective encompasses attention to historical contingency, theory, religious doctrine and texts, and religious practitioners' intimate, personal narratives. The series also highlights the critical realities of migration and transnationalism.

A complete list of books published in Where Religion lives is available at https://uncpress.org/series/where-religion-lives.

Secular Sensibilities

ROMANCE, MARRIAGE, AND CONTEMPORARY

ALGERIAN IMMIGRATION TO FRANCE AND QUÉBEC

....

JENNIFER A. SELBY

THE UNIVERSITY OF NORTH CAROLINA PRESS Chapel Hill

© 2025
The University of North Carolina Press
All rights reserved
Set in Utopia and TheSans by codeMantra
Manufactured in the United States
of America

Some interviews featured in this book have previously appeared in "Romance and the Male Secular Body: The Case of Algerian Men in France and Québec," *Journal of the American Academy of Religion* 90, no. 1 (March 2022): 248–69; "'There Is No Place for the State in the Bedrooms of the Nation' or The Case of Bill 21," in *Key Categories in the Study of Religion: Contexts and Critiques*, ed. Rebekka King, 162–75 (Endicott, NY: Equinox, 2022); "Required Romance: On Secular Sensibilities in Recent French Marriage and Immigration Regulations," in *Secular Bodies, Affects, and Emotions: European Configurations*, ed. Nadia Fadil, Birgitte Schepelern Johansen, and Monique Scheer, 157–69 (London: Bloomsbury, 2019); "Le *bled* en banlieue : le mariage musulman face à l'État français," *Ethnologie française* 4 (2017): 693–705; and "Un/veiling Women's Bodies: Secularism and Sexuality in Full-Face Veil Prohibitions in France and Québec," *Studies in Religion/Sciences Religieuses* 43, no. 3 (September 2014): 439–66.

Library of Congress Cataloging-in-Publication Data
Names: Selby, Jennifer A., author.
Title: Secular sensibilities : romance, marriage, and contemporary Algerian immigration to France and Québec / Jennifer A. Selby. Other titles: Where religion lives.
Description: Chapel Hill : The University of North Carolina Press, [2025] |
Series: Where religion lives | Includes bibliographical references and index.
Identifiers: LCCN 2024045138 |
ISBN 9781469685854 (cloth) |
ISBN 9781469685823 (paperback) |
ISBN 9781469685830 (epub) |
ISBN 9781469687698 (pdf)
Subjects: LCSH: Algerians—France—Social conditions. | Algerians—Québec (Province) —Social conditions. | Secularism—France. | Secularism—Québec (Province) | Islam and secularism—France. | Islam and secularism—Québec (Province) | Marriage —France. | Marriage—Québec (Province) | France—Emigration and immigration. | Québec (Province) —Emigration and immigration. | BISAC: RELIGION / Islam / General | SOCIAL SCIENCE / Gender Studies
Classification: LCC DC34.5.A4 S45 2025 |
DDC 305.892/765044—dc23/eng/20241118
LC record available at https://lccn.loc.gov/2024045138

This book will be made open access within three years of publication thanks to Path to Open, a program developed in partnership between JSTOR, the American Council of Learned Societies (ACLS), the University of Michigan Press, and the University of North Carolina Press to bring about equitable access and impact for the entire scholarly community, including authors, researchers, libraries, and university presses around the world. Learn more at https://about.jstor.org/path-to-open/.

For product safety concerns under the European Union's General Product Safety Regulation (EU GPSR), please contact gpsr@mare-nostrum.co.uk or write to the University of North Carolina Press and Mare Nostrum Group B.V., Mauritskade 21D, 1091 GC Amsterdam, The Netherlands.

FOR ÓSCAR.

Tu eres el aire, yo soy la vela . . .

CONTENTS

List of Illustrations *viii*

Introduction. Methods, Theories, Politics *1*

1. Secularism's Sexual Sensibilities and Body Politic *34*

2. Gender Politics in the Contact Zone *76*

3. Where Immigration Policy and Marriage Meet *119*

4. Coloniality, Kinship, and Desire *158*

Conclusion. Secular Romance *203*

Acknowledgments *217*

Notes *221*

References *239*

Index *271*

ILLUSTRATIONS

Figures

0.1. Bâtiment D in Petit-Nanterre, emptied for demolition *14*

1.1. "Faut-il un pacte avec l'islam de France?" *45*

1.2. Timeline of legislation on secular bodies in France, Canada, and Québec *48*

1.3. "Jihadist radicalization: The first warning signs" *56*

1.4. Government of Québec's 2013 pictogram for Bill 60 *59*

1.5. A soccer field at the Canibouts housing projects, Petit-Nanterre *68*

2.1. "The Republic is lived with an uncovered face" *103*

2.2. "Choose your suburb: Vote for the National Front" *104*

3.1. Nadia and Sofiane on their wedding day, 1971 *132*

4.1. Khalil on his wedding day, 2004 *170*

4.2. Eiffel Tower and snow globes figurines *180*

4.3. "Algerian Wedding" by Bruno Boudjelal *184*

4.4. Amel on her wedding party day, 2016 *185*

Maps

0.1. Petit-Nanterre, France, and its surroundings *15*

0.2. Montréal, Québec *18*

SECULAR SENSIBILITIES

INTRODUCTION
....

METHODS, THEORIES, POLITICS

On a warm afternoon in her apartment outside of Paris in May 2016, bouncing her eighteen-month-old son on her lap, twenty-eight-year-old Nawel explained how she had prepared herself for an appointment at the French consulate in Oran, Algeria, nearly three years earlier.[1] She and her new husband, Khalid, had just married in western Algeria thanks to a familial arrangement. As Algerian nationals seeking to live permanently in France, they needed to validate their Algerian wedding documents at the consulate for their future lives in the outskirts of Paris. As she described her encounter with French officials, Nawel's tone turned quiet. To shield against the sun, the shutters of her fourth-floor, one-bedroom walk-up were nearly closed; the baby's toys and highchair nestled nearby added an air of intimacy to our conversation.[2] She served deliciously cold lemon pudding she had prepared before my arrival and began sharing her experiences of marriage and migration from Algeria to France.

I first met Nawel two months earlier in Nanterre, a suburb northwest of Paris where she also lived, at an "Oriental" wedding show intended for brides interested in North African wedding styles.[3] Nawel had gone for a child-free afternoon with her husband Khalid's sister, who was planning a summer wedding in Algeria. The rented community hall was busy with women and young children who milled among vendors selling dresses, jewelry, catering options, and beauty services. At the center of the room, across from the vendor booths, was a raised catwalk flanked by dark red velvet drapes. Catered halal food in an adjacent room, with child-minding and prayer rooms next to it, meant women could spend the whole day at the wedding show. Near the end of the afternoon, the bridal fashion show began, announced by loud *rai*-style dance music blasting through two raised speakers at either end of the catwalk. The parade of wedding dresses was the main event.

By chance, Nawel and I had sat next to one another on plastic fold-up chairs. Most women had their cellphones readied, prepared to capture inspirational photos. I struck up a conversation, telling her about my research on marriage and migration over the loud music. She looked at me

{ 1

quizzically but accepted my research brochure, agreed to be interviewed, and wrote her mobile phone number inside my notebook. Over the next month or so, we spoke a few times by phone. I had invited her to meet at a café for lunch or a park with her son for an interview about her marriage and migration story, but she had too much to do at home, she said. She canceled twice, so I was especially thankful for this invitation to her apartment. Khalid worked full time as an event coordinator for the local municipality, and therefore was not present. While this ethnography also includes the experiences of French and Québécois men of Algerian origin, I was not able to connect with Khalid.

Nawel grew up in a middle-class family in the western Algerian city of Tlemcen, approximately forty kilometers from the Moroccan border. Her parents owned an export company and, she stressed, loved to tell the story of how they had met in France, when her father was on holiday. Theirs had been a "love" and not an arranged marriage like hers. Unlike most individuals of Algerian origin living near Paris and those in Montréal whom we will meet in this book, Nawel's mother, Maria, migrated from outside of Paris to Tlemcen for her marriage. Maria then settled in Algeria permanently.[4] Owing to her mother's background, Nawel held privileges in France: she spoke French fluently and had a French passport. When she finished her undergraduate degree studying literature at the university in the same western Algerian city, Nawel worked briefly in the family business. But, seeking to escape business and familial pressures, even if only for a year or two, she successfully applied to undertake graduate studies in Arab literature at the Université Sorbonne Nouvelle in Paris. Her parents agreed to the move, so long as she lived with and commuted from her maternal aunt's small apartment in a northeast suburb of the city. Such an arrangement would help with expenses and keep her *cadrée* (centered). Nawel had visited Paris before as a tourist, but now solo she enjoyed the freedoms afforded to her by her metro pass to explore the city and to window-shop. Two years passed. Her studies had gone well, but they did not fulfill her as she had hoped. Mostly, she explained, she could no longer ignore signs from God that it was time to marry.

As she stretched baby Yanis's pants over the clothes hanger to dry next to her, Nawel described how soon after, her mother mentioned in a weekly Skype call that she knew of a young man through a business colleague in Tlemcen. He was only a few years older than Nawel and also lived outside of Paris. Nawel agreed that her mother could share her phone number. She and Khalid began texting each other. They soon met at a café near the Sorbonne. The first meeting went well.

I asked Nawel if she had a mental image of her ideal marriage partner before she met Khalid. She shrugged, downplaying her own role in the arrangement. "Not really. Our meeting was destined, *et c'est tout*! [and that's it!]" Still, in our conversation, Nawel *did* mention criteria in describing her appreciation for him: Khalid already lived in France and knew how suburban Parisian life worked; he spoke French fluently; he had a secure job; his parents lived in Tlemcen like hers, which would facilitate their future transnational lives; and, most important for her, he already held French citizenship. In this conversation, Nawel did not reference the post-2006 French immigration laws curtailing family unification immigration that I examine in this book in tandem with secular laws, but Nawel *was* aware of potential marriage fraud. She worried that an Algerian-born potential husband could seek her out for an arranged union so she would sponsor him. She needed to be strategic. Her pragmatic tone continued when she described their first meeting, stating plainly, "He seemed kind. So, I was open to get to know him." Because of the cost of text-messaging, she and Khalid continued chatting by MSN Messenger in the evenings. There were no red flags. She felt they could build a life together, so, three weeks later, Nawel agreed to marry him.

They shared the news with their parents. The planning happened quickly. Her parents and in-laws took care of organizing two modest receptions in Tlemcen. She focused on purchasing the right eight dresses, including the ornate *chedda* dress and jewels, typical of that region, for the wedding party (see another participant's chedda in fig. 4.4). With these purchases, Nawel began adopting common consumer-culture practices around weddings, here in relation to attire and objects for her nuptials.

Nawel and Khalid had had an arranged marriage. In her words, "It wasn't a love marriage. We didn't know each other. And we didn't have a lot of time to get to know one another because the marriage came together really, really quickly: two months from the proposal to the wedding. So, we weren't very ready. We didn't know what to expect [at the French consulate in Oran, validating their marriage]." "It wasn't a love marriage"—the absence of signs of sexual intimacy between them, she feared, could raise alarm bells for French consular staff. I did not prompt Nawel in our interview to tell me that hers was not a "love marriage"; it was she who framed her relationship with Khalid as a likely problem for state officials at the consulate. She shared her preparations for this appointment in response to my open-ended questions about how she had experienced migration from Algeria and how and where she had married. Because of the short time frame in which the marriage came together—as she noted matter-of-factly, "really, really quickly: two months from the proposal to the wedding"—and because it was arranged by their parents, she had worried about how their union would be perceived at the French consulate. It mattered. Their goal was to settle outside of Paris permanently.

I recount Nawel's experiences to begin to think about how racialized and religionized foreign nationals seeking to settle in France face heightened scrutiny of their intimate relationships and pressure to embody and externalize a range of what I call "secular sensibilities" (cf. Fadil 2009; and Wiering 2017). Without ostensible signs of romance—that is, externalized signs of specific gender and sexual politics to which their relationship conformed—the couple could be accused of "*escroquerie sentimentale à but migratoire*" (love fraud with a migratory aim) and/or have their marriage annulled. This judgment would not only jeopardize their legal status in France and impede their access to a *livret de famille*—the state-delivered "family book" necessary for a number of administrative tasks, like renting an apartment, or applying for a mortgage or other state-run programs—it would also be embarrassing. Their relationship was sincere; they were simply less capable of and willing to perform these intimacies for consular staff. More broadly, Nawel's experience reflects a dynamic that plays out routinely for Algerian migrants who are circulating in the Francophone world to places like France and Québec.

In France and Québec, as racialized immigrants of Algerian origin, many of my participants are recurringly confronted by these sensibilities in the so-called public sphere in ways white, non-Muslim, nonimmigrants may not experience. The presence of their bodies ignites these sensibilities. My focus on one country of origin—Algeria—is deliberate. I hope it allows for a more pointed comparison of nation-state policies regarding colonialism, immigration, transnational marriage, and secularism. Women and men (and others) are often called upon to bracket their religious sensibilities in order to follow abstract liberal principles (cf. Amir-Moazami 2022; Bracke and Hernández Aguilar 2020; Schepelern Johansen 2022). Gender matters, both in how secular sensibilities are imagined by French and Québécois governments and in public parlance (that is, in binary cishet, cisgender, and heterosexual ways) and in how they are experienced by my interlocutors; veiled, racialized women reported experiences of surveillance to the greatest extent (cf. Razack 1998: 13 on "interlocking" privilege). Expressions of romance and signs of intimacy, I will argue, are prominent features of these sensibilities and are reinforced by long-standing ideas about chivalry, seduction, and sexual attraction, as well as consumer cultures. Because immigration opportunities are also at stake in the "contact zone" between the state and individuals I examine, civil marriage offers a performative ritual moment where gender, familial, and religious norms overlap, revealing many of these sensibilities.

A great deal of scholarly attention has been paid to the increasing number of laws in France and Québec that penalize visibly religious bodies. While noting these contributions, in this book, I ask a different set of questions: What are the resulting sought-after sensibilities that emerge *counter* to these restrictions? If we accept that secularism is not solely an abstract principal, what are its visual and affective forces? How do secular sensibilities play out in people's intimate lives, namely in how individuals love (or not) and marry (or not)? I will argue that, among others, these sensibilities delineate acceptable gender performances in the public sphere. Characterizations of religion are part of this register; religion is often depicted as rigid and sexually limiting. Put differently, I aim to move away from solely examining the restrictions against conservative religious bodies in France and Québec to consider, in contrast, the *content* of what is imagined as the "desirable" secular body. What is this emancipated secular body according to the logics in these laws? How does it influence the lives of religious and racialized individuals?

Based on extensive, binational comparative ethnographic research, this book interrogates the secular-sexual-racial politics of the transatlantic marriage and migration of Algerians to France and Québec to theorize coloniality and secularism in legal and state spheres as well as in personal and embodied ones. The content, values, and emotions of secular sensibilities that surface in the contact zones around civil marriage in contemporary France and Québec can be read through several lenses. I focus on their governance related to proper religiosity, sexuality, and race.[5]

To be clear: my interlocutors may or may not identify as "secular." Most do not. I do not recount the sensibilities of expressly secular people. Rather, more phenomenologically, I consider how pervasive secular sensibilities shape the ways my interlocutors love and live. I distinguish between so-called religious and secular bodies for heuristic purposes, with full acknowledgment that, empirically, people do not conform to such fixed categories (see also Burchardt 2020: 43). I trace how appropriate expressions of sexuality, religion, and race are articulated in legislation on *laïcité*, and also, through the long-standing influences of coloniality, marriage, and migration, and how these shape individuals. Visual materials that emphasize religious symbols offer a facile visual assessment of secular sensibilities and radically minimize religious beliefs, traditions, and practices to pass/fail visual cues. In both France and Québec, an almost-required legibility of demonstrable love affects racialized and religionized minorities, in ways that echo colonial politics. The narratives I heard of transnational marriage and migration are thus helpful to interrogate preferred secular sensibilities, whether by state officials, whom I do not interview, or by individuals of Algerian origin, who are my focus. In the early stages of this project, I spent one field season unsuccessfully seeking to broker entry into Nanterre Préfecture, the city's central governmental building, to observe civil weddings (akin to the work later undertaken by Levanchy 2015 in Switzerland). For privacy reasons, my requests to access the civil marriage chambers at the Préfecture were stonewalled. It is no accident that other scholars who have studied immigration policy and marriage migration in France have done so not through state institutions but through activist organizations that lobby for the rights of transnational marriage partners (see Odasso 2016 and Odasso and Salcedo Robledo 2022). Sociologist Julia Martínez-Ariño (2019, 2021) analyzes the work undertaken by municipal workers and politicians in Rennes, Bordeaux, and Toulouse, with attention to how they respond to mundane and pragmatic public requests related to "migration-driven religious diversity" and not that which is marriage related (2021: 4). Martínez-Ariño notes that when related to Islam, these requests typically trigger a counter "normative religiosity" or Catholic response. Also likely for privacy reasons, we do not learn about the individuals brokering these requests. Due to these constraints, on the subject of marriage ceremonies, with the exception of the four marriages I attended, I rely primarily on the retelling of these moments in this book.

Civil marriage is perhaps not an obvious site for an examination of secular contestations and negotiations or the ever-presentness of secular sensibilities. To make this link, I take a cue from secularism studies scholars who suggest that the most generative way of examining secularism is tangentially or "through the shadows" (Farham 2013; Lee 2015: 88; Asad 2018: 3; Lemons 2019; Singh Judge 2020; Schepelern Johansen 2022). My aim in doing so is not to facilely suggest that the surveillance of marriage and romance is a racialized and gendered form of statecraft. Rather, this book's centering of the lived experiences of transnational Algerian and Algerian-origin individuals, couples, and communities aims to take this shadow approach to see where, when, and for whom secular sensibilities are ignited or rendered banal.

A distinction proposed by the anthropologist Michel-Rolph Trouillot (1995) has been helpful to me in situating the lineage, apparently unlikely on the surface, between my interlocutors of Algerian origin and my examination of secular sensibilities: Trouillot separates one's "object of study" from one's "object of observation."[6] This book takes as its object of study the politics laden in legal and policy articulations as well as in public parlance and individual interpretations of state secularism, especially their promise of gender equality and color blindness. At a more surface level, I investigate the narratives of my interlocutors of Algerian origin in France and Québec and their engagements with the state at the time of marriage. The state control of civil marriage matters given how, for some of my interlocutors, family reunification through marriage has served as a central migratory conduit. As we will see, legislation in France in 2006, 2011, and 2021 aimed specifically to curtail non-French and non-EU national marital unions (in Canada, also in 2006, "bad faith" marriages came under scrutiny).

Returning to Nawel, she and Khalid held French citizenship, but in order to return to the suburbs of Paris with the right paperwork for their *livret de famille*, they needed their Algerian marriage documents to be certified by French officials at the consulate in Oran. Overseas departments mirror the laws and scrutiny of the metropole. Nawel was prepared. She had read online forums and gathered tips from a French-born cousin who had married a woman of Algerian origin the year before. She expected questions to be posed to her and Khalid separately to determine their emotional and sexual intimacy. Their paperwork was in order. In theory, she had nothing to be worried about. Following the categories introduced in 2006 marriage legislation, their recent marriage was neither "fake" (known as a *mariage blanc*), "fraudulent" (a *mariage gris*), nor "forced" (a *mariage forcé*), classifications introduced by French legislation curtailing non-EU marriage partner unions and intended to curb "illegitimate" transnational marriage. Their marriage certificate–related request was entirely procedural.

But even if Nawel was unaware of the specific contents of the series of French laws curbing non-EU transnational marriage, she knew the Republic had introduced increased scrutiny to impede "love fraud with a migratory aim." A French government memorandum that circulated in 2010 required marriage officiants and consular staff to better assess couples' sexual and emotional intimacy, especially when citizenship was at stake. According to this memorandum, sincerity can be measured through evidence of the genesis of the relationship, who paid for the rings, the couples' living arrangements, and so on. Some symbols signaled emotional and sexual intimacy, like diamond rings, gifts, and romantic gestures. Others, like some religious symbols, did not, and raised questions about a bride or groom's individual agency. Couples like Nawel and Khalid, who did not yet share emotional, sexual, or financial intimacy at their civil wedding, were disproportionally burdened by the performance of appropriate intimacy. Penalties range from annulment, to deportation, to fines and jail time. Civil marriage, especially for transnational actors like some of my Algerian-origin interlocutors, is thus a site where secular sensibilities are constructed, enforced, and negotiated, and is therefore a helpful "contact zone" to examine interactions between individuals and the state. As the reader is surely aware, legislation and popular parlance do not include concern for the longevity of these unions. Divorce rates in France and Québec suggest that premarital intimacies do not necessarily translate into long-term unions.[7] So, what *is* at stake?

It was this judgment of their appropriate intimacy that made Nawel most nervous about the consular appointment. An unprompted description of how she prepared for the appointment tells us about how she understood these expectations translated onto the body. She woke up two hours early to thoroughly blow-dry her hair. She carefully set a chignon with dozens of hairpins and hair spray. The formality of this hairstyle—a classic French *chignon du cou* (meaning a "nape-of-the-neck bun"), where the hair is swept off the neck and secured in a more formal twist than an ordinary bun—can be read as a marker of femininity, social class, and whiteness.[8] She purchased special hair-styling products. She normally keeps her hair in a ponytail and does not use a hair dryer or hairspray. She applied her makeup in a purposeful "French style," with red lipstick, pink blush, mascara, and no dark kohl eyeliner. Her cosmetics reveal an awareness of the Orientalist tropes associated with dark eyeliner, and, perhaps, knowledge of the signal of sexual availability in her red lipstick. Nawel also intuited that entering this government space wearing a *djellaba*, a long and loose gownlike dress, without visible makeup (or worse, with dark eyeliner applied around her eyes) and with the intention of returning to France with an Algerian-national and Muslim-identified spouse from an arranged marriage, would render her suspicious, undesirable, and unagentic. She had sought to signal her sophistication, and her knowledge and facility with ways of moving and being appropriately feminine before French government representatives.[9]

She also privatized her religiosity. While Nawel did not yet wear a headscarf, its presence at the French consulate would have presumably further destabilized these desirable gendered and secular sensibilities. With a visible sign of religiosity, the onus of performing proper sensibilities through other means—her speech, demeanor or otherwise—would have been even more important. Religious symbols, especially the niqab or full-face-covering veil, impede acceptable performances of femininity.

Nawel's offhand comment about setting her hair and makeup so to be seen as appropriately secular and feminine is an example of what I see as her seeking to inculcate secular sensibilities. With attention to what sociologist Pierre Bourdieu (1977) called "habitus," or socially ingrained habits, skills, and dispositions, I read Nawel's interpretation of a dress code at the consulate as her internalization of the French state's concerns with the visibility of Islam and traditional arranged marriages. She did not plan to dress "disruptively" (cf. Robson 2013: 103). Rather, to "pass" in this potentially volatile contact zone, Nawel aimed to present her body as socially and sexually acceptable in the eyes of the state. She consciously refashioned her body, emotions, and social comportment to render herself a "good" (read: moderate, liberal) Algerian woman. Secular sensibilities in contemporary France paint Islam-related religious symbols (read: modest dress) as especially rigid and sexually limiting, and narrowly contour acceptable public performances of racialized and religionized women *and* men (if less overtly for the latter).

These sensibilities are powerful precisely because they are not clearly articulated top-down requirements. The state's gaze is not all-pervasive. No one told Nawel that a chignon and red lipstick would help her secure her paperwork. Nawel intuited acceptable femininity, as many women do, and woke up early to ensure she had time to comply. Expectations for secular sensibilities—especially as they relate to personal habitus—are powerful because they pair liberal forms of social regulation with individual self-regulation, consumerism, and pleasure. Biopolitical and capitalist expressions are part of the wedding industry, and trickle into rituals and habituses. Expressions of the secular body are not simply imposed by the state. They can be sources of enjoyment. In complex ways, my participants often happily reproduce these tropes in both their contacts with the state and in their weddings.[10]

In Nawel and Khalid's case, perhaps because she marked her body as "secular," or perhaps because she had overestimated the consulate's scrutiny of their arrangement, the couple were *not* subject to separate questioning on their emotional and sexual intimacy, as implied by the 2010 officiant directives I examine, and as experienced by other interlocutors. They received the paperwork necessary for their French family book and settled in Nanterre. They rented an apartment. Yanis was born. The specter of the surveillance of these sensibilities is thus more powerful than their application.

That Nawel prepared herself for this government appointment can be expected. We all perform our social class, gender, values, and politics every day through our gestures, speech, and dress (cf. Goffman 1956). These performances are not necessarily insincere. We learn about dress codes and protocols for different spaces and audiences, especially in the face of power differentials, like when government documents or citizenship are at stake. Still, we respond differently to these expectations. So too, Nawel's contact zone experience with the French state in Oran is not meant to be representative of the diverse women and men of Algerian origin I interviewed. We will see how their narratives evidence wide-ranging responses to how their bodies are imagined and performed in moments of contact with state officials. Nawel, for one, is racialized and self-identified as Muslim. She spoke French fluently and held several other class privileges. She also called herself a "rules follower." Nawel expressly did not want to rock the boat and challenge state officials at the consulate. She just wanted the certificate. Others, we will see, find expectations for the performance of romance more challenging. Some may or may not perform preferred sexual, emotional, and/or financial intimacies. Others eschew the neoliberalism, consumer capitalism, and hyperindividualism that undergird these expectations. We will also see distinctions related to Algerian immigration and settlement policies in both national contexts and how they also shape individual narratives.

"Love fraud," as defined by the French state, and "bad faith" marriages, as delineated by the Canadian federal government, have both individual and collective implications: individual as related to the potential emotional transgression of deception in love; and collective, in a potential illegal transgression of national borders should citizenship be granted. Notions of romance entrench acceptable citizenry and sexual politics based on highly individualized choices that center love and attraction above any other rationale for monogamous marriage, in contradistinction to those based on kinship-organized arrangements, as was the case for Nawel and Khalid. Focusing on an individual and their sexual agency and emancipation dissociates them from their communities (see Bhuyan, Korteweg, and Baqi 2018: 364; and Gaucher 2016: 520 on this mechanism in the Canadian case). Not unrelatedly, legislation in both places in 2010 and 2019 that restricts the wearing of full-face veils does similar work to firmly establish unacceptable religious and gendered bodies as sexually unagentic, lacking desirable individualism, and as eschewing commercialized and cosmeticized norms of beauty and consumption. Niqab laws also do a lot of work to delineate secular sensibilities in relation to gender norms.

Nawel's interpretation of how secular sensibilities should appear on her body relate to three contributions in this book: First, despite their different histories and legal frameworks on religion and secularism, legislation on secularism in France and Québec since 2004, along with immigration reforms since 2006, have dovetailed.[11] Second, calls for a secular readability as a response to political ills have sharpened. In contrast to social scientific literature on the secular body that initially largely argued that secularism is "the water we swim in" (cf. Hirschkind 2011), or that its normativity makes it invisible (Asad 2011; Connolly 2011), I show that contemporary French and Québécois contexts increasing require externalized markers of secularism. They *require a legibility* of secularism on the bodies of men and women. Those who are racialized as Muslim and newcomers may no longer be passively secular. Their bodies and faces must be visually accessible. Ideally, they should publicly demarcate consent, individualism, and rationalism, with homonationalist (cf. Puar 2013) and gender-egalitarian views. Third, in noting which markers of secularism are maneuvered and by whom, I trace the concomitant work that secularisms and their sensibilities do to the categories of gender and race, particularly vulnerable at the border. In this vein, I examine secularism's politics in contemporary France and Québec in relation to what Michel Foucault (2008) calls "biopolitics," to what Walter Mignolo and Catherine Walsh (2018) call "coloniality," and to what Aníbal Quijano (2000) calls the "coloniality of power." I return to this theorization following a discussion of methodologies.

Methodologies

This study draws on a tripartite methodological approach: ethnographic data and 187 interviews with French and Québécois interlocutors of Algerian origin collected between 2011 and 2019; political, legislative, and cultural discursive analysis related to laïcité and immigration policies in France and Québec after 2004; and, more broadly, a binational connective comparison of these two contexts.[12] France and Québec connect in obvious and less obvious ways.[13] I undertook interviews and extensive ethnographic fieldwork in a mostly Algerian-origin suburb fifteen kilometers northwest of Paris called Petit-Nanterre, in different neighborhoods in Montréal, and through two transnational marriage trips to Tizi Ouzou and Ghazaouet, Algeria.[14] Discourse analysis focused on law, policy, and government reports. I draw these methodologies together through a "connective comparison" (cf. Weinbaum et al. 2008) to conceptualize how laws and policies on secularism, religious freedom, and immigration shape how Algerians migrate and marry in ways that are connected and in conversation.[15]

It goes without saying that positionality matters in the world and in conducting research. My status as a white, able-bodied, cisgender, and foreign Canadian Anglophone enabled these encounters in Petit-Nanterre more than in Montréal, where I was less conspicuous. Following Éléonore Lépinard (2020: 81), I mean whiteness not only in terms of racialization but also as "a material, cultural, and subjective location of privilege." I endeavored to consider power dynamics, especially when volunteering in a drop-in community center in Petit-Nanterre, not to engage in any recruitment when assisting individuals experiencing stress or precarity (see Selby 2012: 198n14 on some sharp perceptions by my host family in Petit-Nanterre regarding my weaknesses). Moreover, as I develop in the next section, the colonial underpinnings of this anthropological project infused many moments of this ethnography. I now turn to my two primary field sites.

PETIT-NANTERRE, FRANCE

More tangibly, my fieldwork site in France is located in Petit-Nanterre, a *banlieue* or suburb fifteen kilometers northwest of the Arc de Triomphe, bordering the Seine River on the north side and the Université Paris Nanterre on the south (see map 0.1). I have known several of my interlocutors of Algerian origin from Petit-Nanterre who are featured in this book since I began ethnographic fieldwork there in 2004. In *Questioning French Secularism: Gender Politics and Islam in a Parisian Suburb* (2012), I examined how seventy first-generation Muslim-self-identified North African women living in Petit-Nanterre negotiated their identities postmigration in the context of restrictions on hijabs in government offices and public schools imposed in 2004. The majority of these interlocutors were of Algerian origin, including the family with whom I lived from 2005 to 2006.[16] The seeds of this book were thus sown in that project, as marriage migration was a primary driver for these women's settlement.[17]

Following Franz Fanon (1967), we can see the politics of domination laden in the colonization of this Parisian suburb, in particular the unequal interrelationship between core (i.e., Paris) and periphery (i.e., Petit-Nanterre). The banlieues of France are not the suburbs of North America. They symbolize the fall of industrialization, the failures of colonialism, the realities of racism (in securing the whiteness of urban centers), and racialized unemployment. Racism appears in poverty, school failure, and for young men especially, youth criminality, incarceration, and attacks by (and on) police (Beaud and Pialoux 2003; Wacquant 2005; Selby 2009b; Truong 2013, 2017; Collet 2019, 2023). During my daily commute on public transit from various small rental apartments in the south of Paris, where I stayed with my partner and daughters over the years, to Petit-Nanterre, I regularly witnessed racial profiling and anti-Muslim racism: my whiteness shielded me from a direct altercation. In one case, returning to Paris by bus, tramway, and interurban train, I escaped the carding and suspicion experienced by racialized male youths. Busing works on the honor system, with sporadic ticket checks by RATP (the state-owned public transport) controllers. On this late afternoon on an overcrowded bus, I did not have a ticket or easy access to purchase one, and chose to risk penalty, squeezing in with a dozen others through the back door of an extended bus on its way to La Défense, where the interurban train connects passengers to Paris. When six controllers blocked all three bus entrances two stops later, I knew I would not escape a fine. And yet, I did. I was invisible to the two middle-aged controllers at the entrance nearest to me, who did not even make eye contact to acknowledge I was seen but not targeted. I stood there sheepishly, waiting for them to give me a fine, but they never asked me to show my stamped ticket. A half-dozen racialized young men were their focus and were removed from the bus.

Petit-Nanterre's distance from Paris is not geographical (Selby 2009b). The area was once the location of the largest shantytown in France during the industrial period between World War I and World War II, with more than 10,000 inhabitants (Benaïcha 1992; Charef 2006; Selby 2009b). Sociologist Abdelmalek Sayad, a student of Pierre Bourdieu, wrote his graduate thesis about this shantytown in the early 1950s. Sayad (1995) describes the draw of Petit-Nanterre for Algerians: by 1953, the *bidonville*'s population was fourteen times greater than in 1946. This growth, Sayad (1995: 32) explains, was due to a "phenomenon of contagion," where friends, family members, and acquaintances of Algerian origin incited each other to *se bidonvilliser* (to "shantytown themselves"). The abominable physical conditions—with constant threats of rats, water, mud, and fire—were superseded by more systemic traumas of physical and economic alienation. Moreover, amid the Algerian War of Independence, the Algerian National Liberation Front undertook transnational organizing in Petit-Nanterre. In response, French state surveillance of the area began in earnest. Its flimsy shacks with limited water and other service access were bulldozed in the 1960s, and, in a notable improvement initiated by the state, replaced by high-rise concrete social housing. But, within a decade, the pejorative social implications of these high-rises were felt. A subsequent "Franco" or "white" flight from Petit-Nanterre first occurred in the 1970s. Around the same time, French national immigration policy shifts in the 1970s began to favor family reunification, so many more women and children, especially from Algeria, settled in Petit-Nanterre. Residents describe the demise of industrialization and the loss of employment in the 1980s. A significant drug trade characterized the suburb in this decade, as did malaise and growing Islamophobia and discrimination by law enforcement. Since the 2010s, the suburb has seen gentrification. A tramway line in neighboring Colombes now better connects the area to La Défense, the business district just outside the city's periphery, and then to the RER network and Paris.

Figure 0.1. Bâtiment D in Petit-Nanterre, emptied for demolition, February 2016. Photo by the author.

Tensions between state improvements to the area and state surveillance remained evident through the 2010s. Riots following the deaths of young, racialized men in this area and nearby banlieues in 2005 and 2023 capture the tensions related to police surveillance and violence (Selby 2013; Collet 2023). Social housing conditions and access also reflect changing programs by the state. One of the largest high-rises, a ten-story building known in the neighborhood as Bâtiment D, notorious for its degradation, faulty elevators, and drug dealing, was demolished at the end of 2016. This photograph (see fig. 0.1) shows a middle stage in its demolition, where residents had already moved out. With the destruction of large housing projects like this one, the population of this neighborhood decreased substantially between 2011 and 2016, from 8,800 to 6,900. Mixed public and private three-story low-rise housing complexes have replaced Bâtiment D. Its former residents have limited access to the new builds; most were forced to relocate further away from Paris to areas not yet gentrified, or as well connected via tramway to La Défense.

Most of Petit-Nanterre's residents live in social housing, sometimes inhabiting the same apartment over several generations (see Selby 2014b). Aisha, a woman in her fifties with two daughters, with whom I lived in 2005–6, first moved into the apartment when she married her first husband, whose parents were its first occupants in the 1960s. The family has thus lived in the same social housing unit for more than fifty years. Together,

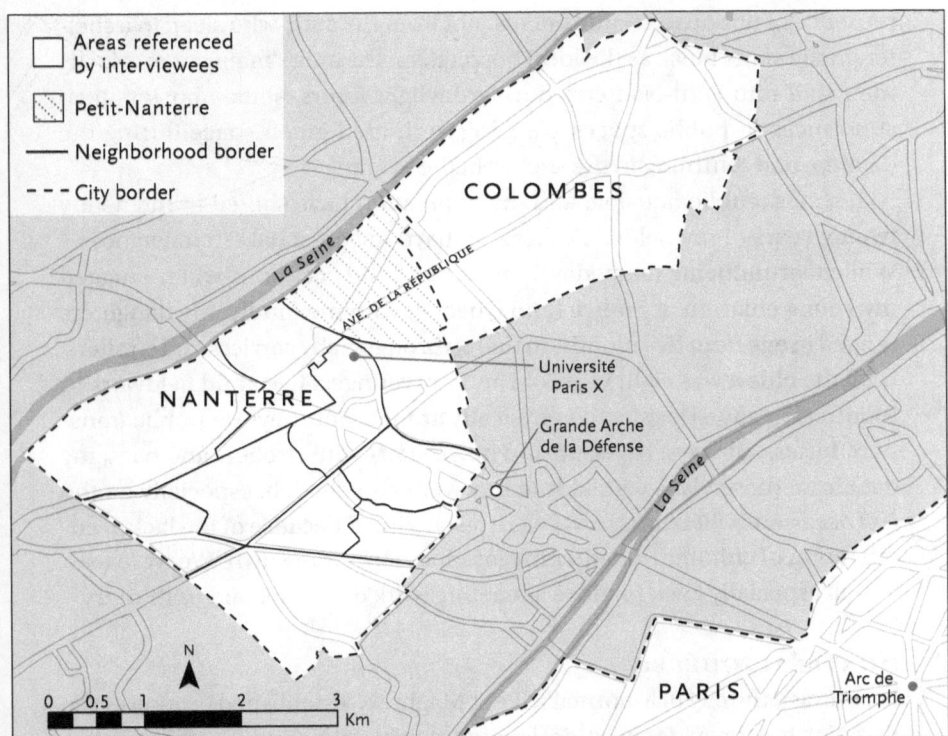

Map 0.1. Petit-Nanterre, France, and its surroundings.

the history of Algerian-based reunification and attraction to paid work, as well as, for some, like Aisha, the stability of living in the same government-sponsored housing, mean that the area is relatively culturally and religiously homogenous compared to other suburbs (Kepel 1987, 2012). Most inhabitants are believing but not practicing Sunni Muslims. The most architecturally impressive building on the avenue de la République is the Sunni, Algerian-based Okba Mosque built in 1974. The local commerce reflects the foodways of its inhabitants: two bakeries offer baguettes and *khobz el dar* (Algerian flatbread); the Greek takeaway restaurant clearly announces that its offerings are halal; and there are also two busy halal butcher shops. Even decades after the initial settlement of so many inhabitants in its shantytown, Petit-Nanterre's population still consists of 30.8 percent first-generation immigrants (INSEE 2015). Unemployment is a significant problem. In 2018, 36.3 percent of Nanterre was officially unemployed (INSEE 2018); this percentage is higher in Petit-Nanterre, the poorest neighborhood in the city of Nanterre. The suburb's disenfranchisement is accentuated by the continued

METHODS, THEORIES, POLITICS {15

presence of unhoused nonresidents, not from the area, who sleep in a shelter on the same block as the local hospital, on the area's main street. Mostly men spill into Petit-Nanterre during daylight hours, some abusing illicit substances in public spaces, sleeping in limited green space during the daytime and returning to the shelter in the evening.

If shops, public housing, and the population have shifted in the nearly twenty years of my fieldwork there, so have my personal circumstances.[18] While tear-inducing many days, I now recall the occasions when I lugged my young children in France (and Québec) with me fondly. My daughters ranged in age from five months in utero, through baby carriers and strollers, until the oldest was eight years old and my youngest five amid fieldwork in Montréal in 2019. Despite the physically arduous journeys on public transport, buses, subways, bikes, up and down stairs with strollers and bags, my data from those visits with kids in tow were equally rich, especially on the few occasions when interviews were rescheduled because of the lack of cooperation of children, whether my interlocutors' or my own. We were usually all especially keen to make a meeting work on the second or third try.

MONTRÉAL, QUÉBEC

In contrast, the city of Montréal's "Petit Maghreb," established in 2009 as the first North African–focused designated neighborhood in North America, appears to signal a concentration of inhabitants of North African origin.[19] The designation is more commercial than residential. Annick Brabant (2017) notes that in 2014, 38 percent of businesses (46 of 120) in the Petit Maghreb were North Africa–related, whether restaurants, grocery stores, bakeries, or halal butcher shops. Also, despite the official designation, the Petit Maghreb is home to a mixed population. In contrast to Petit-Nanterre, Montrealers of Algerian origin live throughout the city. Urban geographer Bochra Manaï (2018) shows that only 12.9 percent of Algerians live in the Villeray–Saint-Michel–Parc-Extension region, which includes the Petit Maghreb, and so it is hardly a concentration. The differing configurations of my field sites—comparing the experiences of people who mostly live in one banlieue of Paris with those who live throughout Montréal—influenced my data. Unlike the number of individuals of Algerian origin in the suburbs of Paris, there are no notable Algerian-focused neighborhoods or mosques in Montréal like the Okba Mosque in Petit-Nanterre (Castel 2010). Most Montrealers of Algerian origin live in the east-end Francophone-focused parts of the island. The Saint-Léonard neighborhood in the northeast has the highest concentration (13.8 percent of the Algerian population; see Manaï 2018: 51).[20] This dispersal influenced how I collected data. Unlike my fieldwork in Petit-Nanterre, the months I spent in Montréal undertaking interviews, also with two research assistants, meant I was walking, biking, and taking buses and metro trains around the city. I did meet a handful of participants in cafés and restaurants in the Petit Maghreb, mostly at the Algerian-owned Table Fleurie pastry café on the rue Jean-Talon Est or at the Algerian Cultural Centre on the same street, but most of my interlocutors lived in the Saint-Léonard, Ahuntsic, and Cartierville neighborhoods, with four living off the island in Laval and commuting into the city to work (see map 0.2). In general, participants in Montréal were more affluent. Methodologically, my data reflect these idiosyncrasies, namely the significant differences in how my participants lived, and where and how I interviewed them.

In Montréal, I had five key informants before I began fieldwork who were friends, or friends and relatives of friends, who assisted with snowball sampling, and whom I got to know quite well, with multiple outings, visits to their homes, and meetings with their families. However, because I spent a total of five months in the city, and wanted a sample that held up to the interviews I conducted in France, the eighty-nine interviews undergirding this part of the research include more than half undertaken by two graduate research assistants, Julia Itel and Kawtare Bihya.[21] While I set the interview schedule for these interviews, their own positionalities and relationships with the interviewees obviously shaped the data they collected. Julia and Kawtare wrote notes about the contexts of their interviews, as well as on the mood and physicality of their informants. I found these notes helpful while listening to, reading, and coding the interviews they conducted, but I was admittedly more detached from their data than the data I collected myself. I would characterize the research conducted in Montréal as more sociological than anthropological, in that in some cases I met interlocutors once or twice to conduct an interview. In Petit-Nanterre, by contrast, I knew some participants for a dozen years before interviewing them for this project. All this is to say that, ethnographically speaking, this project's underlying comparison is far from perfect, but I believe the connective comparative framework still provides valuable insights.

While I separate them throughout my analysis, France and Québec are linked for many individuals. France remains a referent for all my Montréal informants of Algerian origin. Some had migrated to France first and/or believed Québec offered an easier path toward permanent residency and better professional opportunities. Others suggested that Québec was more challenging because of the colder climate and distance from Algeria. Others had visited or had family in France. While a half-dozen interlocutors in Petit-Nanterre had visited or, in two cases, previously lived in Montréal,

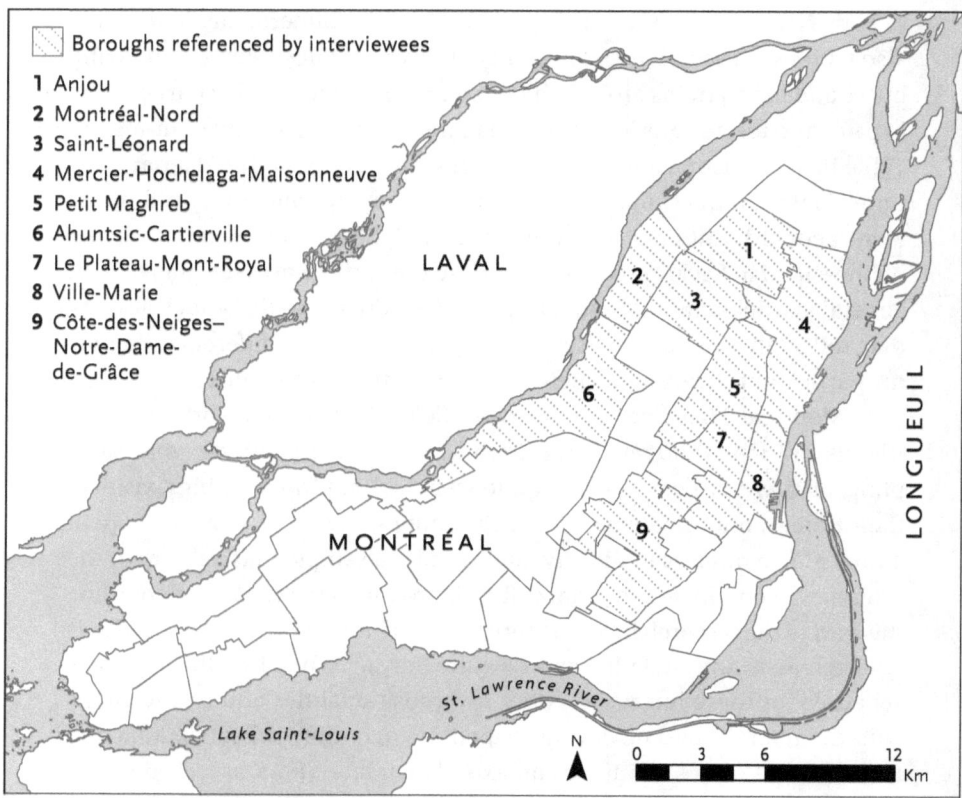

Map 0.2. Montréal, Québec.

Québec was less present in the migratory circuits of my Algerian-origin interlocutors in France. In both instances, Algerians have a complex and long-standing relationship with France given its colonization for more than 132 years. The ongoing impacts of the violence, including torture, and other adverse impacts of this colonial relationship continue to be experienced and debated today.[22] Several of my interlocutors in Petit-Nanterre were born in Algeria prior to its independence in 1962 and held French passports before having ever immigrated to France, facilitating their arrival from the 1950s through to the mid-1970s.[23] In general, interlocutors in Montréal have quite different migration trajectories, largely arriving in the province beginning in the 1990s, as Québec opened to refugees of Algeria's *Décennie noire* (Dark Decade), a period of civil war when between 60,000 and 150,000 Algerians were killed (Stora 1992; Verdier 2018).

Participants

I feature fewer than half of the individuals I interviewed for this project in this book. The voices and experiences shared here are all of people who are tied to Algeria through birth or family lineage. Nevertheless, their shared *algérianité* betrays the diversity among them related to social class, race, belief, practice, ethnicity, and immigration experience. I interviewed more women than men, who were more challenging to recruit (approximately 60 percent of my sample in France and 70 percent in Québec were women); the sample includes only one self-identified nonbinary participant.

Participants' sense of religiosity ranged tremendously, from atheist to nonbeliever, and from believer to conservative practitioner. I aim to take variations of nonreligious belief and practice as seriously as I do religious ones. Attention to a so-called lived religion approach is helpful in taking my interlocutors' religion *and* nonreligion seriously.[24] A lived religion approach allows for a broader metacritique of the secular episteme in the production of knowledge on religion and nonreligion. That is, an overarching secular episteme in France and Québec necessarily problematizes categories of religion for my interlocutors (and for me). Because a lived religion approach positions religiosity as a significant mode of inquiry, it is a useful perspective given this project's broader intellectual situatedness in a largely secular time and place. A lived religion approach thus encourages awareness of how secularisms also possess affect, beliefs, practices, and habitus.

Many of my Algerian-origin interlocutors identified as Muslim, even if only culturally. For most, tradition includes Islam, and also relates to the *Bled*, or Algerian country of origin, to kinship ties, and to Algerian culture and language, whether Arabic, Tamazight (Berber), or French. Participants interviewed in Montréal tended to be both more practicing *and* more atheist or nonpracticing. In other words, there was greater polarization among Algerians there than in Petit-Nanterre (see Selby and Bihya 2025 for more on this polarization among female Algerian participants in Montréal). In contrast, most individuals in Petit-Nanterre self-identified as nonpracticing Muslims but nevertheless fasted during the month of Ramadan. How individuals described their practice is gendered and embodied: for men, being practicing Muslims often translated as dressing modestly, wearing a beard, and attending mosque regularly, especially for *ju'muah* prayer; for women, it often meant modest comportment and dress, especially head coverings ranging from bandanas, looser scarves, hijabs, or, in rare cases, niqab (none of my female participants wore niqab).

The immigration experience inspired some participants to shift their religious belief. Many participants, especially men, became less practicing. Others became more practicing in Canada. Several Montréal participants who migrated to the province in the second wave of immigration, felt a sense of liberation from their families and their beliefs. Tilila, for one, a married twenty-eight-year-old doctoral student and mother of one, said she became more practicing postmigration. In our interview, she explained how her father, still living in Algeria, identified as an atheist. Related to his Kabylian roots, she explained that, in large part, his beliefs reflected a political position against what he saw as an "Arab-Islamic hegemony" in Algeria. According to Tilila, her father would never have accepted her religious beliefs had she stayed: "He [my dad] associated Islam with Arabs. He wants nothing to do with Islam." Three other female Algerian-origin participants in my Montréal sample relayed similar stories of how the distance and new context, with new friends and greater individualism and freedom, allowed them to revert or convert to Islam after they had settled.

In addition to differences in religious or nonreligious practice among participants were distinctions along ethnic and linguistic lines, especially between Kabylians and Arabs. Ethnic tensions in Algeria, especially during the Dark Decade of the 1990s, further entrenched these groups along (imagined) religious and racial categories. Paul Silverstein (1996, 2002) notes that Berber (or Amazigh) identity was suppressed in Algeria during the colonial period, at the same time as it was rehabilitated in France. This situation has served to reinforce the Arab/Berber opposition within Algerian circles, especially in the diaspora.

Approximately 40 percent of my overall sample were Algerians of Kabylian origin.[25] The division figured slightly differently in Montréal insofar as this part of their identity held greater salience. Many Kabylians there were emboldened by Québécois sovereigntist politics. Those who supported secular laws in Montréal tended to be Kabylian (i.e., they agreed with laws curtailing religious symbols), where Kabylian community organizations were active. Rare, but still worth mentioning, were three members of one family I interviewed who situated their *kabylité* as an expression of Indigeneity, paralleling Indigenous politics in Canada, a framework I did not see in France. In both France and Québec, these differences were often cast on racialized lines. Kabylians are more often read as white, not only because of phenotype but also because they tend to be less religiously practicing than Arab Algerians.

Of course, in practice, these binaries, whether practicing/nonpracticing or Arab/Kabylian, are far from neat. Some interlocutors overtly rejected these ethnocultural and religious categories, like Sabrina, thirty-three. Over ice cream, sitting on a bench in the parc Jeanne-Mance in Montréal's Plateau neighborhood on a warm July evening in 2018, Sabrina insisted, "I'm *just* Algerian! I detest how Algerians constantly distinguish [between Arabs and Kabylians]. I've really seen how it leads to hate and separation. What's the point?" While some like Sabrina denied the differences, they mattered for others in their marriage partner preferences. In sum, participants differed not only along social class and religious lines but also on ethnic, linguistic, and cultural ones, even while all identifying as Algerian.

On Ethnographic Refusal and Centering Desire

Ethnographic refusal was central to this project's design and its results. Of course, all scholarship is political and located in the politics it critiques. While my approach aims to be anticolonial and antiracist, this research remains located in a colonialist discipline, undertaken by a white body, funded and employed by an imperial nation-state. Underlying discrimination in France and Québec have certainly influenced all parts of this project, including my thinking and avenues I do not fully explore.[26] For these reasons, my analysis does not rely on grounded theory, largely because of the approach's problematic assumption of neutrality (see Urquhart 2013).

Throughout different stages of this project, I have asked myself, What does it mean to critique the surveillance of Muslim bodies and sexuality while, at the same time, surveilling Muslim bodies and sexuality through ethnography? What is my complicity in the colonial and postcolonial obsession with "Muslim sexuality"? That questions of religion, race, and sexuality are of interest to me reflects racialized and colonial politics of which I am both aware and unaware.[27] Anthropologists have long encouraged reflexivity and a recognition of the partiality of truths (Clifford 1986). Put differently, in seeking to critique the biopolitics and secular sensibilities and their impacts on racialized bodies of Algerian origin, I admittedly also mobilize them. Some of these power moves can be framed methodologically. bell hooks (1990: 353) considers how violence is central to this scholarly engagement and extractive impulse: "No need to hear your voice when I can talk about you better than you can speak about yourself. No need to hear your voice. Only tell me about your pain. I want to know your story. And then I will tell it back to you in a new way. Tell it back to you in such a way that it has become mine, my own. Re-writing you I write myself anew. I am still author, authority. I am still colonizer the speaking subject and you are now at the center of my talk" (cited in Tuck and Wang 2014: 227).

Acknowledging this searing anthropological fascination with "your pain," as well as my overt privileges as a white scholar and author who is neither surveilled by the state nor the victim of racism in the ways my interlocutors experience, I have, when possible, endeavored to, very partially, respond to the potential violence in these power differentials. In addition to interpersonal politics of reciprocity and care, another avenue to consider these power differentials is in engaging in two responses: first, what some scholars call "ethnographic refusal" (Simpson 2014; Tuck and Wang 2014; McGranahan 2016), and, second, by emphasizing desire.

"Ethnographic refusal" refers to when researchers uncover sensitive information that, if revealed, could have social and material consequences for their interlocutors and the communities in which they are located. Lara Deeb (2010), who has written about the politics of care and ethnographic refusal in relation to her fieldwork in Lebanon, discerningly asks, "How do we decide which politics, which context, and which priorities to honor when those priorities, politics, or contexts come into conflict with one another?" In her fieldwork with Shi'i youth in Beirut with Mona Harb, Deeb (2010) explains why she chose *not* to write on temporary marriage in their broader project: its sensationalist repercussions would reify the racist stereotypes they sought to dismantle. So too, in the midst of this ethnography, when a handful of young men shared their marriage partner preferences, they explained that part of their motivation to initiate transnational unions was because they sought virginal brides. Patriarchal at best, and perhaps in part because they were often arranged, some women entered situations of domestic power imbalances and/or violence or what a handful of female interlocutors described as marriages that were forced by their parents. These situations of sexual and gender-based violence reinforce some of the worst fears of many white French and Québécois legislators: that transnational marriage arrangements facilitate sexual exploitation and position Algerian brides in especially vulnerable positions. Even in the happiest of arrangements, these unions *are* many times based on patriarchal ideals. However, chronicling and critiquing some of the patriarchal notions embodied and said by my interlocutors was not the goal of this work. To *not* center these responses thus entailed an ethnographic refusal. To return to Trouillot's (1995) distinction between one's object of study and of observation, my object of study is not arranged marriages. Conducting a quantitative survey on my interlocutors' sex lives would have entailed quantitative surveillance of Algerian-origin sexuality. In contrast, this book's focus is on the impacts of how arranged and other transnational marriages are problematized amid contemporary secular sensibilities, as lived and as delineated by state law and surrounding discourses. For instance, in chapter 2, I consider these marriage partner preferences through the implications of 2021 legislation focused on curtailing virginity certificates, but not on the sexual lives of my participants.

More practically, ethical quandaries and considerations of refusal in this project occurred more in Petit-Nanterre and less so in Montréal. In Petit-Nanterre, in general, my interlocutors experienced significantly more vulnerability than those in Montréal. Because of a greater geographic concentration of participants and participant observation in Petit-Nanterre, I also spent more time in people's apartments and hanging out in shared community spaces. I thus also engaged in greater ethnographic refusal there than in Montréal. For example, in two instances (and thus 0.01 percent of the people I interviewed), I encountered what French legislation deems as a *mariage blanc*, or a marriage of convenience. That is, both parties were aware it was fraudulent and undertook it for paperwork purposes; these were marriages conducted in the express interest of immigration and not of "love" or romance. I engage with them here briefly to show how the situations undergirding these unions involved far more complex emotions and situations than appear on the surface. The first case involved an older divorced woman and a younger man seeking citizenship status who eventually, unexpectedly, moved in with her to better care for her when she developed breast cancer. In ways they did not predict, they developed a relationship that defied monogamous-oriented sociological categories, and that is erased by the surveillance of their financial and sexual intimacy when she sponsored his residency application. A second case involved a bride-to-be with four young children who had entered France through Spain without papers, fleeing intimate partner violence in Algeria.[28] She organized a marriage of convenience as a path to documentation. In this second instance, in the spring of 2012, following our morning meeting at a café in Petit-Nanterre, she asked me to serve as a witness at her upcoming civil wedding. I was equally thrilled to be included so formally, to help someone experiencing precarity, and cognizant of the penalties outlined by the state. A 2011 amendment to the immigration and criminal laws in France meant that those who knowingly witness a marriage of convenience—here, me— could be punished with fines and jail time. After some anxiety-inducing contemplation, I agreed to serve as witness but not write about it here.[29] Not centering patriarchal marriage partner preferences or rare instances of marriages of convenience is thus a form of ethnographic refusal.

A second mode of ethnographic refusal is to move away from the voyeurism that often focuses on the pain of the most oppressed, as the citation by hooks, above, reflects. Focusing on pain over privilege reproduces a settler colonial logic where "pain is evidence of authenticity," as Eve Tuck and K. Wayne Yang (2014: 229) have argued. As an antidote (but not antonym) to these damage-focused narratives, Tuck proposes desire-based research. Desire is not aimed at capturing a lacking or a problem but rather is "exponentially generative, engaged, engorged" (Tuck 2009: 418). Scholarship focused on "integration" is one such damage-focused narrative. This project's foci on the rituals of marriage[30] and the adventure of migration aimed to capture a less troubled entry into thinking about secular sensibilities than the stigmatizing research that analyzes secularism through the lens of conspicuous religious symbols, especially hijabs (a perspective I once took; cf. Selby 2011b, 2012). In other words, rather than focusing on often ill-favored religious symbols of difference, marriage narratives have a universal appeal that allows for theoretical problematization of a common academic overemphasis on religious symbols as gauges of so-called Muslim integration (see Ahmed 2021 on her refusal to focus solely on hijab restrictions in order to disentangle the impact of scholarship on Muslim women's symbols from legislation focused on them). It is attention to desire that spurred my interest in marriage and thinking on the bridges, and not only the burdens, fostered for many through marriage migration from Algeria.

In aiming to move from scholarship that overtly benefits from the pain of others (cf. Simpson 2014: 107), ethnographic refusals can be strategic and hopeful (cf. McGranahan 2016). If French and Canadian colonial apparatuses have historically surveilled Algerian and nonwhite, non-Christian sexuality and family life—which I argue they have—to refuse to solely focus on these subjects can—hopefully—generate a different politics. This positioning also reflects why I did not seek to know or intervene in relation to participants' legal statuses or ask about their sexual lives. Rather, a desired end goal was to critique the unspoken norms laden in secular sensibilities, which, given their situatedness, my interlocutors invariably engaged. The remainder of this chapter situates laïcité in France and Québec in relation to notions of biopolitics, desire, and coloniality, which I contextualize by briefly historicizing the two contexts of examination. I conclude with a brief overview of the book's remaining chapters.

Secularism, Biopolitics, Desire, and Coloniality

A central premise of this book is engaging the interstellar relation between these four concepts. I do not offer a singular normative definition of secularism because of its malleability and also in reference to the ethnography of post-2004 France and Québec underpinning my analysis. Put differently,

I am more interested in how and where it appears, and to what ends, than a solo definition. I start from the idea that secularism is not as a "thing" but an episteme, or a way of framing politics and religion. From this more macro level, we can observe how, for one, secular sensibilities hinge upon a number of binaries, including public and private spheres, the positioning of certain religious symbols as conspicuous and others inconspicuous, a strict separation of what is imagined as conservative and liberal, and a concomitant emphasis on a gender binary, all of which, social scientists will know, fall apart in practice.

French philosopher Michel Foucault's thinking on biopolitics in particular undergirds how I theorize secularism and its relationship to gender and sexuality. Sexuality, writes Foucault (2003: 252), "represents the precise point where the disciplinary and the regulatory, the body and the population, are articulated."[31] Following this insight, I propose that articulations of secularism can be read as expressions of biopolitics, coloniality, or the ways bodies and populations are managed. Foucault (2003: 239–64) defines *biopower* as the systems that control and surveil populations, often accompanied by rationales for their necessity. Tangibly, if a person or group does not behave "properly," they are excluded from the rights and freedoms accorded to citizens. In delineating what he calls "the coloniality of power," Aníbal Quijano (2000) ties biopower to European colonialisms, noting their power to shape knowledge and realities long past the "end" of colonial eras.

The French and Canadian governments' perennial concerns with the constitution of normative, private, and familial arrangements are thus not accidental. Secular legislation in France and Québec is inseparably enveloped within the goals of capitalism, and its related structures of inequality and extraction, which can be traced to European coloniality (Asad 2003: 7; Six 2020). "Stable" monogamous families protect stable capitalism. Polygamous arrangements, for one, threaten this balance of production. A number of scholars have shown how establishing the acceptable contours of marriage and of sexuality have been long-standing concerns for white settler colonial governments (see Morgensen 2011: 52; Surkis 2019). Ann Stoler ([2002] 2010: 47) chronicles this control of sexual politics across colonial European administrations and their subsidiaries. Stoler shows how for more than four centuries, colonial agents, but also "missionaries, investment bankers, military high commands, and agents of the colonial state," were obsessed by "sexual sanctions and conjugal prohibitions." Colonial administrators managed intimacies through the subtle instruction of proper desire (Stoler 1995; McClintock 1995). Policing sexual morality and related sensibilities secured the frontiers of national communities and marked claims to property rights and citizenship. The shaping of secular sensibilities is part of long-standing colonial projects.

In its appreciation of the enduring nature of colonialism, the concept of coloniality engaged by several thinkers helps to explain the biopolitics of the control of marriage, as well as the invisibility of some symbols and sensibilities and not others (see Roy 2005 and Jeldoft 2013 on this point). We will see how the control of so-called Muslim sexualities inside and outside marriage was a central concern in French colonial Algeria and, in a different configuration, in the colonization of Canada, initially focused on controlling Indigenous bodies. Coloniality also shapes an idealized secular body as white. On this point, cultural theorist Sara Ahmed's (2007) work is helpful to map how colonial legacies remain in and on the body. Ahmed (2007: 153–54) writes, "Colonialism makes the world 'white.' . . . Bodies remember such histories, even when we forget them." Whiteness is structurally advantaged through its establishment of what is "normal" or racially unmarked (see also Hartigan 2005; Bhopal 2023).

The constellation of the colonial secular body maps differently across the Atlantic. Obviously, the Canadian province of Québec did not colonize Algeria, but, as part of a French colonial constellation, in different centuries, both Québec and Algeria were colonized by the French. In Québec, this colonial history remains manifest in a long-standing violence toward and erasure of Indigenous populations. Named "New France" when first colonized by the French in the seventeenth century, the Canadian province has its own histories and continued traces of coloniality, which reappear in its legislation on secularism.[32] In both Algeria and Québec, pushes to protect Christian norms were central mechanisms in the arsenal of the French colonial government. While France no longer officially occupies Algeria or Québec, and while these countries are no longer officially tied to the Catholicism, logics of white settler politics echo in the contemporary justifications for secularism. As we will see in considerations of coloniality, the French colonial project in Algeria and in Québec clearly delineated proper religion and sexuality as part of its civilizing mission (see Surkis 2019; Clancy-Smith 1998; Shepard 2012, 2017, 2018; and Massad 2008).

How do these historical frames translate into my participants' experiences? Desire and coloniality intersect not only in the narratives I heard but also with pejorative overtones regarding so-called Muslim sexuality in contemporary cultural references in the North Atlantic world, especially in France. Popular literature and cinema reinforce a pejorative vision of religiously informed bad relationships. True crime narratives of the sexual violence of Muslim men are recounted in dozens of best-selling books

(Razack 2008; Mahmood 2009; Barras 2018); pornography and mainstream cinema also reinforce the Islamophobic narratives of problematic Muslim sexuality (Mack 2017; Peter 2021). For these reasons, I found it notable that, despite these pejorative depictions in popular culture and the surveillance by the state, among my Muslim French of Algerian-origin interlocutors, Algerian-born individuals remain desirable marriage partners, especially for couples who may not share the same first language or upbringing.[33] But this seeming paradox is not paradoxical when we take the Bled and coloniality seriously. Initially, in Petit-Nanterre, I thought these marriage partner preferences could be explained by the highly contentious geopolitical context of the suburbs, where religious symbols and Islam are stigmatized. In this sometimes-volatile space, for some men, women born in North Africa may have been seen as "uncorrupted" by French secularism and gender politics and as possessing more authentic Muslim qualities (see Selby 2009a: 5). However, I now see these marriage preferences as relating more complexly to desire, coloniality, social mobility, and kinship. In Québec, where my sample is more geographically and socioeconomically diverse, I also found that many men sought out partners in these arrangements, despite somewhat different challenges related to distance, both geographical and cultural.

Desire and ongoing specters of coloniality are but two motivations for these marriage partner preferences.[34] Other forces that, literally, *move* people are desires to improve their financial standing, be closer to (or further from) kin, experience adventure, and return to the Bled, as well as a sense of *mektoub* (God-given destiny).[35] Choice is in tension throughout.[36] When interlocutors explained their marital partners as destined by God, they often eschewed both the notion of individual will and a linkage of kinship with colonialism. Particularly for my interlocutors in Petit-Nanterre, who experience greater marginalization geographically, religiously (whether or not they practice), racially, and socioeconomically, to reclaim their abjection by the French state can be a moment of repossessing the Bled in celebratory and intimate ways. If colonial logics work to establish the colonizer and colonized in a violent relation of power, in part, these transnational marriage preferences interrupt and reclaim these relations.

I heard hundreds of narratives about marriage (and divorce) and, for some, migration, and the factors shaping these life moments. One interlocutor, Amel, was a twenty-five-year-old woman born in northern France. She and I spent a great deal of time together, from January to July 2016, in the lead-up to her transnational wedding trip to Algeria. Amel married Yacine, twenty-six, in an arranged union in Ghazaouet, Algeria, that I attended.

In so doing, she participated in a family tradition. Her father and oldest brother also had transnational marriages with women from the same city. Amel was religiously practicing, which, for her, meant praying regularly, being consciously generous and modest, including wearing hijab, and eating halal. She was thirteen in 2004 when hijabs were banned from public schools. With her union to Yacine she did not need to explain her hijab. For Amel, kinship ties were central to these equations. To facilitate her yearly summer trips in her teens, she secured her Algerian passport with an uncle's help. On a number of occasions, and in different ways, I asked her why she had agreed to a transnational arranged union with Yacine, particularly given the paperwork, surveillance, and effort it entailed. Echoing many of the Algerians I interviewed, she pointed to its destined nature: marrying a *Blédard* was mektoub.[37] She was, most simply, following God's will. In the hundreds of hours we spent together in preparations related to her wedding, and in my experience on her wedding trip in Ghazaouet, I also observed how, for Amel, this union effectively ensured her continued linkage with Ghazaouet, and to her grandmother's home specifically. Yacine's parents lived next door. Kinship and a cosmopolitan transnationalism mattered. Amel is not a "post"-colonial subject. Her family and her everyday life are deeply connected to Algeria. Her body and her kin—including now her husband—are testaments to this continued bridge. We will see many examples of these deep and fibrous transnational connections through marriage and migration, and also consider preferences that consciously reject these bridges.

Secular Legal Contexts in France and Québec

Iterations of laïcité in contemporary France and Québec triangulate women's equality with the removal of religious symbols and concern for women's sexual freedom in similar ways. Still, despite commonalities in coloniality, language, cultures of Catholicism, and similarly framed sanctions against religious symbols and niqabs beginning in 2004, the historical and legal parameters of laïcité in France and Québec are shaped differently. While this research is contemporarily focused, the *longue durée* of laïcité in France can be drawn back to the anticlericalism of the French Revolution in the eighteenth century. More than 100 years later, the Loi du 9 décembre 1905 concernant la séparation des Églises et de l'État (Assemblée Nationale 1905) was foundational to the establishment of French state secularism (see Baubérot 1998). A few decades later, laïcité was enshrined in the French Constitution and thereafter often positioned with the national trifecta of liberty, fraternity, and equality.

More contemporarily, in France, since the 2004 ban of conspicuous religious symbols in public schools and government offices, I note a shift to a greater focus on laïcité's delineation of proper sexual and gender comportment, beginning with a number of publicly debated cases that probed acceptable sexual politics for Muslim women. I pay particular attention to a handful of cases in 2008 that capture the surveillance of Muslim women's private sexual lives, and whose content can serve as fodder with which to contrast an idealized secular body. In addition to a ban on full-face veils in the public sphere in France in 2010, as well as bans on bandanas (2005), skirts (2010), niqabs (2011), burkinis (2016), abayas (2023), and, to a lesser extent, debates on Muslim beards, a number of other laws have aimed to "secure" secularism, in response to violent incidents attributed to Islamic radicalism. Numerous incidents of terrorism in France in the post-2004 period—including the attacks on the *Charlie Hebdo* weekly satirical magazine in January 2015, the horrific Bataclan and Paris attacks in November that same year, and other subsequent incidents of religiously framed violence, including the 2016 Nice truck attack and the murder of public school teacher Samuel Paty and three others in 2020—cannot be discounted in understanding fears associated with publicly visible symbols of Islam, linked to terrorism, and how these incidents motivated the subsequent increase in secular-focused legislation.

In contrast, Canada does not have a clear legal separation of religion and politics (see Colorado and Selby 2020), and it has enshrined greater legal protections for religious freedom and multiculturalism, with its Charter of Rights and Freedoms and Multiculturalism Act, established in 1982 and 1988 respectively. Protestantism and Catholicism also enjoy constitutionally based protections in some provinces. At the same time, other traditions have been excluded. At the federal level, the Indian Act of 1876 (amended in 1951 and 1985) has historically violently excluded Indigenous spiritualities (see Klassen 2018). At the provincial level, we can note specificities as well. Established in the wake of French colonialism in the seventeenth century, Québec is often distinguished by an intercultural rather than multicultural model that aims to protect its linguistic and cultural minority status. This model aims to secure a moral contract between newcomer and that province to ensure an established common public culture in which the French language is central (Laxer 2019: 23; Lépinard 2020). In addition to language politics that differentiate it from the rest of Canada, opinion data have also shown how debates in Québec on secularism are more divided than in France, and, with the exception of the regulation of the niqab, engender less public support (Laxer 2019; Tremblay 2022). Put differently, in general,

Quebeckers are more divided on how laïcité should be deployed to regulate conspicuous religious symbols than in France. Still, Canadians and Quebeckers agree that niqabs require regulation (see fig. 1.2). There have been horrifying incidents of terrorism in Canada too, but their violence has been directed *at* Muslim bodies to a greater extent.

In Québec, public and legislative debates on religious symbols and accommodations are more recent than in France. Philosophies undergirding deconfessionalization date to the Quiet Revolution in the 1960s. This period, we will see, engendered an unprecedented "aesthetic revolt," in which French Canadian Catholic symbols and sensibilities were profoundly rejected (Zubrzycki 2016a, 2016b). A flashpoint emerged forty years later in 2006 when some of these sensibilities were concretized in a Charter of Values established by the town council of Hérouxville, 180 kilometers north of Montréal. The Hérouxville Charter focused on pejorative characterizations of imagined-Muslim sexual politics. With significant international attention, the premier of the province launched a commission on accommodation practices (Commission de consultation sur les pratiques d'accommodement reliées aux différences culturelles) to address the Hérouxville Charter and a broader "crisis" regarding religious accommodation in Québec. In other words, as in contemporary France with its 2002 Debray Commission, 2003 Debré Commission, 2003 Stasi Commission, 2006 Rossinot Commission, 2006 Machelon Commission, and 2010 Gerin Commission (cf. Selby 2011b: 457n3), the Québécois government responded to public concerns about Islam by creating a commission. The two government-appointed commissioners, sociologist Gérard Bouchard and philosopher Charles Taylor, traveled to listen to Quebeckers share their experiences with cultural difference. Bouchard and Taylor's primary goal was to make recommendations on the "reasonable" limits for the accommodation of these differences (see Beaman 2011, 2017 on "accommodation" and Selby et al. 2018a for a critique of "reason"). Arguably, the commission whetted the public appetite for a more regulatory approach vis-à-vis visibly religious bodies and their supposed claims for recognition in Québec. Since the publication of the Bouchard-Taylor report (2008), successive provincial governments in Québec have sought to legally delineate secularism.

Following three other legislative attempts to curtail religious symbols,[38] in 2019, the Coalition Avenir Québec (CAQ, Québec Future Coalition) government in the province successfully legislated the Act Respecting the Laicity of the State, or "Law 21."[39] Law 21 introduced a number of articles and focuses on the exclusion of full-face veil-wearing women from all public services (Article 8) and the restriction of conspicuous religious symbols for those who hold state-based positions of authority, including public school teachers (Article 6). Despite protections for the freedom of religion, as articulated in Section 2a of the Canadian Charter of Rights and Freedoms, a notable reason why Bill 21 passed into law was because the CAQ successfully invoked a "notwithstanding clause," which allowed it to circumvent, for a renewable period of five years, federal- and provincial-level protections that the Charter of Rights and Freedoms affords religious minorities. Articles 6 and 8 are especially attuned to the acceptable parameters of the secular body.

Even while contemporary leaders in France and Québec proclaim colorblind or neutral politics, anti-Muslim racism, Islamophobia and white supremacy shade these secular laws.[40] In response to critiques of anti-Muslim racism laden in its most recent secular law, Québec's premier François Legault repeatedly declared that institutional Islamophobia "does not occur" in Québec. Data show, however, that we *can* correlate secular debates on religious symbols with heightened incidents of hate.[41] In this study, I did not explicitly focus interviews with my Algerian-origin informants about their experiences of Islamophobia and anti-Muslim racism, whether in government systems or on individual levels, but in our interviews their narratives almost invariably alluded to these exclusions. They sometimes relate to marriage partner preferences. One interlocutor, Mustafa, twenty-five, explained in a June 2018 interview at a café in Montréal how Islamophobia continues to blindside him years after certain incidents: "All of this pressure from students in high school. And intimidation, insults. They really made me reflect. I changed a lot having gone through all of that." From the vantage point of his mid-twenties, Mustafa saw his high school experience with different eyes. The "jokes" of which he was a target, he now recognizes as intimidation, as insults, as Islamophobia.[42] Still, like many young men of Algerian origin we will meet in the coming chapters, Mustafa dreamed of a good job with a pension and of starting his own family, ideally by sponsoring a woman of Algerian origin to Montréal as his wife. For him, this potential relationship could offer a touchstone, a connection to the Bled and desire. We will see how men like Mustafa grapple with secular sensibilities and here, Islamophobia, in different ways.

A primary contention of this book is that secular sensibilities are fostered in France and Québec alongside mechanisms of coloniality and through legislation on secularism, immigration, and family law. Equally effective, secular sensibilities are transmitted through less coercive soft politics, including cues from government-mandated instructional posters that signal national values, or ways citizens ultimately monitor one another and themselves.

I argue that these secular sensibilities aim to promote, among other things, normative conceptualizations of gender roles and sexuality, and continuing colonial hierarchies that, among other goals, uphold whiteness. These sensibilities appear enigmatic as they claim to remain unmarked, unnamed. I focus on secular sensibilities as they are detailed in legislation, and in how my interlocutors describe how they surface on their bodies, in social interactions, in rituals, and through the minutia of everyday life, including in whom and how they love (or don't), whether through civil marriage (or not). Given states' interest in regulating acceptable religiosity and sexuality, marriage, whether civil, religious, or common-law, is a ripe moment through which to think about how secular sensibilities are imparted, not only in top-down ways but also through colonial histories, contemporary legislation and policy, and, more compellingly, from surrounding popular culture and individual expressed desires.

The chapters that follow situate secular sensibilities in legislative and policy contexts in France and Québec, with particular attention to how they emerge (or not) in the lives of my interlocutors. Beginning in the next chapter, I define what I mean by secularism, secular sensibilities, and the related secular body, building on recent thinking by scholars who articulate secularism not as a fixed entity but as a discursive power operative whose effects can be examined within specific contexts (Wohlrab-Sahr and Burchardt 2012; Modood 2017). I then examine how post-2004 secular legislation on religious symbols constructs a secular-sexuality framework. These sensibilities have a disproportionate impact on women and for racialized and religionized minorities, like for Ilias, with whom I begin. Chapter 2 puts post-2004 legislation in France and Québec on secularism into conversation. In contrast to the 1989–2004 focus in France on regulating religious symbols, a more recent focus on public/private binaries and a cisgender dualism echo in the lives of participants, including expectations of what are publicly acceptable sexual politics and secular bodies. Chapter 3 captures how French and Québécois concern for "love marriage" in post-2006 immigration law can be read through a lens of coloniality, which shapes and constrains migration. In chapter 4, before considering the long-standing silences on historical and ongoing coloniality in recent French and Québécois laws and commissioned reports on secularism, I locate these broader impetuses in my interlocutors' evocative narratives about marriage partner preferences and rituals of marriage. Even if Maya, with whom I open that chapter, overtly rejects an Algerian-origin marriage partner, I see her decision as shaped by transnational interstices of longing and belonging that are, among others, an expression of a coloniality of being (cf. Maldonado-Torres

2007). The book's conclusion returns to romance as a central contemporary secular sensibility in France and Québec. The surveillance of expressions of romance in civil marriage and of visible religious symbols in the public sphere, I argue, does a great deal of work in bolstering secular sensibilities. It perpetuates patriarchal and antireligious ideas that do not "liberate" individuals as secularism promises, whether they are religious or not, whether they are in monogamous relationships or not, and whether they are racialized, married, or not.

To be clear, my critique in *Secular Sensibilities* does not mean to suggest that secularism—variously defined and configured—should be replaced by the promotion of an imagined antisecular or solely religiously informed or visible framework. Secularism is not necessarily a tool of oppression. *But*, and I expressly underline this point, its purported neutrality *is* problematic. For feminists, antiracists, and for those who care about maintaining the visibility of difference (whether religious, ideological, racial, classed, or gendered), the politics of these articulations matters.[43] Drawing on political and legislative discourses in France and Québec since 2004, as well as my interlocutors' experiences of marriage (and, for many, migration), I show how contemporary legislation on laïcité's focus on the visual access to women's bodies and their sexual liberation has repercussions for all of society, including for men, and for those who do not fall into rigid gender binaries. The desirability of romance as an expression of secular sensibilities at the time of civil marriage shields its sometimes-violent implications. For these reasons, I critique these variations of secularisms.

CHAPTER 1

SECULARISM'S SEXUAL SENSIBILITIES AND BODY POLITIC

Ilias, twenty-five, was born in Petit-Nanterre to a family who has lived in the neighborhood's Canibouts section for three generations, in the same apartment of a social housing project block. His paternal grandfather first migrated to the Parisian suburb in the late 1950s when it was a shantytown and, like many, had worked in the neighboring Renault car factory. Ilias's father, who grew up in the housing project, became involved in the drug trade and died young. When Ilias, who had experienced similar trauma, also began using drugs in his early teens, his paternal grandparents sent him to Kabylia, their region of origin in north central Algeria, for three months, to "set him straight." Ilias explained in our May 2014 interview that, inspired by that time in the Bled, he had "rediscovered" the beliefs and practices he had left behind as a child. Like many second- and third-generation young people of Maghrebian origin in France (a 2011 study by the Institut national d'études démographiques suggests almost 80 percent), Ilias had fasted for Ramadan since his teens, but he did not otherwise consider himself a practicing Muslim.[1] Other circumstances facilitated this post-Kabylia reconnection with Islam. His evening job as a waiter in Paris enabled him to attend midday Friday prayers with friends. As part of his new religious interest, Ilias also sought to change how he interacted with women, including in his intimate relationships.

After years of casually dating women of different racial, ethnic, and religious backgrounds, Ilias said he consciously adopted what he called a "grandmother method" to relationships. He wanted to "procéder autrement . . . procéder religieusement" (proceed differently . . . proceed religiously) to seek out a suitable Muslim and Algerian-origin marriage partner. At the same time, he was conscious of not wanting to deal with the administrative hurdles of a transnational marriage, which had heightened with the passage of a series of laws in France in 2006, 2011, and, after our interview, in 2021. We will see how Ilias's marriage story is illustrative of one way racialized

Algerian-origin members of French and Québécois societies tacitly and strategically maneuver in the context of state-articulated secular sensibilities as they relate to marriage and immigration. His narrative of love and marriage captures his transnationalism and sophisticated discernment of French immigration law. Like a good number of other young men in this suburb and in Montréal, he consciously sought out a "traditional" transnational marriage partner of Algerian origin. On the surface, given the laws aimed at impeding this choice, the preference may appear paradoxical. But, when we center kinship and coloniality, we can see other logics and factors.

This chapter examines the content of contemporary French and Québécois secular sensibilities and related body politics. I sketch these sensibilities theoretically alongside legislation and memorandums around marriage and religious symbols, and how their secular sensibilities are experienced by four interlocutors: Ilias in France, and Zohra, Farah, and Firdaous in Québec. While I begin with Ilias, and mention concern with beards deemed "Islamic," secular laws in France and Québec have invariably had a greater impact on the lives of racialized women perceived as Muslim. For this reason, and because of Law 21, restricting niqabs generally and conspicuous religious symbols for people in positions of authority, had passed more recently in Québec, and therefore had a more visceral impact when I interviewed them, I focus on narratives drawn from interviews and fieldwork with Zohra, Farah, and Firdaous in Montréal. Because not all that is done in the name of secularism is "secular," this study is not limited to legislation on laïcité but also considers legislative parameters related to marriage and immigration as related to the notion of coloniality. My aim is not to present one orderly view of secularism. Rather, we will see how, together, these contexts shape an embodied sexuality-secularity-citizenship nexus that upholds norms. I pay particular attention to those articulated in relation to gender and race. Given that a secular body politic in France and Québec disproportionately influences how racialized female immigrants religionized as Muslim live and love, the second half of this chapter focuses on hijab-wearing participants in Québec. Legislation curtailing hijabs for students and government workers had been in effect for some years at the time of my interviews in France, while the timing of interviews in Montréal, in 2018 and 2019, meant participants there felt the new restriction to a greater extent.

Defining Secularism

Before we turn to lived examples of these notions, let us turn to "secularism."[2] Secularism is often understood as a tool of modern political organization that helps states marshal neutrality and/or separate politics from the (negative) influence of religion. Most contemporary liberal democratic nation-states delineate parameters to manage religion. Neutrality, freedom of conscience, and freedom of religion, protection against the overt tyranny of religious orthodoxies, and shelter for religious and other minorities are some of the promises deployed by states under the umbrella of secularism. Secularism has been employed by states (and scholars) in ways that have made it synonymous with neutrality, regulation, and protection. Like many concepts, in practice, secularism is far more complex. It is a multitudinous, polysemic, variegated, and often tautological term, which, in turn, makes it a confounding, malleable, and powerful notion.[3] As the scholar of laïcité David Koussens (2023: 23) notes, "The multiple meanings of the concept upstream result in multiple forms of regulation of religious diversity downstream." Its meanings thus multiply as it is translated through theory, law, and practice. While touted for its neutrality, the concept has also been critiqued as exclusionary, as banal, as cunning, and as decidedly nonneutral. Indeed, secularism can work to simplify complex values, and it typically holds liberalizing goals. Some scholars see it as a fait accompli and delineate a "post"-secular period.[4] For specificity, I employ the term "laïcité" when referring to the geographical and sociohistorical specificities of the French and Québécois contexts and "secularism" to think about the concept—or, as I will suggest, the *episteme*—including how related sensibilities manifest in the lives of individuals. Talal Asad's (2003: 25) observation that secularism is "a concept that brings together certain behaviors, knowledges, and sensibilities in modern life" moves us in the direction of these sensibilities.

To date, anthropologists have argued that secular norms are powerful precisely because they often remain unstated and ubiquitous (Hirschkind 2011; Asad 2011; Connolly 2011). Others have pointed to the secular's "cunningness" (Fernando 2014b: 687; 2014c), arguing that it occupies a paradoxical "problem space" (Agrama 2012), and privilege suspicion as its primary disposition (Asad 2018). Conceptions of secularism are powerful precisely because they can be normative *and* problem spaces. Several anthropologists have shown how, given their malleability and promises of neutrality and equality, secular discourses can be mobilized for a range of political aims (see Mahmood 2015 in relation to contemporary Egypt and Lemons 2019 on how, when the Indian state positions religiosity as private and structures Muslim family law as separate, it sanctions harm on Muslim women). Still others describe secularism's ability to render phenomena mundane or banal (Lee 2015; Oliphant 2021). These characterizations point to subtle ways that secularisms shape social life, in which I would include bodies and ways of being.

More useful than insisting on a specific definition, I suggest, is to read secularism broadly as an episteme. The term *episteme* underscores that the secular is not a *thing* per se; instead, as Foucault suggests in *The Order of Things* ([1966] 2005), it works as an often-unconscious ordering structure that shapes how knowledge operates and forms realities. Judith Butler similarly describes the secular as "the condition of thought itself" (cited in Scott 2018), insofar as it works to delineate objects and, in this way, constitutes a discursive field (cf. Lemke 2001, 2007; and Mahmood 2013). Monique Scheer, Nadia Fadil, and Birgitte Schepelern Johansen (2019: 5) mobilize a helpful metaphor that captures this view, describing secularism in contemporary Europe as a "grammar." In their reading, secularism is a structuring lens that shapes world-conceptualizing lexicons and vocabularies; these, in turn, shape power relations that determine, among other things, what is normative, particularly in contrast to "religion" (Quack 2017).

I mobilize this notion of episteme here in two overarching ways. First, I argue that secularisms shape embodied sensibilities, particularly related to sexuality—specifically normative ideas about the body, the family, and marriage—and race within specific sociohistorical, colonial, and national contexts—for our purposes, in France and Québec. A significant rationale used to bolster legislation on secularism after 2004 in France and Québec is its importance in protecting women's rights. This language of protectionism works to categorize and normalize gender as binary, sexuality as monogamous, and, often through a patriarchal gaze, a view of women needing both protection and being sexually available. We will see how post-2004 legislation on niqabs in France and Québec mobilizes this dual characterization of women. In relation to race, we'll see how, in tandem with histories of colonialism in these contexts, secularism has long been mobilized as a tool of governmentality, which, under the guise of neutrality, has upheld whiteness.

Second, the episteme bolsters seemingly stable and normative binaries—secularism/religion, rational/irrational, male/female, colonial/Other, public/private—that belie underlying instabilities inherent in all cultural and social categories. The religion/secular binary functions capaciously. Some "religions" are more comfortably synchronized with this secular framework than others. Many Quebeckers (82 percent), for instance, see nothing amiss in self-identifying at the same time as secular and as Christian (of whom 75 percent identity as Catholic; see Brown 2012; Lefebvre 2008; Boucher 2021; and Wilkins-Laflamme 2022). Other religious and racialized minorities cannot straddle this religion/secular binary as unproblematically. We have only to look at which symbols are rendered conspicuous (read: unacceptable, offensive, foreign, or *religious*) or as inconspicuous (read: acceptable, heritage, cultural, or *secularized*) to see the political work of these binaries.

Secular Sensibilities

One way to engage with the politics that undergird conceptualizations of secularism is to ask what the legislation and its accompanying mobilization articulate as acceptable. What do they say is unacceptable? How do these delineations materialize? And what are the sensorial, bodily, and affective dimensions of the secular? Nadia Fadil (2009, 2011) describes the "secular sensibilities" of her female Moroccan interlocutors in Belgium that emerge in how they choose to *not* veil and to *not* engage in handshaking with men. Fadil's (2009) conceptualization of the "dominant sensibilities" latent in liberal-secular regimes captures the range of dispositions and responses invoked in this supposedly secular social context (see also Jouili 2009, 2015: 101; and Amir-Moazami 2022). By showing how her participants express concern primarily with managing others' (implied as non-Muslim and non-racialized) affects more than interpreting the state's conception of rights and citizenship, Fadil shows how these are not only top-down prescriptions. These sensibilities are what emerge in habitus-like expressions on people's bodies and in their lives, relationships, and rituals. Other scholars who engage this notion include Talal Asad (2018: 2–3), who defines secular sensibilities as "ways of feeling, thinking, talking," Saba Mahmood (2009: 861), who asks how a "secular affect," in contrast to religion, is disciplined into formation, and, in her analysis of controversies involving Muslims in Europe, Nilüfer Göle (2015: 56), who introduces what she calls the "habitations of the secular," more directly invoking Bourdieu's (1977, 82–83) work on habitus. Göle (2015: 48) shows that these "habitations" are socially constructed and "part of a project of modernity and politics of self that require [for those coming from outside] assimilation and 'acculturation.'"

So too Schirin Amir-Moazami (2013) describes "secular embodiments" in considering how, amid 2012 public debates on the acceptability of circumcision in Germany, an idealized secular sexuality was constructed in contrast to undesirable and harmful Jewish-Muslim sexuality. Circumcised men were thus imagined as Jewish or Muslim, and as traumatized and victims of gratuitous, religiously informed violence (Amir-Moazami 2016: 166; see also Asad 2003: 11). In contrast, the uncircumcised *secular* were positioned as examples of desirable conventionalized masculine sexuality, and the site of normalized sexual pleasure. These notions are not top-down. Rather, they reflect what Alessandro Ferrari (2009: 333) defines as narrative secularism. Ferrari separates this narrative register from a legalistic one, which includes official or legal reports, parliamentary debates, and media reproductions.[5] Secular sensibilities and bodies are best examined through narrative secularism. Along this vein, Ashley Lebner (2015) proposes the notion of secularity, noting its presence in everyday life (see also King 2023: 17–25 on "lived secularity"). In sum, these scholars introduce different prisms that point to secularisms' body politic.

Building on this scholarship, I distinguish between a "secular body," as an imagined spectral ideal, and "secular sensibilities," as they are articulated and appear. To be clear, no contemporary legislation on secularism in France and Québec has overtly delineated an acceptable secular body. The sensibilities I examine are predominantly *non-dit* (unspoken) dispositions, emotions, and social relations that are part of a habitus that remains implicit and normative (see Burchardt and Griera 2019 on how the burqa evokes strong emotion in European public spaces). Nevertheless, as we saw with the example of Nawal's preparation for the French consulate in Oran in the introduction, the individuals I interviewed *do* have a sense of what might be expected of them in their engagements with state officials, and an understanding that these expectations include the performance of secular sensibilities. These sensibilities position some religious symbols and behaviors as ostentatious, exaggerated, or proselytizing. Other symbols are ignored or even "heritagized" and thereby suitable. More convolutedly and specifically, in the contact zone of civil marriage I focus upon, visible appropriate expressions of intimacy—ideally framed as based on romantic love with no other benefits (whether financial, citizenship-related, or whatever else)—become signs of sincerity and appropriate secular sensibilities.

While managing "bad" religion, secular legislation and sensibilities also denote acceptable versions, here related to Christianity. Elizabeth Shakman Hurd (2012: 955) portrays the linkage of religion and secularism in her definition of secularism as a series of legal and political projects that define and manage religion. Hurd's definition captures secularism's common reliance on an irrational, unmodern, unenlightened *religion* counterpoint. In relation to his fieldwork with secular groups in the United States, Joseph Blankholm (2018) captures this dynamic in defining secularism as a "religion-maker." So too, in his theorization of political secularism in Egyptian courts, Hussein Ali Agrama qualifies a secularism/religion relation as a tethering. For Agrama (2012: 29), this duality implies not that religion and secularism "mutually interpenetrate" as equal transhistorical essences but that they are mutually reliant. Saba Mahmood (2015: 25) also captures this interrelation of religion and secularism in Egypt, in denoting "the modern state's disavowal of religion in its political calculus," on the one hand, and its "simultaneous reliance on religious categories to structure and regulate social life," on the other. Katherine Lemons's (2019) brilliant critique of the secular Indian state extends Mahmood's point on disavowal. Lemons shows how when the contemporary Indian state relegates Muslim divorce to personal Islamic law, it effectively renders family law as religious and private. However, when unilateral *talaq* divorce is protected, the state does nothing to protect Muslim women: talaq serves as an external sign of Muslim women's inequality and further demarcates Islam as a "bad religion." Frank Peter (2021) goes further in this line of thinking to argue that, in contemporary France, the governance of "bad Islam" is so pointed that secularism is no longer actually tethered to religion at all. Peter proposes that the French climate promotes a version of secularism without a linkage to religion; instead, he traces a discursive link between secularism and politics of integration.

Peter reminds us that secularism's linkage to normative religion has shifted alongside the colonial projects of Christianity. Formulations of secularism in France and Québec therefore privilege Catholic iterations as part of their colonial legacies. Based on these historical legacies, secularisms privilege different religious traditions. For instance, Jean Baubérot (2004: 139) coined the term "catholaïcité" in France to capture laïcité's implicit Catholic underpinnings. So too Marian Burchardt (2020: 10) argues that Catholicism remains central to the nation-building projects of Québec and Catalunya, Spain (see also Göle 2007; Cesari 2016; Portier 2016). With her notion of "churchstateness" in Canada—which positions a British monarch as head of state while recognizing a limited sovereignty for Indigenous peoples— Pamela Klassen (2018) shows the ongoing support of a secular praxis by the Crown in the Canadian context, and how it relates to colonialism. Under the false auspices of neutrality, since Canada's colonial beginnings, secularism was a useful weapon brandished to protect the Crown. Rendering Indigenous peoples' bodies "secular" or acceptable meant forcibly stripping them of their language, families, and homelands in genocidal conditions (Truth and Reconciliation Commission of Canada 2015). Together, these scholars draw attention to the North Atlantic context that stresses *where* and *which* religious tradition is protected or problematized.

These power plays behind neutrality are often obscure. Gil Anidjar (2006: 62) argues that the "secular/religion overlay" is purposefully tight in order to mask its politics, namely its promotion of the "one and diverse Christianity and Western Christendom." Anidjar is attuned to the invisibility of whiteness in this equation. Christianity remains unmarked in Western distinctions between the religious and the secular, a move that "made religion the problem" rather than Christianity, which itself remains normative (and white). Hussein Agrama (2012: 25) takes a slightly different approach in mapping which religious practices are ignored in the Egyptian legal context. Some religious practices, Agrama notes, have been configured as modern and liberal so as not to oppose liberal secular tenets. Noticing this protectionism allows us to question secularisms' seeming impartiality.

Following a common secular focus on religious symbols is also an expedient way to reveal these power plays. In tandem with moves to secularize, in both France and Québec, Christian symbols have migrated to become symbols of heritage or culture. In Québec, Lori G. Beaman (2020) argues that the lack of contestation around omnipresent Catholic symbols is evidence that the Church remains a subtle yet powerful organizer of social life (cf. Perreault and Laniel 2022). A remarkable example of the "invisibilization" of Catholicism is the protection of a Christian crucifix from 1936 to 2020 in the National Assembly, the provincial government's legislative building in Québec City. For more than eight decades its prominent placement in the parliament's Blue Room was unassailable.[6] Former Québec premier Jean Charest echoed this protectionism: the crucifix was a symbol of Québec's history (cited in Beaman 2020: 73). In 2020, after debate on its presence following the passage of Law 21, the cross was quietly relocated, without a formal acknowledgment of the symbol's potential to evoke exclusionary histories of Christianity and/or colonialism. The political expediency of its removal was no secret. Premier François Legault publicly conceded that it was removed "in order to get as much support as possible [for Law 21]" (cited in CTV 2019). Other crosses in public spaces remain highly visible in skylines across the province, outside public hospitals and schools, and on Mount Royal, towering over the city of Montréal and especially visible with its white lights in the night sky. Arguably, the scale and visibility of these crosses make them normalized, unassailable, and even banal. Moreover, as I will turn to momentarily, given that the secular legislation in France and Québec has focused on the "problem" of religion on symbols on individuals' bodies, these expansive examples remain unregulated. Article 16 in Law 21, to which I turn later in this chapter, explicitly protects "the emblematic or toponymic elements of Québec's cultural heritage" (Assemblée Nationale du Québec 2019: 8), effectively shielding cultural Catholicism and big crosses from scrutiny.

HOW SECULARISMS ENGAGE RACE

Secular discourses also shape discursive treatments of race, namely in their promotion of an unnamed whiteness. With some exceptions (in the United States: Kahn and Lloyd 2016; Hart 2016; Sorritt 2016), fewer scholars have turned to how secularisms promote race-related habitus. Peter Coviello (2019: 235) is one. In *Make Yourselves Gods: Mormons and the Unfinished Business of American Secularism,* he shows how American Mormons became white when they disavowed polygamy and accepted mainstream secularism (see Scott 2016 on when French Canadians became white). With this context in mind, Coviello provocatively and rhetorically asks, "Can there be a secularism apart from whiteness, and its violent aggrandizement?" His goes-without-saying answer: no. Coviello brazenly proposes American secularism as "the racialized theodicy of hegemonic liberalism" (46). His example of Mormons' acceptance of normative Christian monogamy and patriarchy captures how the liberalism and secularism to which Mormons aspired had related racial and theological components. Whiteness is often caught up in ideas about evolution, progress, and civilization.

It is on the point of how secularisms render some expressions and norms as sacrosanct that we can begin mapping their habitus as white (see Jasbir Puar's [2013: 26] aside on secularism). A habitus of whiteness, Sara Ahmed (2007: 157) reminds us, is powerful because it is "invisible and unmarked . . . the absent center against which others appear only as deviants, or points of deviation" (see also Wekker 2016: 59; Scott 2018: 3; Bracke and Hernández Aguilar 2020; and Lépinard 2020: 83). Following this insight, I briefly consider how articulations of secularism in France and Québec have, at times, served as expeditious tools of white governmentality. Their constructed neutrality work in tandem with the unexamined whiteness and Christian project of coloniality (see Ahmed 2007: 154). Contemporarily, purported goals of *laïque* legislation, whether a *vivre ensemble* (living well together) in France or "unity" for the Québécois, take decidedly color-blind approaches. We can read the omission of references to race in state-based secular formulations in France and Québec as a bolstering of implied whiteness.

Coviello's thinking on how sex and race intersect through secular legislation in the United States is instructive, even if based on a very different time and place than the contexts I examine. Coviello shows how American secularism disciplined the carnal theology of early Mormonism. When their polygamy was visible, they were characterized as "Indian, as Mohammedan, as African or Asiatic despots, [and] as slave-live sycophants to domineering theological masters" (Coviello 2019: 172). However, when Mormons formally rejected polygamy in 1890, they reshaped their theology to coincide with normative monogamous settler Christianity and patriarchy. In so doing, they came to be recognized as sexually normative and, subsequently, were effectively embraced by the state as white. The shift was not without theological consequence; their previous support for polygamy was central to their distinctive theological notion of exaltation.

Dispensing this theology effectively rendered nineteenth-century Mormons as normatively liberal in the eyes of the imperial state. Allegiance to this racialized liberalism of mainstream American secular politics meant the former Mormon threat to the nation was neutralized. This pivot also meant an embrace of heteronormative patriarchal sexual politics. There are parallels for Algerians in France and Québec more than 100 years later: depending on whether they are read as practicing Muslims, they are sometimes categorized as white and sometimes as racialized; their sexual politics are also often scrutinized depending on these perceptions. The impetus to publicly perform appropriate nonpatriarchal power relations are heightened for those perceived as Muslim and/or racialized.

HOW SECULARISMS ENGAGE GENDERED AND SEXUAL SENSIBILITIES[7]

Notwithstanding a now-famous comment made in 1967 by former Canadian prime minister Pierre Elliott Trudeau, in the context of revisions to the Criminal Code of Canada to decriminalize "homosexual acts," that "there is no place for the state in the bedrooms of the nation," nation-states are *very* interested in managing the sexual politics of their citizens, both in the public sphere and, for some more than others, in imagined-as-private bedrooms. Foucault's notion of biopower is, again, useful to think through how—as in other colonial nation-states—statecraft in France and Québec is invested in surveilling the seemingly private matters of sex and sexuality. Secular legislation is, again, a useful tool: it has been mobilized in triumphalist ways, as the locomotive of gender equality, and therefore necessary as part of a framework for the equal rights of women. A central logic in these secular frameworks is a binary that locates religion in the private realm where "intimacies" are protected (see Rambukkana 2015: 28). Religions' presence in the public sphere is then problematized for trespassing these boundaries. Such categorizations are made powerful when they are "naturalized." For example, these nation-states actively position monogamy as sexually "normal."[8] Let us now turn to how these ideas are narrativized on and through people's bodies.

Secular Bodies

Configurations of the secular can be examined materially, including through a rendering of a "secular body." My overarching assumption is that secularisms can be studied as something that is practiced, felt, and experienced, and that, like religious traditions, includes a range of social and physical dispositions. Secularism is not, put simply, an empty, neutral container. While it is not a "thing thing," and while I appreciate Lois Lee's (2015: 102) warning that "the notion of a secular body is, then, truly a tricky one," I nevertheless propose that a secular body *can* be stitched together through examination of which bodily practices, dress, comportment, and dispositions are restricted, and, to a lesser extent, which are promoted (see Lee 2015 and Engelke 2015 for their analyses of overtly atheist habituses with fashions, dress and jewelry in the United Kingdom). Coviello (2019: 19) offers a wonderful personification of a secular body. This imagined secular person dresses in "respectable guises" and speaks "in an ordinary and even critical voice." Their posture is "neutralish, cogitative, deflating, [and] always faintly condescending." Adding specificity to Coviello's secular body, and in light of the French and Québécois contexts under examination, I would add: a savvy consumer, rational, white, and a monogamist, who equates sexual freedom with visual access to women's bodies whether or not he is heterosexual. This section engages theoretical work on the secular body and analyzes a caricature from the French daily *L'Opinion* to draw out some common features in France. Such overt depictions are less available in Québec.

Several cultural and political theorists, historians, and anthropologists have critically engaged the notion of the secular body. These theorists—Talal Asad, Saba Mahmood, Nadia Fadil, William Connolly, and others—implicitly agree that there is not *a* secular body but that a significant habitus and performances exist that we can associate with secularism. My goal is not to locate the secular body on those who see themselves as secular or nonreligious but rather, through the narratives of my interlocutors of Algerian origin, to consider what is at stake when "secular sensibilities" aim to shape a common social world, and to interrogate the content of these sensibilities.

My take challenges previous scholarly work on the secular body. Asad (2011: 661), for one, argues that the secular body's normativity and *invisibility* are what grant it power in the world. He contends, "Unless you knew someone well you couldn't tell whether she was a believer or not merely from the way she spoke or behaved. What does this say about the secular body? One answer may be that [religious] belief, where it exists among liberal moderns, is so deeply repressed that it has at best a very tenuous connection with observable behavior." The normativity of the secular body thus necessarily renders religious-identified ones as observable and atypical. We can see some extension of this thinking in Asad's *Secular Translations*

Figure 1.1. "Faut-il un pacte avec l'islam de France?" (Do we need a pact with the Islam of France?) Cartoon by KAK, *L'Opinion*, June 7, 2016.

(2018), where he moves away from the allusion of invisibility into that of suspicion. Connolly (2011) similarly contends that the secular body's expectations are concealed and therefore immunized from challenge.

In contrast to a secular body, the unavoidable visible presence of religion evokes unease, a misgiving, a problem. In his conception of secularism as a "problem-space," Agrama (2012: 34) describes secularism as a questioning power that generates suspicion and anxiety in relation to religion. This framing of suspicion rather than invisibility is more apropos, in my reading. My data show that the secular body is far from invisible. Since 2004, French and Québécois legal projects, including those I discuss related to marriage, are increasingly prescriptive and demanding of proof of secularity—a clear legibility—on the body.

The 2016 caricature (fig. 1.1) by KAK for *L'Opinion*, a French daily, neatly portrays some of the common parameters of the secular body I see in France and Québec in relation to how laïcité and related constructions of religion, race, and sexuality are constitutively imagined. In the cartoon, we see two religiously identifiable men wearing conspicuous religious symbols: the first is a practicing Muslim and the second, standing behind him, a white Catholic priest. Beads of sweat are visible on their brows as they face a bare-breasted bust of Marianne. Immortalized in Eugène Delacroix's iconic painting *Liberty Leading the People* (1830), Marianne has long symbolized the French Revolution and its calls for freedom and democracy. In this caricature and Delacroix's painting, Marianne is young, wears a Phrygian cap, and is bare-breasted. More modest versions exist, but they have circulated less (Almeida 2018). Indeed, Marianne's torso is ubiquitous on statues, on the official government logo of France, on euro coins and stamps in France, in the entryway of public schools. It is no accident that her profile was chosen as the representative symbol of France for the 2024 Summer Olympic games in Paris. The recognizability of her face and cap, and ubiquity of her breasts, captures how common laïque discourses in France frame gender in ways that privilege a heterosexual male gaze. We can also note the tripart Republican values are etched below the bust in the lower base, with laïcité added to the list.[9]

Note the older white-haired Catholic priest who encouragingly calls for "courage" to an anxious-looking Muslim man in the face of Marianne's laïcité and breasts. The priest appears more steadfast. He is older and has more experience with this discomfort. The caricature implies that the body-covering garments promoted by religious convictions, which might not induce these beads of sweat, are too conspicuous, too conservative, too foreign, too religious, too patriarchal. A bright light behind them may evoke even more heat. If we imagine that this light reflects the rational Enlightenment's critique of religiosity, we are reminded that these narrow understandings of the desirability of areligious sexualized feminized bodies are not new. These publicly visible religious men are guilty of transgressing a public/private sphere division, and more egregiously, of inappropriately responding to the democratic Republican Marianne's sexual politics. Their sweat belies them. They embody sexual excess. Compounded for those who are racialized and more socially precarious, KAK's caricature depicts religious men as Orientalized and associated with bad sexuality, which in France often collapses the covering of women with polygamy, gang rape, and homophobia (see Scott 2018: 163; and Farris 2017). As an exemplifying symbol of the French secular body, the statue of Marianne evokes the improper sexuality of these religious men.

Marianne, in contrast, remains stone-faced before these religious excesses. Sexed and static, she cannot speak. Marianne is an oft-evoked figure in French politics. In his take on the burkini debates on the French Riviera in 2016, some of which specifically targeted Algerian-origin women, then French prime minister Manuel Valls stressed to the press that bare breasts "symbolize freedom," adding that Marianne "is not veiled because she is free" (cited in Sims 2016). So too Laurence Rossignol, who in 2016 was the minister of the families, childhood, and women's rights (and later a senator) and a founding member of the Mouvement de libération des femmes, stressed that the niqab cannot be approached under the need to protect an individual's freedom to dress as they wish because the niqab "is a societal project [with] a vision of women's place" (cited in Europe 1 2016). In contrast to women who cover with niqabs or burkinis, Marianne's putative freedom is captured by her nudity and areligiosity, as depicted in KAK's cartoon.

Regulating Secular Bodies in France and Québec

There are generalizable differences between how the secular body materializes in France and Québec. The surveillance of secularism in Québec is not as clearly regimented as in France. For one, conspicuous religious symbols—hijabs—are not (yet) monitored on the heads of children in Québécois public schools as they are on teachers. Mothers wearing hijab in Québec have not been scrutinized on school grounds or on school outings. There is also less specificity in the idealized secular body in the province: bandanas, beards, and abayas have not been formally curtailed by the state, as they have in France. In general, Muslims in Québec have also fared better than self-identified Muslims in France in securing work and in their general socioeconomic profiles (see quantitative data by Hachimi Alaoui 2006; Joly and Reitz 2018; and Laxer, Reitz, and Simon 2019). In addition, historical and contemporary immigration policies shape differences in the response to difference. For my interlocutors of Algerian origin, migration to Québec from Algeria dates primarily from the 1990s; in France, it can be traced to more than a century earlier. Unlike in France, where we see significantly more family reunification immigration, it is more challenging to enter Canada, not only because of its isolated geography but also thanks to a points system introduced in 1967 that moved away from a stated preference for British Protestant subjects; unskilled workers who do not hold diplomas or speak French fluently have fewer options (see a helpful critique of Canada's immigration model in Triadafilopoulos 2013).

Despite these differences, there remain resonances with how the secular body is conceptualized in contemporary France and Québec. Beginning in 2008 with the release of a report and its recommendations on how to manage religion in Québec, formulations of the secular and related secular sensibilities in Québec began dovetailing with those in France. Figure 1.2 plots significant public controversies and legal projects that have shaped the contours of the secular body from 2008 to 2024. I include the broader Canadian legislative context because, while often imagined as wholly different from

	FRANCE
2008	Government probing of private sexuality: High Court of Lille on the "Marriage Annulment" case; and "Mme M." citizenship request is denied
2009	
2010	Gerin Commission and niqab law (law enforced April 11, 2010)
	Memorandum for marriage celebrants
2012	Chatel Memorandum (restricting mothers' hijabs in public schools)
2013	
2014	Baby Loup private nursery case (hijab-wearing woman is fired)
2015	
2016	Proposed burkini bans in the French Riviera
2017	
2018	Sports hijabs pulled from Decathlon store shelves
2019	IFOP Survey: 74% of French feel "threatened" by religion in the public sphere
2020	
2021	Decree from the Conseil d'État to dissolve Collective against Islamophobia in France and Secularism Observatory
	Law of 24 August 2021 Confirming Respect for the Principles of the Republic (Separatism Law) passes
2023	Abaya ban in public schools by Education Minister Gabriel Attal
2024	

ONSC: Ontario Superior Court of Justice **QCA:** Québec Court of Appeal
SCC: Supreme Court of Canada **SCQB:** Superior Court of Québec

Figure 1.2. Timeline of legislation on secular bodies in France, Canada, and Québec, 2008–2024. Figure by the author.

CANADA (FEDERAL)	QUÉBEC (PROVINCIAL)
Truth and Reconciliation Commission of Canada Report and its 94 recommendations	Bouchard-Taylor Commission Report released Launch of compulsory Ethics and Religious Culture course in public schools
SCC decision: *Alberta v. Hutterian Brethren of Wilson Colony* (disallowing accommodation of no photographs on drivers' licenses)	
	Bill 94 (Niqab ban) proposed
SCC decision: *R v. N.S.* (on ad hoc protection of niqabs in courtrooms)	
	Bill 60 (Charter of Values) proposed
Federal election concerns: SCC decision: *Ishaq v. Canada* (Minister of Citizenship and Immigration); and Zero Tolerance for Barbaric Cultural Practices Act SCC decision: *Loyola High School v. Quebec (Attorney General)* (on ERC courses)	SCC decision: *Mouvement laïque québécois v. Saguenay (City)* (to cease reciting prayers at the opening of municipal sessions)
	Bill 62 (Niqab ban) is sanctioned and stayed
ONSC decision: *Christian Medical and Dental Society of Canada v. CPSO* (Canadian Physicians and Surgeons of Ontario)	Law 21 (Laicity of the State) passes Crucifix removed from the National Assembly
SCC refuses to hear appeal on Law 21	Ethics and Religious Culture course abolished
Municipalities in the Rest of Canada rally against Law 21	SCQB upholds most of Law 21 Fatemeh Anvari case in Chelsea, QC (loses job over wearing hijab in public school)
	Culture and Citizenship in Québec (CCQ) program launches in public schools CAQ directive to prohibit worship spaces in public schools
	In *Hak v. Attorney General of QC*, SCQB upholds most of Law 21

the secular politics in Québec, Supreme Court of Canada decisions in 2009 (*Alberta v. Hutterian Brethren of Wilson Colony*) and 2012 (*R. v. N.S.*, regarding the acceptability of the niqab) suggest comparable formulations of a secular body, particularly around the importance of the visibility of faces in the public sphere. A 2015 Canadian federal Barbaric Cultural Practices Act also included specific language and concern with transnational marriage and polygamy. The *sous-entendu* was that the risk of so-called barbarism lay with racialized non-Christian immigrant men. This comparative overview makes evident how the "problem" of religion has been recently lodged primarily in managing conspicuous religious symbols. I do not rehearse each moment in this section. I point briefly to six key directives in relation to their "secular sensibilities": in France, the 2004 law banning conspicuous religious symbols, the 2010 law against niqabs, the antiterrorism prosecularism campaigns launched after the 2015 terrorist attacks, and the 2021 Law of Separatism. In Québec, I look at Bill 60 and Law 21.

CONSPICUOUS RELIGIOUS SYMBOLS THAT IMPEDE THE SECULAR BODY

Public and institutional concern with the visibility of religious symbols in public schools exploded in France in the late 1980s, and in Québec more than three decades later. Hijabs were at the center of this maelstrom and imagined as endangering gender equality, safety from terrorism, and living well together. But why a focus on symbols? And why *these* symbols?

Most obviously, externalized religious symbols visible on the body are simpler to assess and sanction than illiberal or undesirable philosophical beliefs or practices. Understanding religion through its symbols is not new. Clifford Geertz (1973: 80) famously conceptualized religion as a system of symbols that serve to capture the "moods" and "motivations" central to creating an "aura of factuality" for those who engage them. As externalized containers for more complex personhoods, political inclinations, and changing interior sensibilities, among others, conspicuous religious symbols are facile to determine and restrict. When religious conviction exists, a simple piece of fabric—whether a bandana, a wool hat, a long flowing garment, or even a medical cap—can become a conspicuous religious symbol (Woehrling 2012: 10; see also Mahmood 2009: 273). Yet its containment of "religion" is not always straightforward. For instance, women wear hijab for a myriad of nonreligiously informed reasons too, including pattern baldness (Selby 2014b), cancer treatments, custom, and as a shield (like Farida, who we will meet, who sees hers as protection against violence, as she began to wear it in Algeria). Pictograms (figs. 1.3 and 1.4) suggest that the delineation is straightforward. These official descriptions of the secular body in government-issued pictograms radically distill complex lifeways to facile dos and don'ts. An object, visible on the body, is either religiously conspicuous or not. Allowed or not. Chosen or not. Geertz has since been rightly critiqued for the ahistoricity of his reliance on symbols to define religion (Asad 1983; Schilbrack 2005). Religious symbols are not static in their significance and meanings. Religious symbols may not reflect a choice. They may reflect a deep-seated conviction.

Concerns with conspicuous religious symbols—hijabs in particular—began percolating decades before 2004 in France, in the 1980s, also influenced by a number of national and international political happenings, including a 1974 shift in immigration policy, which brought many more women and families to the Republic, and the Salmon Rushdie Affair, that ignited fears related to Islamic symbols. What became known as the *Affaire du foulard* (Headscarf affair) erupted in October 1989 when three middle-school girls in a Parisian suburb were suspended when they refused to remove their headscarves. Media and political response centered on the symbol's dangers.[10] The Cour de cassation (Court of Cassation) ultimately ruled on the case, stating that religious symbols were permissible so long as they were not "conspicuous" or "militant." The decision left interpretation to individual schools (Brulard 1997: 179). In the ensuing years, some school administrators complained that the parameters were too broad and too challenging to apply. The Circulaire Bayrou (or Bayrou decree), issued in September 1994 by then education minister François Bayrou, sought to clarify these categories. It introduced a now-foundational distinction between "discreet" symbols, which "express a personal attachment to [someone's] convictions," and "ostentatious" symbols that constitute "proselytism or... discrimination" (cited in Joppke 2007: 323; see also Laborde 2005; Selby 2014b). This binary distinction between discreet and conspicuous symbols was replicated in Québec, beginning in 2013 with Bill 60 or the "Charter of Values."

Despite the Bayrou Decree's clarification, a pervading sense remained for some that hijab wearers under eighteen were being unduly influenced through the proselytization of their surrounding culturally homogenous and pressure-filled communities, for which *communautarisme*, or communalism, becomes shorthand. This communalism is recurringly contrasted with a more desirable secular sensibility of individualism, and notions of vivre ensemble, which also support the feminist goals of Republicanism. The varying uses and vagueness of communalism are purposeful, says sociologist Julia Martínez-Ariño. Their ambiguity "allows conceptualising practically anything as potentially threatening social cohesion" (Martínez-Ariño 2021: 68). Hijabs in schools become symbols of this threat.

Aiming to further concretize the Bayrou Decree's distinction in public schools, then French president Jacques Chirac appointed a twenty-member team, led by government ombudsperson Bernard Stasi, to determine the application of the principle of laïcité in public schools. The Stasi Commission, or the Commission de réflexion sur l'application du principe de laïcité dans la République (Commission Reviewing the Application of the Principle of Secularism in the Republic), produced a final report that outlined twenty-six recommendations (see Laurence and Vaisse 2006: 166; Weil 2009). Recommendations that did not garner political traction included the recruitment of Muslim chaplains for the French army and prisons, the creation of a national school of Islamic studies, the official recognition of religious holidays outside of Christianity, and ensuring that the teaching of French history included slavery, colonization, decolonization, and immigration (Assemblée Nationale 2004). Notably, the recommendation most quickly legislated was the delimiting of discreet and conspicuous religious symbols in schools, which was enforced with the *rentrée* (back to school) in the fall of 2004.[11] In their immediate recognizability, conspicuous symbols reflect bad religion. Hijabs are the most egregious. A later memorandum from the Education Ministry sought to clarify its definition of "conspicuous" symbols. The subsequent decree therefore noted that the wearer's religion should be "immediately recognizable" or "exaggerated" (Légifrance 2004).

Echoing the Bayrou Decree, the 2003 Stasi Commission report depicts young Muslim women as the most vulnerable to the machinations of bad religion, noting that "sometimes, the headscarf is violently imposed upon preadolescent girls" (Stasi 2003: 47). Significantly, and as with other legislation against them in France and Québec, the commission neither auditioned women or girls who wear the garment, nor did it offer data showing the dangers of hijab for them (Tissot 2011; Amiraux 2016; Benhadjoudja 2018; Laxer 2019; Jahangeer 2020; Zoghlami 2020; Taher 2021). Instead, reporting on the dangers of religious symbols here, and elsewhere, relies on gravitas and other (often white, non-Muslim) women's anecdotal testimonies. Because of the perceived influence of proselytism, those who wear these symbols are unable to rationally assess inconspicuous and conspicuous distinctions.

The legal malleability of interpretations of conspicuousness reappeared in a 2007 case, where the Council of State ruled that a female student who switched her headscarf for a bandana should be expelled. The commissioner in this case noted the importance of "verify[ing] the ostentatiousness of the student's behavior" (cited in Koussens 2023: 107). Surveillance of her undesirable religiosity therefore went beyond the religious symbol itself to her habitus and sensibilities.

The presupposition that undesirable politics can be visually monitored and disciplined through religious symbols was reentrenched seven years later in 2010 with a commission assigned to assess full-face-covering headscarves. A now-familiar six-month-long commission resulted in a 658-page "fact-finding mission on the practice of wearing the full-face veil on the national territory." The report positions the meaning of full-face coverings rather starkly: they are *not* religious symbols. They are political, antiwoman, and "Islamist" symbols. Full-face veils are framed in the report as jeopardizing citizenship and as reinforcing patriarchy. The report's overarching argument is clear: the Republic has a problem—the full-face veil—and a simple solution—its removal from the public sphere—thanks to a sound and just government—here André Gerin, on behalf of the French state (Selby 2011b: 387). The Conseil français du culte musulman (CFCM, French Council of the Muslim Faith), a consultative group created by the state in 2003 to represent the country's diverse Muslim population, corroborates this point that niqabs are not religious symbols (see Caeiro 2005 and Bowen 2011 on the CFCM). To be fair, few organizations, Muslim or otherwise, mobilized to defend full-face veils, not unlike in a half-dozen other Western European nation-states where they have also been outlawed (Selby 2012; Barras 2013). Characterizing them as "an excessive practice" and as cultural and not religious symbols, the CFCM effectively dismissed full-face veils' potential protection through freedom-of-religion avenues. This argument also worked to define the parameters of a domestic-framed Islam (an Islam *de* France) (Assemblée Nationale 2010: 36), which John Bowen (2004: 44) has critiqued as a "hackneyed rhetorical device" to signal state and religious allegiance.

In the same period as this heightened concern for niqabs in France, a series of shocking terrorist attacks in January and November 2015 further ignited fears related to Islam-related symbols. The first deadly attack, on January 7 at the *Charlie Hebdo* satirical magazine headquarters in Paris, was followed by related violence in the Île-de-France region over the next two days. Altogether, twelve people were murdered and eleven injured. The attacks inspired significant political responses, both online and in the streets. The #JeSuisCharlie hashtag became one of the most important in Twitter's history, which complicatedly merged the magazine's views of Islam with solidarity for the freedom of expression (Funk 2017; Peter 2021: 174). Days after these assassinations, between 2 to 4 million people took to the streets for the Marches Républicaines, the largest of their kind in the country's history. Former president François Hollande described these marches as the "esprit du 11 janvier" (cited in Chapuis 2015). An outpouring of sorrow and anger in the public sphere in cities around the country was palpable. These marches were also a celebration of the state and of those deemed ideal citizens. The crowd's prevalent racial and socioeconomic composition was noted by several critics: those who marched were mostly white, urban, educated, and what one philosopher characterized as "zombie Catholics," residuals from "a peripheral Catholic subculture" (Todd 2015: 55).

The *esprit* of fear spread through #JeSuisCharlie and in the state's Vigipirate Alerte Attentat, the highest level of security alert, and a state of emergency, which was extended for over two years, until November 2017. A common refrain—*Plan Vigipirate Alerte Attentat: la vigilance est l'affaire de tous* (Antiterrorist Security Plan: Vigilance concerns us all)—was an omnipresent reminder from 2015 to 2017 of a potential terrorist presence in France's public spaces. Red triangles warning of a "high risk of attack" with the Vigipirate slogan were placed in public spaces during the state of emergency: in stores, at school entrances, in subways, in public libraries. Even in the basement of Paris's National Library, the red triangles were taped on every other desk, reminding researchers of the possibility of imminent attack. I never saw the red triangles postered in the little public library, or outside public schools or the recreation center, in Petit-Nanterre, a reminder of the imagined location of threat. The message: vigilance concerns us all; combatting potential terrorism is a shared responsibility. Individual citizens should be on the lookout. The Vigipirate response also initiated greater police response everywhere, which bolstered an association of domestic terrorism with racialized suburban youth.

Indeed, a contributing factor to the *Charlie Hebdo* attack, argued Prime Minister Manuel Valls, was the "apartheid, territorially, socially and ethnically" of the country's peripheral suburban regions like Petit-Nanterre, recalling former president Nicolas Sarkozy's description of *banlieusards* as *racaille* (or scum) in the context of the 2005 riots. Valls's disparaging comments capture a recurring political exclusion of these spaces and their inhabitants. Suburban youths are, as in the 2005 riots, evoked *and* violently excluded. Valls's allusion to the apartheid-like conditions of the suburbs does not imply accountability for the racial and overt governmental discrimination politics and policing. The banlieue's imagined Fanonian separation of the core from the periphery was thus only worsened in this political moment. If in the 1990s political attention and fear fell on a suburban religious patriarch who enforced headscarves, in the 2000s they fell on hoodied male youths throwing Molotov cocktails at police, with far-reaching implications (see Zappi 2015 and Guénif Soulimas and Macé 2004 for their analysis of a delinquent "Arab Boy"). The banlieue's male Other in this Vigipirate period is arguably less containable: he is more worldly, is active on social media and in global forums, and holds possible connections with international terrorist groups.

Concern compounded in the capital city following a second period of violence in November of the same year. It centered in a northern suburb of Paris, Saint-Denis, and in the city's eleventh arrondissement, with particular terror at the Bataclan Theater, where 130 civilians were killed. The Islamic State (or Daech) claimed responsibility for the attack. Several of the attackers were born in France and Belgium, which compounded fears (BBC News 2016; Durin 2022). I was living in Paris in November 2015 for a sabbatical year, during which I undertook research for this book, and can attest to the heightened sense of immanent violence in the wake of the attacks in the city. Narratives about the victims were overwhelming. Along with the incendiary Vigipirate alert signs, the state of emergency meant bags were searched in many public places by machine-gun-wearing police, fingers resting on triggers, who in addition to subway stations and other public institutions also stood outside a synagogue next to the private daycare my one-year-old attended.

It is in this context of intensified fear and securitization after the January and November 2015 attacks that a poster (fig. 1.3) was introduced by the government as part of its "Stop Djihadism" campaign. It offers more actionable and tangible "signs" of radicalization. As the poster notes, the more these signs are present in an individual in combination, the more citizens should intervene. Signs and behaviors to watch for include declining to swim wearing a revealing swimsuit, rejecting traditional French foods, and refusing gender-mixing. These fears are not new. They echo 2012 comments by then president Nicolas Sarkozy on how the problem of *communautarisme* in suburbs like Petit-Nanterre makes it difficult to manage Muslims, including problems at public pools around gender-segregated swimming, requests for halal foods, and requests for doctors of the same sex (see Beardsley 2012).

This poster (fig. 1.3) also offers visual shortcuts regarding the idealized secular body. Here, an imagined unacceptable religious body, linked to *la menace terroriste* (the threat of terrorism) denies heterosexual engagements (as in the first image), refuses form-fitting dresses (as in the bottom center image), and rejects a staple of the daily diet, the baguette (top right). The poster also advertises a telephone hotline created for reporting these unacceptable behaviors, echoing the hotline promised in Canada in 2015 with the federal Barbaric Practices Act (to which I turn in chapter 3).

Figure 1.3. "Jihadist radicalization: The first warning signs," French poster government. Cited in *Toronto Star*, "Quit Sports? Avoiding Baguettes? French Issues Checklist of Jihadist Warning Signs," January 30, 2015, www.thestar.com/news/world/2015/01/30/quit-sports-avoiding-baguettes-french-issues-checklist-of-jihadist-warning-signs.html.

Repercussions from the 2015–17 state of emergency in France were experienced unevenly. The Collectif contre l'islamophobie en France (CCIF, Collective against Islamophobia in France), founded in 2003 and dismantled in 2020, noted a significant rise in Islamophobia following the January 2015 attacks (CCIF 2015: 14), which surely remained the case that November. The government's dismantling of the CCIF in 2020 also reflects the period following the November 13 attacks and the political response to the assassination of a schoolteacher, Samuel Paty, almost five years later. The two primary goals of the CCIF (2015: 5) were to provide moral, practical, and legal support to victims of Islamophobia and, through its "observatory," to monitor Islamophobia and anti-Muslim racism in France.[12] The CCIF was criticized for mobilizing the term "Islamophobia" (notably by journalist Caroline Fourest, former prime minister Manuel Valls, and journalist and far-right politician Éric Zemmour) and accused of Islamist linkages (most notably by political scientist Gilles Kepel).[13] In a broader context of concern for radicalism and a putative rise in "islamo-gauchisme," particularly among "woke" academics, the French Council of Ministers announced the dismantling of the CCIF in December 2020 (*Le Figaro* 2020).[14] Concern expressed by the then minister of education about "Islamo-leftism," and especially that there is "something at work [in academia] that is ideological and must be made explicit," created a further chilling effect. The accusation of islamo-gauchisme was lobbed at scholars seen as too activist or complacent toward terrorists in their critiques of Islam in France (Diallo 2020; Tharoor 2021; Marlière 2023). Amid this broad anxiety surrounding a perceived rise in extremist violence, and concern related to the notion of Islamophobia itself, the surveillance of and formal litigation against Islamophobia by a not-for-profit organization in France was no longer tenable. Selim Nadi (2021) convincingly argues that the perpetuation and validation of Islamophobia and neocolonialism under leftist progressive fronts like feminism have served to delegitimize Muslim associative organizations like the CCIF (see also Zia-Ebrahimi 2020, 2023). Arguably, therefore, the CCIF's 2020 closure is a tangible example of the political impacts of the islamo-gauchisme anxiety in France, and how secular laws offered a response to these fears. The "war" against "Islamist separatism," as described by President Macron in the 2021 secular Law of Separatism, responds to these concerns.

By 2020, in an effort to counter potential threats and secure these ideas legislatively, legislative reforms to secularism were proposed in France. In a September 2020 speech that sought to address this moment, President Emmanuel Macron outlined what he called the "Projet de loi confortant le respect des principes de la République" (Bill strengthening the respect of the Republic's principles), which became known as the Antiseparatism Bill. The proposal claimed to better combat "the growing influence" of radical Islam and terrorism (République française 2021; see also Bryant 2020; Diffley 2020; Willsher 2020).[15] The decapitation of a history and geography high school teacher, Samuel Paty, in October 2020, in a suburb of Paris, ignited further concerns for Islamic terrorism. The man who killed Paty is said to have been incensed that the teacher showed a *Charlie Hebdo* cartoon of the Prophet Muhammad to his students. Like the attacks at the satirical weekly magazine, Paty's murder was therefore framed as an attack on the freedom of speech. Paty's face, stressed President Macron, was that "of the Republic" (cited in Euronews 2020). By December 2020, the Antiseparatism Bill was formalized. Debates began on its contents in February 2021 in the midst of other restrictions and concerns engendered by the COVID-19 pandemic. Minister of the Interior Gérald Darmanin underscored the bill's continuation of the parameters of the 1905 law, given that it was presented *jour pour jour* (to the day), 115 years later, on December 9, 2020. Despite critiques that it further stigmatizes Muslims, the Antiseparatism Law passed the French Senate in July, by a vote of 347 to 151 (Griffin 2021; *TRTWorld* 2021). Following minor modifications of two of the bill's provisions, the Antiseparatism Bill become law in August 2021 (RFI 2021). The "24 August 2021 Law respecting the principles of the Republic" includes several provisions related to laïcité and Islam, among them increased state control over religious groups' finances, the requirement that civil servants undertake secular training and pledge allegiance prior to accepting state-based jobs, and changes to inheritance law, home schooling, and government procurement (Légifrance 2021; see also Koussens 2023: 36).

The scope of the 2021 Antiseparatism Law is more expansive than other post-2004 legislation in France. Nevertheless it continues to outline acceptable secular comportment and sensibilities through a negative casting of Muslim sexuality. In particular, the law bans virginity certificates, curtails immigration for couples in polygamous arrangements (Art. L. 412-16), increases sanctions against female genital mutilation, and strengthens rules against forced marriage. An explosive marriage annulment case in Lille in 2008 around a virginity certificate, which I discuss in chapter 2, was recalled, as well as news reports interviewing gynecologists on the protection of women from the necessity of such certificates without quantifying their prevalence (see BFMTV 2020; see also TV5 2020). Chems-Eddine Hafiz, rector of the Grande Mosquée de Paris, called the impression that virginity certificates are in demand into question, noting that they are "really the least of Muslims' concerns today" (quoted in de Lasa 2022). With these objects of focus, the 2021 law extends the purview of acceptable comportment beyond curtailing conspicuous religious symbols to more complex signs of social-sexual acceptability, now virginity certificates. The problem of patriarchy is not acknowledged.

Transatlantic resonances are notable. Parts of these laws from 2004, 2010, and 2021—certainly their focus on religious symbols—emerged in Québec beginning in 2008. A 2013 pictogram created by the Parti Québécois that delineated "acceptable" and "conspicuous" religious symbols akin to the demarcation in the Stasi Commission report best captures these reverberations (see fig. 1.4). This visual distilled the primary impetus behind Bill 60, or the wordily named "Charter Affirming the Values of State Secularism and Religious Neutrality and of Equality between Women and Men, and

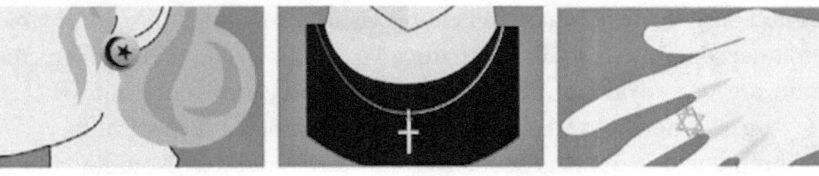

Figure 1.4. The Government of Québec's 2013 pictogram for Bill 60. Cited in Jonathan Montpetit, "Quebec's Charter of Values, Revisited," *CBC News*, September 5, 2016, www.cbc.ca/news/canada/montreal/caq-quebec-charter-of-values-identity-politics-1.3748084.

Providing a Framework for Accommodation Requests." Bill 60 followed Bill 94 and preceded Bill 62, which passed but failed a challenge on religious freedom, and was stayed. See figure 1.2 for a more complete timeline (Assemblée Nationale du Québec 2010, 2013, 2017, 2019).

Also known as the "Charter of Québec Values," Bill 60 was introduced by the Parti Québécois in the last year of its mandate as a minority government; some suggest it was not part of a larger ideological plan but a political maneuver to gain votes (Laxer 2019: 107). The charter aimed to reinforce the so-called secular character of public institutions in the province by providing a framework for assessing reasonable accommodation requests. More controversially, it included the prohibition against conspicuous religious symbols for public servants. Public opinion and briefs submitted in relation to the charter were divided (Laxer 2019: 159). When the Parti Québécois was defeated by the Liberal Party in April 2014 provincial elections, Bill 60 was not formally adopted.

As in France, the conspicuous religious symbols under scrutiny in the Québécois secular debates are also depicted as stable, uniform, and self-evidently religious. They are only located on individual bodies. The inclusion of the crescent earrings and a Star of David ring as an allowable "discreet symbol" implies that symbols can be easily substituted or altered (see Barras and Saris 2020: 3). Again, religion is visually separated into acceptable and unacceptable versions, and reduced to symbols that, in the 2013 pictogram, are located on individual, unracialized bodies, are removable (that is, they are externalized and detachable), and imagined as privatizable.

The pictogram reflects secular "color-blind" politics. Notable is how the featureless faces of those depicted in the color image are white-ish beige or "unracialized." These are not real individuals. Their nondescript, mannequin-like bodies sidestep how the "banned" symbols disproportionally affect racialized Quebeckers. Images of actual individuals wearing the symbols might have humanized and captured the intersecting elements of their inclusion and exclusion. The point is that the "problem of accommodation" or of difference was again distilled as one that could be managed through the disciplining of certain religious symbols on individual bodies. The 2013 pictogram was *not* resurrected with the 2019 Bill 21, but the specter of the distinction between allowed and banned symbols usefully lingered in suggesting that symbols' ambiguities can be sharply reduced. Walid, with whom I begin chapter 2, invoked the violence of Bill 60 in his experiences in Québec following its debate.

Bill 21, or "An Act Respecting the Laicity of the State," was tabled in March 2019 by Simon Jolin-Barrette, the majority CAQ's minister of immigration, diversity, and inclusiveness (a post since tellingly renamed "minister of immigration, Francization, and integration").[16] The bill aimed to affirm laïcité in the province in ways that include prohibiting the wearing of religious symbols by government employees in positions of authority (Article 6). The bill also required those seeking government services to have their face uncovered (Article 8), a clause largely affecting those (Muslim) women who don full-face covering veils.[17] Those who have their faces covered for medical reasons or to do their jobs are exempt from these rules, including the entire population obliged to mask in the initial months of the COVID-19 pandemic.

Like those that preceded it, Bill 21 focuses on religious symbols as defining religiosity, particularly in their "connection with religious conviction or belief." The bill states that "a religious symbol . . . is any object, *including* clothing, a symbol, jewelry, an adornment, an accessory or headwear, that (1) is worn in connection with a religious conviction or belief; or (2) is *reasonably considered* as referring to a religious affiliation" (Article 6 from Bill 21 2019: 7; my emphasis). In this definition, the Coalition Avenir Québec mobilizes the ambiguity and malleability of symbols. Bill 21 does *not* explicitly define what constitutes a "religious symbol." Rather, it more ambiguously aims to assure "laicity," a neologism introduced in the English-language version of the bill (see Selby 2022b: fn6). Article 6 outlines that these symbols include "any object *including* clothing, a symbol, jewelry, an adornment, an accessory or headwear, that is worn in connection with a religious conviction or belief" (Selby 2022b: fn6; my emphasis). The "including" caveat in Article 6's definition is notable and expansive. The bill includes greater specificity in who it considers "persons in authority," devoting two appendices (or "schedules"), four pages or a quarter of the legislative document, to an exhaustive list of those individuals included under the purview of Article 6.

"Religious" tattoos offer interesting counterpoint to consider the privatization and individualization of religious symbols. Religion-related tattoos are *not* included in lists of unacceptable or conspicuous religious symbols in France or in Québec. Their greater individualization, ability to be concealed, and difficult removal may also facilitate their absence from the list. Drawing on a qualitative study of tattooed individuals and tattoo artists in Montréal and Toronto, Amélie Barras and Anne Saris (2021) argue that because they are imprinted on the skin and cannot be easily removed tattoos are not often imagined as external manifestations of religious belief and have escaped regulation.[18] Tattoos are also common among Quebeckers of all races and social classes; one study suggests that more than one-third of Canadians have tattoos (Logit Research 2024). For all of these reasons, tattoos do not provoke secular sensibilities.

Dreadlocks were also excluded from consideration. When asked about them in particular, Minister Jolin-Barrette noted: "No. [Dreadlocks are] part of the body" (cited in Authier 2019). The wigs worn by some Orthodox Jewish women also presumably get a pass, also because they do not disrupt secular sensibilities. They do not shield visual access to women's faces or bodies. In Montréal, the bodies of Hassidic men, who often wear tailored black suits, distinctive black top hats, and long curls framing their faces, are far more visible but have escaped regulation, perhaps because of their social segregation (Amiraux and Desharnais 2015). At the same time as it restricts, Law 21 does protect *some* symbols. The bill stipulates that the province's religious and cultural past must be protected. Emblems of Québécois heritage are not subject to its disciplinarity (Assemblée Nationale du Québec 2019: 6). Premier Legault also clarified that while some symbols might be understood as religious—like the crucifix in the National Assembly in Québec City or the Christian cross perched at the top of Mount Royal in Montréal—Law 21 protects them given their long-standing cultural meanings.

Also excluded from these regulations on secularism are symbols of Québec's colonial past. In a news conference following the provincial election (and before the passage of Law 21), Premier Legault explained, "We have to understand our past.... In our past we had Protestants and Catholics. They built the values we have in Québec. We have to recognise that and *not mix that with religious signs*" (cited in *BBC News* 2018; my emphasis). Protecting *these* religious symbols as part of the "past" or as the "values" of Québec recalls Lori G. Beaman's (2012, 2020) work on how these symbols are made cultural and rendered benign. Prominent Christian crosses are *not* conspicuous religious symbols but relics of Québec's cultural past. As we have seen, some of the ironies of this protectionism became untenable by 2020, when the contentious cross centrally hung in the provincial National Assembly was removed from its position of privilege.

Together these legal landscapes (in France: the 2004 law against conspicuous religious symbols, the 2010 law against full-face veils, and a number of publicized cases related to Muslim women's sexuality, including a 2016 controversy on burkinis and 2021 legislation against virginity certificates; in Québec: Bill 60 and Law 21) draw attention to the individual, outlining unacceptable forms of religiosity and dress and underpinning secular sensibilities. How do these laws translate to people's bodies and lives? The next section examines the impact of Law 21 on Zohra, Farah, and Firdaous in Montréal. These women are disproportionally affected by the legislation because of their gender and because, in Québec, the critique of religious symbols is more recent than in France and thus sharper in their experiences. In the face of Québec's secular body politics, from their different social locations we will see how these three women alternatively push back, reframe, and absorb these expectations. I then return to Ilias, the interlocutor from Petit-Nanterre with whom I opened this chapter, who described how he navigated his marriage partner preference vis-à-vis himself, his fiancée, his family, and the French state when he sought a "traditional" marital match.

Algerian Women's Negotiation of Religious Symbols in Québec

Conceptualizations of secularism and religious symbols appear on the bodies and in the lives of many of my interlocutors. The scrutiny of religious symbols in Québec influenced *all* my Algerian-origin participants, regardless of whether they were women or wore a headscarf. Of course, histories of Islamicist violence in Algeria, which also focused on the visibility of headscarves, shaped these responses. In this section, three women in Montréal—Zohra, Farah, and Firdaous—explain their positions on hijab in ways that differ from my interlocutors in Petit-Nanterre, in part because women in Petit-Nanterre have lived with these debates around religious symbols since the 1980s (see Selby 2012: 87–92 for a discussion of how interlocutors in

Petit-Nanterre grappled with the French 2004 law). Amel, twenty-five, for one, is accustomed to putting on and taking off her hijab throughout the day. She grew up as part of the post-2004 generation and, rightly or wrongly, this reflex to remove is part of her everyday life. It is difficult to predict whether Zohra, Farah, and Firdaous will reflect differently on Law 21 in fifteen years.

The experiences of Zohra, thirty-five, a self-defined Muslim woman and newcomer of Algerian origin, capture some of the effects of Law 21's framing of religious symbols. I met Zohra a half-dozen times in July and August 2018 and 2019 through her aunt, whom I met through a mutual friend and also interviewed. The timing of our meetings meant that we spoke about her responses as a teacher-trainee before and after the passage of Law 21 in June 2019. When we first met, she had lived in Montréal for three years, having settled with permanent residency with the intention of returning to university to complete teacher training. Her postmigration experience highlights some of the blind spots and violences implicit in Law 21's Article 6: first, as a woman who is racialized; second, as a new immigrant whose French accent is not Québécois; third, as a woman who is poor; and fourth as a Muslim who wears hijab. An intersectional approach reveals her vulnerability to the machinations of this version of laicity.

Zohra was quick-witted, self-assured, and charming. Her sparkling brown eyes and easy smile made her immediately likeable. During our first meeting on a warm July morning in the dimly lit living room of her two-bedroom rental apartment in a brick low-rise building in the Cartierville neighborhood north of Montréal, the shades were drawn to keep out the heat. Her children happily and quietly watched cartoons. Her husband slept after his night shift as a parking lot attendant. Zohra was relaxed. She seemed pleased with the cakes and chocolates I brought.

Zohra had chosen to migrate to Montréal and not France because of her hijab and her dream of becoming a high school math teacher. She knew that if she migrated to France, the two would not mix. She explained, "I first submitted my immigration request [in Algiers] in 2008 and I arrived here [in Montréal] in 2015. It was a slow procedure where I was asked repeatedly for my papers and to confirm that I was working in Algeria, that it was a permanent position and that the job was linked to my university degree. But I was really motivated [to wait for seven years]!" Zohra had previously completed university studies in Algiers in math and finance and secured a "good job" at a bank in the business district. Despite its stability and good pay, she described her worry and dismay at the internal corruption to which she was privy. She was close with her family but began dreaming of a life elsewhere.

Zohra had married Samir twelve years before settling in Montréal. They had three children: a daughter, seven years old, and two sons, ages four and three. Samir had needed to be convinced to emigrate. With the expense to apply, the long wait, the cold weather in Montréal, and his sense of duty to care for his divorced mother, he had misgivings. In addition, Samir had an engineering diploma and knew it would likely not be recognized in Québec. Both he and Zohra had cousins who had migrated to Montréal and had warned them about the difficulty of finding good work. Zohra said she worked for years to convince Samir; once their eldest daughter was born, he agreed.

Zohra and Samir arrived with the protections of permanent residency, but their settlement in Québec was challenging. As he expected, Samir was denied a degree equivalency certificate for his Algerian diploma and, after several rejections from job applications in comparable fields, he took a full-time job as a nighttime parking lot attendant downtown. The hours and the exposure to the elements in the wintertime were especially demanding. Compounding their stress, Zohra learned she was unexpectedly pregnant when they arrived, which stalled her plans to enroll in the four-year education degree program at the Université de Montréal. At the time of our interview, three years into her studies, Zohra had just over a year and internships remaining to complete her bachelor of education degree. Even though she would be allowed to graduate because of the CAQ's "grandfathered" concessions, debates around Law 21 had contributed to a climate where some of her superiors in two of her internship placements had felt emboldened to make racist comments. In one placement, her supervisor reported her "foreign" accent as a potential problem in her final report. Zohra also noted that she was regularly expected to complete "demeaning" cleaning or custodial jobs in classrooms, which she suspected might be related to her racialization and hijab. Most pressingly, her hijab would bar her from employment in the province's public education system postgraduation.

In this context, Zohra faced a dilemma: Should she stay in Montréal, renouncing her newfound emotionally and financially expensive degree, and try to find work in one of the city's four private Islamic schools? Should she leave the education field altogether and seek work elsewhere? Or should the family leave their Montréal rental apartment and move to Gatineau, Québec, a city that neighbors Ottawa, Ontario, where the provincial law is not applicable? There they could still live in French, hopefully still secure provincially subsidized daycare spots in Québec, and see if she could find work teaching in Ottawa.

The now-limited future possibilities engendered stress. Samir was not tied to his job, but they had a support network of family and friends in the city, and province-subsidized childcare for their two sons. Zohra had considered settling in Ottawa before they migrated. She would have been able to complete an education degree there in two years instead of four. But when she realized she was expecting and that her baby son had been approved for a state-subsidized daycare spot, she and Samir chose to stay in Québec. She now regretted this decision (see Legault-Leclair 2023 and Hasan et al. 2024 on the migration of Muslims out of the province following Law 21). For now, Zohra pushed on to complete her degree amid heightened tension regarding the undesirable "religiosity" of her hijab. She recognized that hers was not the idealized secular body as promoted by Law 21.

Another interlocutor, Farah, thirty, who was born in Montréal, explained her take on pressures related to Law 21. Her father had settled in the city in 1975 at age twenty to study. Following her father's failed marriage to a white Québécoise, her mother, then working as a French teacher near Annaba, migrated in 1992 for an arranged transnational marriage. In our interview, Farah laughed and described her father's shift in marriage partners as "moving 'Old School.'" Farah was married without children and lived on the northeast edge of the Mont Royal neighborhood downtown. She called herself a "believer" who did not practice. As a teen, her parents did not allow her to socialize freely. She had attended some *halaqa* (Islamic studies) classes with other young Muslims but never found them engaging. Her family celebrated Eid, but she did not fast for Ramadan. Her dad, whom she described as "Americanized," was fine with this decision; he was diabetic and did not fast in any case. Farah admitted that she let her mom believe she fasted "juste pour épargner ses sentiments, quoi" (just to spare her feelings).

Farah met her now-husband at a friend's wedding. He had migrated to Montréal from Algeria with his family when he was seven years old. He was one year older than her and worked as a banker. He was also nonpracticing. Despite Islamic practices not being part of their daily lives, they chose to be married "traditionally" and had a religiously framed marriage ceremony. Farah was happy with the ease in which she could introduce these traditions, which she described as more Algerian than Islamic. She had previously dated a non-Muslim Quebecker and said that she always felt his family didn't like that she was of Algerian origin. The parents of this previous boyfriend expressed "a certain reluctance towards me . . . definitely. When you're young and all that, well I'm still young, but when you're young, you tell yourself, 'It's OK. I don't care if I don't have a relationship with his family.' But, in fact, it's important." Farah does not wear a visible religious symbol. She also expressed unease with religious accommodations: "I tend to disagree with those who ask for these reasonable or unreasonable accommodations, because they put too much emphasis on things that are not religion." Still, Farah could see how the accommodation debates and their overemphasis on so-called conspicuous religious symbols influenced how Islam and Muslims circulate in Québec. "So people, when they think about Islam, they just think of "Oh, the veil" and stuff like that, whereas that is not just Islam. So, I find that it [Law 21] . . . it gives a negative image of Islam." For Farah, Law 21's necessity for the *legibility* of the secular body means that determining "bad religion" is reduced to a visual assessment focused on religious symbols. However, also for Farah, the hijab was not a reflection of what Islam means or how she is Muslim. Still, the narrow visual interpretation influenced how Farah, racialized as a Muslim, even without a hijab, was able to circulate.

A third and final Montréal participant, Firdaous, twenty-three, was born in Algeria and migrated to Montréal in 1998. Firdaous was a confident and expressive young person who considered herself a "cultural Muslim." At the time of our interview, she had recently completed an undergraduate degree in engineering and was engaged to a man of Tunisian origin whom she had met at a *collège d'enseignement général et professionnel* (CÉGEP, college for general and professional teaching), which many Québécois students attend for two years following secondary school. Firdaous explained that because she grew up in the culturally and racially diverse Saint-Léonard neighborhood in Montréal, even though she is a racialized minority, she did not experience much discrimination growing up. When asked, she identified as "a Montrealer," and not as a Muslim or Algerian. She believed that all markers of religiosity should be private and relegated to the home: "I can understand that they [Quebeckers] are not happy with that [visible hijabs], that for them it doesn't make sense. . . . I have always gone under the principle that my religion will be practiced at home. . . . I tell myself it's up to me to adapt rather than asking that I be accommodated. . . . I find that there is a certain effort that must be made on our part as an immigrant when we're born here." Firdaous spent her formative teenage years in Montréal amid public debates about the Bouchard-Taylor Commission and its report. She said she was not antiaccommodation but wanted to "be chill" and didn't want to impose any parts of her religiosity on others. Notably, while she had spent most of her life in Montréal, she considered herself an immigrant. For her, making all forms of religiosity private was part of the social contract of being an immigrant in the province. To create no fuss. She therefore accepted these parameters around the idealized secular body and enforced them in her entourage.

Together, these three women's experiences in Montréal capture the simultaneous specificity around religious symbols and the ambiguity around what Law 21 considered to be acceptable "religious symbols." Firdaous was critical of Law 21 because of a notable subsequent rise in Islamophobia following its passage, but she did not wear hijab and supported the law's implicit sharp delineation of public and private spheres. Farah was more ambivalent toward the law. She could see its impact in shaping a public imaginary, whether rightly or wrongly, around the traditions of Islam as focused on hijabs above all other expressions. She worried that this radically narrow version of Islam—where the hijab was *the* signifier of its traditions—discounted her way of being Muslim. This vision meant that her version of Islam as a cultural Muslim might receive less credence. Finally, for Zohra, Law 21's ban on public school teachers' wearing hijab meant that her decade-long plan and dream in the province was now impossible. She did not see her hijab as optional or removable in the public sphere, as imagined in this secular sensibility. She did not see her response changing. Again, in contrast, in general, in France, given the passage of the comparable 2004 law related to hijabs in public schools and government offices, the passage of time meant that women who wore hijab there were habituated to these restrictions in their everyday habitus (see fig. 1.3).

Ilias on the Secular Body

Let us return to Ilias, whom I first met in 2004, ten years prior to our formal interview, when he was a teenager and I was living and undertaking doctoral research in Petit-Nanterre. His life at that time was challenging: both of his parents had passed away, and his older brother had left France to work in Asia. His good-naturedness seemed to belie the tragedies he had experienced. Ilias liked spending time at the community center and participated in most of its programming. He had close friendships with several of the staff, who had stood by him through the maelstroms he had endured. I had agreed to tutor high school students in English-language coursework two afternoons a week at an after-school drop-in center (see Selby 2012: 16 for more on the history of this organization). My credentials were that I was an Anglophone and steadfastly punctual. I would help students with their homework or share worksheets I found on the internet and would print at my student residence. I had a handful of regular students, most of whom were nearing the end of high school and beginning to prepare for their baccalaureate exams, where English language counted but was less important

Figure 1.5. A soccer field in the center of the Canibouts (or Can's) housing projects, Petit-Nanterre, March 2016. Photo by the author.

than other subjects. While not in the formal study group at my table, Ilias and his friend Azdi (whose marriage story I present in chapter 4) saw me struggling to make English fun.

One afternoon Ilias asked if I would translate one of his and Azdi's favorite hip-hop songs, Kanye West's "All Falls Down," into French.[19] He and Azdi liked to rap the lyrics but weren't sure what the words meant. "Oh yeah. Of course!" I responded, eager to be useful and noting the title in my notebook. I had never heard of "All Falls Down." I enthusiastically looked up the lyrics the next day after I had returned by bus and commuter trains to my student residence in Paris, where I kept my laptop and had internet access. Scanning the lyrics on my laptop—"You cross that line and it's time to say F*ck you"—I laughed. Even if a good exercise to incorporate my French *verlan*, I knew Ilias's grandmother well enough to know she wouldn't appreciate a translation of this language. So, I put stars in the place of the most explicit passages. A few days later, back at the center, I handed Ilias and Azdi my French translation of the lyrics. "But, what's this?! Not cool, Jennifer. Not cool," Ilias said, scoffing at all the stars. When I suggested he could to learn more English to translate songs himself, gesturing to him welcomingly to join me at my table, he laughed. Over the subsequent decade, we did not meet often, but Ilias liked to remind me about my enduring lack of coolness.

When his grandmother passed away in 2012, I wrote him a Facebook message to share my condolences and appreciation for her. While we had a handful of conversations during research stays over three previous summers, what follows draws on a recorded interview from the spring of 2014.

In 2014, Ilias lived in a studio apartment with his wife, Zara. An administrative staff person at the youth drop-in center who knew about my project had told me about his wedding, texted him, and asked him if I could interview him about his marriage experience. Ilias remembered me and agreed to meet. He worked afternoons and evenings as a waiter in Montmartre and preferred mornings for sleeping, so it took several weeks to meet on a late Saturday morning in an empty computer lab belonging to the drop-in center. I brought a bag of pastries and sandwiches for us to share. When he saw me, he chuckled at my further descent into uncoolness, as evidenced by my gray polyester maternity pants and Birkenstock sandals (I was six months pregnant). He wasn't wrong. He inquired about my health and kindly ensured that I was physically comfortable for the interview.

Midway through the interview, Ilias described how he conceptualized his marriage in relation to his newfound religious identity: "In the end [*en fin de compte*], dating wasn't working for me. So, um, I preferred to proceed by other means. And, proceed religiously. And so, there you have it [*voilà*]. So, I started to read [online] and see who was interested in this approach. And, in fact, I found it really interesting to see how reason takes precedence over love. And that's, that was what I was looking for, actually: *that a religious approach is more rational*" (my emphasis). Ilias's last point—about how a religious approach is more rational than a "falling-in-love" approach—is significant to my analysis on romance as a secular sensibility. The point captures a call toward religiosity and the Bled as primary sources that privilege Muslimness, kinship ties, and the Bled above individual goals, chivalry, or romance to explain the road to marriage. My analysis in this book as a whole and in this chapter in particular certainly pays attention to women's experiences. This is no accident. Secularist restrictions are placed primarily on their dress and embodiment, and my sample included more women than men. However, thinking about secular sensibilities "through the shadows" allows us to consider how secular-sexual norms affect men like Ilias as well.

Ilias had married Zara, also twenty-five, two years earlier. Perhaps owing to the fact that I knew his grandmother well, when I asked him about his marriage, he spoke at length about how he had been influenced by his paternal grandparents' migration and marital lives: "For me, my 'method' [of living, of finding love] is my grandmother. . . . I found all of that [referring to his grandparents' marriage] very, very beautiful. Very, very simple. Very natural and I was really supported by that. Those were real commitments [*des vrais engagements*]." Ilias's grandmother migrated from Algeria in the late 1950s following his grandfather's arrival to work in a neighboring Renault car factory, which attracted many young Algerians to the area. Due to its proximity to industrial and construction work, Petit-Nanterre developed from the hilled poppy fields immortalized in Monet's 1873 painting to become the then-largest shantytown in France. Ilias's grandparents had had an arranged marriage in their Algerian hometown, and his grandmother had then waited, with the first of their five children, for her husband to settle and secure employment before joining him in a shack in Petit-Nanterre. In the 1960s, in response to problematic sanitation and safety, the state demolished the shantytown, and the family moved to a social housing apartment in the same suburb. More than a dozen families like theirs still lived in Petit-Nanterre, many inhabiting the same social housing apartments they were initially allocated when the shantytown was destroyed.

That Ilias skipped over his parents and their influence in this telling was no accident. Like a good number of youths of that generation, when Ilias's father was a young man in the early 1980s, he had struggled with school and in finding good work, and became involved in the suburb's then-significant heroin drug trade (Hajjat 2014). His father married his mother, who had migrated from Algeria for the arranged marriage, and who was unaware that he had a drug addiction and was embroiled in crime. Her "traditionalism" and virginity likely promised him a fresh start. Women like Ilias's mother relied upon family networks in their migration and often hoped for glamour and new opportunities in France. Unfortunately, Ilias's Kabylian-born, functionally illiterate mother encountered neither glamor nor opportunity in Petit-Nanterre. She died in her early forties from complications of HIV-AIDS, contracted from his father through his intravenous drug use. His father died shortly afterward by suicide.

When in the face of these traumas it looked like Ilias, at fourteen, might also fall into the local drug trade, his grandparents sent him to live with relatives in rural Kabylia for three months. While he had visited on vacation with his parents a few times, this particular trip affected him a great deal. The Bled became a touchstone for him of a simpler rural place where he found, in his words, *ressourcement* (meaning both "returning to one's roots" and "rejuvenation"). Despite the continued presence of the drug trade and chronic unemployment for racialized young men from the suburbs like him, after this trip, Ilias vowed to stay away from drugs and delinquency. He subsequently looked outside of Petit-Nanterre for employment, and began to turn toward the internet to learn more about Islam. Since beginning to practice the religion, and especially since he chose to grow a beard, Ilias experienced what it meant to be racialized and perceived as a suburban-living Arab-origin and Muslim man (he was of Kabylian origin). He described incidents on the RER A commuter train to his job in the north of Paris, and also, more generally, how "everyone talks about Islam in the suburbs [*l'islam dans les banlieues*]. It's so heavy [*relou*]. It brings everyone down. The problem is that there are so many sheep in France who believe whatever they see on TV."

Ilias explained that given this context he spent some time thinking about how he should proceed to meet a suitable marriage partner. He decided to speak about it with his aunt and uncle, who had become like parents to him after the passing of his parents and his grandparents. The word got out. One of his cousins shared Zara's Facebook profile with him. She lived in a neighboring suburb, but they had never crossed paths. Ilias liked her photograph and sent her a Facebook message. They then interacted by text message, spoke by telephone, and decided to meet in person, agreeing that they wanted to "proceed religiously." For them, this qualifier meant being accompanied by her parents, and his aunt and uncle. Ilias felt that "talking in front of our parents makes it official [*ça fait officiel*]."

The meeting had not all gone smoothly. His aunt initially did not want to participate in this religiously informed matchmaking. He said she told him, "Nous, on essaye d'avancer. Toi, tu recules" (We're trying to go forward [away from the trappings of religion], you're going backward). Still, his aunt attended the meeting and, according to Ilias, changed her mind after meeting Zara and taking part in their conversation. Over several hours at her parents' apartment, the two young people shared their values—where, for Ilias, "the core is religion"—and ideas about a potential future family life. Focusing on their families and on their values allowed them to "d'allumer son cerveau avant d'allumer le cœur" (to turn on the brain before turning on the heart). Ilias sought to center religiosity in their marriage and *not* physical chemistry, intimacy, or romance. The meeting went well. After more correspondence and thought, Ilias and Zara, then both twenty-three, agreed to marry.

Zara was born in Algeria and had migrated with her family to a Parisian suburb when she was ten years old. For Ilias, her upbringing was ideal: she had absorbed notions of modesty and Islamic practice but had already attained French residency status, removing the suspicion and surveillance that accompany arranged and transnational unions, both by the state with the 2006 and 2011 legislation, and by their family and friends. Zara had worn hijab since her teens but removed it every day for her job at a duty-free shop at the Roissy (Charles de Gaulle) airport. Also important for Ilias was that, unlike his mother, Zara spoke French fluently and was well socialized in French secular sensibilities, skills Ilias saw as handicapping his "traditional" and religiously practicing mother's short life. At the same time, Zara understood his "grandmother method" of seeking an arranged match. Ilias was hopeful that, because a number of their family members were involved in making the match "traditional," he and Zara would receive additional support, as well as God's, when they inevitably faced challenges, quite different from the individualized conception of marriage espoused by the French state. Referring to the legacies of two previous generations of transnational marriages, Zara's virginity, and the religious parameters of the match, Ilias added, "It's good to start cleanly [*proprement*]."[20] This shift in his thinking about relationships related to his newfound, more regular religious practice.

Aware of the 2006 and 2011 laws aiming to curb transnational, especially non-EU marriage partners, which I describe in more detail in the next chapter, and with the acute knowledge of his parents' failed union, Ilias stated plainly, "I preferred not to be bothered by all the paperwork [*paperasse*; to sponsor a transnational bride]." Zara's French citizenship mattered. Despite his move away from overt surveillance, with a sponsorship application, governmentality lingered in their union insofar as Ilias knew paperwork for a transnational union would be burdensome. At the time of our interview, I was struck by the consideration Ilias had put into the question of seeking a transnational union or not. I had anticipated that he would spend this long conversation making jokes, but he had clearly carefully considered the administrative parameters of his future married life.

The "grandmother method" he described, which involved a "traditional" marriage partner (i.e., a woman of Algerian origin who was a virgin at the time of marriage, in a union arranged by their families), are precisely factors that the French state subtly aimed to curtail in its 2006 legislation focused on "love fraud with a migratory aim," to which I turn in the next chapter. How Ilias's choice of his marriage partner was influenced by the state is not immediately perceptible. While he *did* want to marry a practicing Muslim, he also sought to protect himself from a *mariage gris* (a fraudulent marriage where one partner seeks access to citizenship), again depicted by the state and in cultural discourse as the most worrisome of transnational arranged marital offenses.

I introduced Ilias's story to think through social and legislative narratives on love and marriage—which I read as partly encapsulated by a normative secular body—and how they relate to concerns for the visibility of religion and the necessity of individualism. Ilias preferred a semiarranged, religiously framed marriage. He took measures that he thought would give his marital life greater longevity than the state-favored parameters. In doing so, Ilias effectively destabilized the prevailing notion of the French state, which conceives of a "sincere" marriage in putatively secular terms and as evidenced by rituals of romance.

Ilias overtly called these signs of authenticity and these values into question. For him, to be religious and traditional was to be entirely modern and rational. Ilias thus reframed the logic undergirding the legislation against transnational marriage where romance, individualism, and attraction ensure legitimate coupling. His position also suggests that "traditional," or arranged, marriages are not anathema to individual choice. From his perspective, and following his online research on Muslim French thinkers, including Tariq Ramadan, Ilias's approach was *more* rational than an imagined romantic love surveyed by marriage commissioners in state-sanctioned weddings.

In her introduction to the concept of "sexularism," historian Joan Wallach Scott (2011, 2018: 176) echoes some of Ilias's thinking in how she unpacks the sexual emancipation focus in legislation on secularism in France. Legislators in Québec have increasingly converged to promote a model of secularism in which liberty and equality are articulated as *sexual* liberty and *sexual* equality. In her work, Scott (2018) debunks the promise of emancipation offered through laïcité, and argues that the discourse of sexularism locates women's agency in the "desiring body" and *not* in the reasoning mind. Ilias also engaged this prevalent logic in his replacement of the "desiring body" with a religious, reasoning mind. This is where Ilias's understanding of the state logic and masterful reformulation of it—by seeing his arranged union as more rational and enduring than one based on romantic love—brilliantly undermines the safety against violence, irrationality, and illegal immigration imagined as safeguarded by what I call "secular romance." Ilias's astute rejection of romance responded to the prevalent ethos on sexuality and secularism in France, which frames Islam in ways that do not do justice to how it serves as a spiritual resource, as a system of knowledge, and as a basis for a positive marital life.

This chapter has outlined how secular sensibilities materialize on bodies and through social relations. Racialized migrants, particularly those who are women, Muslim, and without citizenship status, are disproportionate targets of legislation on secularism in France and Québec, which defines the parameters of the secular body and its sensibilities. I have argued that, especially since 2004 in France and 2008 in Québec, we can map a growing requirement for these secular politics to be *legible* on racialized and religionized Muslims' bodies. That is, it is no longer enough to abide by the laws and to accept the secular formations of these contexts. My participants' experiences in contact with the state captures how a secular legibility has been particularly onerous in the post-2008 period. Still, the narratives I've introduced attest to the myriad ways individuals respond to this pressure on the performance of religiosity and sexual politics. These narratives also reveal the political malleability of the secular, in how it can create a problem space or ignite suspicion with regard to religion, race, and gender.

The always-tethered-to-the-secular "religion"—here, Islam—is positioned as problematic in its sexual conservatism that impedes sexual emancipation, which is no less a racial construct than a sexual one. This conservatism is rendered as irrational and coercive, impeding free choice and individuality. The religious mind, this narrative suggests, is unagentic, as Ilias's aunt assumed when he expressed his preference for a "grandmother approach"-style marriage. There are gendered particularities to this pejorative characterization. Heightened in relation to Islam, religious loyalties are imagined as constraining women's imagined "good" and "free" sexual lives. These mores affect not only many women but men too, as they navigate secular sensibilities that shape and delimit the possibilities in their daily lives. Racialized Muslim men in these equations in France and Québec can be subtly depicted in legislation on transnational marriage with non-EU partners as homophobic, controlling, and patriarchal. Negative characterizations of conservative, undesirable religious sexuality are further subtly reinforced through secular legislation that focuses on certain religious symbols as signs of antiliberalism and polygamy, and which, since 2021, includes special attention to virginity certificates. With these foci, related elements of these realities—race, racism, Islamophobia—are thereby obscured. When held and deployed by the police and controllers on public transit, this imaginary has real consequences in contemporary France and Québec. Ilias, for one, is regularly carded when traveling by public transport to his restaurant job in Paris. His new outward expressions of Muslimness are met with suspicion. More generally, his religiously expressed sexuality is more likely to be surveilled by the state.

Secularism's sexual sensibilities and body politic in France or Québec thus elicit a range of responses, as we saw through the narratives of these Algerian-origin interlocutors—responses that require regulation of intimate realms and one's body in the face of state surveillance in arenas that other citizens might otherwise conceptualize as private. Sometimes these responses can be resistive. For one, Ilias's push against state surveillance and social expectations of romance as a sign of a healthy and long-lasting monogamous relationship are notable. Ilias perceptively rejected the logic undergirding 2006 and 2011 laws in France restricting transnational unions: that romance and individual choice safeguard against "love fraud," and that "traditional" arranged marriages are anathema to love and rational choice.

CHAPTER 2

GENDER POLITICS IN THE CONTACT ZONE

In our nearly two-hour conversation at the Chez l'Éditeur coffee shop just east of the Jean Talon market in Montréal in July 2018, Walid, forty-seven, described the scrutiny he experienced of his and his wife's relationship by paramedics when she fainted outside a grocery store when pregnant. The incident had taken place five years earlier. His telling, which included a description of a six-month return to Algeria after the birth of his second son when they thought they could no longer handle the pressures related to Farida's headscarf in Québec, was emotionally charged. Despite the medical emergency at hand, and the protocols of first responders related to assessing the situation, including potential domestic abuse, the paramedics slipped into questioning familiar to Walid as a racialized person of Algerian origin in Québec regarding his marital life and sexual ethics.[1] How had he met his wife? Was theirs a forced marriage? Why did she not speak French as well as him? Had he obliged her to veil? In sum, How had he contributed to her fainting? In this urgent moment, he felt obliged to respond to their questions. As he noted somberly, "I was in such a state of panic related to her fainting, that I just responded to their questions."

Taking Walid's narrative into account, this chapter looks more closely at civil marriage as a "contact zone" of individuals and the state. It argues that civil marriage is a site where the state's imagined citizens, and desirable delineations of sexuality and religion in particular, are evidenced, negotiated, and surveilled. These machinations figure differently in France and Québec, in part because of specificities in how civil marriage is managed, and in part because of how their immigration policies differ, but they are both "contact zones" where expectations for secular sensibilities shape the regulation and experience of civil marriage and governmentality in other parts of intimate lives.

Walid and I first met on a daylong bus excursion organized by the Algerian Cultural Centre and then again at this coffee shop for a more formal interview, chosen because of its proximity to his workplace. A soft-spoken and burly man with thick expressive black eyebrows, Walid described himself as a nonpracticing believer, adding playfully in our interview, "Don't tell my mother!" He lived in the northern part of the island of Montréal with Farida and their sons, who were nine and six. Because he was nonpracticing, Walid did not usually participate in the Cultural Centre's regular programming, but he had made an exception because his mother had been visiting for a few weeks and the tour was in both French and Arabic. The tour was thus ideal for him, his family, and his mother: "I don't have to drive and my mother is at ease. So . . . perfect!"

Walid first settled, solo, with permanent residency more than a decade earlier, in 2006. Thinking back, he explained that he was motivated to migrate to Montréal so to find a space "to be myself," including moving away from pressures to practice Islam and from his large religiously conservative family. Weighing the options, he saw professional opportunities in Québec more positively in comparison to those of France. Walid explained, "The Canada brand is so . . . so . . . I'm not sure how to say it, like with the Olympic Games! You see Canada with its flag and you think it's amazing [*laughs*]. But then you realize later it's something else [i.e., not so amazing]." His own solo immigration process to Canada had been lengthier than he had expected, taking more than five years, but, in general, it had gone smoothly. Prior to imagining his departure, Walid had completed an undergraduate university degree in management studies at the University of Algiers in Arabic. He was fluent in French, and this, combined with his youth, good health, and education made him an ideal immigration candidate.

Walid had wanted to see more of the world and to find good-paying work. Thinking back to his premigration life, Walid smiled wistfully, recalling his "rose-colored glasses." In his imagination at that time, "Canada was something magical for me, I have to say." As we will see, his vision grew darker after Farida, who wore hijab, migrated to Québec to join him in an arranged marriage. Her presence influenced how others perceived him. With scrutiny of his "traditional" transnational marriage to Farida, he began to experience more overt discrimination.

Walid experienced fewer negative interpersonal interactions with *Québécois de souche* ("Old Stock Quebeckers," by which he means long-standing white Quebeckers) upon his arrival than Farida did, but he also confronted systemic barriers. Like many other male immigrants from the Maghreb in Montréal, once he had settled, Walid had found it difficult to secure work that reflected his qualifications (Grenier and Nadeau 2011: 31). At first, Walid, then single, worked full time in a call center, saving money to pursue a business degree, with which he then secured better employment. Three years passed. Once established, his thoughts turned to marriage. His mother urged him to return home on holiday, to see "what destiny would bring." He knew he wanted to marry a woman of Algerian origin, ideally someone who, like him, was "croyante mais pas trop pratiquante" (believes in God but isn't a practicing Muslim) and who also wanted to raise children.

Their marriage had been arranged easily between their families. They celebrated in Algiers, with Walid then returning to Québec to file the paperwork to sponsor her. Despite laws introduced federally in 2006 that aimed to restrict transnational arranged marriage migration to Canada (to which I turn in the next chapter), Farida joined him with permanent residency seven months later in 2008. This period after the Bouchard-Taylor Commission (see fig. 1.2) can be characterized by a prevalent "discourse of demand," wherein Muslims alone are imagined as making demands of the state, even if data show accommodations for Islam remain minimal (see Barras 2016; and Brodeur 2008). The first legislative attempt to curtail religious symbols, with Bill 94 in 2009, had focused on full-face veils and had not directly affected Walid and Farida.

The cultural atmosphere in Québec grew tenser a few years later with the proposal of a Charter of Values by the Parti Québécois (PQ). Also known as the "Charter Affirming the Values of State Secularism and Religious Neutrality and of Equality between Women and Men, and Providing a Framework for Accommodation Requests" or Bill 60, the Charter of Values sought, most contentiously, to ban *all* public servants from wearing conspicuous religious symbols. While it assured "religious neutrality" in the dispensation of its measures, the PQ's widely circulated pictogram of religious symbols deemed acceptable and unacceptable made clear it was racialized religionists who would be targeted, and that their religious symbols reflected their *non*adherence to the province's values (see fig. 1.4). As with other secular bills that preceded and followed it, Bill 60 was widely supported in Québec. Like with Bill 94, backed by 95 percent of Quebeckers polled, it too had popular support (Angus Reid 2010, cited in Scott 2010; on Law 21 see Meunier and Legault-Leclair 2022). As its title makes clear, at stake were not only neutrality and proper religiously framed accommodation but also "equality between women and men." The unstated equation in the bill's presentation was that conspicuous religiosity impedes religious neutrality and gender equality (Bilge 2010). Yet Islamophobia and anti-Muslim harassment, discrimination, and violence also coincide with this support for the removal of religious symbols, particularly for women, like Farida, who wear hijab (see studies that capture a concurrent rise in violence by Bakali

2015b; Dobrowolsky 2017; Nagra 2018; and Jahangeer 2020). The state was not concerned with these expressions of equality.

As is true for most people's clothing selections, Farida's sartorial choices cannot be reduced to a singular explanation of her identity. She preferred to dress conservatively, and considered herself as nonpracticing. Walid said that Farida's clothing preferences were shaped by her experiences in Algeria in the 1990s, when she had felt tremendous pressure to wear hijab due to pressure from Islamicist groups.

Walid noted, with irony, that in the year before debates about Bill 60, she had begun wearing her hijab less often, which was part of what he called "un processus de dévoilement qui était naturel" (her own natural process of deveiling). Walid explained how the charter heightened stigma against the veil, which shifted this "natural" process for her: "With the debate on the charter in 2014, with everyone who was against Muslims, that was terrible. You know, at that moment, she [Farida] said, 'I'm not removing my veil. I'm *not* taking it off.'"

Remembering this state-informed pressure, Farida now refused to remove her headscarf in Québec. Her experience of the Charter of Values debate echoed too closely her hijab's imposition during the Décennie noire a decade earlier in Algeria. While he said he had not said anything to her, Farida's hijab affected Walid after Bill 60. With the Islamophobic fallout from Bill 60, especially the negative attention toward her hijab, Walid became aware that he was no longer a valued citizen in Québec. He felt more visible. Recalling both this intense period and the negative attention Farida experienced in grocery stores and on public transit in Québec, Walid said these circumstances made him feel terrible: "You know, I think that if I had seen a psychologist [un psy], he would have told me I was depressed. I'm someone who follows the news, and all this [news about Bill 60] made me sick." At the time when debates around Bill 60 circulated, Walid recalled the afternoon when Farida fainted outside a grocery store while pregnant with their second son. Because she was disoriented after her fall, he called for an ambulance. Fortunately, an ambulance had arrived quickly. As the three firefighters attended to her, they were also focused on him. He shared his bewilderment by the white firefighters' "stigmatizing questions." He now regrets that he did not call them out on comments that were not medical-related and that slid into Islamophobia.

I see these first responders' slippage into questions about Walid and Farida's intimate and religious lives as resembling the kind of questioning pursued by French marriage commissioners and the experience of niqab-wearing women in the public sphere in both contexts. Both here and in the questioning by marriage officiants and at the time of immigration, negative specters related to Muslimness, to arranged marriage, and to consent are omnipresent. In the incident Walid described outside a grocery store, the first responders read Farida's physical body—as fainted, weak, pregnant, and hijabed/religionized—as a reflection of Walid's undesirable sexual politics. This narrative captures how secular-sexual sensibilities in Québec also ignite pressures on racialized men, particularly those who are imagined (rightly or wrongly) as practicing Muslims. They have received less attention in the literature to date (Selby 2022a). With their questions and demeanor, the first responders indirectly impelled Walid to *perform* his secularity, to demonstrate his acceptance of Québécois secular-sexual politics. In his case, Farida's physical state, visible hijab, and Algerian-dialect accent made it more urgent to demonstrate the secular sensibility of "romance," even in a medical emergency.

In three sections, this chapter looks more empirically at secular sensibilities in the "contact zone" of marriage between individuals and the state to show how invocations of the secular emerge in relation to the intimate lives of my interlocutors. "Contact zones" is a notion developed by a few theorists (see Pratt [1992] 2008; and Linke 2006). As Pratt ([1992] 2008: 34) explains, contact zones are "social spaces where cultures meet, clash, and grapple with each other" in asymmetrical power relations. States' long-standing interest in delineating the acceptable contours of family life make civil marriage a primary site for the manifestation and assessment of these sensibilities. At the same time, for many couples, civil marriage ceremonies are also performative ritual spaces for consumerism, expressions of sexual emancipation, and narrow performances of gender. More specifically, I suggest that we can read *expectations of romance* as a proxy for a number of liberal values, including free choice, sexual intimacy, and, going further, an idealized secular body. While not directly related, these expectations are buttressed by secular laws focused on the removal of externalized conspicuous religious symbols from the body, and thereby problematize religion more generally.

To make this argument, following theorization regarding contact zones, I begin by casting a longer gaze on how the management of marriage has been central to French and Canadian matrices of coloniality. We will see how contemporary critiques of racialized and non-Christian bodies in the legislation on marriage and secularism in France and Québec echo long-established tropes. I pay particular attention to how the contemporary legislation alludes to an idealized sexuality and, sometimes, an idealized accompanying romance. To grapple with this idea of romance as a proxy for the secular body, I show how, at the time of marriage, individuals of Algerian origin in France and Québec tacitly and strategically maneuver their habitus in light of surrounding secular sensibilities. I turn to five interlocutors—Walid and Waël in Québec, and Rachida, Yacine, and Amel in France—with specific attention to their casting of secularism and sexual politics in relation to their marital and intimate lives before the state.

The Contact Zone

So, what *is* a "contact zone" and how is it a helpful lens with which to consider how habituses form in relation to the state and the sensibilities of its body politics? Mary Louise Pratt ([1992] 2008: 8) defines a contact zone as the "space of imperial encounters" where "peoples geographically and historically separated come into contact with each other and establish ongoing relations, usually involving conditions of coercion, radical inequality and intractable conflict." Pratt situates this contact as necessarily involving power relations that are part of broader imperial machinations. She has been critiqued for her theory's reliance on binaries (see Hall and Rosner 2004: 101), but "contact zones" can nevertheless be helpfully situated on a macrohistorical timeline that relates to Foucault's conception of the state in biopower.

So too, Uli Linke's notion of political contact zones helpfully conceptualizes the life of the state in a Bourdieusian manner, as corporal, sensory, and emotional, and as the socially constructed and ingrained habits, skills, and dispositions that appear on the body (cf. Bourdieu 1977, 1984; see also Göle 2015). In these ways, "modern governments act on and inhabit the body" (Linke 2006: 206). Linke maps how states' ideals are externalized and encroach on people's bodies. These corporal formations include "postures, facial expressions, gestures, and movements, [that] are often habitually enacted" (210; cf. Scott 1990). Following these ideas, through commissions, parliamentary and public debates, as well as through legislation that forces public servants to embody some of the dispositions of the state, the state effectively transmits dispositions and preferences. Linke's notion of the corporality of the contact zone and Bourdieu's (1984) habitus are frameworks that help us reflect upon the secular state's preferred clusters of dispositions and comportments, which, again, include the performance of a publicly secular body and secular sensibilities in general.

The contact zone of civil marriage is evocative not only because of the asymmetrical power dynamics between state representatives and individuals but also because marriage rituals are ripe sites to consider personal, familial, sexual, cultural, and consumer values. The happily-ever-after trope is a mainstay of popular culture and romantic comedies (see Roach 2016). We will see how these sensibilities also privilege monogamy, and cishet female sexual availability, while, at the same time, effacing other considerations, like contextualizations of racism and coloniality.

Indeed, mores around civil marriage and secularism meet within a specter of coloniality. On this point, in addition to their metaphor of secularism as a grammar, Scheer, Fadil, and Schepelern Johansen (2019: 12) helpfully describe secularism as a "boundary-maker." Their point is that, no matter individuals' personal convictions, they encounter this boundary-making as citizens and particularly when citizenship is at stake. Put plainly, for some of my interlocutors, transnational marriage was also about access to citizenship. Anne Levanchy's (2015) ethnographic-based findings of administrative procedures related to civil marriage and civil partnerships in Switzerland articulate this convergence well. Levanchy shows how, as a sociolegal space, the moment of civil marriage allows for a governmental privileging of a number of values, including whiteness.[2] Switzerland, says Levanchy, is a "race-mute" (and not race-blind) country. Whiteness is thus reinforced by the state in silent but consistent ways, namely through how "unspoken racialized categories are mobilized by registrars in critical aspects of their professional mission" (Levanchy 2015: 278). Levanchy situates registrars' actions and racism as proxies of the state, but with some caveats: "I am concerned about possibly giving a false impression of the registrars as racist individuals. Such a labelling would give a biased image of the power and ubiquity of racialization in Swiss everyday life. The registrars fulfill their professional tasks with a huge amount of goodwill and meticulousness. They consider their gate-keeping tasks to be a necessary evil and a 'dirty job,' which causes them a great deal of stress and discomfort" (281).

Levanchy's findings show how suspicion regarding non-EU marriage partners would arise especially when registrars deemed the couple's statuses as asymmetrical. Known administratively as "mixed couples," this category designates potential deviancy. She also reads "mixedness" as a code for a threat to racial purity, "a central concept in Switzerland in reference to the biological renewal of the nation" (286). Not unlike my own analysis, Levanchy thus questions the state's determination of legitimate motives for marriage. As in France, registrars in Switzerland conduct hearings with couples separately to determine the appropriateness of their degree of intimacy. Romance, or as Levanchy states, "romantic love narratives" (284), are an important signal of an ideal marriage, sealed with a kiss following the wedding vows. Together, Levanchy concludes, concerns around racial mixedness and appropriate intimacy in "mixed" couples reveal a desire to maintain Swiss whiteness.

In this chapter, I extend Levanchy's perspective. My project aims to show that secular sensibilities around sexuality and the body are powerful precisely because they are not simply top-down directives based in state surveillance. They are also sources of capitalist consumption and joy. Other factors further shape how proper performance of romance is encouraged in the civil marriage contact zone. If married, the reader may recall their own wedding. Perhaps your grandmother wanted you to wear a traditional western Algerian wedding gown, a chedda, while you may have insisted on a white princess dress, with its own cultural trappings. Perhaps your spouse wanted a religiously sanctioned wedding. Perhaps your sister insisted on wedding rituals related to music, lighting, décor, attendants, food, or drink that were sites of tension. In addition to state and familial preferences, other sources of influence are more pervasive in popular culture, including wedding shows, social media (Pinterest, Instagram), family, and friends. The wedding industry offers both significant guidance and significant costs (Ingraham 1999).[3] Of course, all of these pressures are not necessarily negatively experienced. The inculcation and the performance of romance can be pleasurable.

Politically expressed laïcité in contemporary legal projects on secularism and transnational marriage in France and Québec *does not* explicitly shape my interlocutors' experiences of love and marriage. However, as we saw with the example of Nawal in the introduction, individuals *do* have a sense of what might be expected of them in their engagements with the state. These expectations—whether or not individuals meet them—include the performance of a legible secular body. If marriage is subtly framed as irrational and motivated by love and with no other benefits, signs of romance become markers against insincerity and dubiously based immigration. Notions of and expectations for romance in these contact zones are articulated differently in France and in Québec, insofar as the former outlines these preferences most clearly in state-monitored marriage ceremonies and in follow-up surveillance of intimacy, while my interlocutors in Québec, like Walid, describe state surveillance more in their postmigration lives. The onus of this performance is felt more acutely by those who are racialized or do not have legal status. Again, these contact zones are not new, and, as we'll see in the next section, can be traced back to long-standing histories of coloniality.

Colonial Intimacies

States have a vested interest in shaping appropriate family structures. Nuclear families ensure proper taxation, the appropriate distribution of goods and property, supports for child-rearing and welfare, and the promotion of a moral or "civil" society. Historian Nancy Cott (2000: 1) describes a dual process where "the structure of marriage organizes community life and facilitates the government's grasp on the populace." Echoing Foucault's notion of biopower, the state's control of marriage, in other words, facilitates the government's grasp on the populace (see also Carter 2008: 8; and Beaman 2013). While appearing stable, governmentality on intimacies shift.[4] The changing access to rights for LGBTQ2S+-identifying individuals, including the legalization of gay marriage in Québec in 2004 and in France in 2013, and differing rules around adoption for gay couples in France, are two examples of biopolitical shifts within the broader reinforcement of monogamy (Fassin 2014; Koussens 2023: 102). These debates show how secular-related legislation on sexuality also affects noncolonized actors, including LGBTQ2S+ individuals. Some religious organizations, including Catholic ones in France and Canada, mobilized fiercely against the opening of civil marriage to same-sex couples (Dickey Young 2006; Portier and Théry 2015; Koussens 2023). Still, biopower related to sexuality and the family has long histories, which we can map back to the control of subjects in colonial contexts.

BIOPOLITICS IN FRENCH ALGERIA

The "civilizing" mission of French colonialism in Algeria included infrastructure and resource extraction, and also the imposition of a constructed sexual normalcy. In other words, in tandem with concretizing political and economic control, legal and social reforms aiming to "democratize" the colony were directly aimed at sexual ethics. Historian Judith Surkis (2019: 191) argues that the 1830 French conquest of Algeria focused on religious and sexual differentiation. This push for distinction, Surkis says, maintained Algerians' political and psychic subservience to their colonizers in powerful ways (21). Historian Todd Shepard (2017: 15) similarly shows how, in the case of French Algeria, an "endemic play of difference and sex" allowed so-called proper desire to serve as a driving agent for colonialism. Fears of cross-cultural or cross-national sexual encounters between the ruler and the ruled drove early legislation (see also Clancy-Smith 1998: 161; and Stoler [2002] 2010).

Characterizations of sexual deviancy were gendered. Scholars have argued that, by the nineteenth century, following French military dominion in Algeria in 1832, a heteronormative structure was established where Algerian women were cast as oppressed, and Algerian men as sexual predators. Drawing on early colonial legal documents and newspaper representations, Surkis shows how French colonizers escaped these anxieties. Violent ironies abounded. Colonial officials sanctioned Muslim men's sexual lives while "French law itself left ample room for French men's extramarital sex (and, one might add, marital rape), despite the Civil Code's professed commitment to monogamous marriage" (Surkis 2019: 18). Pejorative sexualized characterizations of the racialized and pejoratively religionized colonized was a central move in the colonial playbook.

The regulation of monogamy was a key component of this control. Pejorative characterizations of polygamy in particular became formidable markers of sexual difference. In French Algeria, this core feature of sexual difference was reinforced with the establishment of a separate Indigenous Muslim family law. There were material, capital, and kinship implications as well (see Surkis 2019: 68). The relegation of the "problem" of polygamy thereby fell squarely on Muslims. Characterizations of sexual depravity were bolstered in popular art and literature; the writings of Montesquieu and the Orientalist paintings of harems filled with languorous Arab men and nude Arab women by Eugène Delacroix and Théodore Chassériau are but a few examples. French advocates for colonial settlement would cite passages from the Qur'an to denote how polygamy encapsulated, according to one publication in the *Revue de l'Orient*, the "multiplicity of women, their inferiority, and men's near absolute freedom over them" (cited in Surkis 2019: 47). Concerns for maintaining white supremacy were primordial: the white European man needed protection from Muslim sensuality and decadence. Alongside recurring negative characterizations of women in hijab, negative sexual depictions of the colonized Arab men echoed widespread Orientalist beliefs about the innately perverse nature of North African sexuality (Clancy-Smith 1998: 159). This "civilizing mission" rhetoric not only critiqued Algerian men for their moral degeneracy but also, as Surkis adds, on a psychological plane, incited "sexual resentment." French women's unequal political rights and suffrage remained untouched in these early critiques of the colonized's sexual ethics.

A second tool of colonial sexual control was a condemnation of homosexuality among Algerian men. Historian Julia Clancy-Smith critiques the purported sexual immorality of the colony in nineteenth-century Algeria, which cast North African Muslim men as prone to homoeroticism.[5] In their examination of colonial portrayals of Algerians in newspapers and popular culture through the colonial period, Neil MacMaster and Toni Lewis (1998) capture a shift in the location of sexual deviancy by the French colonists. They argue that in the post-Independence period in Algeria, sexualized representations of Muslim women shifted from bedroom to battlefield scenes. An initial dominant eroticized representation of the veil and the harem, they show, was shaken by the 1954–62 War of Independence. No longer depicted as sultry harem accessories, veils became overtly politicized and depicted as masking potential anticolonial terrorism. In sum, following the official end of the Algerian War of Independence, when their official colonial relationship was renegotiated with the Évian Accords in the 1960s, these biopolitics continue to mark France-Algeria relations.

The post-1962 "postcolonial" period did not abate these sexual-sociopolitical anxieties vis-à-vis so-called Algerian sexuality. Todd Shepard (2012) directly links a fractured French psyche following the decolonization of Algeria with sexual revolutions in France of the 1960s. Shepard argues that French debates in this decade related to sex work, gay rights, and sexual violence were ways to grapple with questions of empire, colonial violence, and decolonial racism. More specifically, Shepard contends that public debates about sex and sexuality in France in the late 1960s were ignited by postcolonial anti-Arab sentiments. The Far Right's concern in the 1960s and '70s with the so-called sexual deviance of Algerian-origin men in the suburbs of French industrial cities is an apt example of these biopolitics. Far-right campaigns pejoratively associated Algerian men with sexual harassment, homosexual promiscuity, and rape. Doing so, Shepard contends, contrasted the Far Right's "normal and healthy manliness capable of defending the French from their perverted enemies" (Shepard 2017: 124). Given that many men of Algerian origin migrated to the French suburbs as unskilled workers in the 1960s, and tended to live in the disenfranchised suburban regions of large cities, like in Petit-Nanterre, one way to control them biopolitically was through this focus on the postcolonial sexual depravity among Algerian male laborers in the banlieues. Immigration policy in the 1970s followed suit. A focus on family reunification, especially in promoting the arrival of Algerian women rather than on single male workers would, the thinking went, "stabilize" the unacceptable sexuality of men living in concentrated shantytowns like Petit-Nanterre and "contain" them in nuclear families. These moves to control Algerians in the postcolonial period capture a central argument of this book: that these biopolitics, from the colonial period onward, sought to control the contours of the proper family with nonneutral implications.

Jumping forward more than fifty years, these (mis)perceptions of a sexually depraved Muslim living in immigrant-filled suburban housing projects have further reinforced biopolitics in metropolitan France. When riots broke out in the fall of 2005 following the accidental and fatal electrocution of two racialized suburban young men—Bouana Traoré and Zyed Benna, fifteen and seventeen years old—as they fled from police to avoid being carded, the leading center-right Union pour un Mouvement Populaire (Union for a Popular Movement), as well as some public intellectuals, pointed to a well-used trope of a depraved male Muslim *polygamist* as an explanation for the social unrest. The response was extensive: demonstrations took place in 300 towns, suburbs, and municipalities across the country; more than 9,000 cars and several public buildings were burned; 1 person was killed; 217 police were injured; and 4,770 rioters were arrested (see Moore 2005; Fassin 2006). I was living in Petit-Nanterre amid the 2005 riots and curfew (Selby 2012: 37). Media and political discourses depicted suburban-living families, often racialized as Muslim, as nonnormative, and sexually deviant, with a focus on polygamy, even if such unions were statistically nonexistent (making up less than 1 percent of the population, according to the most generous estimates; see Selby 2014c).[6] For instance, the then minister of employment, Gérard Larcher, publicly condemned polygamy and the lack of parental control as the causes of the riots. He extended these problems to explain high unemployment in the suburbs, as well, proclaiming, "If people are not employable, they will not be employed" (cited in *Le Nouvel Obs* 2008b; see also Arnold 2005; and Sciolino 2005). These *banlieusards* did not reflect idealized notions of monogamy, as espoused in French biopolitics, which came to explain all suburban social issues.

Echoing the colonial period, in response to the 2005 riots, questioning the moral positionings and familial arrangements of mostly Muslim suburban families was a potent shortcut to blame the chaos on "their" moral ineptitude. These characterizations of sexual deviancy in the suburbs absolved the state of any wrongdoing, including related to the deaths of the young men who fled from police. Again, these characterizations were gendered. In contrast to the common discourse in France that equates unacceptable Muslim parenting with overdetermining their daughters' choices with regard to headscarves, especially following the 2004 law banning religious symbols in schools, with the 2005 riots, these same parents were accused of hands-off neglect of their boys.

A twelve-day curfew imposed in the midst of the riots by then prime minister Dominique de Villepin bore further colonial vestiges. In 2005, older residents in Petit-Nanterre recalled the previous nationwide curfew that had been applied forty-four years earlier, in 1961, to quell independence movements by the National Liberation Front in the same suburbs (Stora 1992). A handful of my interlocutors in Petit-Nanterre experienced both curfews. The first, in 1961, targeted local factory workers and families in the crowded and muddy shantytown without running water. The second, in 2005, took place in its then–social housing high rises. Residents were stressed. But riots did not break out as violently in Petit-Nanterre as in other locations. A handful of cars were incinerated, but the destruction of property was not on the same scale as elsewhere. Theories differed. One social worker in Petit-Nanterre surmised that the neighborhood's important heroin trade shielded it from more riotous activity and police attention (see Selby 2012: 63–67). Others believed that the families who had lived in the same apartments for more than fifty years prevented escalation. They were invested in this space. Whatever the complex reasons that contributed to its lesser ferocity and duration, and despite the fact that polygamy is not visible in this banlieue, it should be clear that the nonpresence of polygamy does not explain suburban riots in France in 2005, and more recently, in 2023.[7] I knew of two polygamous families in Petit-Nanterre, as well as three women whose husbands had known cowives in Morocco and Algeria, but the practice was otherwise not practiced. The takeaway here is that, long after the supposed decolonization of Algeria, the continuing disciplining of the sexual suitability of racialized Muslims allows for a parallel disengagement of the state's responsibility in fostering conditions of violence.

BIOPOLITICS IN CANADA AND QUÉBEC

Governmental control of monogamous marriage has also shaped nation-building efforts in Canada. Colonial efforts to Christianize settlers and Indigenous peoples, all while protecting capital goals, was assured through the state control of monogamy. Again, we see a similar logic of coloniality: imagined-as-stable nuclear families generate stable economies and maintain the succession of property (Cott 2000; Carter 2008; Gaucher 2016, 2018). "Naturalizing" Christian monogamy in the early colonial settlement of Canada was thus an effective tool to bolster nationhood.

Fears of polygamy emerged in settler colonial Canada as well. Historian Sarah Carter (2008: 11) shows how, in nineteenth-century western Canada, a main justification for colonial intervention was to "save" Indigenous women from polygamous marriages. Now-familiar depictions of lawless Indigenous men and sexualized Indigenous women as promiscuous and too available to white men circulated widely in the mid-1880s. Colonial anti-polygamy campaigns were not only concerned with protecting Christian and Indigenous women from the moral "depravity" of nonmonogamy but also aimed, as in French Algeria, to prevent mixed-race relationships. In the early white European colonialism of western Canada, pushes for monogamy by the state were thus central to both the creation of citizenry and to the expansion and justification of colonialism. Again, as we saw in colonial Algeria, morality was selective. In her archival research, Carter (2008: 32) shares evidence of ignored polygamous marriage arrangements among governors operating in and working with the Hudson Bay Company. The colonial gaze focused on problematic sexual relations with Indigenous peoples, which could jeopardize whiteness and the "Christian two-by-two" ideal.

Recall Shepard's (2012, 2017) compelling argument of how the "erotic thrust" of France's sexual revolution in the 1960s should be read in tandem with the post-decolonization of Algeria. Québec's sexual revolution in the 1960s situated laïcité differently. Under the tenure of the Liberal Party of Jean Lesage, the Quiet Revolution's foils were the previous social controls of the Catholic Church, and a former Montréal-based English elite. With the decline of the former, as for cishet women elsewhere, with greater access to contraception and second-wave feminism, sex and sexuality in Québec were no longer primarily understood in reproductive terms. Birth and marriage rates in Québec fell dramatically (Brown 2012; Gauvreau 2015). A key component of Québec's imagined modernization was its embrace of secularism, framed tautologically alongside democratic, linguistic, urban, and economic shifts that celebrated women's sexual freedoms (see Zubrzycki 2016; and Mossière 2021). The speed of these shifts explains why, with its Quiet Revolution, Québec is often deemed as one of the fastest secularizing societies in the North Atlantic world (Lefebvre 2008; Brown 2012; Boucher 2021; Burchardt 2020). This revolution has also been a powerful myth in the province's collective memory, insofar as it bolsters the notion that laïcité is what ensures Québécois nationalism, language rights, and emancipation. Traditionalist, powerful ideas of Catholic ethnic nationalism were replaced by a leftist, feminist, and a secular nationalism (Bilge 2012; Burchardt 2020: 18).

These examples in postcolonial France and in both settler-period and post–Quiet Revolution Québec show how, with the advent of colonialism and white settler nation-building, top-down, state-led parameters to delimitate "appropriate" family life and the parameters of acceptable sexuality were tools of citizenry. These notions are most powerful when deemed "natural." Continued concern with monogamy, and accompanying desirable race and religiosity are thus pivotal ideological components in both French and Canadian nation-building. Specters of these biopolitics remain evident in present-day concerns with racial difference in delineations of secularism, particularly evident in how they disproportionally affect racialized and religionized individuals.

Post-2004 Legislation on the Secular Body in France and Québec

If in chapter 1 I considered how religious symbols have been mobilized as central expressions of acceptable and unacceptable religion, in this section I turn to how acceptable and unacceptable sexuality are delineated within legislative articulations of secularism. One of the by-products of these determinations is their bolstering of a cisgender binary that renders gender. Put differently, when we look at post-2004 cases and legislation on secularism in France and Québec, we will see that public/private and male/female binaries are key logics in how such laws are formulated. This normalization of sexuality and cisgenderness also disregards asexuality, transsexuality, and other non-cisgender identities. These blind spots are replicated in the secularism studies literature, which has also largely focused on cisgender, heteronormative religious interlocutors, perhaps in part because scholars subconsciously rely on the imbricated binaries of religion / the secular and male/female.[8] Some political debates in the North Atlantic emphasize sexual difference explicitly through delineating sexual genitalia: recall concern for the absence of foreskins in circumcision debates in Germany, and the presence of hymens in legislation curtailing virginity certificates in France. Still, in general, the promotional content for the secular body in France and Québec has emphasized the curtailment of externally visible gendered symbols. These include garments that cover female bodies (hijabs, niqabs, abayas, burkinis) and, to a lesser extent, those that religionize male bodies (*qamis*, beards).

This nearly ubiquitous focus by legislators and schools on women follows other factors. Laws in France and Québec since 2004 have stressed the necessity of enforcing secularism to protect cisgender women's rights. Sociologist Callum Brown (2012: 1) argues that shifts in family demography and women's greater autonomy in sex are "intimately and causatively interconnected" with secularization in the North Atlantic world. Drawing on statistical and survey data, Brown contends that the most dramatic shift during the "long 60s" (from 1957 to 1975) in waning religious beliefs, practices, and church attendance, and the increased age at which women first married occurred in Canada, and particularly in Québec. Brown's observation is worth unpacking. There is little doubt that processes of de-Christianization—or the waning of Christian influence in public institutions and in the public imagination—have led to important improvements to the protections and liberties afforded to cisgender women, and sexual and religious minorities' rights (see Choquette 2004; Dickinson and Young 2008; Gauvreau 2015; and Shepard 2012, 2017). As women gained control over contraception and married life, and were less bound by religious codes of sexual conduct, church leaders *and* scholars have come to position them as principally "secular actors" (see Taylor 2007: 767; Klassen 2019: 19; and Blankholm 2022).

Secularisms' ordering mechanisms vis-à-vis gender appear differently on individuals, depending on the latter's privilege, social position, race, religiosity, and other markers of difference. But there are commonalities, too. Those who are women, racialized, religiously practicing, *and* newcomers are the most vulnerable to the biopolitics of secular laws. In her research on the post-2004 period among young Muslim activists in France, anthropologist Mayanthi Fernando astutely points to how French secularism's maintenance of a public/private binary, effectively allowing for the state's invasion into Muslim women's private spaces, all while maintaining the guise of neutrality. Drawing on two post-2004 cases in France that focus on Muslim women's unacceptable sexuality, Fernando (2014b) maps a tripartite mechanism: the French state first constructs secularism as centering upon a private/public separation, so as to privatize religion. In a second move, it trespasses this boundary by requiring Muslims to share intimate details regarding their sexual lives. And third, Fernando argues, when Muslim women undertake this requirement, the private/public framework necessarily falls apart. Most egregiously, the same religionized (and often racialized) women are held responsible for the mechanism's protective failure (see also Surkis 2010; Mahmood 2013, 2016; Lemons 2019: 25). Mirroring colonial logics, the imagined privacy promised by the secular private sphere is thus unevenly applied and selectively intruded.

The public/private boundary transgression offers further evidence that contemporary laïcité has not made women's emancipation or rights a priority. Joan Wallach Scott proposes that this false assumption is built on a broader binary association of secularism, gender equality, and sexual emancipation (including queer rights), on the one hand, and Catholicism/Islam, gender inequality, and sexual repression, on the other. Most interesting, Scott (2018: 183; see also Cady and Fassenden 2013; Fessenden 2016) adds that the assumed linkage of gender equality with secularism has functioned to conceal the centrality of sexual difference as foundational to modern secular regimes and to perpetuate gender *in*equalities. In other words, women remain problematically associated with their differentiated, sexed bodies, further entrenching a dilemma of difference, ironic given that French universalism has historically sought to discount difference (Scott 2005).

Cishet women's agency thus became marked through their desiring sexualized bodies. Sociologist Éric Fassin (2010: 513) points to a rise in the rhetoric of sexual freedom beginning in 2004. Scott also observes that the period following the 2004 law on religious symbols marshaled a "new French secularism" whose roots were sown in the French sexual revolutions of the 1960s. Sexual freedom, Scott (2018: 157) stresses, became "the most important element of human freedom" (see also Fassin 2006, 2010: 512). Sexual desire became a universal right, but focused on cishet women.[9] Because of the legislative and scholarly foci on hijab-wearing women, others *appear* outside the implications from this binary, but as we will see, they are not.

GENDERED SECULARISM AND MEN

While seemingly absent, cisgender men *are* part of these gendered secular machinations. A trope of the imperiled Muslim woman in Orientalist media and political discourse invokes two other constructions: a "civilized European" and a "dangerously patriarchal Muslim man" (see Razack 2004, 2008: 32; and Guénif-Souilamas and Macé 2004). Like its female counterpart, the secular body, when gendered as male, also promotes individualism, feminism, and female sexual emancipation, but some specificities exist. Schirin Amir-Moazami's (2016) brilliant thinking on the male secular body takes up a 2012 debate on circumcision in Germany. Much more than foreskin was at stake. Amir-Moazami pays attention to negative tropes of Muslim masculinity invoked through the debate. She shows a constitutive link between secular politics and a discursive construction of Muslim men. Public scrutiny of Muslim and Jewish circumcised men, she argues, negatively marked their bodies as traumatized. Examining the ear piercing of girl babies, as a bodily modification ritual which, like circumcision, is sometimes undertaken without children's consent, offers a productive counterexample. Ear piercing is framed as a secular and not religious activity and so is not laden with the same "archaic otherness" as male circumcision. An *uncircumcised* secular body in this debate prevailed as the desirable conventionalized form of masculine sexuality, and as the site of normalized sexual pleasure (Amir-Moazami 2016: 166). The grammar of the secular reduced the circumcised to being guilty of "bad" sex.

A secular body—scientific, rational, individualized, gender equal, and the site of "good" sex—was cast in contrast to this undesirable religious body. Throughout the debate, Muslims and Jews turned primarily to religious freedom arguments. In the end, however, religiously framed arguments were annexed. "Rational" medical arguments were given greater credence (see also Asad 2003: 11, on his reflection of how "modern" pain is medicalized as separate from religion). Again, white German secular parents who pierce their children's ears are exempt from these concerns for consent and violence. The ear-piercing example also captures how, in negatively casting religion, a secular lens shapes the contours of acceptable gender expression too. Ear piercing babies is an acceptable bodily modification and gendering of girls.

We can extend Amir-Moazami's insights to other sights and sites on the body. The length and presence of beards are also scrutinized depending on their wearer (see also Khan 2018 on the secular misreading of his male Pakistani interlocutors' ethical practices as only irrational and violent). One of my interlocutors in Algeria, Yacine, whom I introduce later in this chapter, shaved his beard in preparation for questioning by French state officials on the legitimacy of his transnational marriage. Like Nawal in the introduction, Yacine intuits that a clean-shaven face will pass more readily. A handful of social scientific studies confirm Yacine's assessment. One shows how when a bearded man asked strangers at a subway stop in Paris how to find the Sorbonne, the question was read differently than when he asked how to find the Grand Mosque of Paris (Aranguren et al. 2021). Another study illustrates how white converts are racialized differently depending on their gender: white Muslims who wear beards are religionized far less than white Muslim women who wear hijab (Galonnier 2021a, 2021b). Political contexts matter too. Émilie Gastrin's (2020) study of beard wearers in France argues that the January and November 2015 terrorist attacks intensified critiques of their presence in the city (see also Touzeil-Divina 2020). The French and Québécois legal spheres have seen fewer cases related to beards. A 2020 legal decision in favor of a bearded male surgical intern in the Paris suburb of Saint-Denis reminds us that beards are typically not included in the conspicuous/inconspicuous binary reserved for religious symbols.[10] In the Saint-Denis case, the judge determined that the intern's beard was *not* a conspicuous religious symbol but warned that the subjective intention of its wearer did not necessarily protect it from scrutiny (Gastrin 2020; Jacob 2020). Like bandanas, long dresses, and abayas worn by women, beards may also fall under future regulation.

GENDERED SECULARISM AND WOMEN

In the remainder of this section, I consider depictions of the secular body that emphasize its femininity, and concurrent heterosexuality, and sexual availability. Because its content in France is presented more sharply, I pay more attention to examples from there than Québec. In France, as we saw in the previous chapter's caricature (fig. 1.1) of the bare-breasted figure of Marianne, depictions of women's unclad bodies are central to the visualization of Republican mores of freedom, democracy, and anticlericalism. Delacroix's personification of liberty in *Liberty Leading the People* (1830) emphasizes a bare-breasted woman. The painting was completed in 1830, on the cusp of the French colonization of Algeria, where concern for head coverings and female modesty came to partially justify colonialism. Surveillance of hijabs thus percolated for more than 150 years, culminating in the late 1980s with the "headscarf affairs" in France (Bowen 2007; Scott 2007). In the ensuing debates, clearer prescriptions on dress and sexual values emerged by 2004, recalling Fassin's (2006) argument of a "sexual democracy" articulated in France (which I extend to Québec). Laws and memorandums subsequently focused on eliminating the visibility of religious symbols. Accessing these symbols, here headscarves, veils, niqabs, burkinis, and abayas, offers material for understanding secular sensibilities. For these reasons, I begin this analysis with the 2003-4 debate on conspicuous religious symbols.

The 2003 government commission that preceded legislation in 2004 against religious symbols in public schools and government offices in France focused on Muslim girls' sexual and political emancipation. Not unlike in the preceding colonial period, according to the Stasi Commission report, the veil in France became a short form for young women's forced and willing submission to undesirable religiously informed patriarchal forces. *Forced* because of religious patriarchal dynamics and *willing* because "choice" was motivated by irrational religiosity. With the 2004 law, the logics behind the idealized parameters of the female secular body were clarified. In her work on the 2004 law, Mayanthi Fernando (2014c: 210) observes that to be unveiled in France is to be "sexually normal." A number of high-profile court cases in France emerged following the 2004 law mirror this concern for "proper sexuality," wherein the state trespasses into the private sexual lives of visible Muslim women. I turn to three examples. Together, they capture the extent and range of how symbols of Islam are disciplined:

- First, a 2008 virginity annulment case in Lille. When a bride inaccurately portrayed herself as a virgin, her wedding was annulled twice, first by the state, and then the annulment was annulled;
- Second, a 2008 citizenship case where the state concluded that niqab-wearing Mme M.'s sexual politics were not reflective of Republican values, and so excluded her from citizenship rights;

- And third, the Baby Loup case (so named for the association that ran the children's nursery) ignited when a woman was fired after she began wearing hijab at her job in a private daycare.

In all of these cases, women's freedom is linked to their sexual and visual accessibility. More than curtailing conspicuous religious symbols in schools and government offices or condemning virginity statements, the cases reveal how women's bodies should be "free" from religiously informed restraints in courtrooms, in supermarkets, and in private businesses.

The first case, a 2008 marriage annulment case in a civil tribunal in the northern city of Lille, stemmed from a request from "Monsieur C." for an annulment from his then-bride, "Mme H." At issue was her misrepresentation of her "essential qualities." More plainly, Mme H. lied about her virginity before the marriage's consum255ation. Initially, Monsieur C. was granted the annulment. There was no mention of their religious beliefs in the court documents. The subsequent appeal's request alluded to a "*community* [i.e., Muslims] where *tradition* [i.e., Islam] stipulates that one's spouse must remain a virgin until marriage" (cited in Monnin 2008; my emphasis). These allusions to "tradition" in a "community" signal an aberration from a preferred rational and individual secular woman.

Monsieur C. and Mme H.'s Muslimness was masked in the initial annulment process. But when their religious affiliation and Monsieur C.'s requirement of virginity were leaked to the press, a maelstrom erupted. Pundits held that virginity could not be accepted as a reason to annul a marriage. A public opinion poll published in *Le Figaro* (2008) revealed that 73 percent of respondents were "shocked" by the decision to annul on these grounds of misrepresentation. Public intellectuals and well-known French feminists opined extensively on the case's implications. Philosopher Élisabeth Badinter deemed the initial annulment "sickening," stating that it would encourage young practicing Muslim women to run "to hospitals to have their hymens repaired" (cited in *Le Nouvel Obs* 2008a). Sihem Habchi, then president of Ni Putes ni Soumises (Neither whores nor submissives), who like Badinter was also later invited by the Gerin Commission to testify against the acceptability of face-covering veils, called the initial marriage annulment a "fatwa against women's rights" (cited in Rosen 2008).

Few public voices expressed concern for the public airing of Mme H.'s private sexual history. Far from protecting her from violence, the controversy after the ruling subjected Mme H. to public humiliation and exacerbated anti-Muslim views that positioned religiously framed sexual values as unacceptable. Rather than shut down discussion of speculation regarding

Mme H.'s choice, following a great deal of media interest and a petition, the minister of justice, Rachida Dati, who initially supported the annulment to protect Mme H.'s privacy, doubled down to suspend the initial annulment. Politicians across the political spectrum agreed that annulling the annulment would protect the "modernity" of French law (Surkis 2010: 532). The political and public interest in the Lille marriage annulment case reflects a heightened social concern with so-called traditional communities' impediment to women's sexual emancipation. It is no accident that thirteen years later, the 2021 Antiseparatism Law on secularism in France banned virginity certificates in the name of protecting women.

In a second case from 2008, "Mme M.," was denied French citizenship by the French Conseil d'État on the basis of her "insufficient assimilation, other than linguistic competence" (cited in Assemblée Nationale 2010: 166). I read her "insufficient assimilation" as a direct consequence of her unacceptable sexual politics, reflected in her niqab. More generally, a handful of excellent qualitative studies have studied the perspectives of women who wear niqab in France and in Canada (Parvez 2017; Clarke 2013; Daro 2017; Bakht 2020). There are few studies of these women in part because few women wear them.[11] Natasha Bakht's study, for one, offers a rare perspective, in characterizing the niqab as a bold statement against state intervention and a patriarchal gaze, and in situating it as a sign of freedom of expression.

Mme M., thirty-two, was a woman of Moroccan origin who had married a French national eight years earlier. The couple had three children and lived thirty minutes outside of Paris. Mme M. spoke French fluently. But she also wore niqab, a practice she adopted since having migrated to France. In my reading of her case, it was her *voile intégral*—read as an antiwoman symbol based on radical religiosity—that ensured the rejection of her citizenship request. The Conseil d'État, the governmental body that serves as a legal adviser to the Supreme Court, did not explicitly name the niqab in its recommendation (see Bowen 2011 for more on the role of the Conseil d'État). Its report gestures in vaguer ways to Mme M.'s "radical" religious practices, which are incompatible with gender equality, an "essential value" of the French state.

State biopolitics are visible in the court's surveillance of Mme M.'s body and social comportment. The determination of her unacceptable gender politics was partly based on state-initiated personal interviews and notes from social workers who visited and observed Mme M. and her family (for more on these materials, see Selby 2014a: 443). That the government commissioner in the case cited details garnered by physically following Mme M. in her daily life, including into supermarkets, reflects the incursion of the state into her private life. Her niqab meant that her private religiosity became a matter for adjudication by the French state. These intrusions went so far as a positive comment, in a social worker's report, on how Mme M. had nevertheless accepted to be the patient of a male gynecologist (Prada-Bordenave 2008, cited in Selby 2014a: 444). Not only are Mme M.'s sexual ethics unacceptable but her related conspicuous symbol is too. One report cited in the Gerin Commission report, which preceded the 2010 law banning niqabs in the public sphere, concludes that Mme M. and her husband are Salafists, the branch of conversative Islam that became shorthand for terrorist threat in France (Assemblée Nationale 2010: 31; Selby 2011a: 389). Her face-covering niqab was the most egregious example of the incursion of undesirable sexual and Islamic religious politics onto her body. Combined, this evidence meant that her citizenship request was denied.

Mme M. is cited as an example of unacceptable French gender and sexual politics in the Gerin Commission report, published following a six-month commission investigating the niqab's permissibility. Because there are so few quantitative data on the number of women who wear niqab in France and their experiences of violence, anecdotes or "gossip" like hers serve as evidence of a problem (Amiraux 2007, 2014, 2016). In July 2008, a member of parliament from the French Communist Party, André Gerin, noted a "rising tide" or radical Islamism—as evidenced by women wearing niqab—in his district in a suburb of Lyon, but he provided no data. Fifty-eight other deputies agreed (Resolution no. 1725 on June 9, 2009) and cosigned a decree calling for a national commission. President Sarkozy echoed this concern, describing women who wear niqab as "imprisoned behind a grid, cut off from society and deprived of [their] identities" (cited in Gabizon 2009). Sarkozy subsequently formed a thirty-two-person Mission d'information sur la pratique du port du voile intégral sur le territoire national, also known as the Gerin Commission, appointing Gerin as its chair. Similar to the Stasi Commission, the committee met for six months and invited 211 individuals to address the panel. Also like the 2003 Stasi Commission (see Baubérot 2004; Bowen 2007), no women wearing niqab were invited to speak (see Zoghlami 2020 and Taher 2021 on the exclusion of Muslim women in commissions undertaken in the Québec context).

While not invited to the Gerin Commission to offer her perspective, Mme M. publicly disagreed with the allegation of Salafism in both a rebuttal statement to the Conseil d'État and in a 2008 *New York Times* interview (cited in Bennhold 2008). Her appeal was denied. While I am, of course, not privy to all the data that informed the decision to deny Mme M.'s request for citizenship, her unpalatable religiously informed habitus was certainly part of the equation. The inclusion of deeply private information about Mme M. by the state—the gynecological record, as well as observations of her interacting with her husband and father-in-law—are examples of the blurring of public and private spaces. Again, in order to be accepted as French citizens, while surveilled, Muslim women must perform specific sexual politics.

The third case focusses on Fatima Atif, who, also in 2008, began wearing hijab while on a two-year maternity leave. When she returned to work, she was fired from the private Baby Loup daycare in the town of Chanteloup-les-Vignes, about twenty-five kilometers west of Petit-Nanterre. Prior to her dismissal, Atif had worked at the daycare for sixteen years, but without wearing hijab. She sought damages and approached the Haute autorité de lutte contre les discriminations et pour l'égalité (High authority for the prevention of discrimination and for the protection of equality), which initially ruled in her favor. At stake was the extension to private businesses of the 2004 law banning conspicuous religious symbols in government institutions (see Etkin 2016). Atif's firing signals a slippage of the state's surveillance of religious symbols into a "privately" operated daycare. The societal notion that daycares socialize young children, a "particularly suggestible and sensitive audience" (cited in Badinter et al. 2012: 65), arguably allowed for the disciplining of secular sensibilities in this private business. Wearing a headscarf, Atif could unduly influence the children in her care. Her hijab, in this reading, was an affront to an internal regulation that required "philosophical, political, and confessional neutrality" (cited in Amiraux and Koussens 2013: 12). The children's vulnerability trumped Atif's religious freedom claims *and* her economic vulnerability. As in the other two cases, public opinion did not support her. A 2013 opinion poll from *Le Figaro* found that 84 percent of those polled in France agreed that women in private sectors should be impeded from wearing a headscarf (cited in Jacobsen 2017).

Following Atif's dismissal, the case went through several courts over six years. Ultimately, a 2014 decision from the Cour de cassation (Court of Cassation) determined that Atif had violated the religious neutrality requirements of the nursery's company policy (Hunter-Henin 2015: 717). With this decision, the parameters of neutrality were extended beyond government offices.[12] The Baby Loup case's outcome also reflects a significant divergence from the 1905 understanding of laïcité in France, which championed individual liberty, to a far more prescriptive and individualized version (Daly 2016). As I have noted, the post-2004 period has meant that racialized and religionized women can rarely be passively secular. That Atif's clients were small children further upped the stakes. Her areligiosity had to be legible, her secular sensibilities obvious.

Together, these three cases capture the increased necessity to outwardly perform one's secular politics in France. They also served as precedents for later secular legislation in France, namely against niqabs in 2010, and memorandums extending the public school's neutrality to visitors and to school trips in 2012, and against abayas in 2023.[13] In contrast to those focused on women's bodies, cases related to beards and circumcision on male bodies have received less public and legal attention. The visibility of niqabs especially trigger concern for proper sexuality. Niqabs are portrayed as particularly unagentic and as impeding acceptable secular and sexual sensibilities.

THE NIQAB'S ATTACK ON THE FEMININE SECULAR BODY

On the question of the niqab's acceptability in the Republic, the 2010 Gerin Commission report offered a resounding *no*. In the resolution that led to the creation of the Gerin Commission, full-face veils are depicted as "an attack" on "a woman's dignity and on the *assertion of her femininity*" (Assemblée Nationale 2010: 4; my emphasis). The resolution states that full-face veils exclude and humiliate women. They impede visual access to the female body. A personal choice example from the Gerin Commission report, which I see capturing this patriarchal exhortation to unveil, comes from André Rossinot, then mayor of the city of Nancy (see also Selby 2014a: 448). Seeing face-covering veils as necessarily imposed by men, Rossinot bemoans to the commission that the niqab represents the loss of women's sexual freedom: "When women do not have control of their image, they are not free to show themselves, to exist on the outside, *even less to seduce*" (as cited in Assemblée Nationale 2010: 110; my emphasis).

Rossinot's sexualization of women and call for access to women's bodies in the public sphere was, notably, not critiqued in the French press. This remark appears to have been unremarkable. Granted, Rossinot is but one of more than 200 individuals who testified before the commission, but this patriarchal-based fear that niqabs impede visual access to a woman's body, and her sociosexual freedom, situates cishet male desire as the basis for a woman's identity. Women are responsible for seducing men. Full-face veils impede this obligation. Again, Joan Wallach Scott's (2007: 158) point regarding how a cishet male gaze is key to a woman's subjectivation is worth reiterating. Visual access to women's faces and bodies brings women into being *as women*, just as the ability to see women's faces and bodies brings men into being *as men*. Again, the gender binary is central to how the secular body is affirmed. Within this framework, the niqab becomes not only an assault on women's femininity and men's masculinity, and the notion of biological and sexual difference, but also, more broadly, on women and men's existence as subjects.

It is not solely white male politicians like Rossinot who insist on visual access to women's faces and bodies. Several women who spoke before the Gerin Commission bolstered a conceptualization of women's bodies as "most free" when they are visually accessible. Four women's testimonies are cited extensively in the Gerin Commission report: philosopher Élisabeth Badinter, feminist Olivia Cattan, politician Danièle Hoffman-Rispal, and activist leader Sihem Habchi, then president of Ni Putes ni Soumises, a Maghrebian banlieue-based feminist organization. Their common message: Niqabs impede women's sexual power. To make this point, Badinter references a 2009 film starring Isabel Adjani, *La journée de la jupe* (*Skirt Day*).[14] The film chronicles a high school teacher who loses control of her suburban-living, racialized male students and decides to hold them hostage. Their worst offense is their questionable sexual ethics. In her presentation before the commission, Badinter references her experience watching *Skirt Day* with a middle-school class in Paris's eighteenth arrondissement and her shock at how few Maghrebian-origin female students (read: Muslims) wore desirable short skirts (Assemblée Nationale 2010: 334). Badinter also cites the 2008 Mme H. virginity case from Lille in noting how, problematically, women who wear niqab are likely imposed virginity at the time of their marriage (Assemblée Nationale 2010: 97). Mme H. did not wear niqab, but her well-known unacceptable sexual politics were more telling than factual accuracy.

A second speaker at the commission, Olivia Cattan, president of Parole de Femmes (Women's speech), takes Badinter's point on *Skirt Day* further and argues that, in a similar context where she teaches, there might be "one girl" who wears a skirt. For Cattan, this lack of femininity, combined with an alleged rise in *garçons manqués* (tomboys), reflects a problematic deviation from mainstream French femininity (cited in Assemblée Nationale 2010: 135; see also Wesselhoeft 2011). Cattan characterizes undesirable too-long abaya-like dresses of Maghrebian-origin girls as a defense mechanism against the potential violence of young Muslim men in the suburbs. This linkage casts young men of North African origin as culpable for the erasure of the girls' desirable femininity. This refrain on paternalist protection against religion-inspired violence should sound familiar. As we saw in the 2003 Stasi Commission report, young Muslim women in the suburbs require state intervention to free themselves from their religious communities that foster violent Muslim men, whether their fathers, brothers, or others.[15]

A third participant, a Socialist member of the National Assembly representing Paris's sixth arrondissement, Danièle Hoffman-Rispal, agrees that the Adjani film represented problematic gender politics and the niqab in France: "*Skirt Day* is not just a film, it's every day" (cited in Assemblée Nationale 2010: 596). These three accounts are corroborated by Sihem Habchi. Positioning herself as a privileged insider of the Maghrebian-origin suburban experience, Habchi testifies, "*Our* daily lives become routinized by a [religious] schedule, and respect for a prescribed dress code when the skirt is banned and where, ultimately, sexuality is controlled and gauged via a sacrosanct virginity" (cited in Assemblée Nationale 2010: 98; my emphasis). These words were given greater gravitas in Habchi's testimony at the commission. Sociologist Sylvie Tissot (2011: 45), who attended, notes that when, in her testimony, Habchi declared that she was not ashamed of her body, she removed her jacket to reveal her bare shoulders. The panel applauded this gesture, indicating its pleasure at the visibility of her body and the performance of undressing (cf. Fadela Amara of Ni Putes ni Soumises on her testimony for the 2003 Stasi Commission in which she stressed that, as a teenager, it was "natural for us to wear short skirts, tight-fitting jeans, low-cut blouses, and short T-shirts" (cited in Selby and Fernando 2014).

To be clear: *Skirt Day* is not a film about niqabs. It *is* about a white, middle-aged feminist female teacher who valiantly—or violently—fights suburban Muslim masculinity for an appropriately sexualized secular body. Here again, the character's fought-after appropriate secular body is not "routinized" by religion: the body she fights for can wear skirts and short dresses, be an individual uncontrolled by male members of her religious community, be a nonvirgin and therefore effectively seductive and sexually available, and have control over her sexual life.

According to the antiniqab report, the idealized woman wears short skirts, and her face is not "concealed" or, as figure 2.1 states, is not "dissimulé." Art historian Nadeije Laneyrie-Dagen (in Assemblée Nationale 2010: 511) acknowledges the broader socialization of the "naked" face: the idealized nakedness of the female face is mitigated by the beauty industry (and, presumably, surgical interventions and injections). Laneyrie-Dagen's primary point is that women whose faces are covered, especially by a religiously and community-oriented garment, are anathema to the shared Western cultural heritage that France rests upon. Niqabs therefore impede access to full membership in "Western civilization." In contrast, a naked face is primordial because it carries an individual's soul, reason, and personality. Laneyrie-Dagen explains that "for us [in France], it's a *secular cultural heritage* [to see the face]" (Assemblée Nationale 2010: 590; my emphasis). Laneyrie-Dagen brings gravitas to this statement by invoking an "us" (French citizens) in contrast to "them" (niqab-wearers). Her invocation of heritage is a protective move (cf. Beaman 2020). Laneyrie-Dagen effectively links this secular body with French heritage status. The heritage assignation of the naked face renders it a reflection of national identity and a requirement for vivre ensemble (living well together) and *mixité* (the comingling of men and women). There is much at stake.

The 658-page, single-spaced report details a half-dozen rationales for why face-covering veils should be banned, including gender equality, women's freedom and dignity, security, and neighborliness (see Selby 2011a: 385). But who would read this copious document? Visual materials work well to collapse complex arguments about religious symbols into facile arguments. This poster (fig. 2.1), circulated by the government to promote the 2011 law, relies on the familiar symbol of Marianne and references the law's primary thrust: that women cannot cover their faces in public. In contrast to a niqab-wearing woman, Marianne is an iconic representation of liberty, reason, and femininity. She reflects acceptable secular sensibilities. In the poster, she is young, white, and wears her characteristic small Phrygian cap, referencing freedom in the French Revolution. In contrast to the Delacroix depiction, in this rendition, her gendered secularism is less sexualized and more mannered. The poster mentions concrete locations where the law is enforced, including stores and commercial spaces, and cites the date of the law's implementation, April 11, 2011.

This second image (fig. 2.2) is a photograph of a promotional poster for the far-right Front National party (now the Rassemblement National). The poster instructs the idealized sexualized secular woman, who again, is contrasted to one wearing niqab. It situates danger in the suburbs; this Marianne's nonwhiteness is a further marker of her suburbanness. The tagline "Choose Your Suburb," effectively locates the problem of the niqab as within the country's suburbs, recalling a Fanonian demarcation of space I describe in the introduction. That I saw this poster in the thirteenth arrondissement and not in Petit-Nanterre also may say something of its intended audience. We see the face and invocation of Marianne, which again serves an instructive function, signaling the idealized secular woman. The contrast favors the woman on the left, whose naked face is visible and even adorned with French tricolor flag face paint. Her cap is a nod to the Revolutionary Marianne. The eyes of the woman wearing the niqab appear frightened, capturing the poster's emotional register. These are all qualities that the secular body is not.

Niqabs are most targeted in characterizations of an idealized female secular body, but burkinis have also served as foils to secular sensibilities. Long after Marianne's nudity in Delacroix's painting, bare breasts came

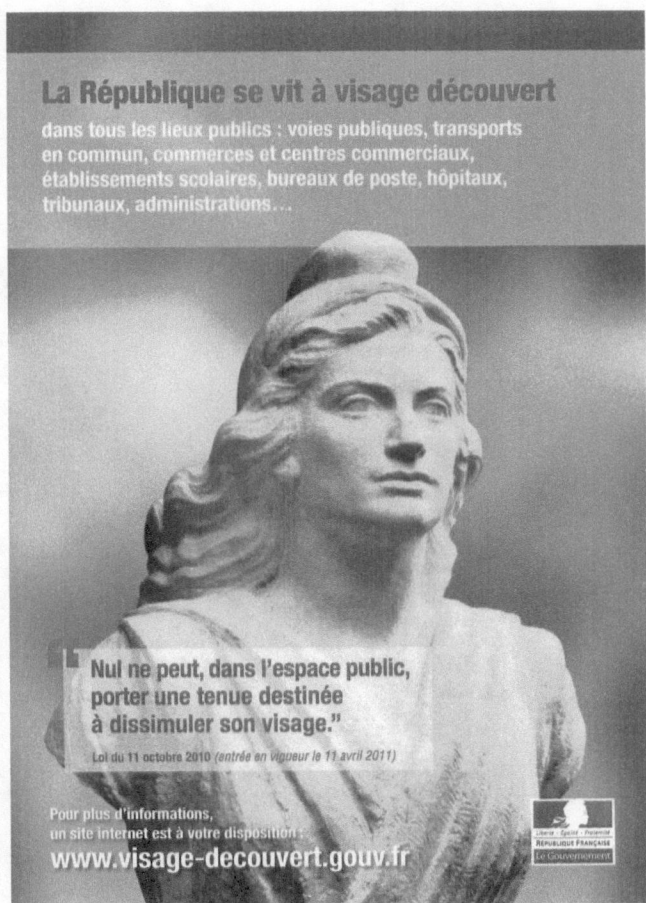

Figure 2.1. "The Republic is lived with an uncovered face." Gouvernement de la République française, Archives départementales du Var, accessed October 22, 2024, https://archives.var.fr/article.php?laref=11188&titre=affiche-la-republique-se-vit-a-visage-decouvert.

into mode on the beaches of Saint-Tropez in the midst of France's sexual revolution in the 1960s. They were associated with indifference, aestheticism, relaxation, and sexual freedom (Kaufmann 1995). Restrictions against burkinis are more recent. They heightened in the summer of 2016, when a series of terrorist attacks occurred across France, including in Nice on the fête nationale (July 14), claimed by the Islamic State.[16] Thirty-one municipalities on the French Riviera sought to institute fines for women wearing body-covering swimsuits at their beaches. Decrees in Cannes (July 28, 2016) and Villeneuve-Loubet (August 5, 2016) were rapidly overturned on appeal (Koussens 2023) but concern for burkinis went viral. Others suggested that Manuel Valls's outspoken position, to which I now turn, was a smoke screen against a controversial labor law—the Loi travail (n° 2016-1088) allowed for

Figure 2.2. "Choose your suburb: Vote for the National Front." Photo by Christophe Petit Tesson © picture-alliance/dpa.

greater ease in firing employees, and other labor law shifts—then being debated in France (Almeida 2018: 23).

President Sarkozy overtly linked the presence of burkinis on France's beaches as impeding a shared national identity (cited in Beardsley 2016). Others noted the "courage" necessary to stand up against the burkini. The Socialist prime minister (and former interior minister), Manuel Valls, echoed that burkinis were impediments to secularism and women's rights in France. In a speech to fellow Socialists, Valls noted that, in the spirit of Marianne, "bare breasts symbolize freedom" and that "Marianne has a naked breast because she is feeding the people! She is not veiled, because she is free! That is the Republic!" (cited in Beardsley 2016). In Valls's equation, therefore, as with Marianne, bare breasts reflect women's equal rights and freedoms. Beachside burkini restrictions were not formally legislated like antiniqab legislation. Still, even if the French courts overturned many of the bans as unconstitutional, their pejorative impact remained in the contouring of secular sensibilities.

SECULAR-SEXUAL BODIES IN QUÉBEC

The post-2004 interpolation of secular sensibilities in Québec is drawn less sharply, but in its antiniqab legislation also focuses on the importance of a naked face as an assurance of proper femininity. Beginning in 2009, a series of bills proposed by different Québécois governments reveal significant dovetailing with French legislation on laïcité. Four provincial bills have been proposed that attempt to "solve" the province's so-called reasonable accommodation problem (Bouchard and Taylor 2008; see also Rousseau 2012; Bilge 2013; Barras 2016; and Selby, Barras, and Beaman 2018).[17] Québec differs from France in that it has no ultraright political party (Laxer 2019: 81). A number of political parties in the province have sought to restrict religious symbols. Articles 6 and 8 that focus on the removal of religious symbols in the 2019 Act Respecting the Laicity of the State (Law 21) shed light on the Coalition Avenir Québec government's idealized secular sensibilities. Article 8 especially calls for a naked face to protect clearly gendered emancipation and thereby, proper relations in a "healthy" Québécois nation (Assemblée Nationale du Québec 2019).

Beginning in 2010, other provincial governments in addition to the CAQ—the provincial Liberals and the Parti Québécois—have proposed different iterations of secular laws focused on religious symbols. All of these imply or mention an idealized female "naked face." Mandatory masking amid the COVID-19 pandemic in Québec did not inspire Premier Legault to reopen the question of the acceptability of face coverings (Pelletier 2020). Those who cover their faces for medical reasons or to do their jobs were exempt from the restriction. The reason behind covering the face mattered most. As in France, critiques of cosmetics or other alterations are absent, but these are presumably accepted.

In the context of discussion surrounding a first iteration against full-face veils, the report on secularism by the Québécois government-funded Conseil du statut de la femme (CSF, Council on the Status of Women) (2011), for one, affirmed the patriarchal dangers of the visibility of religiosity on women's bodies in relation to the proposed Law 94. The report argues that women's faces must be bare and their bodies areligious in order to be "neutral." It proposes that a neutral dress code and bare face protect women against patriarchal religious traditions and, symbolically, ensure access to social and civic rights, including the rights to vote, to divorce, and to receive an abortion. Given that these rights came later to this province—women in Québec gained access to voting rights in 1940, far later than suffrage in other Canadian provinces and in France—and the dramatic shift in sexual politics that took place with de-Christianization in the 1960s, gains in these rights feel recent. The logic of the report is that to promote an areligious female body serves as an assurance against organized religiosity, whether Catholicism or Islam. Yet even as the CSF report attempts to fit niqab bans into this broad narrative, its repeated invocations of and attachment to a bare face index a particular problem with head-covering garments in Islam and a grounding in specific norms and gender performativity integral to Québécois values.

Like in France, a specific 2010 case helped to spur the minister of justice that March to propose Bill 94, also known as An Act to Establish Guidelines Governing Accommodation Requests within the Administration and Certain Institutions (see fig. 1.2). Neither the title nor the contents of Bill 94 overtly name the niqab or the 2010 Naima Atef case, but even a superficial reading of the bill makes the full-face veil target clear. Atef, an Egyptian-origin newcomer, began wearing niqab after she settled in Montréal. She made headlines when she was dramatically expelled from a state-run French-language training class because of her refusal to remove her full-face veil. Shortly after, the Parti Québécois introduced Bill 94, which spelled out clear restrictions for women who wear niqab. It did not pass.

SECULAR-SEXUAL BODIES IN THE REST OF CANADA

Many Canadians imagine the rest of Canada's approach to religion as profoundly different from Québec's (see Selby and Barras, forthcoming). But I would suggest, on the secular body, the differences are not as great as they may seem. Three subsequent federal legal decisions in Canada suggest very different undercurrents that *do not* support the visibility of religious symbols in the public sphere. A seemingly unrelated 2009 Supreme Court of Canada case on a conservative communal Christian community (*Alberta v. Hutterian Brethren of Wilson Colony*), the Hutterite Brethren, shows that the Canadian courts were not going to be open to arguments framed using religious freedom and group rights in a case surrounding the visibility of the face. This community sought an exemption from being photographed for their driver's licenses due to their interpretation of the admonition against graven images in the Hebrew Bible (Exodus 20:4). The Supreme Court's majority decision (4–3) determined that infringing the religious freedom of this group was less deleterious than the potential security harm of not correctly identifying an individual through their driver's license (Esau 2008; Berger 2010). Seeing the naked face on a driver's license was imperative, here for security reasons.

In a second case, *R v. NS* (2012), the Supreme Court of Canada's majority decision promoted an ad hoc response to the acceptability of niqabs in the courtroom. At issue was balancing the effects of the allowability of the niqab in an alleged sexual assault case, with concern for demeanor evidence and the rights of the accused (see Bhabha 2013; and Bakht 2020, 2021: 346). In her majority opinion, then chief justice Beverley McLachlin determined that the court could not make a unilateral decision regarding the acceptability of niqabs, and therefore, with reference on the Charter of Rights and Freedoms, did not offer a blanket protection for the garment. In her dissent, Justice Rosalie Silberman Abella questioned the portrayal of niqabs as potential obstacles for the assessment of demeanor: "trial fairness cannot reasonably expect ideal testimony from an ideal witness in every case, and that demeanor itself represents only one factor in the assessment of a witness's credibility" (*R v. NS*, paragraph 107). Niqabs were not granted unequivocal protection in Canadian courts.

Third, in 2015, in the midst of a federal election, the federal Conservative Party banned niqab-wearing in citizenship swearings-in, specifically that of Zunera Ishaq. The oath of allegiance is the last step in the process toward becoming a Canadian citizen. Under the Canadian Citizenship Act, a prospective citizen must take the Oath of Citizenship in order to become a citizen and their mouths must be visible uttering the oath. As a devout Sunni Muslim whose interpretation of religious beliefs meant she wore niqab in public, Ishaq did not want to remove her face-covering veil in the ceremony. Anecdotal evidence led to the law. A former Conservative member of Parliament phoned the federal immigration, citizenship, and multiculturalism minister, Jason Kenney, to complain that he had just witnessed four women taking the Oath of Citizenship with their faces fully covered (Alibhai 2023: 104). The restriction was then implemented quickly.

The impact of this decision reverberated outside the specifics of Ishaq's oath-taking ceremony. Perhaps most significant, when the ban was announced, the Conservative Party leader's popularity rose. Stephen Harper noted that according to normative interpretations of Islam, Muslim women are not required to cover their faces in public and "most moderate Muslims support the [niqab] ban" (cited in Chase 2015; see also Alibhai 2023). There would be no protections for Ishaq under religious freedoms assured in the Charter of Rights and Freedoms. Eventually Ishaq *was* able to participate in her swearing-in with her niqab because of a technical error in the judgment.[18] I mention these three decisions in Canada because they reflect a clear legal directive to show the face, and the support of this sensibility by the Canadian high court and public. In sum, these series of post-2004 laws in France and Québec that reference secularism and sexuality and that focus on niqabs, burkinis, and other forms of unacceptable coverings can also be read as sources of more appropriate national sensibilities.

Narratives of Romance and Civil Marriage

Waël and Walid in Montréal, and Rachida, Amel, and Youcine in Petit-Nanterre had their own engagements with the secular-sexual framing of secularism in the contact zone of their civil marriages. In this section, we will see how they, alternately, pushed back against, reframed, and absorbed these expectations, which held differing implications for them in each of their specific social locations.

In our formal interview in 2016, Rachida, forty-two, who lived in Petit-Nanterre, shared a narrative of romance in describing how she met her now-husband, Farid. Rachida and I had spent months together in the same outreach organization over four years, where she worked part time and I volunteered three mornings a week (see Selby 2017 for more on this organization). Rachida's framing of how she met Farid surprised me given her general no-nonsense approach to life. Rachida was sympathetic toward those who came to the community association for help with their paperwork. Many did not have the literacy or French language fluency to grapple with complex requests. She was quick to laugh and deescalate tense situations at the organization when they arose. Rachida had a lot going on: she had three living children, Farid worked full time for the national railway (the Société nationale des chemins de fer) and was often away.[19] As the primary parent to their three children, she worked part time. She had two married brothers who lived nearby who relied on her too. Rachida had a sporty look and kept her dyed platinum-blond hair very short, which accentuated her large round brown eyes. Because her French was flawless, I wasn't aware she had grown up in Oran until several months into our knowing one another.

In our interactions at the community association in Petit-Nanterre, Rachida made it clear that she did not want to speak with me at work about, in her words, "anything personal." Instead, she invited me one Saturday for a couscous lunch at her family's three-bedroom apartment. Rachida had moved to France from Oran and first settled with her husband in another nearby suburb, which she preferred over living in Petit-Nanterre. The other banlieue was "plus calme," closer to the market, and the streets were cleaner. But that apartment was too small for them. Their oldest son was now a teenager, and the waiting list for a three-bedroom social housing apartment was long. The new apartment was at the edge of Petit-Nanterre, across from a popular halal butcher shop.

Because of her busy schedule and her no-nonsense demeanor, I wasn't sure what to expect at her apartment. She welcomed me warmly when I arrived with flowers, and insisted we eat together in the living room—"a rare moment of peace"—while her husband and the children helped themselves and ate in the separate kitchen. It was a cloudy day, and with the two windows facing north, the living room was dark. She lit some incense. I sat down and she turned on a lamp behind me. She had not expressed a lot of interest in me in the previous months, but as we traded confidences, she became more relaxed.

More than twelve years earlier, in 2004, Rachida had migrated to France for her marriage to Farid. Before then, she said she had no clear aspirations to immigrate. Rachida had attended public school in Arabic, but was immersed in French culture and language at home thanks to her mother, who had been educated in the French colonial education system, spoke French flawlessly, and had spent her own career teaching French in a private high school, all while raising Rachida and her three brothers. Rachida's mother had insisted the family speak French at home, which now served them as three of the four lived or worked in Petit-Nanterre. A few months after this interview, in July 2016, I had the opportunity to stay with her parents in Oran (after Amel and Yacine's wedding in Ghazaouet; they did not know each other) and quickly saw why Rachida's French was impeccable. Her mother was a Francophile, an avid reader of French literature, and watched the news in French every night. Like her daughter, she had a no-nonsense manner, which Rachida said was necessary to deal with her father, who was "difficile."

Over couscous, Rachida narrated her story of marriage and migration to France with allusions of romance. Like in a romantic-comedy film, she stressed repeatedly that their coincidental meeting in Oran, while he was on vacation from France, was fated. For her, God had willed their paths to cross. They fell in love. After completing her undergraduate degree at the Université d'Oran Ahmed Ben Bella, Rachida began working for an advertising agency. She smiled as she remembered how stylish and sophisticated she had been before her children were born, stressing she has never worn hijab. As she told it, one afternoon, when she was walking from work in downtown Oran, she saw Farid across the street. He waved at her and crossed the street. He then followed her, requested her phone number, and over several weeks persistently tried to woo her by phone. Her telling invoked a well-circulated romance trope of miscommunicated love signals that were eventually understood. She said he was drawn to her because of her rare combination of "modernity," in her unveiled and stylish business suit, and "purity," as a practicing Muslim woman from a conservative family. This blend, she said, was rare among young women of Algerian origin in France: "He [Farid] was looking for a woman who didn't have a past [i.e., was a virgin]. Who was modern, who was . . . everything you want. Who came from a good family. There you have it [*voilà*]. Who hasn't dated. Who's serious. So they [Franco-Algerians] like to test this when they meet us." Rachida explained that Farid sought a *Blédarde* as a marriage partner. His holiday in Oran included a wish for "destiny" to take hold; he hoped he might meet "la femme de sa vie" (the woman of his life) on this trip. Also as in many rom-coms, Rachida passed an unspoken test in not responding too quickly. It was important that she refuse his initial invitation. Eventually, after several conversations and a handful of meetings, Rachida's parents encouraged their daughter's migration for marriage. She says she herself had more reservations. She had not met his family in person and had not seen him in his own environment. And, most significant, the marriage implied a radical change in her life course: she would leave Oran to live in France, which she had visited only once on a short family holiday.

Once she agreed to marry Farid and migrate to France, challenges emerged. Rachida noted that the planning of their wedding celebration was a source of tension between them. Farid had pushed to marry civilly in France to expedite Rachida's reunification immigration file. In their case, it was Farid who had interiorized the state's concern regarding their transnational wedding. Rachida was not keen on this wedding plan, but accepted it. The idea, therefore, was that Rachida would apply for a visitor visa and they would marry when she arrived. Farid would then file paperwork so she could receive a longer-term visa. Farid assured her that this elopement plan in France would be intimate and romantic. Rachida reluctantly accepted this plan and forwent the traditional dresses, which she had imagined she would wear, for a plainer white dress, and the usual big wedding celebration common among her entourage in Oran.

Rachida and Farid were married in 2006 in a civil marriage outside of Paris, which meant they could skip a step that others who marry legally in Algeria must undergo—like Nawel and Khalid, and Amel and Yacine—of having their wedding certificate translated and certified at a French consulate in Algeria and then arranging an official reception of this document in France. Rachida acknowledged that Farid's plan had been a good one: she had received her *carte-de-séjour* (residency card) quickly and without any hassle. In the end, only one of Farid's sisters and his parents were able to attend the civil ceremony at the city hall in Colombes, which neighbors Petit-Nanterre. Her parents' visitor visa requests had been rejected, and they were not able to attend. Her brothers had migrated only after she did. Most disappointing, Rachida recalled, was that after the ceremony, she and Farid had celebrated alone in an inexpensive restaurant in the banlieue: "C'était pas un grec, mais presque" (it wasn't a kebab, but almost). The meal had a fast-food quality that was nothing special.

For Rachida, in addition to these disappointments about the day's rituals, celebrating the wedding in France meant conflicts and the impossibility of finding the right "ingredients," which for her meant not only the meal but also the necessary components of a proper wedding ritual: missing were her extended family, the right good food, location, ambiance, and right garments. Rachida had felt alone and far from the celebration she had imagined. Moreover, the planning had been "annoying" and "haphazard," and her wedding day and her party in France "without taste":

> Honestly, the [wedding's] location is important. In Algeria, it's better. Why? It's a different audience [*public*]. The guests are not at all the same. And there [in Colombes] they have a mentality that's a bit... they're neither Algerians nor real French people. All this cultural mixing makes them a bit *out*. However, if you go to Algeria, if you celebrate it in Algeria, you have everything: you have the necessary guests. You have the necessary ambiance. The music. Everything....
>
> *Au Bled* [back home], when you're there, you don't need to tell anyone to do this or that. Everyone knows things go like this and not like that. But here, you have to explain why. Here [in France], a wedding is a debate. You try to make a traditional cake, but here you can't find the ingredients you need. The cake will be good, but it won't be the same. For all of these reasons, it's better back home.

Rachida was certain that a wedding party in Oran would have been easier to negotiate. The main problem with her wedding ceremony in France was that, for her, Farid and his family were neither fully Algerian nor fully French. The ceremony also marked the beginning of tremendous transitions for her: "J'ai dû changer de pays et changer de caractère. Ici il faut lutter pour tout. C'est pas facile." (I had to change countries and change my personality. Here you have to fight for everything. It's not easy.) Despite these challenges and compromises, Rachida was committed to shaping the arc of her migration life as one based on a God-ordained romance, perhaps in part because she thought I would appreciate this trope. This telling was perhaps also enabled because their meeting had been haphazard, prior to their families' involvement. It was not a familial arrangement suspicious for the French state.

Waël, thirty-two, also invoked secular sensibilities and romance in his telling of his marriage story. Waël migrated to Montréal via Paris, where he had completed a master's degree in economics, which, in turn, had facilitated his application for permanent residency in Québec. At the time of his interview at the Ginkgo café near the Université du Québec à Montréal (UQAM) on the rue Sainte-Catherine, he was a married doctoral student. He explained to Kawtare how hard he found initially migrating to his aunt's apartment in a Parisian suburb from Boumerdès, Algeria, in 2007, mostly because of his constant stress around money.[20] Life in Paris was exponentially more expensive than in Boumerdès. After finishing his studies at the Université d'Évry-Val-d'Essonne, he had been unable to secure a good job in France to begin repaying his student debt. His thoughts turned to North America. Waël admitted he was more attracted to the United States than to Canada, but because he didn't speak English, he applied for permanent residency in Québec. An uncle who lived in Montréal was a bonus. Even if their relationship was estranged, he felt he could count on the uncle in case of emergency.

Waël recalled the "marathon" of his permanent residency application in the year before his departure for Montréal, which included leaving a non-Algerian, French-born girlfriend. He was tired:

> When I arrived in Montréal, I wanted to take a break. So, I worked for, I worked in a call center. Actually, that's a typical immigrant thing, which I did for like two, three days. Then I said, fuck this! And after, I think I worked at a gas station, just to pay my bills and all that. But I was going out a lot. I wanted to just live, discover, watch TV, not to worry about the future or my career. And then, little by little, after a year and a half or so, I said, "Come on, what do you want to do?"
>
> And then, I went back to school at UQAM. I did a master's in economics; I did my master's and then my director saw that I could do it [academia]. And then he asked, "What do you think? If you do a doctorate, we can find some funding." So I said, why not? And I did my dissertation.

Waël had done some research online prior to migrating. He knew that many Algerians began their work lives in Québec at call centers. But the cubicle life didn't work for him. The gas station was more interactive and, he stressed, motivated him to apply for a Québec-based second master's degree.

Feeling his values had changed a great deal since his life in Algeria, Waël did not seek out Algerian friends in Montréal, or seek to join country-specific networks, including the Algerian Cultural Centre.

On a few occasions during the interview, he stressed that while "there are things of which I'm proud," he "doesn't share the same values" as many Algerians in Montréal. He cited an example of a visit with a male friend to a café in the city's Petit Maghreb neighborhood: "Someone asked [pointing to us], 'Are these gays?'" His implication was that he was not gay but also not homophobic, and that other Algerians who hang out in the Petit Maghreb neighborhood in Montréal are. His point was that, compared with his compatriots, he was more cosmopolitan and had more modern values.

It was during this period of renewed study that Waël met his now wife, Megan, who had also been studying at UQAM and was part of the same social circle. In describing how he met his wife, a white Franco-Ontarian atheist, Waël underscored the sexual normativity of their meeting. Theirs was not arranged, destined, or related to his Muslimness or Algerian past.

KB: And so, how did you meet her [his wife, Megan]?
W: Here in Montréal, through friends. You know. *Normal* [said in English].
KB: OK, so you met. You liked her. She liked you, and—
W: Yeah, I really liked her. I think she liked me, actually I'm sure she did. Then after, we lived together, and when she moved to Ottawa, I went with her. And that's it.

Here Waël implies the normativity of a secular romance: they met through friends. Theirs was a relationship built on mutual attraction. It was "normal" and not like those he implied were usual for his compatriots, based on destiny or familial arrangements. So too, when Kawtare asked him about how he and Megan were raising their two-year-old, it was Waël who brought up the question of circumcision. The couple had chosen to circumcise their son, but he stressed that their decision was based on extensive medical research and "scientific reasons." Irrational religion did not influence his decision-making.

Waël said he became an atheist as a response to having lived through Algeria's Décennie noire in the 1990s and its religiously framed violence. One of the questions in our interview schedule asked those who had lived in both France and Québec to consider their secular debates comparatively.

Waël stressed that for him the restrictions against niqabs in both places made sense for two reasons. First, he critiqued what he called "un truc anglosaxon" (an Anglo-Saxon way) that "sacralizes the individual and the liberty of the individual; you do what you want." He saw a greater harm in allowing any kind of veil, hijab or niqab, be present in the public sphere. Answering his own question, he asked, "When you live in a society where there are interactions, does the fact that you wear a veil, does it cause problems in a public or an administrative space, or not? Yes, it does."

Waël's second argument against full-face veils replicated logic introduced in the Gerin Commission report in France around the legibility of a woman's body. Unprompted, Waël noted, "I don't think we should aspire to this way [to accept niqabs]. I want to see a woman as she is. My future dream society does not include a woman who wears the niqab. I want to see her, and I really don't understand why she wears it." Here, Waël reinforces a posture of the necessity and desirability of visual access to women's bodies. He wanted to see a woman "as she is," implicitly referencing the notion of the naked uninhibited face. A full-face veil impeded "proper" social interactions between men and women.

In a similar vein, like Walid, with whom I opened this chapter, Waël emphasized that his transnational marriage was based on romance and attraction and not familial or religious preferences. He also made sure to mention that neither he nor Megan were virgins on their wedding night. I mention this comment as a way to consider the potential social benefits in revealing their sexual histories, particularly given that, as part of an ethnographic refusal I explain in the introduction, I did not pose questions on this subject. I suspect that Walid and Waël shared this detail because of their reading of Kawtare and me as liberal, nonpracticing women. These men's willingness to "overlook" virginity served to signal their liberalism. Their positionality differs from Rachida's, who is conscious of her husband's politics and her desirability as an Algerian-born virgin. Still, her adoption of a love-at-first-sight narrative in her telling of her marriage story does similar work in situating her in well-known tropes.

In a final example, I turn to Yacine, twenty-six, who has a different perspective as a transnational marriage partner, that is, as a man who migrated to France owing to an arranged marriage with a French national. The real and imagined surveillance of his sexual ethics was omnipresent on his wedding day in July 2016, given that his marriage to a second-generation, twenty-five-year-old French-born woman of Algerian origin, Amel, implied his immigration to France. I first met Yacine by email when he had helped me with paperwork for my tourist visa to attend his wedding in Ghazaouet, a small coastal city in western Algeria where he grew up.[21] Amel had invited me on her weeklong wedding trip. Amel knew the challenges and scrutiny she would face in sponsoring Yacine but had nevertheless sought an Algerian-born groom. Despite the potential power differentials in their union, they both attributed their union to mektoub. Amel's father and eldest brother had also had transnational France-Ghazaouet marriages, and her affective ties to the region were significant. Still, their union's arranged, transnational, and religious aspects were precisely the concerns laid out by the French state in its 2006, 2011, and 2021 laws sharpening rules against transnational unions.

Given that their union had been arranged, and their limited contact prior to their nuptials, at their evening wedding party in a rented hall in downtown Ghazaouet, I was struck by Amel's eagerness to enact what she described as "modern" expressions of romantic love, including staged photos and a candle-lighting ritual. The couple's staged longing gazes were not based on premarital social or sexual intimacy. Perhaps sensing that I was more familiar with romantic poses than the hired local photographer, Amel asked me to take these photos with my camera. At the reception, which consisted of an elaborate gender-segregated meal followed by a party where guests danced and mingled, Yacine accepted these rituals and followed Amel's cues. She wore eight dresses; he wore a black fitted suit with shiny black shoes and had shaven his thick beard short. Even if these photos would be later evaluated by French state officials in Yacine's residency application, Amel appeared to take great pleasure in their staging, which also allowed her to display her eight dresses and accompanying hijabs and jewelry. She was pleased with three matching candles she had customized in France, and had carefully packed in her suitcase. One featured her first name, another the groom's first name, and a third *amour* (love).

Sharing this ritual of a newly ignited flame mattered to her. She happily performed romance throughout the evening's activities.

Two days after their late-night wedding party, Yacine and Amel drove from Ghazaouet to Oran to have their marriage certificate translated and approved at the French embassy. Amel only had a few holidays from a new job as a radiology technician, so they planned to then fly from Oran and return to Amel's one-bedroom social housing apartment near La Défense, outside of Paris, hopefully with the paperwork in hand. As they picked up Amel's luggage from her grandmother's house where I was still staying with a dozen other visiting relatives, I could see they were both nervous about this administrative procedure. Amel expected they would be individually questioned on the legitimacy of their relationship, as per the 2010 memorandum. Yacine had shaved his beard completely. In the flurry of familial congratulations, hellos, and goodbyes, I could not ask him whether the shave was strategic, but a cousin commented on it and thought it was. Six hours later, Amel's younger brother shared a text message: "Everything's cool." Amel and Yacine had not been questioned separately and had received their paperwork without issue. Indeed, few transnational marriages have been annulled in France since the laws against "love fraud" and the memorandum for marriage officiants (Belmokhtar 2006). The impacts of these laws are in their spectral politics and not in their enforcement. Moreover, with this translated wedding certificate, Yacine's engagement with the French state was only just beginning. Once he receives his permanent residency, the couple will be surveilled in the first four years of their marriage. Their wedding can be annulled by the state at any point for thirty years if deemed fraudulent.

We have seen how these six participants engage differently with state officials in their expectations of romance in the contact zone of civil marriage and in describing their "love" stories. Walid, with whom I opened, experienced the sexual politics surrounding the 2013 Charter of Values when his wife Farida, who wore hijab, migrated to Montréal for marriage. Walid's sexual politics were called into question by paramedics in his association with Farida, who was deemed vulnerable when she fainted, as a racialized Muslim-identified newcomer who struggled with French. Others engaged these tropes differently. Amel, like Rachida, found pleasure in the expectations of romance in her own wedding ceremony with Yacine in Ghazaouet. Yacine chose to remove his beard when he engaged with the state.

Secular sensibilities are powerful precisely because they are not only top-down. They circulate in ways that are pleasurable. They can signal social and economic capital. Amel's delight *and* sophistication in enacting these rituals of romance at their wedding party are notable. Even if Rachida was profoundly disappointed by the kebab she ate after her wedding ceremony outside of Paris, she found greater meaning in a "star-crossed" telling of when she first met Farid than one based solely on God-framed destiny. Waël framed his relationship outside of these parameters, eschewing religiously framed reasons to explain his relationship with Megan. In sum, these participants' marriage and migration experiences are not solely tales of pejorative surveillance and biopower by the state.

Building on chapter 1's theorization on secular sensibilities and their shaping of religion, race, and gender, this chapter has sought to investigate how contemporary discourses of and legislation on secularism articulate appropriate sexuality. We have seen how these ideals can be traced back to colonial preoccupations with the establishment of capitalism and Christianity. Jumping ahead to the secular and immigration legislative period of my interviews in the 2010s, we also saw how these interlocutors in the "contact zone" of their civil marriages, particularly those who are racialized and religionized non-EU citizens who also seek entry, offers a window into preferred sensibilities and habituses of these ideals. I conclude with two broader points on the religious symbols that capture these mores and on the expediency of pictograms and images in their promotion.

In the first place, we have seen that antiniqab and antiburkini legislative attempts are especially evocative of the parameters of secular-sexual sensibilities in contemporary France and Québec. Women who wear these garments are especially vulnerable to these directives in that they have received little support, whether in public opinion polls, from feminists, from fellow religionists, from mainstream Muslim organizations, or from non-Muslims in the legislation passed restricting them and imparting their unacceptability. The ways these garments cover women's bodies are particularly offensive to secular sensibilities. Niqabs especially are therefore expeditious targets of secular legislation. Debates about them offer data on what the secular body is *not*: a security threat, covered, unfeminine, unreadable, repellant, unagentic, unfashionable, uncivil, unneighborly, nonsexual, a victim of false consciousness, governed by religiosity and communitarian pressures, and so on. Put simply, these garments are the most problematic for idealized versions of femininity and sexuality.

Bans on niqabs and other religious symbols delineate both unacceptable religiosity and acceptable sexual agency. Despite all the energy, time, and money spent in France and Québec to restrict these garments, because they remain rare, their surveillance and instructive impact are, in fact, more tangible for non-niqab wearers than for niqab-wearing women. Moreover, without having to dismantle forms of patriarchy or structures of inequality—whether racial, gendered, or class-based—anti-face veil legislation allows governments to facilely position themselves as "protecting" women. In sum, the work of these commissions and laws to restrict niqabs remains more performative and ideological than practical.

In the second place, it is notable how pictograms in both contexts and, in France with representations of Marianne, work to solidify facile binaries of acceptability and unacceptability, here related to religion, sexual mores, and conceptions of gender. These nonneutral images do a great deal of work in promoting secular sensibilities. Recall the bust of Marianne in KAK's caricature in chapter 1 (fig. 1.1), whose breasts reverberated through the antiniqab and antiburkini political discourses in France. Marianne remains a symbol girded in a heteronormative and patriarchal male gaze. She promotes "liberty" through her sexual visibility and availability. The sexual liberation of secular women through the visibility and sexual accessibility of their bodies, ironically, acts as marker of their equality. I have argued that consumer culture and ideals of romance and chivalry further blur these politics. For these reasons, this chapter has argued that romance in the contact zone shields these gender politics, a point to which I return later.

In sum, these secular sensibilities remain powerful because they rest on facile binaries and because they are sources of pleasure, particularly for those (mostly white, cishet men) who legislate them. More theoretically, with reference to the logics underpinning secular legislation in France and Québec, we saw how a reliance on binaries—including private/public, conservative/liberal, and others—further entrenches sexuality in a male/female cisgender binary, and, arguably, privileges this male cishet gaze. More practically, we saw that these sensibilities are not solely manifest in top-down, state-driven directives. Equally powerfully, they are also interpreted by and replicated through ritual and social performances, as sources of happiness and pleasure. For these reasons, the contact zone of civil marriage and attached wedding rituals are useful spaces in which to map the enactment of these sensibilities.

CHAPTER 3
....
WHERE IMMIGRATION POLICY AND MARRIAGE MEET

I t would take two days for me to appreciate my flippancy in describing my newly single and eligible thirty-year-old cousin in Manitoba, Canada, to Boussad, twenty-seven, when I joked that they could be a marital match. Boussad and I first met in the arrivals area at the airport in Oran, Algeria, on a hot, clear July afternoon in 2016. I had flown from France for the wedding of Amel, my friend and a key interlocutor in this ethnography, to Yacine. Boussad had agreed to work as a research assistant for me, and had driven from Ghazaouet with his cousin and Amel's brother, Mohammed, twenty-three, to pick me up. Boussad insisted on pulling my carry-on luggage to his rusty two-door Renault. I insisted on sitting in the backseat. We settled in for the three-hour drive west to the seaside city of Ghazaouet, en route to the large two-story home of Amel, Mohammed, and Boussad's grandmother. As we made small talk, Boussad turned the conversation to life in Canada, asking whether it was expensive compared to France. Was it difficult to immigrate? Did I know anyone looking for a truck driver? "You know, we could go there together!" he said to Mohammed, who lived in France but was underemployed as an on-call truck driver.

Over the radio blasting and wind blowing through the open windows, I shared a few examples of friends from Algeria who had migrated to Montréal and my experience of sponsoring my own partner to become a permanent resident in 2007, shortly after the increased scrutiny of transnational unions I describe later in this chapter. My take: it wasn't too stressful if you could figure out all the forms, could afford all the medical tests and paperwork, and could score OK in Canada's elite points system, which in Québec favors French fluency, high levels of education, youth, and health. There's also quite a bit of waiting, I warned, longer waits, it seemed, than for migration to France. Thinking of Hichem, whom I introduce later in this chapter, I said, "You know, probably the fastest way to come to Canada is if you're sponsored through marriage." I then added, whimsically, "Actually, I have

{ 119 }

a cousin who's thirty. She's great and she's actually single right now. She's beautiful, kind, smart. Imagine if you could meet her!" I added.

Boussad seemed keen on this idea, again enjoining his cousin: "You see, Mohammed! I wouldn't even feel the snow. I would be in love in Canada! In love with Jenny's cousin. My toes would be heated by love." We laughed. When we arrived in Ghazaouet, with the excitement of seeing Amel and meeting many relatives who would be staying at the house for the wedding, I promptly forgot about this conversation.

Two nights later, Boussad invited me to join a group going to an internet café.[1] It was 10 p.m., and seated on the floor in an upstairs bedroom, I welcomed the interruption. I was into hour two of placing pastel-colored mints and tiny octagon-shaped wedding favors into small white shiny boxes, fastidiously looping small bows to close them. When, twenty minutes later, five of us arrived to find the café was closed, Boussad insisted we drive three hours to Oran, to an overnight café. Sensing my reluctance, he pushed: "Jenny, I really want to see a picture of your cousin! You know, the one I could marry!" My cousin? . . . It took me a few seconds to process. Then in a flash our conversation from the car ride from the airport a few days earlier returned. He meant the cousin I had mentioned who was single. He wanted to see a picture of my cousin, and have me arrange an introduction.

While we were already clearly very differently situated, that moment further laid bare the deeply uneven social class, race, mobility, and Global North privilege that separated us (cf. Oliphant 2021: 26 on how these inequalities also facilitate fieldwork). I had completely forgotten about what, for me, had been an offhand and meaningless remark about introducing him to a younger cousin. I never *actually* thought my cousin would be interested in conversing with him by Facebook Messenger, and be open to the potential of marriage and sponsorship. I had been flippant, too cavalier about a possibility that was impossible for many reasons (even if Hichem's story, which I will introduce shortly, showed that it was not entirely unreasonable). Boussad was a resourceful person. He had clearly thought about it. He surely knew that the other ways he could legally migrate would require a degree of fluency in French, and other forms of capital, that he did not possess. Marriage migration was one way to a different life.

This chapter does not suggest that Algerian young people like Boussad are clamoring to migrate to France and Québec. They are not.[2] Rather, I consider the narratives of a handful of my participants in Montréal and Petit-Nanterre who described their transnational marriage experiences in order to consider how state-based notions around marriage, sexuality, and Islam meet the secular sensibilities and the specters of the secular body I focus upon among these interlocutors. Boussad's willingness to drive to Oran in the middle of the night captures some of the emotion, adventure, financial hopes, and high stakes that were part of transnational marriage experiences for many of my interlocutors. To his credit, Boussad had been willing to make himself vulnerable in briefly sharing his desire to leave Algeria with me.

Alongside mapping the experiences of eleven of my interlocutors—Boussad (who lives in Ghazaouet); Halim, Sofiane, Nadia, and Fatima (who live in Petit-Nanterre); Sami, Adel, and Randja (two brothers and their mother who live in Montréal); Nouara, Thuraya, and Hichem (who also live in Montréal)—this chapter looks comparatively at how French and Canadian immigration policies shape my interlocutors' transnational lives, in what I emphasize are contexts of coloniality that have long monitored the intimate lives of those who are, or are imagined, as Muslim. I draw on Encarnación Gutiérrez Rodríguez's (2018: 20) insight that "migration policies [operate] as devices operating within the logic of coloniality [that] have racializing effects." In other words, building on the sexuality-secularity-citizenship nexus I introduced in chapter 1, I sketch historical immigration policy flashpoints and trace their effects within the wide-ranging migration narratives of my interlocutors in France and Québec. "Coloniality" is a useful term because it envelops the concepts of habitus and secular sensibilities that are at the core of my thinking. It also underscores historical and contemporary realities of France and Québec/Canada, namely in how immigration policy contexts shape my interlocutors' lives in different ways.

These policies shape individuals' marital and migratory possibilities. National "cultural frames" (cf. Small et al. 2010) found in discourses, policies, and public institutions trickle down into people's lives, including influencing whether and how they marry. A national models approach is useful in this connective comparison and contrast of these two contexts' parameters of immigration (see also Laxer 2019: 20). Most pronounced, France has historically remained committed to a universal Republicanism, where cultural differences are relegated to the private sphere and where expressions of difference—whether race, religion, or gender—are diminished. Political scientists have compared this color-blind integration civic approach to immigration with Canada's, known for its endorsement of multiculturalism and official recognition of minority cultures, as expressed in the Canadian Multiculturalism Act and the Charter of Rights and Freedoms (see May 2016: 293; Lépinard 2020: 51). Québec sits somewhere between these models with its promotion of interculturalism (cf. Bouchard 2012), where the advancement of cultural and religious diversity nevertheless promotes a common

Francophone culture (Québec controls some of its immigration).³ At the same time, this characterization, which positions France's model as rigid and integration-focused, does not capture how access to immigration in France is more liberal than in Canada. Commonalities exist too. Both countries remain largely silent on how their colonial pasts shape their engagement with difference.

More contemporarily, immigration policies in both countries began to curtail family reunification through marriage sponsorship in 2006. In France, I focus on the implications of 2006 legislation against love fraud with a migratory aim, and a 2010 government memorandum that formulates guidelines to assess marital sincerity for marriage officiants (ministère de Justice 2010). Further amendments in 2011 and 2021 sharpened the surveillance of polygamy, marriage, fraud, and virginity certificates. In Québec, sexual and secular politics are less sharply delineated, but the federal Conservative Party's 2011 campaign against "bad faith" marriages and its 2015 Zero Tolerance for Barbaric Cultural Practices Act (Bill S-7) pushed for greater evaluation of the "authenticity" of the marital relationships of couples where one is sponsored for citizenship through the union. These are Canadian federal legislative bills that are applicable in Québec.

Civil marriage is a fruitful moment that connects biopolitics with the control of sexuality, the family, and property. It can also be a gateway to citizenship. We will see how these immigration processes of marriage migration are gendered. Approximately half of the men of Algerian origin interviewed in Montréal sought out "traditional" brides from Algeria and sponsored them in migrating (twelve of the twenty-seven men in my Montréal sample); the percentage was slightly higher in France due to proximity and greater pressure to enact algérianité in Petit-Nanterre. In the Québécois context, socioeconomic class neither promoted nor dissuaded desire for these unions.⁴ I only met undocumented individuals of Algerian origin in France, where geography and larger networks make life as a *sans papiers* slightly more manageable than in Canada.

In general, despite the relative smoothness of administrative procedures, my interlocutors described significant challenges in their encounters with the state—through paperwork, costs, procedures, and securing multiple appointments and interviews—where the symbolic also felt egregious. A tension often emerged. On the one hand, several interlocutors show how the specter around engagement with state officials, who many about to marry assume will invariably racialize and "Muslimify" them (cf. Amir-Moazami 2022), is greater than the outcomes of the engagements. On the other hand, we will see in what follows how for Muslim non-EU foreigners, governmentality has moved into surveillance of the most intimate domains, including the selection of sexual partners, and the surveillance, at marriage ceremonies, of clothing, living arrangements, and social comportment.[5] Certain signs and symbols are read as the externalization of undesirable religious and sexual values; again, certain individuals are more compelled to prove their integration of secular sensibilities than others (see Norton 2012; Amir-Moazami 2022; and Peter 2021 on the so-called Muslim Question). We will also see how, from a comparative perspective, their differing geographies and histories of colonialism have meant Algerian migrations to France and Québec have different timelines and welcomed slightly different populations. Connective comparison helps elucidate the historical and ongoing interconnections between these jurisdictions related to colonialism and imperial forms of governance. While I focus on restrictions, it is important to stress that, with few exceptions, my Algerian-origin interlocutors sponsored through family reunification ably passed through the immigration hoops in both France and Québec.[6]

How Immigration Policies Shape Kin Relations

In contrast to the scholarly attention granted to laïque laws and policies in France and Québec, and despite their significant impact on my interlocutors—whether or not they migrate, on whom they marry and/or love—immigration rhetoric, policy, and law have received less sustained scholarly attention in France and Québec than the topics of Islam and secularism. For reasons of history, France remains present in the horizons of Algerians in Québec, while interlocutors in France have few experiences with Québec. Put differently, an Algeria-France colonial connection looms in the lives of Algerian migrants in Québec in that almost all of my interlocutors born in Algeria had either thought of moving to France, had family in France, or had lived in France prior to migrating to Québec. France is closer to Algeria on a number of fronts. Still, Québec beckoned to others with a sense of New World possibilities in employment and housing. Two women's experience in Québec show some benefits and challenges in this migration, particularly as they relate to kinship relations.

Nouara, a thirty-seven-year-old mother of two, captured this sentiment. In our long conversation on a bus rented by the Algerian Cultural Centre (the organization had allowed me to join an organized twelve-hour day trip to the Thousand Islands in Ontario), Nouara noted that, despite the unexpected challenges she has faced, she has chosen to stay in Québec for her children:

There are so many problems there [in France] *and* so many Algerians. Québec was our dream because it's like America, but French-speaking. Because we knew each other as students, it's been a long-time dream for me and my husband to come to Canada. We also had a friend who was already here. My dad's friend who was here, he encouraged us to come. He had told me, "I can really see you here. You're going to like it."

So, France, no. We have a lot of family there, but we said to ourselves, we are not getting away from it all in France: it's like Algeria there. We won't feel that we're really far away, that we've really changed our culture or our way of life. France is practically . . . it's like Algeria! It's just slightly improved, I think. It's the same way of life, the same routines. On the other hand, here in Québec it's a different world. . . .

We had moments where we were like, "Oh my God. Let's just let it go [*on va laisser tomber*]." But we didn't. More concretely, we supported each other in this decision. Then we had kids here afterward, so we had no choice [but to stay]. That's it, we won't go back now because of the kids.

Nouara liked the potential for adventure in a "Francophone America"; she felt the daily routines of France were too close to Algeria. Based on their premigration research, Nouara and her husband expected they would not initially find good work in Québec and so, prior to settling in Montréal, they saved funds to both pursue education degrees as international students, which they have since completed, enabling both to secure jobs in junior high schools. They did not regret having chosen to migrate to Québec over France. Doubt lingered in having left familial supports in Algeria.

In contrast, Asma, sixty-seven, a mother of two and a formal agricultural engineer who became a researcher in pharmaceuticals when her degrees were not recognized in Québec, admits that France was really not an option. Even if she would have preferred migrating to France, Québec was necessary to flee violence in Algeria the 1990s: "In fact, we came to Canada because, you know, it's the only country that received us as refugees. To go to France . . . listen, I have lots of family in France. . . . Back in the days when we came to Québec, those were the days of terrorism [in the 1990s]. There were a lot of people who went to France, and they have not had it easy there at all. Canada advertised immigration. So we opted for Canada."

Asma explained that her diploma and facility in French made her an ideal recruit (on the importance of education in Québec's elite immigration schema, see Belhassen-Maalaoui 2008; Asal 2014; and Manaï 2015), even if she was unaware of the high levels of underemployment that Algerians continue to face upon arrival.[7] Thinking back on her experience, Asma concluded somewhat bitterly that "Québec is no Eldorado." She felt frustrated because her emigration had been a matter of survival rather than choice.

Nouara and Asma's mixed feelings about settling in Québec capture some of the joys, compromises, and challenges in migrating from one continent to another. In the remainder of this chapter, I situate discussion of Canadian and Québécois immigration policies in relation to the marriage stories of individuals. We will see how despite historical differences in these nation-states' approaches to immigration, they demonstrate comparable end goals, with concern about "love fraud with a migratory aim" in France, and about "barbaric practices," including "bad faith" transnational marriages, in Québec and Canada. These immigration politics can be read in a longer arc of coloniality and continue to shape with whom and how folks of Algerian origin marry, if they do at all.

IN FRANCE

For the sake of brevity, I focus on French immigration and family laws introduced in 2006, 2011, and 2021 and a government memorandum to marriage officiants in 2010 aimed at curtailing non-EU transnational marriage. These laws and memorandums can be read within a longer timeline in French-Algerian relations, namely that for 132 years, Algeria was a part of France. With some legal qualifications, Algerians were French. Algeria would remain under French control until 1962 (Tunisia and Morocco until 1956). The relationship between these nation-states was violent.[8] Only in 2018 did the French government admit to systematic torture of Algerians during the War of Independence (see Chrisafis 2018; and Stora 2021). These relationships of domination and resource extraction shade the broader contexts within which marriage and migration occur. I separate Algerian migration to France into four primary waves: 1914–61, 1962–74, 1975–2005, and after 2006.

A Post–World War Industrial Wave (1914–1961)

When millions of mostly men died in World War I, concurrent with France's Industrial Revolution, the country's growing manufacturing industry required unskilled laborers. Recruiting men from France's former colonies aimed to bolster its postwar economy. These immigrants were expected to be temporary. Many long-standing residents of Petit-Nanterre reflect this wave that followed the Algerian War. Its then-open fields and proximity to the Renault car factory meant that men, most solo and sending remittances home to Algeria, settled in the area's shantytown.

One interlocutor in Petit-Nanterre, Halim, seventy-one, migrated from Algeria in this pre-Independence economic wave. At the time of our interviews he was a first-generation retired "Chibani." This term (from the Magrebian Arabic for "old" or "ancient") typically refers to male Maghrebian workers who came to France to work in construction between 1945 and 1975, like Halim. Halim had journeyed alone to Strasbourg, in eastern France, at age sixteen to work in construction. His family had few resources and so, because he was able, he was expected to send remittances. Like the French government, he had meant this to be a temporary stay, but he has remained for almost sixty years. Halim's transnational marital life was significantly affected by France's immigration policies prior to recent laws focused on the surveillance of transnational marriage and "love fraud." But his experiences of migration and marriage show that even if greater scrutiny is now in place (with the aforementioned 2006 law, 2011 and 2021 amendments, and the 2010 memorandum), that implicit surveillance of sexual mores in France is part of a long-standing project based in colonialism.

Halim and I met a half-dozen times in Petit-Nanterre in the spring and summer of 2014 in the main floor common room in the residence building where he lived. We first met when my babysitter had canceled and so my two-and-a-half-year-old came with me to this drop-in center. On this day, she refused to sit in her stroller and insisted on exploring the space solo. At one point, when she leaped out, the stroller fell back from the weight of my backpack resting on the handles. My seven-months-pregnant body bending over to right it, alongside my daughter running in the opposite direction created a small spectacle. Halim saw me and walked toward us, trying to distract her by crinkling his face and heavy eyebrows to make goofy faces, which I appreciated, even if she did not.

Halim was retired and lived alone in this dilapidated residence originally built in the 1960s for male temporary foreign workers on Petit-Nanterre's main street, avenue de la République. Above the common space on the main floor, it included single rooms with a single bed, a small kitchenette with table and chair, a phone on the wall, and washrooms shared with other men on his floor. A local association with which I volunteered hosted social gatherings they called *cafés sociaux* around mint tea and sweets at the building's entrance two mornings a week. Many older men stopped for tea and brought along their administrative mail if they required assistance. Younger men in their twenties and thirties of West African origin also lived in this residence. With few exceptions, these younger men worked long days in construction and tended not to participate in the more Maghrebian-focused social activities, like the cafés sociaux, intended for all residents. Halim dropped in regularly, always in the same pressed three-piece navy blue suit. He was quiet with deep brown shining eyes. He moved gingerly. After decades working in construction, he walked with a cane to support his sore back. Halim had moved to Petit-Nanterre only three years earlier from Strasbourg, after a social housing apartment he lived in there was torn down. Forced to relocate, he found the housing project in Petit-Nanterre appealing on paper, given its relative proximity to Paris and location 200 meters from a public hospital. But its crowded and dilapidated state quickly became evident. Homeless men lived in lean-to shacks outside the entrance, and garbage outside the door drifted into the lobby. Like many of the other Chibanis living in this residence, he was married and lived alone.

Halim described how he returned to Aïn Achache, Algeria, from the Strasbourg region at age twenty-two to marry sixteen-year-old Alma, who had been selected by his mother. His intention had been to resettle in Algeria after the wedding. Halim's tone was matter of fact when he described the wedding day. The couple's first official meeting took place at the fatiha, or religious contract signing, in her parents' home. Despite the high stakes in this meeting, Halim said in one of our two recorded interviews that he felt *tranquille* (peaceful): "I was told about the woman, what she's like. She was described to me. And no worries [*pas de soucis*] on that front." They spoke alone for the first time "before the end of the party when we were alone in the bedroom," prior to the consummation of the marriage. He later admits that she had not been completely unknown to him: "Without our parents' authorization," they had shared photos of one another through his older sister. "But that's a secret," he told me self-consciously, as though his parents might find out about this lapse in protocol fifty years later. Hundreds of guests attended. Finances were tight in his family; his father had two wives, and Halim was one of fifteen siblings (nine brothers and five sisters). Halim had paid for the wedding meals with his French wages. There were no glimmers of romance in his telling. In response to my inquiry about his fondest recollection from the wedding, a question I posed to all participants, he didn't hesitate: the main course of *méchoui*, a grilled lamb dish. It was "simply delicious."

Returning to work in France shortly after his wedding had not felt like a choice: "There was no work over there [in Aïn Achache]." Also, the War of Independence was underway, and he thought it smarter to support his family financially from France than try to live amid the conflict. Early on, he had established a routine where he would work in France and return annually for two months, usually around the month of Ramadan, no matter what time of year. During that month, escaping the residence was especially appreciated: "Ramadan isn't . . . it isn't easy to cook something [alone] in the evening." Solo in France, he missed the ambiance of iftars, and so prioritized returning for this month. The rest of the year, he sent remittances to support Alma, their children, and his neighboring extended family. Meanwhile, as he worked and lived away, he and Alma's family expanded to include seven children.

Over the course of their nearly fifty-year marriage, Alma had never visited France. Initially, Halim says, she did not feel she could. She cared for their seven children and his parents (including his mother and his father's first wife) in their home. In addition to these caregiving responsibilities, they did not have the means for tourist travel. Still, more recently, since the passing of his parents and as their children had grown older and started their own families, she had tried to visit. Alma had unsuccessfully applied three times for short-visit (under-ninety-day) tourist visas, each costing €100, a considerable sum for them. Halim believed his wife's visa requests had been rejected because of fear that she would remain in France illegally; in addition, her age and poor health, as well as Halim's single bedroom, did not facilitate her application attempts. Her application for a visitor visa included specifications regarding the size of the host's accommodations. They could not afford a hotel and did not have family or close friends in France who could serve as hosts. Many of my informants described their frustration with visa requests to bring family to France, even on holiday, believing that refusals were how the Algerian consulate generated funds.[9]

Halim explained that once their children had become adults, he and Alma imagined living half the year outside of Strasbourg and the other half in Aïn Achache. With restrictions on Algerian tourist visas and his unwillingness to bring Alma to France illegally, his binational dream was never realized. Moreover, he did not read or write well in French, which impeded his ability to appeal these decisions. On this topic, Halim grew quieter; his eyes clouding and his face straining when I asked him whether he regretted returning to France after his marriage to Alma. He mentioned his children only when I directly asked him about them. His transnational life had severely limited their relationship. Now that international phone rates were less expensive and did not require visiting a taxi-phone shop (as men did when I first met some living in this high-rise building a decade earlier), Halim now spoke to his wife briefly every day. He remained estranged from his children, however. None of them had sought a tourist or student visa to visit him. Despite circling back to this topic a few times in our conversations, he made it clear he would not elaborate further. In our interactions over that spring and summer, Halim's mood on this topic was one of resignation, not anger. He has never considered permanently returning to Algeria.

The French state has clearly benefited from Halim's single laborer situation. It has also impeded family reunification for his wife and hindered his return to his family home in Algeria in his retirement (because of rules then in effect regarding pensions and residency).[10] More poignantly, Halim now realized that he had spent his adult life, which he marked as beginning with his marriage, in a situation he had always imagined as temporary (cf. Sayad 1980). He was lonely. His illiteracy did not facilitate retired life in France. Yet Halim did not feel rancor toward the French administration. He told me he was grateful to have earned his salary, to have sent remittances, and to now have access to good medical care: "It's thanks to France that I have my pension. And that—and my retirement monies—is what allows me, my wife and I, to live." He has preferred living in residences in Strasbourg and now, Petit-Nanterre. Still, his half century residing in housing meant for temporary workers reflects his continued precarity in relation to the state. He has been unable to enter the civil marriage "contact zone" to sponsor Alma, even as a tourist. The Algerian and French state's impediment of their reunification requests also tells us something about the importance of social class in the contact zone. Halim's marriage story of remittances and solitude is one experienced by many Chibanis. Others with better health return to Algeria in their retirement.

Post-Independence Migration (1962–1974) and
New Family Reunification (1975–2005)

The number of Maghrebian immigrants to France continued to increase with World War II, the end of the Fourth Republic in 1958, and the Algerian War of Independence in 1962. Thanks to the Évian Accords, Algerian nationalists remained authorized to enter, live, and work in France with facility. Male migrants settled in greater number in the 1940s through the 1960s. Immigrants in this period often had lower levels of educational attainment than native French and worked in low-skilled employment like the factories in the suburbs of large cities and, like Halim, in construction jobs. Men continued to migrate to Petit-Nanterre from Algeria into the late 1960s. With the end of the War of Independence, attention turned to the behavior and delinquency of single men in the suburbs. Men from former North African colonies in the suburbs of industrial cities attracted the attention of politicians and journalists (Shepard 2017, 2018). Historian Todd Shepard (2017: 124) shows how in the post-1962 "post-decolonization" period, far right journalists characterized Arab men in France's suburbs as sexually deviant, linking "Algerian men to rape, sexual harassment, and homosexual promiscuity." These pejorative distinctions follow broader European postcolonial politics, which sought to maintain clear distinctions between colonized and colonizer, colonies and metropoles, through hierarchical sexual values (cf. Stoler [2002] 2010). In other words, in the early years of France's sexual revolution of the 1960s, which pushed for more liberal, "secular" sexual values, former colonialized North Africans were very negatively cast. Arguably, this uncertain period encouraged sharp distinctions between "French" men and men from the colonies, binaries constructed between sexually normal and abnormal, healthy and perverted. Only presumably secular white men on the right embodied "normal" sexuality.

In this context, the arrival of Algerian-origin women to the suburbs was imagined as a stabilizing force. Family reunification became a way to tamper perceived male delinquency in the mostly male migration to the suburbs (Koven 1992: 26). Coinciding with this shift was the shantytown's replacement with public housing. Many North African immigrants began living in subsidized housing complexes (HLMs) in banlieues like Petit-Nanterre. The conditions in Petit-Nanterre's shantytown improved significantly. Most of my participants in their fifties, sixties, and seventies in Petit-Nanterre fell into this wave, including Aisha, who had migrated from Algeria to marry her husband, and with whom I lived from 2004 to 2005 (see Selby 2009a: 7–8). She continues to live in the same apartment her deceased husband's parents were allocated when the high-rises were first built.

By the early 1970s, there were fewer industrial jobs outside of France's larger cities. Reflecting a broad-scale economic recession and declining employment opportunities in factory labor, President Valéry Giscard d'Estaing (1974–81) temporarily suspended immigration of non-European male workers. This shift led many immigrant workers to settle permanently in France, and to bring their families with them (Silberman, Alba, and Fournier 2007). These family reunification laws meant that with proof of funds and lodging, men were able to sponsor women to join them with relative ease. Many more Algerian women migrated to the suburbs. By 1974, the country thus officially ceased its more open-door posture to immigration and offered lump sum payments to encourage workers to leave. At the same time, after 1973, an immigrant married to a French citizen was no longer automatically eligible for French nationality; separate scrutinizing measures were developed (Ferran 2009; Macmaster 1997). Together, these immigration and housing shifts meant that the number of single male North African workers like Halim fell, and the visibility of women and children—particularly those wearing visible religious symbols—grew. The "white flight" of the 1970s also meant suburbs like this one were becoming more culturally, religiously, and racially homogeneous. In sum, in this period, family reunification became the most expeditious way to enter France legally as a non-EU migrant.

Sofiane, fifty-nine, and Nadia, fifty-eight, were also part of this group of couples who held French passports and whose migration was eased through family reunification in the early 2000s. I have known Nadia since 2005 (see more about her in Selby 2009a: 6). Nadia is brazen, hard-working, generous, stubborn, and exudes a joie de vivre. At the time of our formal interview in 2016, she had lived in France for fifteen years, having followed her youngest child from Algiers when her daughter chose to pursue medicine in Tours. When her daughter's studies did not go as planned, they both migrated north to this Parisian suburb where two of Nadia's sisters had previously settled, echoing a common pattern of family reunification in this suburb. Nadia's mother was born in France but had moved to Algeria following her marriage to Nadia's father, a polyglot Algerian journalist. The family had lived briefly in Morocco, where Nadia was born, but she spent most of her childhood in Annaba, Algeria's third-largest city. Nadia attended a French lycée and grew up bilingual in Algiers; in addition, her mother had been a schoolteacher in the French colonial system. I briefly introduce her and Sofiane's narrative of marriage and migration as a very ordinary one from this period.

Over a lunch of shared odds and ends in the bright kitchen of a community association, Nadia explained that she and Sofiane chose to marry in Algiers as students in 1971 when she became unexpectedly pregnant. They had been quietly living together since 1968, when she began living in a *cité universitaire* (student housing) to attend university. She explained that life was much more open then, that her parents "savaient qu'on vivaient ensemble sans le savoir" (knew without knowing that we were living together). However, with their unplanned pregnancy, the lightness of the relationship ended. In a separate conversation on the bus as we headed to Nanterre Préfecture, near which she lived and where I would sometimes take the RER train to return to Paris, Nadia told me she had considered an abortion or moving to France to have her baby, with or without Sofiane, as she was not interested in a traditional marriage in Annaba where she would remain at home and raise children. Her mother was invested in the idea of a traditional wedding, however, and promised to do the whole "tra la la," in Nadia's words, for her in Annaba. The wedding and all her dresses were ready within a month. No one said a word about her pregnancy.

In a separate interview, Sofiane similarly remembered the pregnancy situation matter-of-factly. In a mid-afternoon interview at the kitchen table

Figure 3.1. Nadia and Sofiane on their wedding day, 1971. Nadia is three months pregnant with their son. Courtesy of study participant.

in his social housing one-bedroom apartment while Nadia was at work, he explained, "We were both university students. We had lived together [in Algiers] for several years before getting married. Nadia was pregnant, so we decided to get married" (fig. 3.1). Later on, he said, laughing, "We were only twenty years old. It was more of a mutual adoption [of each other, as children] than a marriage!"

Sofiane's experience of migration to France was radically different from Halim's due to his generation, his facility in the French language, and his social class. Nadia described Sofiane's family as "bourgeois" and "conservative." Through her, he gained French citizenship. Nadia became motivated to undertake the paperwork for her French passport when their son, born in 1972, sought to attend university in France and had trouble obtaining a residency card. Her citizenship solved his residency problem. With the continuing violence in Algiers even after the 1990s, when her daughter was eighteen years old and wanted to study in Tours, they all decided to emigrate to France.

Nearly fifteen years later, Sofiane had not yet found work in his area of expertise as a software engineer and remained unemployed (cf. Sayad 1999). Nadia was the family's primary breadwinner. She worked full time in a community association, where she was not well paid. They both acknowledged they were fortunate to live in a well-maintained social housing apartment close to the interurban train to Paris. They were also both in good health and able to return to their family homes in Algeria annually. But, as Sofiane explained, life postmigration had been marked by the challenges his non-practicing children experienced as young adults. Sofiane attributed these challenges to both "too many choices!" and to racism. Weighing the costs of their decision to migrate to France as a family, he said, "Thankfully she [Nadia] has found work here. But ten years ago, our son moved to London and our daughter to Chile because there is so much discrimination here" (June 18, 2014). Sofiane had fought to emigrate to France imagining better opportunities for their children, but both had left.

Like Sofiane and Nadia, many Algerians who settled in French suburbs like Petit-Nanterre migrated to France through marriage and family reunification migration from the mid-1970s until the mid-2000s. In the 1980s, President François Mitterrand's government sought an immigration policy of "insertion" to discourage North African workers from returning home. Mitterrand strove to normalize their status and supported their right to vote in local elections (Brulard 1997: 109). Yet at the same time, in the midst of an economic recession and significant job loss, the Far Right began to flourish under the leadership of Jean-Marie Le Pen. Le Pen formed the Front National (FN) in the early 1980s with an anti-immigration platform. With a cultural and religious agenda, the FN was successful in its intransigent opposition to religious and cultural pluralism (Wieviorka 1993: 55; Bréchon and Kumar Mitra 1992: 63; Nilsson 2018), particularly in cities, like Paris, that experienced rapid economic development followed by unemployment. Muslim North African ethnic minorities, like my Algerian interlocutors in Petit-Nanterre, often lived in the outskirts of these industrialized cities and were the symbols and targets of this rhetoric (see fig. 2.2, for example). Appealing to a populist electorate, the FN claimed that forms of religious and cultural "countercolonization" (i.e., symbols and behavior associated with Islam) threatened French culture and identity. One of the party's campaign slogans was "On n'est plus chez nous" (We're no longer at home).

With a sharp decline in industrial employment beginning in the 1980s, workers without French language proficiency experienced increased difficulty in obtaining legal jobs. This loss of work affected more than wages and remittances for Algerian men. Petit-Nanterre is part of the Paris region's *ceinture rouge* ("red belt"), a former industrial area north and east of the capital characterized by racialized minorities, strong unions, and Communist Party–based community support (Wacquant 2005: 77).[11] The red belt is industrial and masculine. The advent of automation in the early 1980s did not ameliorate the employability of suburban-living North African migrants. By the 1990s, the foreign workforce in France had been reduced by half (Hargreaves 2007: 53). Historically, men in the red belt mobilized through union and municipal organizations (Wacquant 2005: 175), so the loss of employment in factories significantly affected community ties.

These factors contributed to the "white flight" from the suburbs in the 1970s and 1980s and further entrenched Fanonian dynamics in Petit-Nanterre. Several scholars of immigration have examined the pervasive colonialism-informed correlation between the immigrant and the worker in France (see Sayad 1997; and Hargreaves 1998: 90). The context of coloniality means there is little tolerance for the unemployed suburban immigrant. These factors have led North African immigrants to increasingly occupy what Alec Hargreaves (2007: 146) describes as the "lowest ranking in the ethnic hierarchy prevalent in France" insofar as their ethnic and religious visibility marks their socioeconomic and political exclusion. More concretely, this situation means that men like Sofiane have been unable to secure stable employment, and this, of course, shapes their economic, personal, familial, and marital lives.

*Migration after 2006: A Push for "Chosen"
Immigration and against "Love Fraud"*

Coinciding with a desire for more selective immigration, laws adopted in 2006, 2011, and 2021 focused on impeding a perceived growing number of forced and fraudulent marriages from non-EU nationals, imagined as especially vulnerable sites for entry into France's citizenry.[12] In 2005, French minister of justice Pascal Clément cited data that one-third of marriages in France were with non-EU nationals for whom citizenship was then possible: "Marriage has, in effect, become a major stake in migration. . . . Joining a spouse has become the main motive of family immigration. . . . We must recognize that the number of frauds reported by mayors and consular and diplomatic agents to the public prosecutor have not stopped rising" (ministère de la Justice 2006).

In addition to this rising-tide discourse, Clément also offered a number of rationales to justify sharpening immigration laws—namely, to shelter immigrant women from conjugal violence, especially from *mariages forcés* and, citing the legislation, to protect the "purity and integrity" of French citizenship from "love fraud" (République française 2005). In response, rules aiming to impede "love fraud with a migratory aim" were established in 2006. The parameters and penalties for this offense became graver in 2011 and 2021. Significant to note is that marriage officiants in France hold interpretative power, insofar as all legal marriages in the country are conducted in mayoral offices or, if they take place abroad, must be legitimized by French consulates that apply the same directives. Also, beginning in 2003, imams could be fined €7,500 or be subjected to three months in prison for granting a religious marriage certificate prior to evidence of a civil marriage (Monnin 2008).[13] The memorandum for marriage officiants detailed directives on "love fraud." Fraudulent love would include marriage contracted for reasons other than romantic love. I see this concern for the "scamming" of love as reflecting some of the concerns for sexual freedom and agency lodged in pervasive secular sensibilities. That the consequences and fines for men who impose niqabs are similar is notable; in both cases, the perceived danger is gendered. "Love fraud" constitutes an especially egregious offense against the ideals of emancipation and passion lodged in the equation of sexual emancipation with reason and laïcité.

Under these laws, once married, transnational non-EU couples in France became subjected to further surveillance. Investigation extended to unannounced follow-up visits to couples' homes in the first four years of marriage. In her work with advocacy groups, sociologist Manuela Salcedo Robledo (2011: 5) notes the symbols French police look for to assess marital sincerity: wedding photos on display, whether spouses wear their wedding rings, and the physical presence of the spouse and their shared children, among others. Social comportment is likely also assessed. Officials have up to thirty years to annul a marriage deemed fraudulent (Légifrance 2011). Few French citizens remain married for three decades.[14] In relation to similar surveillance in the contemporary United Kingdom, Anne-Marie D'Aoust (2013: 263) describes the state's quantification of love focused on garments and financial entanglements: "By submitting certain artifacts such as bank statements or wearing specific clothes, objects come to stand for the reality of a loving, committed relationship (submitting bank statements and phone records is a common practice in application files in all European countries, and wearing expected wedding apparel also diminishes suspicions)." What serve as evidence of love and appropriate romance in the UK are similar in France.

A twenty-three-page memorandum, sent to French marriage officiants in June 2010 in France and its overseas departments to assess potential fraud, offers more substantive data regarding the ideal version of a monogamous marrying couple and their wedding in the Republic. Following legislation in 2006, with this 2010 *circulaire*, the then minister of immigration, integration, national identity, and codevelopment, Éric Besson, granted more discretionary power to marriage administrators to determine and report marriage fraud. More generally, according to the front part of the document, marriage is "primarily" about "living together and sharing family life, so that unions contracted with an eye to other benefits, including citizenship, can be considered fraudulent and then impeded or annulled" (ministère de la Justice 2010; see also Robledo 2011; and Selby 2017). The memorandum lists two pages of questions officiants may ask prospective marriage partners separately to assess the mood of the ceremony and, in my reading, their premarital economic and sexual intimacy. These questions outline that officiants should note, among others, details about the ceremony, including the atmosphere, emotions, who paid for the rings, as well as the couple's premarital living situations. Other evidence of sincerity can come from an acceptably long period between the engagement and the day in the officiant's office, and the extent of engagement celebrations: Who attended the party? Who organized it? Were photos taken? Were there engagement gifts? Expressions of choice and sexual intimacy on areligious bodies are ideal. The questions also evidence a preference for signs of consumer culture. The penalties for "love fraud" show the gendered assumptions regarding religiously marked bodies. Signs of coercion or aggression among religiously identified men are unnamed but are implicit as the worst offenses.[15]

Several of my participants, like Fatima, thirty-two, experienced this postmarriage surveillance by the French state (see also Selby 2017, 2019). Fatima's mother-in-law, Safia, who attended French literacy classes at an organization where I had volunteered in Petit-Nanterre since 2004, arranged for us to meet. In the spring of 2012, in a conversation with other women in the afternoon class, Safia had shared the work she undertook to locate for her French-born son a bride who was from the same western Algerian city that she came from. She noted that the potential bride's hometown mattered more to her than religious practice or other marriageable skills. A common geography would facilitate cooking and other shared cultural codes.

After a handful of attempts over a four-year period, Fatima and I met twice at the McDonald's in the La Défense shopping center in 2016. By that time, she had been married and living near Petit-Nanterre for almost four years. The first time we met she brought her youngest son, who would not settle in his stroller, so after we ate quickly, we walked around the mall together, chatting and agreeing to another interview with just the two of us. When Fatima and I arranged to meet the following week, Safia had generously agreed to babysit, and in this second, child-free interview, Fatima described her experience of a police visit two years after she received her permanent residency papers through marriage. Fatima was an Arabophone fluent in French. She and Safia's son were married in Algeria and she then returned with him to the suburb where he grew up.

Fatima wore her long black hair pulled back in a high ponytail and dressed in trendy matching sports clothes. In our interview, she explained how, for her, even if her arranged marriage had evolved into what she called a "love marriage," the fear of not performing appropriately, of not incorporating romantic ideals of love in the presence of police, was real. For the law enforcement seeking evidence, proof of marital intimacy in unannounced visits included wedding photos on display, wearing a diamond engagement ring, and the physical presence of the spouse and their shared children. The couple could be questioned on their partner's favorite color, literature, film, or music, and even the time of their last sexual encounter (Robledo 2011: 5).

Fatima detailed how, in a fifteen-minute visit, the three police officers asked about the couple's day-to-day lives and requested to see printed photos of them together in France after their Algerian wedding. Fatima had just given birth to her first child. As Fatima pointed out, the visit could take place at any point in the first four years of marriage:

> F: Three days after [I delivered my son]—imagine—the police came to our home. The police came to our house to see if we were really married. They looked at photos. They questioned my mother, who was visiting [from Algeria] for the birth. So, they saw my mother, they looked at the photos, and my son, and my husband. So, yeah, there was an investigation [*une enquête*] about it [our relationship], to see if we were really married.
> J: Did they let you know in advance?
> F: Not at all. They don't warn you. They knock at the door. And you have to be ready.

The police also questioned her French-speaking mother. My point is not to characterize this intervention as traumatic for her. As she recounted the 2011 visit five years later, Fatima was nonplussed. She saw this state check-in as "*normal.*" She had not otherwise had a specifically negative administrative experience involving her marriage and migration to France. These forms of surveillance are normalized for many interlocutors (see Zine 2022 on the interiorized impacts of state suspicion, which is neither contingent nor accidental). That the police arrived on that day was, in a way, fortunate. Her baby served as a clear marker of a relationship with her husband.

A more considerable effect of the 2006 and 2011 legislation on transnational marriage for Fatima was knowledge that she could not leave her husband for any period for fear the police would discover a separation and her citizenship possibilities would be jeopardized. This concern was particularly challenging in the couple's first year of living together. After their wedding in her hometown, they lived for six months in her husband's parents' apartment before securing their own one-bedroom apartment. Fatima said that when they moved into their own place, having never lived away from his parents' supervision, her husband got into *niaiseries* (foolishness). When he began staying out all night with his friends without consulting her, Fatima was stressed. She did not want to involve her in-laws and had little other recourse to critique his behavior: "Heureusement, il s'est beaucoup calmé depuis" (Thankfully, he's calmed down a lot since then). Even a temporary separation could have, in the worst scenario, meant police interrogation, a marriage annulment, the end of her French citizenship process, and expatriation.

In my reading, the 2010 memorandum, particularly the suggested questions to be posed to couples separately, delineates an idealized performative secular romance. Evidence of sexual intimacy serves as cues to proper French sexual behavior and access to citizenship. These ideas are further reinforced by the unannounced follow-up visits by police, where photos, wedding rings, and behavior are assessed. Marriage without these signs—including unions where couples marry in familial arrangements owing to their "traditionalism" or conservative sexual beliefs attributed to their religion—become suspect. As we will see in the next section, in its mid-2000 anti-marriage fraud campaign, Canadian immigration policy on family reunification immigration shared striking parallels with the laws against love fraud with a migratory aim in France.

QUÉBEC

Canada's immigration policies have long been inflected by colonial and racial citizenry aims that have worked to quell Indigenous sovereignty and bolster whiteness (cf. Gutiérrez Rodríguez 2018). The most significant immigration shift in recent history that directly shaped Algerian migration to Canada was the institution of the points system in 1967. As a response to racist and restrictive policies during World War II, the points system formally replaced an overt preference for white British Protestant immigrants. Points are allocated to applicants with knowledge of its official colonial languages, formal education or skills, youth, and able-bodiedness, and those responding to perceived needs of the country's labor market (see Chowdhury 2018). Even if the points system aimed to curtail institutional racism in Canada's immigration system, scholars have noted ongoing inequalities, particularly in relation to gender biases. The framework privileges elite migration and male workers who could come to Canada without a family (see Chowdhury 2018: 282; and Dauvergne 2020). More generally, since the mid-1990s and to a greater degree beginning in 2006, Canada's immigration policy formally shifted from one focused on family migration to one centered more on attracting economic immigrants (Bragg and Wong 2016).[16]

A participant in Montréal insightfully explained how shifts in Canadian immigration policy have affected Algerians who live there. Yousra, sixty-two, helpfully differentiated between two waves of Algerian migration to Québec in our interview. Yousra is a divorcée who was able to acquire a visa for the United States (and not for Canada) during the Décennie noire. In 1994, at forty-two, she knew she needed to flee terrorism and potential violence in Algiers with her two daughters. She explained, "Personally, I decided to leave [Algeria] because the rise of Islamism meant that there was more and more social and religious control over women." Her goal was to settle in Montréal and so, once in the United States, she made her way to the now-infamous Roxham Road crossing at the US-Canada border, where she successfully requested refugee immigration status. Yousra situated herself in the first immigration wave: "There are two main waves. The one within which I arrived is the one where Algerians asked for refugee status. The [second] wave in the early 2000s was the preselected economic immigrants chosen based on their backgrounds and qualifications. It's funny because these two waves, they're not only related to immigration status, but they also reflect the *catégories* of Algerians. So, in my wave, it was mostly Francophone Algerians, who did a good part of their schooling in French."

These waves can be distinguished by time period and commonalities around immigrant class (whether refugee or economic class), language fluency (whether French or Arabic), and whether individuals undertook their schooling in French or Arabic.[17] Yousra's own French fluency stemmed from having attended a French colonial school. She emphasized several times how her public-school education primarily in French mattered in how she was later able to settle in Québec. With suitcases and two small children in tow, Yousra's success can also be attributed to her grit.

Unprompted, Yousra's daughter, Meryem, now thirty-two, commented in a separate interview on how hard her mother worked in this resettlement: "She had a vision. She was never idle. She didn't waste a second." Meryem also remarked how, in their long journey from Algiers to Montréal through New York State, her mother shielded her and her sister from the tremendous precarity they faced. She also noted how well supported they were as new refugees in the pre-9/11 period in Montréal: "We were treated with such dignity." "Even if sometimes it's humiliating [being a refugee], we were able to eat. We were able to dress ourselves. We could even sing."

In this section, I follow Yousra's distinction of two immigration waves of Algerians to Québec—from the 1990s to 2005 and from 2006 on—and add a third wave that began in 2019. We will see how, in general, Algerian migration to Québec has been significantly lower in number and more recent than migration to France, almost a century later. Migration to Quebec largely began in the 1990s and grew substantially after 2000. Even if both countries have long histories of colonialism and, in Canada, the suppression of Indigenous peoples and Indigeneities, unlike France, Canada has never had a formal colonial relationship with Algeria.

The First Wave: 1990–2005

With France's greater scrutiny of unqualified workers beginning in the mid-1970s, as well as growing unemployment in industrial and construction sectors, Québec became increasingly attractive as offering greater economic possibilities for more elite migrants. The 1980s saw more male Algerians settle following their university studies in the province.[18] Most migration in the 1990s responded to the often-traumatic experiences of the Décennie noire.[19]

Traumas and negative experiences with Islamic terrorism in this decade significantly shaped participants' lives and their later interactions with religiosity and secular debates in Québec. Generationally, immigrants in this wave also grew up under French colonialism in Algeria and attended colonial French public schools. First-wave immigrants typically possessed greater proficiency in French and familiarity with its secular sensibilities. Yousra explained how her family held deeply political ideas about headscarves and French colonialism, so that expressions of religiosity for them were always politically framed. Algerian Independence shaped her family's engagement with the headscarf. Her father did not imbue the garment with religious meanings. She did not wear a veil, but her sisters did: "I remember that when Independence happened [in 1962] my father said to my sisters, 'You can take off your veils now.' So, you see [the veil] was an act of resistance, it was not related to religious practice at all. So, I never wanted it myself, and that's it."

In general, many of the women I met in Montréal who fled Algeria during the decade of acute terrorist violence supported the legal initiatives that sought to restrict religious symbols in Québec since 2009. Randja, fifty-five, is one such individual. We were introduced by a mutual friend and met several times at her bright walk-up two-bedroom apartment in the city's Côte-des-Neiges neighborhood; she lived there with her husband, who traveled a good deal for work. Randja was an articulate and passionate person whose Kabylian identity became more important to her postmigration.[20] Formerly a junior high school math teacher in Algiers, she arrived in Montréal with her husband and two- and five-year-old sons as refugees. She sought to flee following the assassination of her brother, who had been a journalist. Randja reflected on the multiple traumas associated with her migration to Québec in our interview on a quiet June morning in 2018.

> Having to immigrate was not good news for me. It was a failure at all levels: I left my adored land, my homeland. I left my village, my family. And as a citizen, I failed in my country's national construction project [*le projet de la construction de mon pays*]. Canada might have been telling bullshit beautiful stories. But I knew in advance that immigration is not a dream. It's hard. So I was not surprised or disappointed by my immigration experience here, because I know the reality of immigration. For me, it was not arriving in Québec that was a problem. It was leaving Algeria.

In a separate conversation over dinner at a Thai restaurant down the road from her apartment, she described this departure as a "wound that cannot be healed." When she fled Algeria following her brother's assassination, she knew life would never be the same. Government support for religious symbols in Québec thus has an emotional impact for Randja. She cannot support the visibility of Islam in the public sphere. She expressed relief with the passage of Law 21. In contrast, migrants from the second wave who settled in the mid-2000s tended to be more practicing Muslims who generally articulated disappointment at the sharpening of Québec's position against conspicuous religious symbols.

The Second Wave: 2006–2018

The second phase of Algerian migration to Québec has been more strictly focused on economic-based migration, that is, individuals who gained entry primarily based on their professional credentials. This phase parallels a shift in immigration policy in Canada in 2006, which further privileged elite highly skilled workers over refugee and family reunification migration. Most Algerian migrants to Montréal settled in this period; the highest numbers to date are recorded as arriving between 2011 and 2016.[21] I set the end of this wave in 2018 to mark how 2019's Law 21 in Québec has shifted access to certain government jobs, as well as heightened Islamophobia. This period was significant on a national level given policies and legislation introduced that targeted "bad faith" and polygamous marriages.

"BAD FAITH" MARRIAGES AND THE "ZERO TOLERANCE FOR BARBARIC CULTURAL PRACTICES ACT" IN QUÉBEC AND CANADA

In the post-2006 period in Canada, the federal Conservative Party introduced legislation against marriage immigration fraud that focused on "bad faith" marriages. This legislation is not as detailed as the French tripartite categorization of marriages of convenience (*blancs*) and ones that are forced (*forcés*) or based on fraud (*gris*), but Section 4.1 of the "Immigration and Refugee Protection Regulations" stipulates that the relationship should be "genuine" (Government of Canada 2024). The "primary purpose" of marriage cannot be "for status or privilege" (quoted in Pringle 2020: 8). The practice of arranged marriages is not an inherent problem, so long as it is "customary" in the cultures of the couple in question (cited in Government of Canada 2008: 11).

Two changes in Canadian politics further concretized concern for transnational unions in Canada. The election of the Conservative Party as a minority government in 2006, following thirteen years of a more centrist Liberal government, fostered an immigration policy shift toward "labor market" needs. More conservative immigration policies accelerated when the Conservative Party held a majority government from 2011 to 2015, notably its anti-marriage fraud campaign (May 2016: 294). The campaign in Canada was presented as a top priority in the 2011 Speech from the Throne, as read by then governor general David Johnston (2011; cited in Gaucher 2014): "Our government is committed to protecting the integrity of our immigration system. It will introduce measures to address marriage fraud—an abuse of our system that can victimize unsuspecting Canadians and vulnerable immigrants."

In general, the Harper government engaged in a discourse of distrust vis-à-vis claimants for refugee and immigrant status (Carver 2016). Beginning in 2009, the minister of citizenship, immigration, and multiculturalism, Jason Kenney, called for a sterner and more formal "crackdown" on marriages of convenience, termed "bad faith" marriages. Kenney characterized marriage "fraudsters" as queue jumpers and system cheaters who must be blocked from eroding dominant culture and abusing the welfare state's social services (see Citizenship and Immigration Canada 2012b; Gaucher 2014: 190; Bhuyan, Korteweg, and Baqi 2018: 348). The legislative reform plan aimed to impede fraudulent marriage at the source and introduce greater punishments for violations that came to light postapplication. At that time, Kenney and Immigration, Refugees, and Citizenship Canada (the IRCC) suggested that more than 1,500 individuals were involved with this marriage fraud annually; between 2010 and 2014 three individuals were found guilty of marriage fraud in Canada (Standing Committee on Citizenship and Immigration 2014, cited in Pringle 2020: 10). One 2011 news story suggested that three dozen criminal investigations were launched, of which charges were laid in seven, leading to the three convictions (*CBC News* 2011). In general, however, there is little empirical evidence of a rise in fraud that would render it a national concern.

The policies introduced meant that, upon arriving in Canada, a couple should live conjugally in a genuine relationship for two years before the sponsored spouse or partner could apply for permanent residency. According to Kenney, the objective of this measure was to "weed out people trying to use a phony marriage as a quick and easy route to Canada" (cited in Citizenship and Immigration Canada 2012a). Media reports of spouses and partners who "disappeared" upon arrival to Canada circulated in tandem with IRCC-expressed concerns for abuse. Most of the anti–bad faith marriage rhetoric focused on individuals of Indian, Chinese, and Filipino origin (Gaucher 2014; Bhuyan, Korteweg, and Baqi 2018). In sum, racialized international marriages where migration, tradition, and religion were part of marital arrangements were rendered suspicious and greater obstacles introduced before accessing citizenship. The combat against marriage fraud also aligned well with the Conservative government's "strong families" campaign, effectively bolstering anti-immigration and profamily rhetoric in one fell swoop.

These immigration law amendments affect married women. Despite its rationale to protect them, several scholars have shown how the concern with marriage fraud in Canada starting in 2006 made women *more* vulnerable. More specifically, a clause that instituted "conditional" permanent residency—which was enacted between 2012 and 2017, and then repealed by the subsequent Liberal government—put sponsored wives, who make up more than 60 percent of these arrangements, in precarious positions (see Dobrowolsky 2017 and Pringle 2020: 18). Recall Fatima's situation in France, in which she could not leave her French-national spouse in this conditional period.[22] In 2012, also with the aim of reducing opportunities for marriage fraud, the government extended the sponsorship surveillance of permanent residents or Canadian citizens who had immigrated to Canada as sponsored spouses/partners, increasing it from three years to five years (Bhuyan, Korteweg, and Baqi 2018: 356). For these reasons, the specter of marriage fraud in Canada created a chilling effect for racialized immigrant women especially, along with partners in other non-cishet unions.[23]

We can see these logics at play in publicly available decisions on transnational unions in Canadian courts. Let us turn to one case that captures how demonstrable affection and the performance of romance enter judges' thinking in determining the sincerity of a transnational union in Canada.[24] The 2007 *Dhaliwal, Jaswinder v. M.C.I.* case involved a previously married Indian woman, Ms. Raja Dhaliwal, thirty, who had two young children from her first marriage. Once divorced, she agreed to an arranged second marriage with an Indian national, Mr. Jaswinder Dhaliwal, six years her junior. Mr. Dhaliwal had never been married and did not have children. The case noted both were Sikhs. Reports provided in the decision from the visa officer summarized Ms. Dhaliwal's criterion for a spouse: "that he did not drink alcohol nor eat meat and that he shall treat her children well" (para. 4). She also sought "companionship, financial and emotional support for herself and her children" (para. 9). It was the potential husband's imagined motivations that were red-flagged. The justice cited the visa officer's report that "at the interview . . . [the husband] could not provide *reasons* for his marriage to a divorced woman" (my emphasis). Justice de Montigny also waded into theological territory, noting that Sikhism did not generally promote a union with these "uneven" backgrounds. Their unevenness stemmed primarily from her Canadian citizenship, her previous marriage, her children, and her age. The visa officer also deemed their wedding photos as "staged," that their three-times-a-week transatlantic communication was insufficient, and that there was *not* a "great deal" of demonstrable affection between them in their joint interview (para. 11). The point: Their performance of romance was weak. Lastly, Justice de Montigny did not accept the rationale of "destiny"—which some of my interlocutors in the next chapter describe as mektoub—as an explanation for the arrangement. The rejection by the court of destiny as an appropriate rationale for marrying in often familial-organized arrangements is significant.[25] Theirs was, in short, determined by a state official as a "bad faith" marriage.

In addition to focusing on "bad faith" marriage, the federal Conservative Party proposed and passed the Zero Tolerance for Barbaric Cultural Practices Act (Bill S-7) in June 2015 (Parliament of Canada 2015). In general terms, the bill purported to protect women from violence said to be perpetrated in the name of culture, and focused on forced marriage, polygamy, and honor killing (see Gaucher 2016). The bill amended the Immigration and Refugee Protection Act, the Civil Marriage Act, and the Criminal Code to make an anti-polygamy position clear, and to highlight the *"free and enlightened consent* to marriage" (my emphasis). While polygamy was already illegal in Canada, the act framed it as a primarily foreign practice that would threaten Canadian national values.[26] Related to these concerns, as part of their campaign promises, the Conservative Party pledged C$12 million over four years to set up a "Barbaric Cultural Practices" hotline. The proposed hotline would be run by the national Royal Canadian Mounted Police, and average Canadians could report "barbaric" practices when observed (Power 2015). When the Conservative government lost the federal election in 2015, the hotline did not materialize. The Barbaric Cultural Practices Act empowered immigration officers to deem a sponsored spouse or partner inadmissible if suspected of entering into or resuming a polygamous relationship after immigrating to Canada, or undertaking a fraudulent marriage. Pejorative characterizations of Muslim sexuality were entrenched amid this act. Even if the title "Barbaric Cultural Practices" was partially repealed by Justin Trudeau's Liberal government in 2018, the contents of the bill remained similar and the framing of certain behavior and sensibilities as "barbaric" significant.

Together, these shifts in immigration policy and legislation against "bad faith" transnational marriages, and the passage of the Zero Tolerance for Barbaric Cultural Practices Act, meant that family-class applicants in Canada were evaluated with greater scrutiny based on the performance of the "sincerity" of their relationships. Authenticity here maps onto liberal notions of the monogamous marriage of individualized relationships (in contrast to religious or cultural communities) based on signs of love and attraction. Akin to what Mahmood Mamdani (2002) coined as "culture talk" post-9/11, "Barbaric Cultural Practices" followed an overrehearsed trope of positioning imagined-as-Muslim, immigrant, and racialized men as more prone to violence, and rendering encultured women as "imperiled" subjects in need of saving through state surveillance and punitive controls. Indeed, the bill and hotline received considerable scholarly critique for their characterization of gender violence as located in racialized and immigrant communities (Abji et al. 2019: 797; Gaucher 2016: 529; Stolow and Boutros 2015; Zine 2022). Following colonial logics, these frameworks position white monogamous Canadians as exemplars of gender equality, "civilization," and "good" marriages. They also position religionized immigrants as less capable of *"free* and *enlightened consent* to marriage," as outlined by the Zero Tolerance for Barbaric Cultural Practices Act (Bill S-7). Again, even if none of my Algerian-origin interlocutors were directly affected by the anti-"bad faith" marriage laws, suspicion of transnational unions remained.

The Third Wave: 2019-Present

I distinguish a third distinct wave of migration of Algerians to Québec in order to capture the different atmosphere around settlement in Québec I observed as I completed interviews in Montréal in 2019. While political and public debates on religious accommodations and Muslim symbols have been ongoing in Québec since 2009, the passage of Law 21 in June 2019 introduced a new polarizing dynamic as conspicuous religious symbols became banned among individuals in governmental positions of authority (Article 6). The ban on niqabs did not emerge as a concern among my participants (Article 8). Several Algerian-origin immigrants like Zohra who wear hijab expressed regret about having chosen to migrate to Québec. Both she and Thuraya, fifty-nine, noted in separate interviews that while France appeared more rigid than Québec in its regulation of visible religiosity, the province hid the social and financial costs of its immigrant reception better than France. While there had been different attempts to legally regulate religious symbols since 2010, this shift to greater legislation against religious symbols had been unexpected for them both. Zohra, for one, now aimed to migrate to Ottawa or consider a larger city outside the province with a Francophone population where she might find a teaching position. Beginning in this period, women of Algerian origin navigated polarization around visible religious symbols. They were forced to position themselves for or against the law in ways that did not exist beforehand (see Selby and Bihya 2025).

Narratives on Transnational Marriage

Building on the notion that immigration laws and policies in France and Québec are shaped by histories of coloniality and my overview of immigration waves and recent legislation on marriage, I now turn to how participants in this study navigated these rules in their own transnational unions. I focus primarily on men—Hichem, Amin, and brothers Adel and Sami in Montréal—largely because they were more invested and involved in transnational arranged unions than women. As we saw with Ilias in the opening of chapter 1, despite how these punitive laws could have discouraged immigration through marriage, many of my male interlocutors experienced few hiccups in sponsoring their wives.

Hichem, born in Tizi Ouzou, in the province of Kabylia, was forty-four when I interviewed him in 2019. He had married a non-Muslim Quebecker he met online in 2012. He described himself as a "musulman laïque" (secular

Muslim). In his own words, "J'ai mon éducation, je crois à Allah, mais tout en étant laïque" (I have my [religious public schooling] education and I believe in Allah, all while being secular). I had met Hichem almost eight years earlier, in April 2011, when I traveled with his sister, Leila, who lives in a different neighborhood in Nanterre, and her then-husband, Mouloud, to visit their families for a few weeks in Algiers and Tizi Ouzou.[27] Leila, Mouloud, and their youngest son, Yaseem, had traveled to Algeria on vacation, in part to attend Mouloud's cousin's wedding. Mouloud's cousin and her fiancé were both of Algerian origin, but they lived in Lyon. They had chosen a destination wedding because of the allure of the food, atmosphere, the low catering costs, and the greater number of family who could attend without having to secure French tourist visas. Hundreds of relatives congregated at the wedding in the small village high in the Kabylian mountains. Leila knew I was hoping to start a project on marriage migration and had generously invited me to join them; their older two children remained in Nanterre.[28]

I first met Leila in early 2005 when she began part-time work in an association where I volunteered assisting new migrants with their "integration" to France, including French language and culture classes (Nadia, whom we met earlier in this chapter, had taken over Leila's job when she moved to a different employer). Leila worked very hard inside and outside her home and, despite her understandable exhaustion, maintained an elegant and gentle demeanor. In the over twelve years I had known her, I saw how, with her impeccable French, chin-length dyed-blond hair, pale complexion and tailored style, she often passed as white and French.

Despite her chicness and her education degree and previous work in Algiers as a high school teacher in a private school, Leila had trouble securing good work outside Paris that would allow her to return home before 5 p.m. to care for her three children. Mouloud was an aerospace engineer, also of Algerian origin, and had completed his training in France. His workplace outside of Paris facilitated their paperwork. They sought to rent a three-bedroom apartment (a *cinq et demi*) but did not have access to one through social housing, and so they rented a small one-and-a-half-story home just outside Petit-Nanterre. Despite its sole bathroom that had to be accessed by going outdoors, it was expensive. It also did not have a washing machine, so Leila washed by hand. She generously invited me a half-dozen times for meals at their home over the twelve years we had known each other.[29]

Seeking to leave Algiers in the midst of the Décennie noire, Mouloud had accepted a position and tried settling in Montréal. It was, he explained, too cold and too far from his mother, then a widow in Algiers. So he returned. When he found work outside Paris, he rented the small house and the couple began making arrangements to migrate to France. At that time, Leila was pregnant with Yaseem and anxious to leave Algiers. Like the other Kabylian-origin women in her family, Leila self-identified as a Muslim, but she was "discreet" and did not wear hijab. She began to receive death threats in the streets and verbal abuse from parents in the private school in Algiers where she worked. Unwilling to put on a hijab and feeling unsafe, she had pushed Mouloud for their departure. Once settled next to Petit-Nanterre, she did not work outside the home for the first few years. But when Yaseem began primary school, their high cost of living encouraged her to seek out nearby part-time options. She took up a position in a community association in Petit-Nanterre where we met.

When we arrived by car from Algiers to Leila's extended family's shared home in the outskirts of Tizi Ouzou, I could see why she cherished her extended family. Seven of her twelve siblings lived together in the three-story structure with their aging parents. She was the oldest of thirteen. The siblings shared twenty-four-hour care for her father, who was ailing with Alzheimer's disease. Leila had two married sisters, both hair stylists, one who lived in Petit-Nanterre (and was going through a divorce), and the other in Tizi Ouzou. Four younger sisters lived at home; three of them worked in the city. With their mother, the two married brothers worked as jewelers, making and selling intricate silver necklaces, bracelets, and earrings that featured Kabylia's prized and distinct red-orange coral. The three of them worked together in a small workshop adjacent to the television room; they sold their wares through a shop in Tizi Ouzou with Hichem's assistance. All the siblings contributed to the food, cleaning, and ambiance of the home. Two other women had joined the household when they married two of Leila's brothers. One of these couples had two small children, and one of these women was pregnant with her third child when we visited. The large kitchen was the central space of the home. It hummed with constant activity; the women rotated cooking and cleaning duties. Two large tables meant they could eat together.

Despite tragedy—including the infertility and late-stage cancer diagnosis of one sister-in-law, and the domestic-abuse, divorce, and return home of another sister—the family was quick to share stories, laugh, and embrace one another. In the two weeks I spent in their home, they lived and worked in relative harmony. Tall clay fences surrounded the house, and a beautiful lemon tree shaded a small sitting area outside. When I commented on the loveliness of their garden, Leila's divorced sister remarked, "It's a beautiful prison." This sister was grateful to have fled her violent marriage without family stigma, but life outside the confines of the family home was more difficult. She had not found paid work yet and dedicated her days to the care of her parents, housework, and ceramics. She would likely never leave, unless it was to marry again.

Hichem was the sixth of the family's thirteen living children. Of medium height and build, he shared Leila's round face and fairness. He was single and a favorite uncle. When we arrived at the house, Yaseem, fourteen, ran to Hichem first, and they hugged and kissed and began an earnest discussion in French about Lionel Messi, a star player on their favorite soccer team.[30] Because there were more than a dozen family members around, the cousin's wedding celebrations to prepare to attend, and interviews for me to conduct during the trip, I only spoke at length with Hichem three or four times in 2011. He drove Leila, Yaseem, and me around during the day, and also did odd jobs in town, assisting his two older brothers in their jewelry business, and driving his sisters to their jobs in a retail shop and in a separate hair salon downtown. I joined them a few times on these excursions. Hichem was very sociable.

In the evenings, a shared desktop computer in a corner of the family living room was a sought-after space. Everyone in the house between twelve and thirty-five years old had Facebook accounts (including me). I staved off jet-lag by reading French newspapers by lamplight well into the evening, and Hichem was typically there, also up late using the computer. One of his sisters told me in a hushed tone that he was likely chatting on MSN messenger with Jeannette, whom he had met online through a good friend who had migrated to Québec a decade earlier. Because he was clearly and understandably not interested in discussing the matter, I did not push for more details.

A year later, in 2012, with my then-nine-month-old daughter in tow, I saw Leila in Petit-Nanterre over coffee at the new association where she worked. Leila shared news and gossip about her siblings: "You won't believe it, Jenny. Hichem is getting married to *a Canadian*!! A woman he met on the internet." Jeannette, the Canadian, had visited Hichem at the family home for two weeks, and the meeting had gone very well ("love at first sight!"). At the end of the visit, they decided they would marry. Hichem met her eight-year-old daughter in a Skype call and that went well too. Jeannette would return in six months for the ceremony. It was always clear to both of them that he would move to Montréal. In Hichem's words, "She asked, 'Do you want to come?' I said, 'Yeah. Sure.'"

Not until more than six years later, when Hichem and I met several times for coffee, walks, and meals in Montréal in the summers of 2018 and 2019, did I learn the details of his marriage to Jeannette and his migration to Québec.[31]

A key moment in his future marriage migration, confided Hichem, was when Jeannette arrived in Tizi Ouzou: "Jenny, elle a eu le coup de foudre!" (Jenny, she fell head over heels!), he said, laughing. And that was that. In a recorded interview in 2018, he shared more:

> Well, imagine: I had a friend [from Tizi Ouzou] who was already here [in Montréal].[32] He was in the same class as Jeannette [at a CÉGEP, a public school that provides the first years of postsecondary education in Québec]. They were in the same class and they were friends. So, every time we talked, he mentioned her. A few times, he told her about me. Then he presented us to one another [online]. We [he and Jeannette] started chatting [*jaser*]. It went from there. So, it started when we started talking, getting to know each other on the internet.

Hichem was the first in his family to migrate to Québec and the first to meet a spouse online. Perhaps due to stigmas around online dating—a mechanism deemed detached from mektoub and ripe for fraud—when speaking to me he noted a few times how it was all aboveboard and supported by his parents: "Our relationship did not take place in secret [*en cachotterie*]. I was in the presence of my parents, with the blessing of my parents [for the marriage]." The speed of their engagement and his related departure meant that some in their circles questioned whether theirs was a love match. But Hichem stressed he had not been looking for marriage when they started chatting: "There are people who say, 'Yeah, you did that [the transnational wedding] for your papers.' But it wasn't that at all.... I was fine before any of this happened. No, it came on its own, afterward, gradually."

Once their conversations shifted to the possibility of a relationship, they agreed they needed to meet in person. Hichem would likely not receive a tourist visa, so they decided Jeannette would visit; her mother cared for her daughter. Because of the success of that visit, they decided that they would marry at his parents' home in Tizi Ouzou. Hichem would later migrate to Montréal once his permanent residency paperwork was in place. He did not want to live illegally in Québec, like one of his older brothers who lived in France. As he stressed to me several times, he preferred to do everything "by the book." Within days of his arrival in Montréal, Hichem found work in a recycling material factory with a boss who was also of Algerian origin. While his boss was a practicing Muslim and he was not, they got along well. The boss also helped him find a cheap used car and, later, a bachelor apartment.

Hichem's marriage to Jeannette did not last. In a conversation in July 2018 over coffee and donuts along the St. Laurence River in the Honoré-Mercier

Park, he explained that, in retrospect, he felt Jeannette had wanted a husband who would take care of her and of everything in her life. He explained that the day he arrived in Montréal, she quit her job and then mostly stayed in bed. Having never seen her in her own environment, he had not realized she suffered from depression and other mental illnesses. "You know, once I arrived in Québec, she stayed in the apartment all day, just taking her medications." Because she had not disclosed these challenges, he felt betrayed and overwhelmed with caring for her and her daughter. They did not find a resolution. Within two years, they legally separated.

Now single, Hichem worked more than sixty hours a week in the same factory job. These overtime hours helped to pay spousal support for Jeannette and send remittances to his family. Despite these challenges and the cold winters, Hichem stressed he had no regrets about migrating to Québec. He enjoyed the adventure. He had made some good friends. He attended a few Canadiens hockey games, and had gone camping in the summertime. The last two winters he went with friends on weeklong holidays to Cuba. Both times he chose to tell his extended family in Tizi Ouzou about the trip after he returned because it helped him defer pressure to spend his vacation time in Algeria. He smiled when I asked him whether he was open to marrying again. "Absolutely," he replied. He was open to remarrying, even transnationally.

Again, despite marrying after the 2006 laws in Canada that aimed to curtail transnational marriages, Hichem's paperwork for permanent residency went smoothly. His postmigration separation also highlights how, because he was able to arrive in Québec with permanent residency, he was less subject to state surveillance. In addition, because he secured unionized work and found an Algerian network quickly, he was also able to leave his marriage. In contrast, recall again Fatima's situation in Petit-Nanterre. While she did not characterize her relationship as abusive, her husband had not treated her respectfully at the beginning of their marriage. Her options were limited. She knew that a separation in the first five years of marriage might jeopardize her options for permanent residency. She did not have paid employment or a support network. The risks associated with the surveillance of sincere relationships are gendered. In Fatima's case, she had no residency status, employment, or external network upon which to rely.

Transnational unions are gendered in other ways as well. Mothers are active marriage brokers for their sons in both Petit-Nanterre and Montréal. In Montréal, Fahed, twenty-eight, said he trusted only his mother to find the right match. Another participant, Ali, forty-three, noted how he had tried to meet someone in Québec himself. Only when he felt it was impossible did he agree to a transnational arrangement organized by his mother. Like Ilias, whom we met at the opening of chapter 1, Amin, thirty-two, had dated non-Muslim and non-Algerian women in Québec since his solo migration to attend university. But, with his mother's long-distance pressure to marry, he was beginning to change his mind. In our interview in a park in the Vieux Montréal close to his office where he worked as an engineer, Amin described his marriageability and his view that an arranged marriage with a woman of Algerian origin would ensure longevity: "I was open to a lot of things [dating], there was no problem [meeting women]. But, *t'sais* [you know] it's the same culture. [With an Algerian bride] you can go back [on vacation, for retirement].... In contrast, a Québécoise can get bored of you, tomorrow, and just say, 'Bye bye.'... And, well, there are all kinds of other *comportements à côté* [ways of doing things] that make things easier, longer lasting."

Amin had lived with a white Québécoise in a common-law relationship for two years after his studies. He never told his parents about the relationship. In his words, he felt that the relationship ended when their cultural differences became too great. His parents regularly pressured him about formally settling down when they Skyped. When his common-law partnership ended about six months before our interview, Amin said he had joined some online dating and marriage websites like Weshrak (Arabic for "What's up?"). His mother agreed to this strategy. But if Amin was unsuccessful, she would take over. Soon.

Still in Montréal, two brothers capture differences between them on transnational union, despite their common upbringings and shared apartment as adults. Adel, twenty-eight, and Sami, twenty-five, had different takes on the question of transnational arranged marriages, and relatedly, acceptable versions of sexuality and their algérianité (see Selby 2022a). Their differing positions about the acceptability of these sponsorships capture how they navigate between their own preferences, those of their families, and the sociopolitical expectations that surround them regarding gender politics, marriage, and visible religiosity. In a lively debate on a hot and humid July evening in 2018, over takeout Chinese food at the kitchen table in their shared two-bedroom apartment in the Snowdon neighborhood, the brothers shared their visions for their future lives. We will see how, as single, racialized, and imagined-as-Muslim young men, the brothers replicated and absorbed macro-level concerns with fraudulent "bad faith" marriages.

The brothers were born in Algiers and migrated to Montréal with their parents in 1996 when they were two and five years old. Their parents fled the violence of the Décennie noire, especially heightened for them following the death of their maternal uncle, a young intellectual and journalist, murdered by the Groupe islamique armé (Armed Islamic Group). Adel explained that it was their father, who had lived and studied in England and, from there, visited France, who insisted that Québec offered a better sociopolitical and economic *climat* for their family (I met their father twice but did not formally interview him). The young men still held Algerian passports but had not visited for more than ten years in order to avoid mandatory military service. Adel's service obligation had ended the previous year, but he preferred to return with his younger brother Sami, whose service obligation had not yet expired.

The brothers had very different styles in their approaches and in their dress. Sami wore a sleeveless matching T-shirt and baggy basketball shorts and was generally less formal in his tone and presentation than his older brother. He worked full time as a personal trainer, focused on lightweight boxing. Adel sat up more properly and wore a short-sleeved button-down red-checkered shirt. Adel explained that his *gagne-pain* [bread and butter] for the last ten years had been working as a high school tutor. His real passion, though, was psychoanalysis, for which he had undertaken some training—specifically in what he called "transgenerational psychology." That fall, Adel would begin a four-year special education program at the Université du Québec à Montréal, with the goal of becoming a special needs teacher.

In contrast to Sami, Adel was keen for a transnational arranged marriage. Adel remembered the stress of leaving Algeria as a refugee, and saw a reconnection to his past as vital for his future and that of any potential children. "Until now, I've mostly dated Québécoises," he explained, by which he implied white women born in Québec. But, he said, increasingly, and in keeping with his understanding of psychic wholeness, he envisioned a Kabylian marriage partner "for the transmission of my values to my [future] children." According to his preferred timeline, he needed to marry upon the completion of his degree in four years in order to have four children before he turned forty. He wanted to work toward this goal. With an earnest tone he explained, "I've discussed it [returning to Algeria to seek a marriage partner] a lot with Mom. You know, absolutely.... If it's a choice [for the woman and for me], it's a super good option."

At the same time, he would "rather avoid" a "religious marriage," or the involvement of an imam. Instead, he said, "a Kabylian or Berber ceremony is something that would make me very happy. There are some rituals that are very, very old. You know, the union of two families, the union of two people, the spiritual symbolism of the thing and all that. These are all important." This description coincides with the brothers' self-description as "spiritually

Kabylian." Adel's interest in a transnational bride was recent. He had dated for a decade and had not met anyone of Algerian origin. The preference reflected a desire to foster closer ties to the Berber language and culture of his imagined past. He wanted to know more about his Algerian Berber roots and had begun an online Tamazight language class a few months earlier. For him, a partner's desirable "values" did not include Islam but did include the Berber language and culture, best facilitated through a Kabylian woman.

In keeping with the light and teasing tone of the evening, Sami laughed at his brother's reflection. He then gestured, as though standing in an assembly line, "Yeah, and you gotta find a young one [*une jeune*]!" Adel gave a restrained smiled and then responded, again seriously, that he would prefer to marry someone who was Kabylian, so that all the transmission of Amazigh culture would not fall on his shoulders alone. He elaborated, "Would I like to have a family with a Kabylian woman? Yes, absolutely. For all the cultural reasons. But I mean, in reality, that's not what happens. I'm, I've been going out with Québécoises so far. And so, I tell myself that the entire responsibility for cultural transmission [to my potential children] will rest on my shoulders."

In response, Sami memorably threw his arms up in the air and exclaimed: "What? Are you nuts? [*T'es fou?*] But you're not even Muslim!"

Sami's disdain of his older brother's plan in part stemmed from his perception of the social costs of such an arrangement. He knew the scrutiny that such an "antiquated" and "sexist" match could bring. Sami's connotation was that his brother's transnational marriage migration preference was outdated, unmodern, and, therefore, religious. In contrast, Sami framed a future common-law partnership as potentially resting on romantic love, and not such a transnational arrangement. Unlike his older brother's plan, Sami described his vision for the future of Québec as built on people mixing until all ethnic groups were indistinguishable. In this vision, there would be no *pure laine* Québécois or Kabylians. These markers—of not wanting a religiously practicing wife, of not seeking a transnational arrangement—allowed Sami to perform a more socially desirable secular masculinity. All the men in my larger study expressed to me some awareness of how in the recent legislation against "love fraud" and "bad faith" marriages the state positioned their bodies as sites for potential sexual excess.

Returning to my larger pool of male interlocutors, it is clear that immigration laws made it both easier *and* more challenging to sponsor a husband or wife to France than to Québec, largely due to proximity and social networks. Socioeconomic class does not appear to make a substantial difference in

Algerian-born marriage partner preference, insofar as men in Montréal across socioeconomic levels expressed this preference. My sample in France was more homogenous in terms of socioeconomic and educational backgrounds.

The way my female interlocutors in Montréal experienced marriage and migration differed. The fifty-nine Algerian women interviewed in Montréal were, generally, more likely to have migrated with their partners, or to have been divorced. Also, many more of my female informants under forty lived in common-law relationships and/or with non-Muslim or non-Algerian-origin partners than my female interlocutors in Petit-Nanterre. Living in religious but not legal marriages (i.e., common-law arrangements) was more difficult legally in France since the 2002 law against a religious marriage prior to a civil one.

I met Imane, forty-five, employed as a social worker, at her workplace in Laval near the Henri-Bourassa metro station during her lunch break during the month of Ramadan in 2018. She was tall, confident, and wore a bright hijab wrapped on her head in a turban style. She began wearing hijab when she migrated to Montréal following the death of her first husband (a white Protestant who converted to Islam when they married). She had lived first in France for ten years and then, with him, in the Netherlands for ten more. She had migrated to Montréal alone with her two children. One of her brothers supported her; he had lived in Laval for more than thirty years. While her first marriage to a white non-Muslim was based on "love at first sight," she described marrying her second, Algerian-born husband in Montréal as a pragmatic decision: "We aren't civilly married. Religiously, yes, but not civilly. So we are common law. We chose this option because he was coming out of a divorce and, for me, a civil marriage wasn't important. . . . We met here [in Montréal]. Some friends introduced us. And two weeks later we were religiously married."

Imane's desire to marry only religiously, and not civilly, was related to an affirmation of her religiosity as pivotal to her life. Unlike in France, in Québec one may legally undertake a fatiha (a religious marriage), which was insisted upon by her husband, without holding a civil marriage certificate. Imane did not think this request for a religious marriage was a big deal. In fact, she spent much of our interview laughing and comparing her Dutch and Algerian husbands and the cooking challenges of now being an "Algerian wife." Also significant, reflecting her personal story and distance from Algeria, was that the particularities of her second husband's Algerianness (i.e., his family there, his city of origin) did not matter to her. She planned to return to Algiers with her older teenage son the following summer for his first trip, but otherwise the regional particularities of the Bled were not as significant as they were for those who lived in Petit-Nanterre.

A last participant, Célia, twenty-seven, shared how her ideal of marital life was derailed by racism and discrimination among the family of her former husband, a white Quebecker. Her ex-husband could neither see nor confront this violence. Célia was studying for her master's degree in sociology in Montréal, having grown up in France but migrated to Québec with her family when she was in high school. She recalled the tensions that led to her divorce:

> I'm like, OK, *their* culture [Quebeckers] is the culture we learn. We celebrate it. We [Algerians] are folklore. We will be our whole life. And I also lived it with my in-laws, my ex. We will always be pretty, in the way we're portrayed as the Oriental woman. You know, we're going to be pretty women with long hair, dancing and eating weird food and listening to *rai*. . . .
>
> You see, it was with his [her ex-husband's] family that I experienced moments of racism at the dinner table. *Joy* [said sarcastically]. . . . All the time when I went to Chicoutimi, Saguenay, or whatever, I was constantly apprehensive. I knew there was going to be a time when they were going to tell us a *fucking* racist or a sexist thing.

Célia was agnostic. She did not wear hijab. She regretted her marriage to a white non-Muslim man but did not then see these concerns as mitigated by marrying within Algerian circles. She recognized that in the contemporary political climate in Québec, such differences were heightened. The broader context of Québec meant that the couple could not escape suspicion around her potential religiosity. She would not legally marry again, whether to a non-Muslim or a Muslim.

In sum, like other women I interviewed in Montréal, Imane and Célia capture a broader range of concern around marriage partners than I saw with men in Montréal. Imane was older, a widow, and could support herself financially. Perhaps for these reasons, a civil marriage was of no importance to her, while, as a practicing woman, a religious one mattered. Célia, whose family had immigrated to Montréal as economic migrants in the second wave, pointed to public debates about the acceptability of religious symbols that affected her far more than immigration policy changes—namely, the racism expressed by her former husband's family in northern Québec. She regretted the union and had turned away from marriage altogether.

This chapter has connectively compared immigration policy and experiences in France and Québec, especially as they relate to transnational marriage. I have sketched out different waves of immigration in both contexts and how different policies affect individuals. I have noted how in both France and Québec parallel concerns emerged around "love fraud" and "bad faith" marriages, beginning in 2006.

These policies shape how people marry and whom they marry, influencing them long past their wedding days. The specter of possible annulment and deportation, despite the seeming lack of enforcement of these laws, shapes my interlocutors' lives in both obvious and subtle ways. Halim was never able to enter the "contact zone" for his transnational marriage. Boussad too hoped for a possibility when there was none. Others, like Hichem, navigate the system with greater ease. The women I mention, particularly those in Montréal, enter into relationships in more varied ways, while for some young men in Montréal, marriage migration remains attractive, even if complex given the broader secular sensibilities that problematize arranged "nonromantic" religiously informed unions. The next chapter theorizes these preferences through the notion of coloniality.

CHAPTER 4

COLONIALITY, KINSHIP, AND DESIRE

In a May 2018 interview in her Montréal apartment, Maya, thirty-six, described how her taste in men shifted in her early twenties, from assuming she would marry an Algerian, to considering dating a Quebecker, to finally "want[ing] a European. A French man." She recounted these shifts as reflecting her feelings about Québec, Algeria, and France, and what kinds of relationships and gender roles she understood were encouraged in each: "When I look back at my previous boyfriends, I definitely had a period where I was attracted to guys who were dark. Brown, *basanés* [tanned] . . . typical Algerians! I listened to a lot of Arab music then too. And then . . . that's it. After that phase, *pffffiou*, I was finished. Then it was more like, I want a European. A French man. And finally, I married a French man."[1] Maya's relationship chronology implicitly invokes how conceptions of race intermingle with desire. She specifies French and European men as desirable (and white), and "typical" Algerians as a phase and as "dark." A woman of Algerian origin living in Montréal, Maya's narrative encapsulates various registers of coloniality in her understandings of desire, kinship, and marriage partner preference and marriage rituals.

Coloniality, I argue in this chapter, shapes participants' relationships to the Bled, in dynamic "intercolonial" ways.[2] Invoking the term "coloniality," I hope, captures how contemporary migratory patterns relate to long-standing imperial legacies. Expressions of coloniality surface in contact zones and on individuals' bodies and, more broadly, in how realities are shaped and knowledge produced. In other words, coloniality undergirds "universals" in Western knowledge systems, including modernity, global capitalism, and secularism, that are often imagined as neutral and apolitical (Mignolo and Walsh 2018). Following this thinking, Aníbal Quijano's (2000) "coloniality of power" points to the overarching idea that the very disparities of modern power are structured by colonizing processes. Following these insights, this chapter examines how the effects of coloniality can be traced within interpersonal relationships *and* as undergirding contemporary legislative efforts on secularism in France and Québec. While on the surface these appear as disparate sites of inquiry, both are shaped by legacies of coloniality.

Maya migrated from Boumerdès, Algeria, to France with her parents and three siblings amid the civil war in 1996. She did not recall this initial migration traumatically, recognizing retrospectively how her parents shielded her from the violence surrounding them. Unable to work in France legally, her parents spent ten months living on their savings. One of her father's brothers lived in Montréal and encouraged them to apply for permanent residency as refugees, which they were granted ten months later. Maya described her excitement at the idea. "I was like, 'Oh wow, that's amazing!' You know, as a girl, I dreamed of going abroad." Then fourteen, Maya's favorite television show was a French-dubbed *Beverly Hills, 90210*. She knew Montréal and Los Angeles differed but admitted she saw *l'Amérique* as sunshine- and green-grass-filled possibilities. She laughed, recalling her first day at the high school near the Plamondon metro station in the city's West Island region: "I was so disillusioned! It was like I had agreed to a con." It was March. Her school was surrounded by brown melted slush and everyone wore multiple layers of gray and black clothing. There was no sun-kissed skin or hair or convertibles in sight. Life in the Snowdon neighborhood of Montréal was, in short, nothing like what she had imagined.

Maya and her two younger siblings attended the Collège Marie-de-France, a private France-based international school in the Côte-des-Neiges–Notre-Dame-de-Grâce neighborhood.[3] She could now see how attending this French lycée shaped her peer group, her sense of self, and how she related to Algeria and Québec. Once established in Montréal, Maya and her family returned to the coast near Boumerdès on vacation every other year. These visits were initially uneventful. When she visited the summer after finishing high school, however, she saw it differently. She described feeling overwhelmed by the patriarchal structures that had been previously invisible to her, namely how women in her family were treated, herself included. She felt "suffocated." Maya had taken up long-distance running in high school but did not feel like she could run in Boumerdès: "Everyone is looking at you [in Boumerdès]. When you're a woman there, you can't go for a run wearing shorts. And it's not that they're just going to look at you. They're going to bother you. . . . I think it's freedom, yeah. Safety also, especially as a woman. I suffocate in Algeria. People are aware of what you are doing all the time. There is no privacy, *et c'est ça*."

Equally difficult, alongside her perceived surveillance of her body, was the realization that she was no longer considered "Algerian enough" by her relatives there. Unlike the positive experiences we will see for young men,

Maya's presence engendered what she called a "nous ici et vous là-bas" (us here and you over there) demarcation that made her feel rejected, a feeling that was acute in late teenage years when she sought acceptance there: "This realization really pained me. I remember how going there [to Boumerdès] made me cry often." In general, unlike for the men and women of Petit-Nanterre, and the men from Montréal, women from Montréal in my sample like Maya expressed less connection to Algeria. Part of her sense of rejection may have been amplified by the fact that Maya was nonpracticing. Young men often shared opposite experiences on their summer trips, describing their *reversion* to Islam following these visits.

Maya added that this "phase of rejection" that began in her teens was amplified when she began university in Montréal. No longer in her French school and family "bubble," for the first time, she was fully immersed in what she called a "Québécois environment": "I had a lot of difficulties [in classes, at the university] because every time I spoke, I felt that—maybe it was just in my head—but I felt that I was being watched or seen as different, because of my accent, my way of speaking. And that confused me for a while."

Looking back to her postmigration childhood, Maya explained that her earlier socialization at the France-based Marie-de-France school meant that, even in adulthood, she was less at ease in Québécois circles. She didn't necessarily understand the cultural references or the jokes, and felt her French accent made her stand out. These opinions translated to her adult relationships. "Québécois de souche" (Québec-origin men), she felt, did not share her "traditional" vision of gender roles and the family. Maya sensed that a traditional marriage to a "provider" would be less possible with a white Francophone Quebecker.

> You know, I'm sure there are Quebeckers who are very family [-oriented], but the idea I had, from the few people I met and from the image I was given, was that Quebeckers don't get married, or that they separate quickly, for no apparent reason [*pour un oui ou pour un non*]. Those were ideas that, I don't know, shouldn't be generalized, but they're ideas I've had. Like sharing the bills: my husband is the one who pays, who takes care of our family. Which is also a bit like Algerian culture where the husband takes care of the family, the finances. This [distribution of responsibilities] reassures me.

Maya imagined the Frenchness of her husband as being closer to the nuclear and patriarchal construction of family she had idealized. She met her white, French-origin husband through her running group. He was open to settling in Québec and his foreignness would create no issue in sponsoring him.

Race appears to have also been part of the equation. Maya had a previous long-term "tanned" boyfriend of Tunisian origin, which was part of what she saw as a "phase." A "European" was more desirable for her. Despite these proclivities for white European culture, she accepted to wear two Algerian-style dresses for their wedding reception in Montréal, mostly to please her mom and her mom's Algerian-origin friends. Her princess gown was, nevertheless, the *coup de coeur*: "I had always dreamt of having a white dress for my wedding."

Maya's country and racial preferences in a future husband highlight a significant point of difference in my qualitative data among Algerian-origin women in Québec: in contrast to Algerian-origin men in Montréal and men *and* women in Petit-Nanterre, none of them sponsored an Algeria-born man as a spouse. In addition, many more women from Montréal had mixed non-Muslim, non-Algerian unions or lived in common-law relationships than did women from Petit-Nanterre. Some Algerian women in Montréal were in common-law relationships where they were religiously married (an arrangement that is illegal in France; see note 13 in chapter 3). Equally important, women of Algerian origin in Montréal enjoyed more social mobility and privacy than women in Petit-Nanterre, where cramped space and social housing may have influenced greater homogeneity (Lapeyronne 2005; Selby 2017).[4] Drawing on the marriage stories of more than twenty-five participants, in what follows, I show the ways coloniality, kinship and desire are interwoven. Before turning to these narratives, I begin by introducing the notion of "coloniality" and how the Bled, or home country, referring to Algeria, relates to it.

Conceptualizing the Ongoing Legacies of Colonialisms

Colonialisms reverberate in all of our lives, including for many of my participants of Algerian origin who live transnationally. Colonialisms shape social systems, individual and collective imaginaries, myths of inferiority and superiority, taxonomies of difference, and epistemologies of knowledge. From the point of view of settler and not Indigenous sovereignty, colonialisms are a condition of modernity (cf. Bhambra 2007). Colonialisms' legacies remain generations after the official succession of colonial administrations, which, in French Algeria, was in 1962, and in Québec, again, from a settler and not an Indigenous perspective, legally concluded in 1763. To conceptualize this ongoingness, I prefer the term "coloniality." Nelson Maldonado-Torres's (2007: 243) definitional distinction is helpful:

> Coloniality is different from colonialism. Colonialism denotes a political and economic relation in which the sovereignty of a nation or a people rests on the power of another nation, which makes such nation an empire. Coloniality, instead, refers to long-standing patterns of power that emerged as a result of colonialism, but that define culture, labor, intersubjective relations, and knowledge production well beyond the strict limits of colonial administrations. Thus, *coloniality survives colonialism*. It is maintained alive in books, in the criteria for academic performance, in cultural patterns, in common sense, in the self-image of peoples, in aspirations of self, and so many other aspects of our modern experience. In a way, as modern subjects we breath[e] coloniality all the time and everyday [*sic*]. (My emphasis.)

In fairness, I am appropriating and extending Maldonado-Torres's definition, despite his call to restrict coloniality to the Americas and to those specific colonial relations of power. I have found that "coloniality" resonates beyond this time and place and therefore extend it this French colonial web of relations. Maldonado-Torres's (2007: 242) notion of the "coloniality of being" also captures the "effects of coloniality in lived experience and not only in the mind." In other words, as a corollary of Foucauldian governmentality, the coloniality of being shows how "coloniality survives colonialism" through the bodies, minds, and relationships of individuals. To be clear, it is an etic term.

Zohra, thirty-five, an interlocutor in Montréal, grappled with her coloniality as a newcomer in Québec. She was one of only a handful of participants who struggled with her place in contemporary politics. I am grateful to her maternal aunt, whom I also interviewed, for having put us in touch over tea and cookies at her apartment in Laval. When we first met in her two-bedroom apartment in the Cartierville neighborhood in the north of the island of Montréal, Zohra was a mother of three and a full-time student. She was well-spoken, smart, and very, very busy. In a handful of our conversations, she had begun questioning her place amid the longer purview of the history of Québec, a province she had previously idealized as open to all, tolerant, and multireligious. More concretely, until recently, she had never imagined herself as a settler. In chapter 1, we saw her describe her fears for her future employment in the province: the passage of Law 21 in June 2019 meant that women like her who wore hijab were no longer employable as public school teachers. In her daily life, she had experienced hurdles—racism, xenophobia, Islamophobia—since migrating to Montréal as a woman who was visibly Muslim, racialized, and poor. But she now also shared a sobering realization of her own complicity in the province's mechanisms of race and racism. She too was a settler. Given her lifelong critique of the French colonization of Algeria, this awareness generated unease:

> You know, it's [this realization] among the reasons I've thought about leaving Québec: because I realized that finally we [Algerians who have migrated to Montréal] are settlers. We are immigrants, yes, but we're [also] settlers. There are Indigenous people here. It's the same thing as in Algeria [with French colonialism].
>
> Before coming, I didn't inquire a lot about the history of Québec and all that. I didn't have the time with my kids, my work, and everything. But since I've been here, it's been a bit shocking because, finally, these things [power, imperialism] are everywhere. But I've swallowed it for now [*j'ai gobé ça*]. I've tried not to think about that for the past three years. I've swallowed this reality, but there it is [*mais voilà*].

"There are Indigenous people here." With this acknowledgment, Zohra verbalized her complicity in the power structures of coloniality that had been invisible to her as she undertook the long immigration procedures and organized her family's move to Montréal. For her, because of France's violent colonial history, migrating there had been out of the question. But now, having settled and having experienced exclusion on both individual and institutional levels in ways she had not anticipated, Zohra no longer saw Québec with the rose-colored glasses she had worn premigration. She could now better see her involvement in the violent mechanisms of colonialism. With this realization she stressed her desire to "teach my kids about it [the French colonialism of Québec]." This was her strategy to process her experience as a migrant settler (cf. Lentin 2019 on the "double settler-colonizer"). More practically, Zohra had also begun imagining a future living in Gatineau and working in Ottawa, which she saw as less influenced by secular laws, but she knew this would be challenging to make happen.

Most individuals featured in this chapter (myself included) do not articulate their relationship to colonialism as openly as Zohra or as Michi Saagiig Nishnaabeg writer Leanne Betasamosake Simpson does in her short-story collection *Islands of Decolonial Love* (2013). More common among my interlocutors was engagement with the notion of the Bled, the concept of "home country" to which I will return shortly. If we assume, as I do, that histories of coloniality shape the contexts of individuals of Algerian origin when they engage with the state at the time of marriage, how are post-1962 relationships for transnational Algerians best theorized? What language is most appropriate? Postcolonial? Decolonial? Anticolonial? Or, as I suggest, the notion of "coloniality"?

Some scholars have argued that the term "postcolonial" may falsely imply that the processes of colonialism ended with independence in 1962. Others find the term useful to demarcate an aftermath rather than an end, like Alana Lentin (2019), who uses it to describe "being worked over by colonialism" (see also Macías 2022). Sociologist Nacira Guénif-Souilamas (2006: 24) aptly notes that, given that in real life politics rarely play out through binary categories but instead are enacted in ways that are constantly shifting, power dynamics in France are "still colonial *and* already postcolonial" (my emphasis; see also Barclay, Chopin, and Evans 2018; Evans 2012; McCormack 2010; Silverstein 2018). Guénif-Souilamas's tautology of "still and already" captures the nonlinearity of these power dynamics. Todd Shepard (2017: 62) also offers a reformulation of these terms. He coins a "post-decolonization" formulation to describe the ongoing Algeria-France relationship, thereby complicating the end date. Shepard explains that the "post-de" prefix makes evident that French colonialization did not abruptly end in 1962. Again, I find "coloniality" more convincing. The "post-de" designation in the Canadian settler context is awkward because the colonizer is never "going home." Still other scholars have argued for expressly "anticolonial" (or "uncolonial") positions, which effectively center politics and positionalities against colonialism.

In relation to this ethnography, we could ask, How do the continuing legacies of the colonial reverberate (or not) in the marriage partner preferences and ceremonies that often privilege Algerian culture in France and Québec? Could these preferences be explained by "anticolonial" perspectives that reject the French Algerian histories of biopower and sexual imperialism? Zohra, for one, might not find the "anti-" prefix helpful to frame her thinking, in that it gives the false impression of a space outside of colonialism. In fact, Zohra articulated her recognition that she cannot stand outside its power dynamics. The "anti-" component also implies a negative position, which does not capture the life-affirming element to these transnational commitments to Algeria and the sophisticated awareness of systems of power that make renewed kinship with individuals in the Bled at the time of marriage desirable.

Yet other scholars have proposed a "decolonial" posture. This appellation shifts the "locus of enunciation"—or from where one is located—from the so-named Western subject to the colonized or subaltern subject (Mignolo 2007). The language of the "decolonial turn" was largely inspired by scholars focused on Iberian (Spanish and Portuguese) colonial pursuits in the Americas.[5] Decolonial thinkers argue for a causal relationship between these colonial pursuits and the development of European "modernity." This relationship, they argue, is foundational to the global imposition of a racial capitalist hierarchy that has facilitated European/Western political economic hegemony in the Americas and elsewhere (Smith 1999). With a larger group of scholars, sometimes called the Modernity and Coloniality Group, Aníbal Quijano (2000) argues that the colonization of what is now Latin America and the Caribbean generated a "coloniality of power." Notably, despite the violence of these hierarchies, these decolonial scholars and activists emphasize that Indigenous peoples and enslaved Africans have contested the social, political, and economic effects of colonization. Colonial violence, they argue, never succeeded in erasing local, place-based knowledges, and such knowledges are the basis of current decolonial resistance, that is, of life-promoting ways of living and being (Mignolo and Walsh 2018).[6] Colonialisms thus also breed new resistances and new cultures.

Also based in the Americas, Eve Tuck and K. Wayne Yang's (2012: 3) critique of *de*colonial formulations, namely that decolonization efforts should necessarily relate to land and its repatriation to Indigenous peoples, helpfully centers ongoing and necessary Indigenous claims to land rights. Tuck and Yang argue that decolonization is not a metaphor and, in the Americas, "is not equivocal to other anti-colonial struggles" (31). Tuck and Yang's critique, like that of Maldonado-Torres (2007), makes evident that the decolonial has a geographical specificity in its politics, one that is not entirely reflected in my interlocutors' description of desire and its relationship to the Bled.

Engaging with the notion of coloniality, and removing different prefixes, I hope, nods to the enduring structures of colonial oppression in the contexts in which my interlocutors live and in which I write. I do not make a direct causal link but do note that even those cognizant of the difficulties of marriage migration and the challenges of living in arranged partnerships nevertheless seek traditionalism at the time of marriage, with expressions lodged in tropes of Algeria, like the notion of the Bled. These tropes are related to Islam, particularly with articulations seeking to focus on brides' and grooms' sexual purity and the *nikah* (an Islamically sanctioned union). However, desire for the Bled is not only about Islam. Chifia, whom I return to shortly, was sought out by her mother-in-law, and is not practicing. Her mother-in-law did not want a woman for her son who wore a visible religious symbol but did want a young woman who would accept the family's transnationalism, Algerian food and cultural traditions, as well as her (the mother's) centrality in family decisions. With this example and others in mind, the Bled's continued presence in Petit-Nanterre therefore cannot be collapsed as a desired expression of authentic Islam but is better understood as an expression of reclaimed coloniality through kinship.

This notion of coloniality echoes slightly differently in the contemporary sociopolitical contexts of France and Québec. Fewer Algerians live in specific ghettoized neighborhoods in Montréal. Their precarity in Québec becomes more evident in statistical data that record their under- and unemployment (Côté-Boucher and Hadj-Moussa 2008; Lenoir-Achdjian et al. 2009). Indeed, in this context, as Zohra articulated and as we will see in secular legislative efforts in contemporary Québec, the erasure of Indigenous peoples from narratives of life in Québec reflect a different space for Algerians in the ongoing colonial narrative in that province than their statuses in France.

These differences also appear individually among this study's 187 participants. Practically speaking, some return to Algeria regularly, some never do; some remain closely tied to daily political life there, others do not. Some fled as refugees during the violence of the Décennie noire in the 1990s, and others migrated for school or work, for marriage, or for adventure. Algeria is a repository of a wide range of values and preferences, including ones that are sociocultural (via holidays, foodways, dress, etc.), political, familial, sexual, and religious-infused. Given the centrality of the notion of the Bled in these formulations, "coloniality" more than other terms offers a way to understand migrant and Algerian-origin citizens' positionality, as well as the ways individuals create and frame preferences around transnational marriage and partners of Algerian origin.

Desire, Coloniality, and the Bled

While acknowledging colonial inheritances in my interlocutors' marriage partner preferences and marriage rituals, it should be clear that none of my interlocutors conceptualized their preferences by signaling colonialism. More emically, participants invoked the Bled, which implies the seeking out of tradition, or expressions of mektoub, or what is fated or written by God. The Bled indicates relationality with Algeria, which we will see is sometimes sought after, and sometimes not. Still, in most cases, conceptualizations of colonialism shape belonging and longing. The preferences for "traditional" marriage partners among my Algerian-origin interlocutors in a northwestern Parisian suburb and, to a lesser extent, in Montréal are therefore part of a web of relations and desires tangled with colonial politics. For cisgender men more than women, this desire was articulated with the concept of the Bled.[7]

As we have seen, transnational unions are often imagined as a religious response to a secular France, but to unequivocally explain these preferences as only about Islam is inaccurate. Granted, in the face of systemic and personal discrimination based on racialization, social class, and religion, individuals of Algerian origin surely seek partners they imagine will value these parts of their identities. But, as we will see, Islam (here conceptualized as religious values, practices, beliefs, and habitus) is sometimes referenced and sometimes ignored. Many young marriageable Algerian Muslims in contemporary France are *croyants* (believers) but not *pratiquants* (practitioners). So too in Montréal. Religious practice is thus not necessarily a factor in whether one marries transnationally, but concerns with kinship and belonging are ever present.[8] The symbolic and geographical meanings of the Bled even differed among brothers in the same family, as we saw with Adel and Sami in chapter 3. My point is to consider the ever-presentness of these relations.

"Le Bled" is a term sometimes used pejoratively and is most commonly circulated in Petit-Nanterre. In Classical Arabic, "bled" means "country," but in colloquial dialect the term is a gloss for "village" (and familiar French has borrowed it in this latter sense). "Le Bled" is often used to mean "homeland" or "home country."[9] This usage stems from the colonial period and descriptions of Algeria's *bled paumé*, or rural backwaters (see Tetreault 2013, 2015; Selby 2014b: 514). In general, the term remains more abstract than situated. For many of my participants, the idea of the Bled acts as a contiguous space that functions in tandem with and as an expression of differentiation—even a foil—to their lives in France or Québec. The Bled is transnational and not diasporic: it sustains continued exchange, deep affiliations and sociality spanning nation-states (Vertovec 2009).

The notion of the Bled can thus invoke and reclaim coloniality. As we saw for Ilias in chapter 1, and as I will consider for Amel in this chapter, France is home, but the Bled acts as a touchstone of "authentic" culture or "tradition," including but not solely related to religion. Again, for many of my participants, this social bond was primarily expressed through kinship ties in marriage and occasionally by a wedding ceremony or celebration in Algeria. I define "tradition" not as a reflection of orthodoxy but as a dynamic "ensemble of practices and arguments that secure the social bond and provide cohesiveness" (Salvatore 2009: 5).

These ties run deep. Fouad, twenty-eight, was engaged to be married to an Algerian woman whom he would sponsor to join him in Montréal. He had met his fiancée during his last visit to Algiers on summer vacation, and, he noted with a smile, his mother took care of the rest. Now "I'm going to sponsor her [*lui faire les papiers*], and she's going to live here with me. She's going to conquer the West with me!" Fouad characterized her Algerianness as a key factor in their nuptials. She was practicing but did not wear hijab. Their idea was that, once settled, she would start postgraduate studies at Université du Québec à Montréal, perhaps in sociology, which would facilitate employment afterward. He worked as a chemist for a pharmaceutical company in Montréal, having first migrated for his studies four years earlier.

Fouad described how Algeria was at the heart of all of his kinship ties: "Algeria's like your mother. You can't choose her. My mother is Algeria, *c'est ça là* [that's it]. You can't choose. But you're always attached." By sponsoring a woman from Algeria, he felt an ally from the Bled would be joining him in Québec. Together they would "conquer the West." While the reader might critique Fouad's explicit colonial allusion to a settler positionality of claiming land and space, when pressed, he explained that the reference was more implicit for him: a cowboy-like conquering was about adapting to Québec together. His Algerian-born wife would be an ally. He and his future wife both spoke French fluently *and* had deep cultural ties to Algeria that would continue. Fouad saw these qualities as uniting them in their partnership in the Francophone context, while their roles would remain unquestioningly traditionally gendered.

The Bled is not only a place for deep reflection and finding oneself. Many men of Algerian origin in my sample returned for fun, on vacation, bolstered by their spending power (in other words, the strength of the euro and the Canadian dollar there) and the heightened patriarchal context that gave them more and preferential treatment in private and public spheres. For Anas, twenty-five, a participant who had been in Montréal for two years as an engineering student at the Université de Montréal and planned to stay in Québec, Algeria was not a place to encounter the everyday challenges of life, but its climate made it a great antidote to snowy Montréal: "On holiday, you wake up at noon, you go to the beach, you have your car and everything. But real life is not that." As a self-described "traditional Muslim," still single, Anas envisioned an arranged marriage with a transnational wedding there, where there is better "ambiance."

Anas had moved to France for his undergraduate degree and then migrated to Québec afterward, because "let's face it, life is easier here." He called himself religiously practicing and "traditional." Despite not having a prospective bride at the time of our interview, he had a good deal to say about how he envisioned his future wedding day: "Me, when I marry, well,

I'll have the civil ceremony here, but I will have the party in Algeria." Because the cost of live performers, catering, and venues was imagined as less expensive in Algeria than in Québec and France, and because large extended families were often not able to travel due to financial and visa restrictions, hosting a destination wedding there made sense for many.

Young men's limited social and financial capital in France often expanded significantly in Algeria, as for Mohammed, Amel's younger brother whom we met at the beginning of chapter 3, in ways that they did not for his sister. In general, men of Algerian origin in Petit-Nanterre often described the freedom and fun afforded to them in Algeria that nearby Paris restrained. Recently divorced and with two children, Khalil, thirty-eight, often returned from Petit-Nanterre to his hometown of Oran for a beach holiday with his daughters when they were in his care. Khalil generously spent a day with me in Oran in July 2016 when our trips there overlapped and showed me his favorite places to eat and hang out. Having also spent a day with him in Petit-Nanterre in the association where he worked part time, the contrast was not lost on me. In Oran, he could afford to drive a car; gas was cheaper. His mother happily took care of his children. He did not need to work and could afford to go to restaurants, bars, and nightclubs—all impossible in Paris on his salary. The sun shone more brightly. As he himself noted, in Algeria he could be young again. But he also enjoyed the fashion and possibilities available to him in Paris. Figure 4.1, a photo of Khalil, captures his creative interpretation of the ritual of arrival on his wedding day in Paris in what, in his hometown in Oran, would have been his arrival by horseback. He was about to meet his fiancée at the municipal office in the city's eighteenth arrondissement for their civil wedding.

Other men were focused on fun for their later years. Mohammed, forty-four, a married mechanical engineer, had lived in Montréal since 2012. He began imagining a future binational life during his first winter in Canada. He spent a decade having a house built near his childhood home, with the plan of moving there when he retired. Unexpectedly, however, his Montréal-born children were not interested in spending time there. This was a painful realization, but Mohammed remained hopeful: "Algeria will always be a part of me, I spent my youth there. Hopefully one day I can spend time there to get away from the Montréal winters." For these men, the Bled ensured ease and sunshine. Their returnee-retiree-vacationer positionalities afforded them economic and sociopolitical power they did not necessarily hold outside of Algeria.

The Bled also acts as an identarian touchstone. As we saw with Ilias in chapter 1, the Bled also took on a greater meaning for Mustafa, twenty-five,

Figure 4.1. Khalil on his wedding day in 2004 in the eighteenth arrondissement of Paris, substituting his bike for what would have been an arrival by horse in Algeria. Courtesy of Khalil.

after he returned to Kabylia on a monthlong vacation for the first time at age sixteen, four years after migrating to Montréal from Algeria. Mustafa included France as part of his transnational life. The French suburban banlieue aesthetic connected him to a global North African–inspired urban style that acknowledged his social precarity: "You know, they [North Africans in the French banlieues] talked about gangs, and we were like, 'wow!' We [he and his friends] were really fascinated by all that." Unlike his older brother, who was a "model immigrant," Mustafa described how got into petty crime and *voyoutisme* (hooliganism). While squatting in buildings and smoking cannabis in the outskirts of Montréal (when marijuana was illegal in Canada), "we listened to French rap and thought we were thugs [*p'tits voyous*]." He added, laughing, "We had so many references to the [French] banlieues, in their way of speaking, but also in their way of dressing, in our clothes. We wore Air Max, *les Requins*." These social influences circulate amid all three locales.

For Mustafa, the return trip to the Bled at sixteen was "very illuminating." Looking back, he noted that "during those four years [when they arrived in Montréal], I now see I really had a huge thirst [*une soif énorme*] for Algeria." In contrast, his parents wanted to leave behind the violence of the Décennie noire. While they did not dwell on their socioeconomic losses, they had been well-to-do premigration (his mother a cardiologist and his father an architect) and had struggled financially postmigration. A few weeks into his stay in Kabylia, Mustafa saw his life in Montréal from a new vantage point and recognized the richness of his Algerian cultural connection:

> Returning to Algeria for the first time, I could finally see all my alienation from all my distress in Montréal. And I saw my friends in the Bled who were hanging out and playing guitar and all that and I said to myself, "How can I be struggling in Canada, while they are in Algeria? And look how cool they are. They're so peaceful. Look at me, I'm doing fuck all [*je suis en train de foutre la merde*] in Canada." . . .
>
> I had problems here in Montréal. I wasn't well. So, when I went to Algeria, it really clicked for me. I felt, like, a revolution when I came back. Finally, I felt like I could express algérianité in Montréal. I didn't need to always refer to France.

For Mustafa this trip made him question his attachment to French banlieue culture and its romanticization of drugs and delinquency. In sharp distinction from the young men in the French suburbs, his friends in Kabylia were peaceful. This "revolution" in his thinking about the Bled meant that his algérianité became a point of pride and a *repère* (touchstone). His desire for an Algerian marriage partner has been part of ensuring that these traditions remain present in his adult life.

Youcine, twenty-nine, also described Algeria longingly in his interview at a café in downtown Montréal. At that time, Youcine was engaged to a woman in Algeria whom he planned to marry in three months and then sponsor. He had left Algeria with his parents when he was eighteen months old, migrating first to France and then to Québec, where they were able to secure permanent residency. He described how, as he got older, he was increasingly drawn to Algeria, particularly as he became more religiously practicing. He noted that he was disappointed his parents had not "inculcated" much of the culture of his origins in his youth: "I don't know why [they didn't]. I think my father immigrated quite early to France, and then, like, I don't know. And my mother [pauses; becomes quiet] . . . that's it: they went to study in France then, I don't know, they didn't teach me about Algeria [*ils m'ont pas inculqué ça*]. I don't know why."

As he entered his late twenties, his desire to know more about Algeria and Algerian culture also shaped his openness to marry a woman of Algerian origin, contrary to his parents' wishes. Notably, Youcine did *not* make this link, stressing that their meeting was "fated." He met his fiancée, Katia, on Facebook when she came up as a potential friend, and he saw she had the same last name as him. He liked her photo, added her as a friend, and they began chatting, discovering they were not related. Once they made this e-connection, they began conversing more regularly, always in French, and, over the weeks that followed, their conversation turned to the possibility of marriage. Their parents also met, by Skype. The discussions went well. Youcine then traveled to Algeria with his parents for a religious marriage with Katia, and then began sponsorship proceedings. Although they had not envisioned this arrangement for him, because he planned to live permanently in Québec, his parents accepted his decision. The timing was good. Katia was about to finish her studies in biology. Twice during the interview Youcine mentioned that Katia wore hijab and knew more about the traditions of Islam than he did. For their future children, Youcine noted, "I don't speak Arabic very well—and most Algerians speak Arabic well because they speak it with their parents. We didn't really do Ramadan [growing up]. We didn't do religious festivals . . . so, like, I know that if I marry a Muslim Algerian, she will be able to pass these aspects on to them [our future children]." Youcine positioned Katia as a religio-cultural expert on Islam and Algerian language, a guide that he and his future children would need to learn Arabic and more about Algerian traditions. His future children, he said, would not "suffer to know their origins" as he felt he had. Youcine's narrative resonates with that of Adel, twenty-eight, who, in the previous chapter, described his wish for a potential marriage partner "for the transmission of my values to my [future] children."

For young men of Algerian origin in Petit-Nanterre and Montréal, the Bled is a sign of authenticity as related to culture, Islam, food, kinship, and sexual politics. In general, young men more than young women described a need for connection to the Bled, influencing their marriage partner preferences. Young men in Petit-Nanterre most often used the term, reclaiming it from its connotation of a backward, unsophisticated rural place (see Selby 2014b). Despite the greater distance and challenge to visit, young men in Montréal reference the Bled, too. One participant, Younes, thirty-five, who was born in a Kabylian village where he lived until he was eight, laughed when I asked him about Algeria. Unprompted, he referenced the Bled, noting how, as an adult, he now claimed it as part of his identity. "When I do conferences [in Montréal], I tell people, 'I'm a *Blédard*. And I'm proud of it!'"

To be clear, the desire for rapprochement to Algeria through marriage was highly gendered. Men in my sample recurringly expressed how their wives would bring them closer to their culture through marriage. At the time of our interview, Amir, twenty-three, who migrated to Montréal with his family at twelve, was single. He was not sure how this perspective on the Bled would translate into his adult life. Would he, in his words below, "ethnicize" love? While single, Amir was emphatic that he wanted to marry one day. He was nearing the end of his degree in political science, and the question of marriage had begun to feel more pressing for him, especially as related to whether language should play a central role or not:

> I don't know if I need to ethnicize love. Should I opt for an Algerian who already lives the same reality of me? Or a [non-Muslim, non-Algerian] Quebecker? Or any other person? These are the questions that are still unclear to me. The question of language, for example. I mean, I attach a lot of importance to it. As much as I can have complicity or intimacy with a Québécoise, at some moment I will want to speak my own language, I'll want to speak with references that she may not necessarily have. And so, these are questions and doubts that I have. The question of religion . . . *perso non* [personally, not important] . . . and would our wedding be traditional or not? I don't know [*laughs*].

After having lived in Montréal for more than a decade, Amir planned to settle in the city. There is ease in sharing a cultural repertoire, but he was assured his belief that Allah will decide on the origins of his future wife.

Other men saw transnational marriage as less than ideal but better than nothing. I was introduced to Ali, forty-four, through his cousin, whom I had met at the Algerian Cultural Centre in Montréal. Ali's large brown eyes and what appeared as dyed-black hair made him look both younger and older than he was. Ali was a tall, lanky man who had completed a PhD in computer engineering in Algiers and had lived in both cities working for a tech company for more than fifteen years. On a warm afternoon sitting on a picnic table during his lunch break, Ali explained that, after hoping and trying to meet a woman in a more traditional arrangement in Montréal the year before, he had given up and agreed to a transnational match, coordinated by his maternal aunts and mother "back home." Ali emphasized that this arrangement was not his first choice: "I *really* looked here before, before I was introduced to someone [in Algeria], but I couldn't find anyone. It's not easy here. Québec is big and the majority of women my age already come here in relationships [*en couple*]." We spoke in July 2018, a month after he had traveled to settle his engagement. They had met in person and agreed upon the match. He was scheduled to return over his holidays in December for the legal wedding and to begin the sponsorship process. In his case, it was his sister and mother who knew the family of the *fille* he had agreed to marry.[10] In his telling, Ali seemed to be rallying himself for the administrative work that lay ahead but was pleased with the prospect of this marriage.

Meeting eligible women for marital arrangements in Québec was challenging. Houcine, forty-four and a civil engineer, had sought a transnational marriage two years after settling in Montréal in 2003. With few work prospects in Algeria, he had applied for permanent residency in Québec. The process took two and a half years. He migrated to Montréal alone, excited for the challenge. Houcine and I met several times in the reception area of the Algerian Cultural Centre, located on the third floor of an office building on the rue Jean-Talon Est, in the northeast part of the city, not far from the Petit Maghreb neighborhood. Houcine had a quiet and kind demeanor. He volunteered at the reception desk every Monday night. He felt grateful for this opportunity, particularly because he identified as nonreligious and was not practicing. The first time we met, when I undertook preliminary fieldwork in Montréal in May 2016, he noted how he made a point of changing out of his business suits into a track suit when he volunteered, to "set the mood" as relaxed and comfortable at the entry of the association. When I first shared the topic of my research project, Houcine had been hesitant to share his story. "It's just so boring," he stressed. "I don't want to waste your time." In retrospect, the implication in his reluctance was that because his marriage was not based on "romance," it was somehow less interesting to tell.

A year later, in the summer of 2019, after we had crossed paths a few more times, he agreed to be interviewed. As he leaned back in the swivel chair in the reception area, he recalled how, when he arrived in Montréal, he took "every course I could take," having heard that local accreditation would be important to find well-paying work. Once established, Houcine was lonely. He was the eleventh of twelve children and had never lived alone: "It was painful. I missed my nephews and nieces especially." He felt ready to start his own family. Unlike Ali, Houcine appreciated the orchestration of his love life by his family members abroad. He smiled when he described his mother's adeptness at matchmaking. *La candidate*, Basira, lived about 200 kilometers east of his hometown. Despite his dislike of plane travel and the cost, Houcine made four trips from Montréal within the year: to meet her, for the religious marriage, when the paperwork was secured and he could begin the sponsorship process, and for their marriage celebration with their families and friends. While many only have one party to mitigate the costs, he pointed out how the series of parties allowed him and Basira to get to know each other better over the year, prior to the stresses of living together abroad in Montréal.

When she arrived in Montréal, Basira completed training in early childhood education and found work in a daycare, a common employment entry point for women settling from Algeria in the city. To their great regret, Houcine and Basira were never able to have children. While they prayed for many years, eventually, he said, he focused his attention on his volunteering role at the Algerian Cultural Centre. Another benefit of fewer constraints on their finances was that the couple traveled to Algeria annually.

Younes, Youcine, Amir, Ali, and Houcine in Montréal vested importance in the Algerianness of their marriage partners. So too did men in Petit-Nanterre, but with one significant difference: the geographical specificities of Algeria were more salient among interlocutors there—that is, the region (especially when it was Kabylia), town, or city mattered. For instance, Azdi, twenty-four, born in Petit-Nanterre, knew he would marry a Kabylian. I first met Azdi a few years before our formal interview at an after-school program where I volunteered. His mother, Nesrine, whom I had also interviewed, felt strongly that I should meet this son (she had three; Azdi was the only one married to date), perhaps because her transnational marriage experience contrasted with her son's.

Nesrine had had a forced and unhappy marriage, which ended with the death of her husband, twenty years her senior. She married in Algeria when she was nineteen and immigrated to Petit-Nanterre. Her marriage story is mired in domestic violence. She explained that once she accepted her life in Petit-Nanterre, learned some words in French, and had the companionship of her three sons, she felt happier. Her husband died in his early sixties, making Nesrine's life both easier and infinitely more difficult. In our two-hour interview in December 2015, I asked Nesrine whether she experienced scrutiny of her forced marriage at the border. Laws introduced beginning in 2006 might have impeded a union like hers. She shook her head vigorously. She would not have admitted to an agent that she had not consented to the marriage. Her family's reputation was on the line and she spoke little French at that time. Thanks to the local community center where she attended drop-in activities, and to watching French television, she gained fluency in French.

Nesrine insisted that this March 2016 interview take place after a *bon couscous* she had prepared for the three of us for lunch; I brought along a bakery-bought cake. Seeing them together in the familial apartment made it clear that Azdi and his mom were close. They spoke a mix of French and Tamazight. Because he worked full time at a youth center across from the high-rise apartment where she lived, they often ate lunch together. Azdi had married three years earlier and now lived in a neighboring suburb with his wife, Thiziri, also twenty-four. After lunch, Nesrine declared she wanted to give us privacy and feigned busy-ness in her small kitchen while Azdi and I spoke. More than once, she was not able to contain herself and shouted information from the kitchen when Azdi had forgotten a detail, like on the order of events on their wedding day.

Azdi had lived in Petit-Nanterre his whole life. He was a diminutive young man known for his quick smile, his kindness, and his growing beard. When asked, Azdi self-identified as a *Franco-Algérien* and as a practicing Muslim. Attending Friday prayers and observing Ramadan were important to him. When I asked him how he envisioned marriage, he explained that he knew he wanted to marry a woman of Algerian origin, but, like his friend Ilias, he was not interested in brokering the cultural differences and administrative hurdles of a transnational match. He sought to avoid the traumas, migration, and power differentials he had observed in his parents' marriage. Azdi knew Thiziri from high school. The Bled's ethnocultural specificity—here, Kabylian culture—played a significant role in their union, despite his emphasis on the destined romantic nature of it. He insisted: "L'amour il a frappé là. J'ai pas choisi !" (Love struck. I didn't choose!)

Like Ilias's wife, Zara, Thiziri had migrated from Algeria to France with her parents as a toddler. Azdi laughed when he recalled speaking to her father about the wedding proposal. According to Azdi, Thiziri's father's sole condition was that she marry someone from Kabylia: "Once he knew that, he said, 'If my daughter says yes, good for you. If she says no, well, life goes on!'" Nesrine again intervened from the kitchen to explain how she had pushed the couple to hold the celebrations in Tizi Ouzou, the Kabylian capital where she and her deceased husband were from. Azdi and Thiziri preferred to rent a hall in France, within driving distance of Petit-Nanterre, so that their friends could attend. After I turned off my voice recorder, Nesrine pulled out a photo album of Azdi and Thiziri's wedding day from a tall cabinet in the living room. Seated on the same couch, the three of us scrutinized each photo. Azdi was proud of their elaborate photo shoot, and now amused at the seriousness of their poses. Their wedding had been *la classe* (very classy). The couple had saved and borrowed money to pay for it themselves and had spared no expense on the flowers and outfits, incorporating what he saw as French and Kabylian styles. Thiziri wore a white princess dress and an orange-colored Kabylian dress. Azdi wore a tuxedo. They hired an Algerian caterer. For this young couple, references to the Bled acted as receptacles of family lineage. Again, Thiziri was an ideal partner for Azdi: she understood the continued cultural practices, but she was not as vulnerable as Nesrine or Ilias's mother had been as young foreign nationals in *rapports de force* (power differentials).

THE BLED AND WOMEN OF ALGERIAN ORIGIN

The notion of the Bled differed significantly for many of the women I interviewed, both for travel and for marriage partners. For women like Hala, fifty-three, imagining her older years in Algeria was difficult. As we drank herbal tea at a shopping-mall food court in Laval, just outside of Montréal, she explained how her husband, who was ten years her senior, would retire in two years, and dreamed of returning to his hometown in the winters to escape the cold. The couple did not share children (he did from a previous marriage, but all three were now adults). Hala agreed on the cold, but in our conversation, she outlined her hesitancy to leave her federal government job, give up driving (I drove with her on a handful of occasions—she was an excellent driver), and live closer to her family (from whom she was estranged since her previous divorce). She also noted the preparatory work that the return trips took for her. With every trip, she felt pressure to purchase gifts and undertake care work among their relatives when she was there, not unlike a depiction from *Algé-rien de France* by the cartoonist Gyps (Karim Mahfouf) ([1998] 2009).[11] His graphic novel captures the emotions and pressures of the trips by car from France, and the critiques of the immigrants' expectations, their money, their gifts, and even their presence. And yet, despite all the work it took to arrive, once there, leaving was also difficult.

I interviewed several women who had immigrated to France from Algeria as transnational brides. I met Chifia, thirty, through her mother-in-law, whom I knew from a French-language class in Petit-Nanterre where I had volunteered over a twelve-year period. Chifia preferred to meet outside her small apartment. We met in early 2016 for a coffee at the Pomme de Pain café in the La Défense shopping center. Chifia explained in her own words why she had agreed to marry Samir and migrate to this Parisian banlieue seven years earlier. Samir was a second-generation officer who commuted to the central police station in Paris's fifteenth arrondissement. Samir was not practicing and grew up with one younger sister in a household Chifia described as "completely open" with regards to their agnosticism. She explained that it was his mother who insisted on a *Blédarde* (a woman from the Bled) as a marriage partner, specifying she did not want a woman who wore hijab. Samir's mother wanted for her son a woman who would ensure a transnational link for him in his adult life but be "modern" enough to thrive in France. Reserved and well-spoken, Chifia explained her take on the criteria involved in deeming her the best option:

> They [Samir's parents] really wanted that the woman be, I mean, of Kabylian origin, of Algerian origin and everything, so that she can understand them. So that she can be completely in the same mentality as them. . . .
>
> If she [her mother-in-law] brings him back a girl from there she knows she can mold her however she wants. She can talk to her however she wants, she can . . . tell her what she wants. And since, too, we're from the same region, it's the same and everything, it's like she's married a family girl. So, she can speak frankly with her without being judged or anything.

As we have seen, mothers influenced these arrangements. The groom's mother's desire for a *Blédarde* ensured a compliant daughter-in-law with whom she could be at ease in speaking *franchement*. Chifia understood cultural kinship codes and respected her mother-in-law's authority. That she was Kabylian, did not wear hijab, and (while this went unstated) was not racialized as Black, mattered. Religiosity was not articulated as central to this match. Chifia was familiar with the preparation and presentation of flavors, spices, and specific dishes from the same region as Samir's parents. She and Samir lived in their own apartment, but given that they did not (yet) have children, Chifia and her mother-in-law spent time together. Again, these were gendered preferences: no one worried about the cooking skills of Algerian-born men who migrated for marriage.

Farida, thirty-one, migrated to Montréal in 2015 for a transnational arranged marriage to her husband, Slimane, who was also born in Algeria. She was on maternity leave with her first child at the time of our interview in the summer of 2018. Seated on a stool in her apartment kitchen in the Saint-Léonard neighborhood, in the central-northern part of the island, where she lived with Slimane and their son, she explained how her sponsorship application had moved quickly, despite the federal clampdown on transnational marriage in 2006 that I discuss in chapter 3. Farida was unaware at the time that greater barriers had been introduced, capturing how impediments to "bad faith" marriage may have been more symbolic than actual. Farida was granted permanent residency four months after their legal marriage in Algeria. She considered herself a cultural, nonpracticing Muslim. She described her husband Slimane in loving and glowing terms (I did not meet him, as he was at work and expressed no interest in being interviewed). Her primary complaint postmigration had been the challenge of finding suitable work. Farida held a diploma in commercial sales, completed in Algeria, but she had not found comparable work in Montréal. She attributed this struggle to her difficulty in mastering French.

She shared that she had met Slimane online on a dating website and that they connected through food:

> [I know] when my husband fell in love with me—he told me because I asked him—he told me on the sixth day we spoke on Skype. I had asked him, "So what have you eaten today?" He told me, "I ate *boureks à la viande hachée* [fried rolls with minced meat]." It's a traditional Algerian dish. And he said to me, "Oh damn [*putain*], I can say *boureks* and you understand what I mean!"
> Like, it's just, in everyday life, we don't need to change it [our way of speaking, of being] for someone. He told me, "You got it. And there I fell in love." He told me, "That's the detail," I swear [*je te jure*]. Because he had dated Québécoises. They're great to live with, but he feels more comfortable with me. . . . It's not a question of religion, it's a question of how we are.

The specificity of their mutual love for *boureks* was meaningful for Slimane, who had grown up in Montréal in a culturally Algerian home. When asked how she mustered the courage to move to Montréal to marry someone whom she had initially only met online, her tone became coy: "The only thing that matters to me," she noted, "is that a man is circumcised." She continued, matter-of-factly, over tea and while her baby napped: "It's a detail maybe, but for me, no way. Now, whether he's a Muslim, Christian, Jew, I don't care [*je m'en fous*]. Just about the circumcision." With this lurid detail, Farida suggested that the specificities of religion had less bearing on their connection. Their shared love of Algerian culture and his circumcision mattered more. This detail also produced a shock factor that she seemed to enjoy; it countered the imagined narrative of transnational brides as sexually inexperienced.

While Farida painted her migratory experience only positively, women who migrated to France shared their disappointments regarding the promise of postmigration cosmopolitanism. Amel's Ghazaouet-born sister-in-law, Sara, is an example of a bride who experienced this frustration. Sara had excelled in her high school studies, winning a scholarship to attend university in nearby Tlemcen, where she studied and again shone in English- and French-language studies. She wore stylish light and colorful hijabs and

Figure 4.2. Eiffel Tower and snow globe figurines, July 2016. Photo by the author (taken with permission).

took a lot of care with her makeup and clothing choices. Sara's beauty and French-language skills were surely qualities that bolstered her transnational marriageability. She met her husband Rayan through her younger brother, as they played pickup soccer together when Rayan was in Ghazaouet on holidays. More practically, marrying Amel's brother would allow her to send remittances to her family.

My visit to Sara's parents' apartment in Ghazaouet made evident how Sara's education and life in France also reflected her mother's dreams. Her mother served tea and *tcherek m'saker*, delicious almond-flour-based sugar-coated cookies shaped in elegant crescents, when I arrived with Sara and two of Amel's cousins. They accepted the modest bottle of maple syrup I had purchased at Carrefour in Paris, as though it came from Québec.[12] The older couple were clearly pleased to host Sara and their son-in-law from northern France, who were staying with them for a few days to attend the wedding. Her mother had stopped attending school at age twelve and had some rudimentary French-language skills. She was a homemaker. The family lived in a second-floor apartment. Their living room was sparsely furnished, with a long couch and some kitchen chairs. Her mother and I made small talk about Amel's upcoming wedding. I noticed a small metal Eiffel Tower knickknack and a separate Eiffel Tower snow globe displayed prominently on a low armoire near the door to the kitchen. "Have you visited your daughter in France?" I asked, gesturing toward the souvenirs (she allowed me to take the photograph in figure 4.2). "No, not yet," she responded. "But we really hope to, one day." Her joy in describing her daughter's life in France was evident.

"I hope my son will go to Paris to study," she added, pointing to the sixteen-year-old lounging with his long legs hanging off the chesterfield, Game Boy in hand. "One day I will visit the Eiffel Tower with my children," she stated. Her son acknowledged us but remained embroiled in his game. While invoked with these ornaments, Paris felt very far away.

Sara described her marriage match with Rayan as destined but also knew that because of her husband's close ties to Ghazaouet, she would continue to return to see her family, even if she had limited funds to do so.[13] Her marriage migration also ignited familial aspirations. Her mother might have the opportunity to see the Eiffel Tower in Paris in person. Women like Chifia, Farida, and Sara who accepted transnational unions that involved migrating to France and Québec did so for a number of reasons, which included but were not solely economically framed, as they are often imagined.

While a minority, eight of my female participants in France sponsored Algerian-born male partners. In the remainder of this section I focus on two, Amel and Dalia, to consider differing gender politics they navigated. In sharp contrast with Maya, with whom I opened this chapter, Amel and Dalia's preferences for *Blédard* spouses reflect the importance of transnational kinship ties, religiosity, and gendered cultural expectations at the time of marriage.

Amel, twenty-five, clearly privileged kinship ties in her marriage to Yacine, twenty-six, of Ghazaouet. Amel's marriage followed a familiar familial pattern. Amel's mother, Wafa, had had a failed transnational marriage to Amel's father, who was born in France. Amel's older brother Rayan had wed Sara, also from Ghazaouet. The family's continued ties to this western Algerian city may have been destined, but they also had practical benefits. Born in northern France, Amel, for as long as she could remember, had spent summer holidays at her maternal grandmother's home in this small seaside city not far from the Moroccan border. Coinciding with her nonpracticing father's departure in her early teens—leaving her mother alone to raise five children—Algerian familial ties and Amel's religious practice took on greater meaning for her. Her father's whereabouts were unclear. Thanks to support from some female friends and information from the internet, Amel became more invested in Islam and began wearing hijab in high school (though not *at* high school because of the 2004 law). Amel had since maintained strong ties with her mother's family and, unlike her three younger siblings, was fluent in Arabic. Given her mother Wafa's limited earnings as an office cleaner, Amel saved her teenage earnings babysitting and working fast-food jobs for plane tickets. Returning to Ghazaouet had been a lifelong touchstone for her. She returned every summer for at least a month.

Amel's transnational life meant that, in real ways, she lived two lives. Summer days in her grandmother's breezy multigenerational three-story concrete home in western Algeria differed significantly from her life as a single working woman living alone in a small student-only studio residence just outside Petit-Nanterre. Family life in Ghazaouet revolved around playing with and caring for her younger cousins (their mother, one of Amel's mother's sisters, had a degenerative disease and was bedridden), laughing and visiting with her cousins, keeping house, schlepping and hanging clothes to dry on the flat roof's clothesline, and preparing and washing up after large shared meals. In the five days before her wedding, in addition to the four adults and two children who typically lived in her grandmother's house, more than twenty additional family members slept on floor mats and ate together at makeshift white plastic tables set up in the cooler lower-level garage.[14] Amel's life outside Paris was also busy, but there her days were filled by two paid jobs, shopping at La Défense, seeing movies with her friends, traveling solo by metro, and eating ready-made meals in the evenings alone in her studio apartment.

Amel met Yacine during her annual summer visit two years before their wedding. Following the death of her maternal grandfather, her grandmother had moved the three-generational household next door to his parents' home. This move had improved the possibility of their "destined" arrangement. While I had heard about him and even corresponded by email with him over several months, I met Yacine for the first time in person briefly on the evening of the wedding party. By all accounts, he was a very suitable marriage candidate: he was a generous and attentive host. He had completed some university education in the nearby city of Tlemcen, spoke some French, and was open to migrating to her Parisian suburb, a move understood in the match. Amel especially appreciated that he was at ease in boisterous familial environs like her grandmother's home. Yacine's family was middle class by Ghazaouet standards, but it was clear that his potential euro earnings and remittances would be beneficial for his parents and younger siblings. Yacine's specific ties to Ghazaouet (and this street) also ensured that, after their marriage, Amel would continue to be a presence in her grandmother's house. In a number of ways, their union sealed her transnational life. Yacine was now her husband, but he was also a bridge between Algeria and France. Amel successfully orchestrated most of the wedding arrangements single-handedly with a maternal uncle standing in for their fatiha, or religious marriage contract, in the absence of her father.[15]

Still, tensions arose around a few ritual components. Negotiation around Amel's wedding attire in Ghazaouet launched an eight-month debate on the order of the dresses for the wedding party. Amel's mother, Wafa, fifty-six, may have held regrets about her own choices. One evening in Ghazaouet, as we washed and peeled potatoes preparing to make French fries for the large group staying with Amel's grandmother, Wafa told me she was glad her daughter was not moving into her in-laws' home, as she had done after her own wedding and migration: "I worked in their home from morning to night, doing exactly what she [her mother-in-law] said"; "I was like a slave." Her relationship with her husband was never positive, making for challenging years when her French-language skills were weak and she had young children. He had been physically violent and controlling and had left offering no subsequent support when her youngest children, twins, were eight years old. Wafa then religiously divorced him. Despite the seemingly negative outcome of her migration, her oldest son, Amel's brother Rayan, and now Amel, had both formed transnational unions with Algerians from Wafa's hometown, having met and arranged them during summer visits.

Debate emerged between mother and daughter related to a white princess dress, to be paired with a tall silver crown and attached white hijab. Amel wanted to wear the white gown first. It would be most visible, in the car procession around the city, and as she arrived at the venue where they would host the event. As this Algerian seaside photograph of a recently married couple by Bruno Boudjelal (fig. 4.3) captures, following international bridal trends, the white dress has become popular as the primary wedding dress. For Amel, the princess gown was a marker of her sophistication and Frenchness; it would also be easier to wear in the July heat. In contrast, her mother, her aunts in Algeria, and her grandmother insisted she wear a traditional chedda (see fig. 4.4). For Wafa, the chedda ensured custom and decorum, likely deemed vulnerable because Amel's was a transnational marriage and she was born in France. The debate about the chedda centered on proper tradition and decorum.

Given their cost, Amel rented her chedda and accessories from Djouer, a hired wedding coordinator who was also a makeup artist, hairstylist, dresser, and personal assistant in Ghazaouet. Djouer's role as a ritual expert, especially in ensuring that the chedda was worn first, cannot be discounted. Amel's responses to her mother's, aunts', and grandmother's calls for tradition were reactive; she saw them as lodged in the past. As a third party and a professional aware of local trends and fashions, Djouer was a more effective enforcer of marital tradition. On the day of the wedding, as she finished applying her makeup, Djouer coached Amel: "You must be your most beautiful and presentable as you enter the hall. We [have] all found the chedda's weight difficult." These words were repeated by Djouer that evening in French in the dressing room at the hall, perhaps to translate the point and to rally my support. As Amel left the upstairs bedroom at her grandmother's house to walk down the stairs toward the

Figure 4.3. "Algerian Wedding," Zéralda, Algeria, 2012. Photo by Bruno Boudjelal, Agence VU.

event, Djouer stressed, "Elle est lourde avec la tradition" (It's heavy with tradition).

In the half dozen family events where we met, I observed that, for Wafa, her five children's social acceptability in her Algerian hometown mattered a great deal to her. To this end, Wafa appeared to avoid any action or conversation that might be perceived as reinforcing stereotypes of migrants to France, namely of those who returned to the Bled with suitcases (and sometimes cars and trailers) filled with sought-after household goods and gifts, or airs of pretention, judging the practices and habits of those left behind. Wafa had worn a chedda first at her own arranged transnational wedding to Amel's French-born Algerian-origin father, as did her mother and grandmother in Ghazaouet before her. So, Wafa decided, would her first-born daughter. Amel entered the debate in a weak position: she wanted to marry a "traditional" Algerian in Algeria. In agreeing to celebrate the wedding in Ghazaouet, she had already implicitly accepted an unstated family contract: the "traditional trappings" of a family-focused Algerian wedding. Ultimately, Amel conceded to wear the chedda first, seemingly as a gesture of belonging.

In contrast, Dalia married her husband of Algerian origin in Petit-Nanterre. Like many wedding stories, in choosing her marriage partner Dalia, forty-three at the time of our interview, negotiated a number of factors: an expressed desire by her parents to see her marry an Algerian; her five siblings' urging that premarital social and sexual interactions be

Figure 4.4. Amel wearing her rented chedda at her grandmother's home in Ghazaouet, Algeria, on her wedding party day, July 2016. Photo by the author.

restricted; her own aspiration to marry a "modern" man whom she loved and with whom she shared the same religious background; and the state's interest in the timing of her halal or religious marriage and in controlling the citizenship status of her husband-to-be.

When we met in the spring of 2014, Dalia was a sophisticated and well-spoken mother of three. Exceptionally, our interview took place with three other women one rainy Saturday morning in the same community center space where I had interviewed Ilias. Over instant coffees, fruit and pastries, two babies and a handful of young children running around, she, the other women, and I shared a laughter-filled morning, thanks in good part to another woman's lewd stories about her first sexual encounter with her now-husband. These intimacies set a conspiratorial and fun tone, perhaps inspiring Dalia to share the pushback she had received from her gynecologist when she requested a virginity certificate, as well as to tell her own transnational marriage story. Dalia had been prescribed birth control pills to regulate painful menstrual cramps when she was a teenager. To preclude suspicion that she had taken them as a form of birth control, she had asked for a certificate from her non-Muslim gynecologist, with the idea of producing it if any questions emerged. The gynecologist had been reluctant but eventually signed a note. I did not ask participants about virginity certificates, but Dalia is my only participant who described having one. She did not end up sharing it.

Like many Algerian men of his generation, Dalia's father had migrated from Algeria to the then-shantytown of Petit-Nanterre in the early 1960s and later, once he had access to a social housing apartment, sponsored her mother in a traditional arrangement. Their six children were born and grew up in Petit-Nanterre. Childhood summer vacations revolved around long stays in the Bled. Identifying as Algerian and speaking its Arabic dialect were important to her. Dalia considered herself as *pratiquante* and began wearing hijab shortly after completing her university studies, a "bac + 3" (equivalent to an undergraduate degree) at the nearby Université Paris Nanterre. Twenty-three at the time, Dalia was looking for work but felt pressure to marry, to find the right match. She rolled her eyes as she described how her brothers "called me '*Madame, la princesse.*' Because the princess is very demanding." In addition, her mother had not been well, and she did not want to cause her stress; Dalia knew a good match would please her. At the time, Dalia's parents were unsuccessfully organizing meetings with Muslim men of Algerian origin in their apartment in Petit-Nanterre, a familial marital initiative she says was based on "une mentalité heu... à l'ancienne, quoi. Traditionnelle" (an old-style mentality. Traditional). Four young men and their parents had visited the family's apartment, each visit preceded by exhaustive cleaning and the preparation of elaborate Algerian-style baked goods and tea. These candidates fit her family's criteria but not her own longing for a love-based match.

Dalia smiled as she described her confusion when she first met her fair, blue-eyed Algerian-born husband, then undertaking engineering studies, in a food court at the La Défense shopping center a ten-minute bus ride from Petit-Nanterre. Dalia conveyed her excitement telling how, one early evening while she was with friends sitting in the food court, she met a suitable candidate on her own terms, *and* while she wore hijab. This combination was important because she sometimes took it off, and she wanted to ensure that her religious and cultural beliefs were clear to any potential suitors.

[When we first met,] my husband introduced himself as "Alain." Because at the beginning, it's true, I told myself he must be half-French, half-Algerian because he has blue eyes. I said to myself, "He's white!"

So I told my friend, "His name's Alain. Drop it." . . . [But] he was joking with me when he told me his first name. After he told me, "My name's Abdelkader." [*Laughs*]

Well, that changes everything! And then he told me he's from Maghnia, the city that's not far from where my parents are from. And I told him, "Listen. Here's how it's going to be: It's not, I'm not an easy kind of girl. I have brothers who are behind me." And so, what happened was that within a month we talked about marriage.

Abdelkader's first name and Bled connection "changed everything!" for Dalia. If it worked out, theirs would be a transnational endogamous union. Dalia's narrative did not explicitly name Algeria as a criterion, but she did express a desire for "traditionalism" that she considered impossible with a non-Muslim, French-born *Alain*. Abdelkader's perceived whiteness also rendered him unavailable but, admittedly, attractive to her. That Abdelkader was educated, fluent in French and in the social norms of Maghnia, and, she made sure to mention, "handsome," were further evidence their union was mektoub (destiny). They exchanged phone numbers, but she made it immediately clear she was not interested in dating casually; her goal was marriage.

Secrets and lies on Dalia and Abdelkader's wedding day in France capture the real and imagined borders of their potential union, particularly reflected in their parents' emotions and actions on that day. The wedding took place before the heightened surveillance of "love fraud" through transnational marriage by the French state in 2006, but still, Abdelkader's simultaneous migration and potential citizenship were sites of familial tension as they wed. He was in France with a student visa. He came from a large family, but few were able to travel to Petit-Nanterre. Abdelkader had one sister also studying in Paris, and his parents were able to procure visas and afford the plane tickets to travel from Maghnia to attend. According to Dalia, her in-laws were anxious about the civil ceremony. The religious ceremony was no issue: their fathers had signed a *nikah* (Islamic marriage certificate) privately with an imam the day before. They had a civil marriage scheduled, which is likely why the imam agreed to the religious marriage without the certificate. Most significant, because the civil marriage ignited tension around Abdelkader's marital motivations, the couple sought to separate themselves from a discourse of expedited immigration by focusing solely on the religious part of their union.

For this reason—and a key moment in their transnational wedding story—Dalia and Abdelkader *skipped* their scheduled civil marriage appointment at the local mayor's office on the day of the formal celebrations. Concerned that their son might be perceived as aiming for expedited entry through a fraudulent marriage, his parents sought to disassociate themselves from any part of the ritual where they could be seen as interlopers. At the same time, because her parents had insisted on the legality of the union, Dalia lied to them and said they *had* stopped to get their legal papers at the *mairie* (city hall) before arriving at the wedding party. His parents were clearly aware of this choice; she revealed the lie to her parents only a few weeks after the wedding.

Dalia explained that on the "jour J [big day], . . . Mon mari il se sentait comme . . . comme [si] on . . . on ne lui fait pas confiance" (My husband felt like we didn't have faith in him), that his intentions could be fraudulent. Given that his student visa was soon to expire, Abdelkader felt stigma around *mariage gris*, or love fraud with a migratory aim. His stalling to go to the *mairie* was thus a gesture to demonstrate that the paperwork was not his first priority. Abdelkader wanted the guests to see the romance of their union so as to alleviate these fears; the "irrational" gesture of skipping the civil union was part of this performance of love. His parents concurred that the religious part of the wedding needed to take precedence over the civil and legal one; they too sought to separate themselves from a discourse of expedited emigration to France. In general, male interlocutors in Petit-Nanterre and Montréal who sponsored Algerian-origin brides did not feel compelled to ensure that immigration was not part of the wedding as Amel and Dalia did.

Despite these competing pressures from their parents, it went without saying that Dalia would sponsor her husband for permanent residency in France. The civil marriage did take place two months later, at her father's insistence, to protect, in Dalia's words, her "legal interests and reputation." The couple then contended with state-influenced concerns around their trans-Mediterranean union. That he only had a few months left remaining on his student visa meant they could not ignore these administrative procedures.

For Dalia, the Bled was both a real and imagined concept when she married Abdelkader. It was real in the legal implications of their transnational union, and imagined in the cultural lineage he brought to their marriage and future family. Key to their subsequent marriage was that he was from Algeria, and specifically from Maghnia. His French engineering degree, social class, exotic fairness, and kinship links to the same region from where her parents migrated further enabled the destined nature of their union.

In contrast, I had only one participant from Montréal, Sabrina, who contemplated this kind of transnational marital arrangement. In both places, men's motivations for accepting a transnational union were under less scrutiny than those of women. Both Amel and Dalia were regularly questioned in their entourage, directly and in "jokes," on their spouses' motives for these unions. Again, in Dalia and Abdelkader's case, the sense of scrutiny was intense enough that they forwent their scheduled civil wedding ceremony and pretended they had gone to the city hall. In the critiques of transnational grooms, a common concern was whether new male migrants would find suitable work in France or Québec, and whether they would accept France's more liberal gender politics. Again, fewer concerns emerged among family members and friends as to whether women would find good paid work or adapt to the new sociocultural context, likely because of expectations that their future lives in France or Québec would revolve around maternity and childcare.

THE BLED AMONG ALGERIAN-ORIGIN WOMEN IN QUÉBEC

The contexts of their migration shaped the experiences of women in Québec differently. Contrasting Amel and Dalia's sponsorship of transnational grooms with six women of Algerian origin in Montréal—Sabrina, Imane, Selena, Samar, Nour, and Maya (whom we met at the opening of this chapter)—captures how the Bled is less positively framed for women of

Algerian origin in Canada. Certainly, there are practical concerns: it costs more to fly to Algeria from Québec; and, depending on the time of year, there is a five- or six-hour time difference between Montréal and Algiers, and only a one-hour difference with Paris. Women of Algerian origin in Québec articulated criticisms of the religious and gender politics of Algeria and the violence of the Décennie noire to a far greater extent than men. They were not as keen to maintain ties that would ensure regular contact. Recall Maya, whose ties to France and feelings of separation from Québécois culture influenced her choice of a French-origin marriage partner. She was not keen to return to Algeria after her last visit as a teenager.

Sabrina, thirty-three, was one outlier. Generally, her feelings about the Bled were mixed. Sabrina had lived in Montréal for one year when we first met in July 2018 on a daylong bus excursion to Ontario organized by the Algerian Cultural Centre. She was soft-spoken but confident. Sabrina grew up in Tlemcen. While attending university and living with her parents, she applied for permanent residency to immigrate alone. Her main motivation, she said, was for "a big adventure." It took six years for her application to come together and be approved. This dream did not materialize out of thin air: immigration to Québec had also been her father's dream. But as a professor of geology in Tlemcen, he had visited but never settled, despite decades-long attempts to secure a permanent academic position in Québec. His desire to immigrate peaked after surviving a terrorist attack on a bus during the Décennie noire. But he did not want to migrate without a job secured. His unexpected death of a heart attack in his sixties emboldened Sabrina to risk migration solo.

She smiled as she noted how her plans had shielded her from her mother's insistence that she marry in Tlemcen. Sabrina hit the ground running in Montréal. She completed a master's degree in management prior to immigrating and had excellent fluency in French. She quickly found full-time work as a project coordinator in a small architectural firm. She rented a two-bedroom apartment in the Ahuntsic neighborhood in the northern part of the island so her younger sister could join her to begin studies at the Université de Montréal in public relations (her older brother had married in Tlemcen and was settled). Her mother visited her daughters in Montréal for extended periods thanks to a long-term travel visa.

When we met, Sabrina said she felt ready to marry. She was in her early thirties. She wanted to have children. At the same time, preferring a more traditional arrangement, she did not want to date. Meeting a potential match in Montréal had been more difficult than she expected. "I mean, look at me!" she said exasperatedly during one of our two formal interviews in 2019, gesturing to her body. She was, in her words, "invisible" when she circulated in the city. She surmised that because she did not wear hijab and dressed conservatively, but not in an "Oriental" style, men found it difficult to "read" her: Was she Muslim? Was she Arab? She was light-skinned, with long, dark brown wavy hair, which made some question her background. Sometimes she was mistaken for Italian or Portuguese. More than once, men of Maghrebian origin had asked her whether she was Arab or Kabylian. With frustration in her voice, she explained that the question was not about ethnic origin or geography. It masked sexual politics: Kabylians, she said, are known in Québec as less practicing, and more likely to drink alcohol, and be open to dating and sex before marriage. Not only did Sabrina find the question offensive, but, as I mentioned briefly in the introduction, she eschewed the Kabylian/Arab division. She saw it as separating Algerians in ways that had led to violence.

When I saw Sabrina in 2019, she remained disappointed by her prospects. Before immigrating, she had imagined an abundance of cosmopolitan, practicing Muslim men of Algerian origin in Montréal. But "here, everything is blocked [*bloqué*]. I haven't met anyone. And when I'm on the subway or even walking, no one talks to me." She needed to take matters into her own hands: "You know, Jennifer, if things continue like this [i.e., not meeting someone], I'll definitely have to go back for someone. I won't have much choice."

Over hummus and a falafel plate at the Jean Talon market on a Sunday evening, Sabrina seemed to grow bolder in her position; she felt she could no longer be passive. She knew she wanted to marry a Muslim, but whether her potential groom was Algerian was becoming less important. With her sister hoping to stay in Montréal after her studies and her mother visiting often, Sabrina did not feel especially tied to Tlemcen, not the way Amel, from Petit-Nanterre, was with Ghazaouet. Sabrina saw no need to secure a transnational bridge. In addition, she had reservations about a transnational partner: Could she support this person, complete the arduous paperwork and find him work? Would this person accept a small and intimate wedding in Montréal, rather than a large gathering in Algeria? "J'aime pas les protocols" (I don't like protocols/expectations), she stressed. She felt intimidated to browse online for a potential marriage partner and was ready to turn to her mother to broker a match. We met again after the pandemic at a café near the Université de Montréal in June 2023. Amel had not returned to Algeria but in 2021 had met and married her husband, of Algerian origin, through mutual friends. He had lived in the city for a half-dozen years before they met and did not need to be sponsored. She was really pleased by this turn of events.

Common-law relationships were more common among my female interlocutors in Montréal.[16] Recall Imane, forty-five, introduced in chapter 3, who married religiously but not civilly. Reflecting her personal story and geography and distance from Algeria, the particularities of her husband's Algerianness (i.e., his family there, his city of origin) did not matter to her. A more common situation was captured by Selena, twenty-six, who had migrated to Montréal as a refugee when she was three years old. Selena's relationship was more typical of the young women in Montréal in my sample who had "mixed" (with non-Algerians) and common-law relationships. Selena's father had been a journalist who felt his life in Tlemcen was in danger. She had two older sisters, who were ten and seventeen years old when they left. The family spent one year in France before migrating to Montréal.

Selena and I met in her one-bedroom apartment in the city's eastern Francophone neighborhood of Hochelaga while she prepared dinner. Her partner was home but studying in the bedroom with noise-canceling headphones. Unbeknown to her parents, at the time of our interview, she was living with her white, atheist, Québec-born boyfriend, Gabriel. Selena and Gabriel were both law students at the Université de Montréal; her parents understood she was living alone. She claimed she could not date an Algerian: "They're too macho. Well, maybe not the men here, but definitely the ones in Algeria." Later in the conversation she conceded that she had actually never dated anyone of Algerian origin but that this gender-based conservatism was her impression.

Now several months into it, the stress of her secret cohabitation arrangement was mounting. Selena described feeling "blocked" about what to do. She portrayed her parents as "political rebels" who, nevertheless, cared a great deal about social propriety and the perception of their daughters' social esteem, more than about religion. On Islam, she described how her family kept Eid traditions but "really tried to keep everything cultural. What was religious is really less present." Living "outside-of-marriage," especially with a white atheist, would not be OK for them. Moreover, the recent "traditional" marriage of her middle sister, Katia, had not helped her cause: "Katia [Selena's older sister], she really did everything traditional with her husband, who is a Muslim too. She lived with my parents until she got married. Me, I left my parents' house when I was nineteen to live with friends. So, I really haven't done the same thing. . . . Katia is really attached to Algerian culture, more than my parents! Even more than religion. My parents *loved* her wedding."

In a separate interview, her sister Katia explained that, yes, she and her now-husband did everything "dans les règles" (according to the rules) but that, "really, it wasn't following my parents' wishes, it was my own thing." Still, Selena and Katia's father had insisted on a symbolic dowry when Katia married as a sign of "cultural" respect. While they described themselves as nonpracticing, the lines between religious and cultural expectations were blurred.

For Selena, part of her fear of telling her parents about her living situation was that she could not imagine a possible compromise in wedding celebrations between her father, her partner (Gabriel), and his atheist family who lived in Drummondville, about 100 kilometers northeast of the city. "Better to avoid that conversation altogether!" she said, wincing. A traditional Algerian wedding with her family and Gabriel's would be impossible: "[Even] if I actually wanted to marry Gabriel, it would be so difficult. The traditions of Quebeckers are really not the same. For instance [*déjà*], for Gabriel and his family, there is no question that there would [have to] be an open bar with alcohol. But I can't do that because my aunts and my uncles and my father *vont capoter* [will freak out]. Honestly, a wedding day is really difficult to visualize. It would be really complex. All that stresses me out, so I prefer to not even think about it." Selena was focused on completing her law degree. But, because her parents assisted her financially with her studies and because she respected their opinions, she had a great deal to lose if she were forced to choose between her relationship with them and their financial help, and her life with Gabriel. She would wait until the right moment to tell her parents.

Samar's narrative captures a similar situation, in which, even though her parents were not directly involved in whom and how she married, she felt pressure to secure her parents' blessing (Shaw 2001: 323 calls these "arranged love marriages"). Samar, twenty-nine, had migrated with her family to Montréal as refugees from Algiers in 2000. Samar remembered the socioeconomic shift most sharply. In Algiers, her father had worked in government, and her mother had been an Arabic teacher; they had comfortable middle-class lives in a large house. But when they arrived in Montréal, the family relied on her father's salary as a taxi driver and moved into a two-bedroom apartment. It was a stressful transition.

Samar explained how she had dated non-Algerian, non-Muslim men before meeting her now-husband in high school. At the time of our interview, Samar, like Maya, was on maternity leave with her first baby from her job as an inventory analyst at a large grocery store. Now that her daughter was almost one, she had decided to start part-time business training. Samar did not wear hijab, saying she preferred to keep her religiosity private. For similar reasons, she and her now-husband had kept their teenage relationship secret from her parents for seven years. Her parents—her father especially—were far more conservative than his parents. She laughed when recalling all the efforts she went through to hide their relationship from her parents. When they finally decided they wanted to marry, she, her husband, and his parents went through the motions as though they had not known each other well before their engagement: "So, something a little amazing, and maybe I will surprise you a bit, but I dated him for seven years. For *seven years* my father wasn't aware we were together. I had known my partner's family for seven years, so we had to pretend that no one knew each other. And it's sad, but that's how it is. It was better to fulfill my father's will and do as he wants."

Samar said now that they were religiously and civilly married, their non-"halal" beginnings were no longer significant. But she would never tell her parents about their prior relationship. On several occasions she mentioned how much she had learned from her husband's family about "healthier" ways to live out Algerian traditions. She remarked that despite the fact her family and her now-husband's family had arrived as refugees in Montréal around the same time, they had very different settlement experiences. Because they were religiously visible, her mother had never secured work outside the home and her father did not advance professionally outside of the taxi business. Samar associated her parents' religiosity with a more challenging adaptation in Montréal.

The fifty-nine women of Algerian origin whom Julia, Kawtare, and I interviewed in Montréal thus expressed their coloniality and the prospect of transnational partners very differently from women in France and men in France and Québec. Of the three groups, these women's relationships to Algeria and the notion of the Bled were the most estranged, whether through their marriage partner preferences or in visits, as with Maya's pejorative characterization of Algerian (and Québécois) men and visits there. Expressions of coloniality at the time of marriage in this group were more sartorial, restricted to wedding dresses and party provisions. As we saw with Maya, when selecting multiple wedding dresses, several interlocutors sought "Oriental"-style gowns. So too, when Nour, thirty-four, a self-described atheist, married her now-husband, a non-Algerian whom she met online, she wore a princess white gown but also included styles that were not Algerian per se but, in her words, "Oriental." Nour specified that her dress was a Moroccan caftan that she styled with Indian-inspired jewelry: "But, it went together! It was [all] Oriental." Samar, twenty-nine, to whom we were just introduced, wore three "traditional" outfits, but she was not concerned with regional particularities in the food or dress at her celebration. Instead, she noted, "I wanted things to feel really traditional, so I only put on Algerian music."

The lack of Algerian specificity in the "Oriental" components introduced by married women in Montréal suggests that, for them, direct geographical or cultural connection to the Bled is less significant. Maya, Nour, and Samar invoke pancolonial ritual elements—dresses and music—to invoke the Oriental, and, in my reading, "perform coloniality" on their terms. Again, examining ritual-related decisions and constraints at weddings—whether through dress, food, processions, music, ceremonies, dances, gazes, and other forms of habitus—offers a window onto personal and collective values (cf. Stephenson 2015). For the Algerian-origin women I interviewed in Montréal, coloniality remains less entrenched in relationships or visits to the Bled and instead summons an ambiguous "Orient" *without* directly invoking the geography and history of the Bled.

French and Québécois Secular Bills and Coloniality

Colonial ties do not only appear on people's bodies and in their relationships. This last section takes a macro view and, building on the brief discussion of coloniality in chapter 3, locates ongoing structuring logics of colonialism in contemporary reports and laws on secularism in France and Québec. More specifically, I examine four state articulations of secularism in France and Québec since 2004 through a colonial lens—whether prefixed as anti-, de-, inter-, post-, or other—to reveal the extent to which these commissions and their recommendations, as well as one law on secularism in Québec, obscure how state control of religious symbols is tied to capitalism and long-standing settler colonial biopolitics. All four documents presume *terra nullius*. They also encapsulate "bad religion" through conspicuous religious symbols, which reinforces religion as ahistorical and apolitical. In so doing, these documents effectively excise colonialism from consideration. So too, the depictions of the "Nation du Québec" in media discussions surrounding Law 21 introduce a historical chronology that begins with the Quiet Revolution or accommodation debates in the 2000s, and not the colonialization of New France in the sixteenth century (Selby and Barras, forthcoming). In so doing, these laws and commissions effectively detether themselves from colonial pasts.

For brevity's sake I limit my comments to, in France, the Stasi Commission report (Stasi 2003) and the Gerin Commission report (Assemblée Nationale 2010), both named after their commissioners and both preceding the adoption of secular laws prohibiting conspicuous religious symbols in government offices and public schools (2004) and full-face veils in the public sphere (2011); and, in Québec, the Bouchard-Taylor report (2008) and Law 21 (2019) (see more on the introduction of these laws and their full titles in the introduction). The Bouchard-Taylor report first iterated the need for greater regulation of the secular in Québec and preceded four attempts to legislate against religious symbols. The Act Respecting the Laicity of the State, or Law 21, is the first passed and enforced law that regulates conspicuous religious symbols in Québec.

In the French context, neither report addresses the country's long history of colonialism. Of the two, the tone of the earlier and shorter seventy-eight-page Stasi Commission report (published in 2003) is not as triumphalist in how it imagines the "civilizing force" of the secular. Generally, it iterates that the history of laïcité in the country is *not* a "tale of an inexorable march toward progress" (Stasi 2003: 10). In its brief opening overview of secularism in France, the report includes a historical sketch that references "ambiguity" in the application of the "universal principle" of laïcité in Algeria, pointing to how Muslim and Jewish personal status law was introduced in Algeria's legal code to differentiate religious groups (Stasi 2003: 11–12; see also Surkis 2019). Still, there is no acknowledgment of the parallels of the forced removal of the veil from public schools and government offices (recommended by the commission and passed into law in 2004) with the compulsory unveiling as part of the "civilizing mission" of French Algeria. The Stasi Commission report also never names other ongoing *outre-mer* protectorates in the Caribbean, in New Caledonia, Mayotte, Réunion, and elsewhere, where the application of these laws is complicated by differing legal structures and histories.

Significantly, *pro*colonial legislation in France followed the implementation of the 2004 law. Legislation in 2005 imposed an obligation for public school teachers to teach "the positive role of the French presence overseas" and also included a yearlong public celebration of France's overseas departments. The proposal to officially celebrate colonialism ignited responses across the political spectrum. Christiane Taubira, a member of parliament for French Guyana and sponsor of a 2001 Taubira Law that recognized the slave trade and slavery as "crimes against humanity," was one of several protesters against these nationwide celebrations. The minister for overseas territories, Marie-Luce Penchard, answered, in response to critiques, that "2011 must not serve as an occasion to reinterpret history," insinuating that any critical reconsideration of colonialism constituted a rewriting of history. Shortly after, in 2012, the massacre of Algerians in Paris on October 17, 1961, was officially recognized by the state. In the altercations on that day, more than 100 protesters (presumably mostly Algerians) were killed by police, an event still remembered vividly by residents of Petit-Nanterre. Given the number of Algerians who lived in the city in 1961, a throughway boulevard in Nanterre had recently been renamed to remember the date (*Libération* 2011). Discussions of colonialism—particularly as they relate to the Algerian War of Independence—are typically absent from these accounts.

The content of the French 2004 law outlining undesirable religious symbols was sharpened in its focus on the unacceptability of full-face veils in the 658-page 2010 Gerin Commission report. Like that of the Stasi Commission, the Gerin Commission report was preceded by a similar "fact-finding" commission with a subsequent report and recommendations. It too invited experts to share their concerns regarding religious symbols. Again, those who wear these garments (i.e., Muslim-identified women) were mostly excluded and legislation impacting some of them followed (Assemblée Nationale 2011). Despite its length and comprehensiveness, with the exception of testimony from one interlocutor—French historian Benjamin Stora—the Gerin Commission report is also mostly silent on France's colonial past. In his recorded testimony, Stora directly links socioeconomic issues in the suburbs, neighborhoods he sees as sites of communautarianism and radicalism, to the country's colonial past (Assemblée Nationale 2010: 55). Stora goes on to describe the perpetuation of *l'esprit colonialiste* (the colonialist spirit) in the damage evident among young *banlieusards*, like many of those from Petit-Nanterre featured in this book. Indeed, Stora's linkage of life in the banlieue to ongoing colonial politics echoes the broader argument of tying marriage partner preferences to colonial politics. Discourses of decolonization and sexual politics in the 1960s carry over more than fifty years later.[17]

In the Québécois context, laïque reports and legislation have similarly excluded discussion of the province and country's colonial pasts. This exclusion may have been notable given that both the Bouchard-Taylor report (2008) and Law 21 (2019) include short historical narratives to situate the bans on religious symbols. To their credit, the Bouchard-Taylor commissioners' final report *does* briefly address the noninclusion of Indigeneity. Bouchard and Taylor note that, due to its vastness and complexity, what they call the "aboriginal question" was not included in the provincial government mandate to address accommodation (34). The commissioners explain the omission as due to provincial resolutions that call for "nation to nation" relations only. Still, there is no public record of efforts made to pursue a discussion of Indigenous concerns related to reasonable accommodation. Indeed, to date in Québec and in Canada, Indigeneity has been conceptualized as wholly separate from questions of diversity and reasonable accommodation (see also Cornelier 2016: 81).[18]

Gérard Bouchard's preferred intercultural model, mobilized in the 2008 report as a made-in-Québec framework, is presented as necessary to protect the province's distinct society. Contrasted with Canadian multiculturalism, interculturalism emphasizes social cohesion in Québec through shared communal values (Bouchard 2012). Indigenous peoples and questions of race are never named in this equation. Éléonore Lépinard (2020) charts the erasures within the intercultural model in Québec in relation to settler colonialism. Lépinard writes, "Interculturalism acknowledges racial difference, but mainly as cultural difference. The fact that Québec is historically a white settler colony is not mentioned in these discourses" (99).

Interculturalism proposes to include newcomers in a color-blind system. But the intercultural model does not acknowledge the structural issues of racism, xenophobia, classism, and sexism. The model is premised on a meeting of two "sides" so that the broader system is never questioned. In their report, Bouchard and Taylor (2008: 243) note a Québécois "multicultural crisis" and implore the majority to reconcile with the presence of immigrant others. Again, in these relations, Indigenous peoples are presumably included but, again, are never named. They are invited to the Eurocentric state, but they are not granted foundational status nor is their sovereignty acknowledged. Geographers Laura Schaefli and Anne Godlewska (2014: 228) similarly conclude that the absence of Indigeneity in the Bouchard-Taylor report works as a "mechanism through which colonial logic is reproduced and settler continuity ensured." The omission of Indigeneity and the collapse of Indigenous peoples into settler-migrant relations is therefore no accident in these reports and laws on secularism in Québec (cf. Klassen 2018 on "churchstateness" in Canada).

More than fifteen years later, and following the publication in 2015 of Canada's Truth and Reconciliation Report,[19] 2019's Law 21 silencing of Indigenous matters, and its call for the protection of the "Québec Nation" is notable. This suppression is emboldened by how the category of "religion" is employed—as the problematic foil to laicity and as an ahistorical and apolitical concern. Even if the secular bills in Québec were not written with concern for Indigeneity or any form of reconciliation, Law 21 *does* refer to a history of distinctiveness in Québec in order to argue for a "laicity" as part of its "nationhood" (Assemblée Nationale du Québec 2019: 5). How would the inclusion of the colonization of Indigenous peoples in this history change the parameters of the secularism laws? The ruse of laïcité's neutrality and protection against incursions of religiosity could not be more apparent.

The response of Coalition Avenir Québec's immigration minister Simon Jolin-Barrette, who proposed and championed Law 21, on the omission of Indigenous peoples and perspectives is telling. Jolin-Barrette's press secretary noted that "Bill 21 is not intended for Aboriginal people," adding that

Indigenous peoples' school commissions are part of a distinctive legislative regime and therefore unaffected (cited in Authier 2019). The press secretary appears to assume that Indigenous peoples would not hold other positions of authority (i.e., as judge, police officer, doctor; for a full list, see Assemblée Nationale du Québec 2019: 11–14, schedules 1 and 2) or have other recourses through sovereign legal frameworks. Moreover, as the reader also knows, not all Indigenous-identifying people practice Indigenous spiritualities or wear Indigenous-related symbols. Because the law does not take Québec's history of Indigeneity, colonialism, or forced conversion to Christianity into account, it is unclear whether an Indigenous-identifying person working in a public school who wore a Christian cross (sometimes an expression of Indigenous spirituality) would be sanctioned or not. This question is particularly pertinent given how the Truth and Reconciliation recommendations (particularly recommendations 48 and 49; see Truth and Reconciliation Commission of Canada 2015: 9) call for a greater inclusion of Indigenous symbols and rituals in the Canadian public sphere as gestures toward reconciliation. On this point regarding the presence of Indigenous symbols and rituals in the public sphere, Carlos Colorado (2020) insightfully argues these expressions are central to the processes of reconciliation in Canada. Colorado (2020: 76) reads the Truth and Reconciliation Commission's Calls to Action as implying a restoration and celebration of traditional teachings, as well as spiritual practices and worldviews of Indigenous cultures in Canada (see also Berger, forthcoming).[20] Like the Indian Act, we can see an *intentional* misrecognition of Indigenous spiritual jurisdictions in this most recent articulation of the separation of church and state in Canada. Historically, this misrecognition, Klassen (2018: 125) explains, has been "central to the assertion of colonial power over and against Indigenous sovereignty."

We can assume that in the drafting of Law 21, the CAQ saw Indigeneity as completely separate from its project of secularism. From the CAQ's vantage point, protecting laïcité was not part of the ongoing problematic settler-colonial relationship. Yet, as several theorists have argued, and as these four expressions of laïcité in these French and Québécois reports and legal projects exemplify, coloniality shapes contemporary formulations of secularism. Secular politics have been a long-standing tool in the erasures undertaken within colonial projects. Of course, the dismissal of the ever-presentness of colonial politics is widespread.[21]

Two moves in these reports and related legislation enable this erasure. First, the "problem" of difference is placed on religion and then relegated to symbols that are positioned solely on individuals, and as ahistorical and apolitical. This annexing of accommodation issues to problematic symbols, which reflect undesirable sexual politics, allows for a silencing of broader structural and systemic issues. Given the Truth and Reconciliation Commission's federal-level recommendations in 2015, which include proposals for greater visibility of Indigenous ceremony, this overt omission is notable.

Second, leaders in both contexts invoke "color-blind" approaches that lean on an imagined "neutrality" of secularism. Republican values have long espoused an idea of an undifferentiated French identity. Lépinard (2020) captures the taboo of intersectional thinking in France, and how race and racism are consistently located outside its national borders (see also Keaton 2010 and J. Beaman 2019 on the disavowal of race and racism in the Republic). In Québec, the majority center-right Coalition Avenir Québec provincial political party has similarly denied that Law 21 can engender harm, whether anti-Indigenous, antisemitic, xenophobic, racist, Islamophobic, or other.[22] In responding to questions on symbols and the purview of the bill, Jolin-Barrette's "color-blind" approach underscores that the bill does not intend to target any one religious group: "It's applied to all religions. It applies to all Christians" (cited in Lau 2019). In sum, the omission of Indigeneity and colonial histories in the conceptualizations of secularism within these reports and legal projects effectively lays the groundwork for an ahistorical and apolitical focus on religious symbols and a broader invisibilization of the violences engendered by colonial histories and relations. The notion of coloniality with which I engage, in contrast, highlights how, in their marriage partner and ritual preferences, interlocutors of Algerian origin engage and disengage coloniality.

The narratives of participants presented in this chapter have aimed to grapple with how relations at the time of marriage—whether to marry, with whom, and how—reflect kinship relationships, particularly as they are manifest in relation to a real or imagined Bled. The chapter has also sought to show how colonialities are present in their absence within post-2004 secular legislation in France and Québec. Because of how coloniality is far from "post," I have preferred this term, with attention to what Maldonado-Torres (2007: 242) conceptualizes as the "coloniality of being," to capture its lived expressions.

Could these expressions of coloniality—in the marriage partner preferences or in the wedding rituals of some interlocutors—be expressions of "decolonial love"? In the opening of *Islands of Decolonial Love*, Leanne Betasamosake Simpson (2013: 9) cites novelist Junot Díaz, who explains how his characters live and love within specific contexts of coloniality: "The kind of love that I was interested in, that my characters long for intuitively, is the *only kind of love that could liberate them from that horrible legacy of colonial violence*. I am speaking about *decolonial love*... is it possible to love one's broken-by-the-coloniality-of-power self in another broken-by-the-coloniality-of-power person?" (my emphasis).[23]

Díaz's wish for decolonial love allows for the "broken-by-the-coloniality-of-power self." He shows how the practices and legacies of European colonialism are interconnected and shape ways of knowing, including expressions of desire and love. Still, if we assume, as Díaz does, that love is reparative and liberatory, then *decolonial love* can also push back against colonial violences. The kinds of marital relationships and preferences I describe here are not "broken-by-the-coloniality-of-power" ones. Nor are they "decolonial." But they reference French-Algerian and French-Québécois-Indigenous "coloniality." Brian Noble's (2015) distinction, articulated in "Tripped Up by Coloniality," between "coloniality as oppositional encounter" and "coloniality as milieu," is helpful to thinking through how civil marriage might operate as both a site of oppositional encounter *and* as a contact zone. So too, as we saw in chapter 3, the niqab has operated as both a negative symbol of coloniality and of the secular body, that is, as a site of opposition *and* of collusion.

Geographies matter, and, in part, shape whom and how my interlocutors marry. We saw how the particularities of Algeria—related to its specific provinces or ethnicities (that is, a division between Kabylian or Arab)—mattered to my interlocutors more in Petit-Nanterre than in Montréal. This relation is evident in wedding-day rituals. The most noteworthy comparative difference between country of residence and gender is with my female-identifying participants in Montréal. With the exception of Sabrina, who was, reluctantly, open to a transnational arranged match, among the fifty-nine women interviewed in Montréal, several had migrated *with* their husbands, but *none* had sponsored an Algerian-born husband in ways that men of the same age, religious-belonging, and migratory histories had. Contributing factors to this disparity include the aforementioned distance between and geography of Montréal and Algeria. In addition, women in Montréal were more likely to have settled as refugees than those in France, and therefore negatively associate Algeria with previous trauma. They also enjoyed more socioeconomic privilege and privacy in Montréal. This access to privacy can sometimes be literal, as for Selena who, at the time of our interview, had managed to keep her common-law relationship with Gabriel a secret from her family. Moreover, unlike Amel and Dalia in Petit-Nanterre, in general, young Québécoises did not aim to spend extended periods of time in the Bled. They therefore neither sought out transnational bridges through a marriage partner nor found Algeria a space of *ressourcement*, as Ilias and other young men did. This disparity highlights the genderedness and socioeconomics of transnational relations, particularly as they relate to marriage, love, and religion. For Maya in Montréal, France, and not Algeria, is privileged as central to her transnational life, first in attending a French lycée and then in her marriage partner. In contrast, we saw how, for others, arranged marriages consist of a rejection of the secular sensibility of individual choice that is central to the protections imagined by romance.

While there is an apparent tension in the desire for the Bled at the time of marriage among some participants, on the one hand, and increased scrutiny by these states (by the French, of forced, fake-love, and fraudulent marriages, and in Canada, of "bad faith" arranged transnational weddings), on the other, in practice they are not really at odds. State annulments of these imagined inappropriate marriages are negligible. Still, state surveillance causes considerable stress, and incidents of anti-Muslim racism occur. While rare, some, like Halim, the elderly Chibani we met in chapter 3, whose wife has never gained legal access to France, or Boussad, with whom I opened chapter 3, who may never leave Algeria, are significantly affected by these national borders. More generally, however, the specters of these laws on transnational marriage *are* worth noting. It is precisely these laws' instability, their imagined apolitics and ahistory, that gives them what historian Judith Surkis (2019: 17) calls a "fantasmatic authority." For this reason, despite these forces, desires for transnational marriage partners and rituals can be read as a formidable and embodied reclaiming of the Bled and kinship ties in the face of their erasure through contemporary colonialities in France and Québec.

CONCLUSION

SECULAR ROMANCE

Candlelit tables. Dreamy, posed gazes. Heartfelt vows. Sentimental music. A white, princess-style dress. These familiar tropes of romance at the time of marriage are beautiful and often expensive. They are also infused with politics. Romance in the North Atlantic world reflects a range of normative values, including monogamy, consumerism, individualism, property, patriarchal chivalry, and often narrow cisgender scripts. As we see in legislation against "love fraud" in France and "bad faith" marriage in Canada, romance is also— less obviously—a potential vehicle for state- and cultural-based surveillance and enforcement of secularism on individual bodies. Its affective forces play out in aesthetic practices and within intimate relationships. Romance is powerful because of its variegated meanings. Wedding rituals are not top-down directives. They are rehearsed in consumer culture and the wedding industry. They are desired and policed among my interlocutors themselves. The performance of romance can serve as a proxy of authenticity and consent in relationships, as a site for the performance of gender and sexual cultural norms, and as a location where consumer culture blends with the power of the state. Altogether, therefore, romance is a ripe, if unexpected, site of secular sensibilities in contemporary France and Québec.

This reading of secular romance builds on a theoretical view of secularism as an episteme, in that secularisms shape how we know what we know. Also, by employing a "lived religion" approach, we can consider secularisms' discursive and practical contents. In other words, I have assumed that the habitus, affects, and sensibilities of contemporary expressions of secularism can be analyzed in their own right, reading secular bodies and their sensibilities through the prisms of coloniality and race, and by rethinking why symbols have been so expeditious in the governance of secularism in France and Québec. I conclude by considering how expectations for romance in the "contact zone" of civil marriage move in tandem with secular logics.

On Secular Bodies and Their Sensibilities

To map desirable secular bodies and their sensibilities, I have focused on what has emerged as the sought-after sensibilities *counter* to recent secularism-based public debates in the media, and laws and legal projects in France and Québec between 2003 and 2023. If we accept that secularism is not solely an abstract principle, in employing a "lived religion" approach, we can consider its habitus and affective forces. Rather than determining whether secularism has "failed" in its promises of neutrality or distanciation, I have preferred to examine how increasing expectations for secular bodies in France and Québec emerge in the narratives of individuals of Algerian origin, no matter their religious or ethnic self-identification, to consider its political machinations. To better capture secularisms' complexities, I have not limited focus to explicitly self-defined secular people. My focus on individuals of Algerian origin connects these expectations of legible secularity in relation to colonial histories, especially in France, but also indirectly in Québec, which, of course, was once also a French colony.

Racialized and religionized women are most often targeted in France and Québec by secular legislation that focuses on conspicuous religious symbols and visible gender comportment. The onus of secular legibility of their faces and bodies is greater. While the pressure points and foci differ, an idealized secular body includes sharp delineations for men, too. In this comparative research on civil marriage, I therefore explicitly sought to interview women *and* men (and others, although my sample was almost all cisgender and heterosexual). In general, an idealized secular body in contemporary France and Québec is typically imagined as wholly rational (whether through science or reason), autonomous, and, for cisgender and heterosexual women, sexualized and sexually available. Given these parameters, it is no accident that antiniqab legislation in particular narrowly delineates acceptable sexual and gender norms and has been a key source for the content of secular sensibilities (I will return to this point shortly).

The specificity of Algeria as country of origin among my interlocutors was deliberate. It allowed for more pointed thinking on "coloniality," and namely in how transnational movements and power dynamics "survive colonialism" (Maldonado-Torres 2007: 243). The notion of the Bled has been helpful to contextualize participants' experiences of desire, kinship, and coloniality. Considering these preferences from this vantage point can also offer a move toward what Eve Tuck has described as "desire-based" research (cf. Tuck 2009; Tuck and Yang 2014), or examining what drives people rather than solely focusing on restrictions, as much of the literature on secularism in France and Québec has done to date. The Bled thus emerges as an unlikely site where, for my interlocutors, the "coloniality of being" (cf. Maldonado-Torres 2007) and the surveillance of national norms overlap. Connective comparison of France and Canada's distinct colonial and contemporary approaches to the regulation of immigration and religion also allowed me to argue how, since 2006, their legislation on secularism and immigration policies have dovetailed in their focus on religious symbols and in their color-blindness.

In addition to my argument about the centrality of kinship relations for many participants who preferred transnational arranged marriages, I initiated this study because I was especially interested in examining how desire for the Bled at the time of marriage should be situated within colonial legacies. I found that my male interlocutors in Petit-Nanterre and Montréal expressed greater desire for marriage partners from the Bled. In Petit-Nanterre among both women and men, I noted greater specificity in the ethnicity, language, and Algerian regions among marriage partner preferences than for my male interlocutors in Montréal, due primarily to distance, both colonial and geographical.

Women of Algerian origin in Montréal, whether first or second generation, were the outliers of this trend, as illustrated by Maya in the opening of chapter 4. I suggested some explanations for this difference, including a dis-ease with traditions in Algeria lodged in familial memories of the civil war in the 1990s, and perceptions of Algeria as a location of undesirable patriarchal norms. Like many Québécoises, women of Algerian origin in Montréal tended to be more critical of traditional marital relationships and felt less social pressure to marry. Moreover, in general, they had greater social mobility and privacy than Algerian women in Petit-Nanterre, many of whom live in high-rise spaces. In addition, in Québec, and not France, where imams are legally impeded from performing a religious marriage without a civil certificate, couples can marry religiously without having to marry civilly. Recall Imane, in Montréal, who married her second husband, also of Algerian origin, religiously only. Still, despite these differences, almost all the women in my sample, who were almost all cisgender and heterosexual, remained bound to ideals of romance (like the consumer-culture trappings of pervasive wedding-culture narratives) in ways that men were aware of but, arguably, had more space to exit.

Colonializing and secularizing projects in France and Québec share a need to delineate acceptable expressions of religiosity, gender, and race. The establishment of racial and sexual difference was a central way the violences of colonial conquest were justified (see Coviello 2019; Lépinard 2020;

and Benhadjoudja 2022). In other words, secular sensibilities also include conceptualizations of race. In the post-2004 government commissions and legal projects in France and Québec I have examined in this book, what is notable is the almost complete absence of mentions of race or colonial histories. This extraction of questions of race, racialization, and racism invisibilizes their presence in this secular legislation, and replicates a false sense of their apoliticality.

At the same time, if cues related to race are largely absent from those written governmental documents, they do subtly emerge in the visual aids created by French and Québécois political parties as guides to help delineate acceptable religiosity and desirable secular bodies. Several government-created posters promoted the parameters of acceptable symbols and bodies, and depicted the unacceptable ones. The pictogram issued by the Parti Québécois alongside Québec's Bill 60 (fig. 1.4), for example, depicts religious bodies as white-beige or "unracialized." The individuals wearing symbols deemed as conspicuous or inconspicuous have mannequin-like bodies. I argued that the pictogram's color-blind approach has two broad implications. It relieves the viewer of explicitly associating the removal of these symbols with racialized Quebeckers, who are disproportionately affected by Law 21. And, in imagining symbols apolitically and ahistorically, this color-blind approach masks ever-present systemic violence, here in relation to Québec and Canada's colonial legacies and relations.

On Religious Symbols

Religious symbols are at the center of the regulation of secular bodies and behavior in France and Québec.[1] Of course, the containment of religiosity to symbols is not new, but some of the implications are notable (cf. Durkheim [1912] 1995; Geertz 1973; Woehrling 2012; and Zubrzycki 2016 on symbols). The distillation of the problem of vivre ensemble to the removal of certain religious symbols was clearly articulated in France in the 1980s but follows a long-standing project of the removal of headscarves in colonial Algeria. In Québec, the so-called reasonable accommodation debates in the 2000s also came to focus on religious symbols, and, in the 2010s, different political parties focused first on curtailing full-face veils and then on other conspicuous symbols. This focus on symbols, rather than on other expressions of religiosity or difference, allows for facile visual assessment of acceptability. It is premised on simplistic dichotomies that separate the conspicuous from the inconspicuous, the conservative from the liberal, the private from the public, and the male from the female, as though these were always wholly discrete entities. The logic's marking of "bad" religion and emphasis on sexual difference (and not other elements, like race or class) is particularly remarkable.

Symbols are easy to monitor. They facilitate visual assessments of appropriate habituses to pass/fail visual cues *and* allow for a radical minimization of more complex and changing religious beliefs, traditions, and practices. In pictograms and legislative delineations, they are conceived as stable and uniform. They are depicted apolitically and ahistorically. Public debates, commissions, and legislation restricting headscarves in France almost never mention the history of French colonialism and the garment's restriction in French Algeria (there are a few lines in the 2003 Stasi Commission report only). The conceptualization of some symbols as conspicuous, and thereby consigned to the private sphere, also conceptualizes religious symbols as externalized and detachable, and thereby privatizable. Religious tattoos, for one, have escaped the purview of the regulation on religious symbols, perhaps because they are imagined as more individualized and, as imprinted on the skin, less easily privatized. Like dreadlocks or sidelocks (*payot*) worn by some conservative and Orthodox Jewish men, they are thus not easily removed and reworn. But, perhaps more significant, tattoos remain unregulated because they do not interrupt secular sensibilities around religion and sexuality.

A RELIANCE ON THE VISUAL FIELD

When centered on symbols and simple binaries, visual materials are especially efficient in transmitting secular sensibilities. The figure of Marianne has become the emblem par excellence of the desirable feminine secular body in France, and both French and Québécois governments have produced pictograms that delineate acceptable secular bodies and comportment.

The French Revolution's figure of Marianne, most famously depicted in Delacroix's *Liberty Leading the People*, has been a central representation of idealized secularism and femininity ever since, coinciding with the French colonization of Algeria. Her image is affective. She appears on everything from postage stamps to coins and has been incarnated by famous female actors like Brigitte Bardot, Catherine Deneuve, and Laetitia Casta. According to the president's office's official website, Marianne "is the embodiment of the beauty and vitality of the everlasting Republic" (Élysée française 2022). Jean-Pierre Rey's black-and-white photograph *La Marianne de mai 68*, which features a young blonde woman on a man's shoulders holding a flag of Vietnam in a protest in Paris's Latin Quarter, circulated internationally, including in *Life* magazine, and became emblematic of the social movements of May 1968 (Leblanc 2017). More conservative depictions of Marianne have not stood the test of time.

It was therefore no accident that Marianne's face was featured in the official advertisements for the 2010 law banning niqabs in the public sphere (see fig. 2.1). The poster focuses on a young, bright-faced, white sculpture version of Marianne, capturing her steadfastness. In this version, she wears her traditional Phrygian liberty cap with long flowing hair underneath it, and the byline, "The Republic Is Lived with an Uncovered Face." More often than not, Marianne is depicted in a more sexualized way with partially or completely bare breasts, including in statue form in the entrance to public schools. The sexualized visibility of her body stands in sharp contrast with the problematically body-covering niqab, burkini, and abaya, which are imagined as racialized, repressed, and religionized, especially in public schools.

Like with this poster, Marianne's presence often invokes or relates to an imagined undesirable religious body. KAK's caricature of two religious men, a Muslim man and a Catholic priest, who encounter an exaggerated sexualized bust of Marianne captures the retrograde religionist imagined counter to Marianne (analyzed in chapter 1; see fig. 1.1). The men's clear discomfort with her bare breasts reflects their immature sexuality and inability to deal with her breasts and the now quadric national motto of France: liberty, equality, fraternity, and laïcité. To critique the explicitness of this idealized but naked female statue would be tantamount to illiberalism or the impediment of freedom of expression. So too, the National Front's poster (fig. 2.2) outside a metro station in Paris's thirteenth arrondissement was not subtle in its comparison of acceptable and unacceptable forms of femininity: acceptable is the face-visible young woman wearing a knit tuque (an update of Marianne's cap) with a French flag painted on her cheek. Her liberalness and loyalties are clear; her body is also completely visible. Unacceptable is the obscured niqab-wearing woman. The National Front poster also followed well-known tropes of localizing unacceptable racialized femininity to the country's suburbs, like Petit-Nanterre. Marianne is ubiquitous. Her continued centrality to French sensibilities is apparent in her inclusion in the logo for the 2024 Summer Olympics in Paris, featuring her sharp feminine lip and the mascot's personifications of her Phrygian cap.

Government-created pictograms delineate these secular sensibilities even more sharply. Heightened following the 2015 state of emergency and the Plan Vigipirate response to combat terrorism initiated after several devastating attacks in France, the government released a visual guide that outlined "The First Warning Signs" of potential homegrown terrorism (see fig. 1.3). Reducing the unpredictably and terror associated with these incidents to easy actionable signs, the posters surely sought to quell fears. Not accidentally, real bodies are never depicted. The poster features sanitized gray-colored male and female stick figures who reject, among other things, swimming (a subtle reminder of burkini debates), "impure" male/female relations (a reminder of religiously informed social-sexual deviance), baguettes (and French culinary culture), and form-fitting dresses (a not-so-subtle reminder of debates related to undesirable religiously informed long dresses and abayas). Again, the poster is subtly related to race insofar as racial and ethnic identities are effaced in these depictions. In this way, because of this erasure, the idealized secular body, contrary to these problematic sensibilities, remains a de facto white one.

EXPRESSING AND RESPONDING TO SECULAR SENSIBILITIES

A central focus in *Secular Sensibilities* has been to analyze how these secular sensibilities were experienced by my interlocutors in the "contact zone" of civil marriage. With her chignon and red lipstick, Nawel, with whom I opened this book, sought to embody an Islam-free femininity at the French consulate following her arranged marriage, so as not to alert the civil servants to potential social-sexual deviance. She intuited an idealized feminine performance and woke up early to style herself accordingly. Muslim-imagined male racialized bodies are also surveilled, predominantly in their association with religious-appearing women (see Shryock 2010: 10 on Islamophobia and the "Good Muslim man" stereotype). Recall how Walid's sexual politics were questioned by first responders in Montréal when his pregnant, hijab-wearing wife, Farida, fainted outside a grocery store. Farida's foreignness, hijab, and lack of fluency in French intensified the onus on his performance of the right sexual politics. Some of the men I interviewed had beards that, depending on the context, could be read as religious and thereby conspicuous. Yacine discerned this gaze and shaved his beard before his appointment at the French consulate in Oran following his arranged marriage to a French national in Ghazaouet, Algeria, where, despite their not knowing each other well, the couple felt compelled to enact several romantic wedding rituals.

I also shared how these pervasive mores translated into interviews. Some of my interlocutors were keen to demonstrate their acceptable secular-sexual politics to me, mentioning, unprompted, that they were not virgins at the time of marriage or emphasizing the romance of their meeting to dispel a sense of arrangement. Sami's critical response to his older brother Adel's wish to sponsor the immigration of a traditional Algerian-born bride to Montréal captured a pervasive discomfort with and consciousness of the political perception of transnational marriage. Given their family history of fleeing Islamism in Algeria as refugees in the 1990s, the fact they were not practicing Muslims, and the marriage being hardly "cool," Sami expressly did *not* want his older brother to sponsor an Algerian-born woman in an arranged marriage. At the same time, across the Atlantic in Petit-Nanterre, in his preferred "grandmother"-style arranged marriage to Zara, Ilias brilliantly assessed the state surveillance a transnational wedding would engender and made an express choice to meet his future wife locally, but in an Islamically informed manner. These examples capture the range of ways my interlocutors navigate these sensibilities in their relationships, families, and within their broader cultural contexts.

DEMARCATING "BAD RELIGION"

Historically and contemporarily, secularism in law and public parlance in France and Québec has been employed as a tool to regulate religion, determining what is acceptable and what is not. "Bad religion" in these contents is similarly constructed. Based on historical influence and demographics, first Catholicism and then Islam have been imagined as the culprits of the curtailment of liberties. Sustained legislative efforts have thus aimed to counter their social influence. The regulation of these traditions is not analogous, however. In France and Québec, in contrast to the visibility of symbols of Islam, scholars have shown how many Catholic symbols and sensibilities have been protected, invisibilized, and even banalized as sources of heritage (see Beaman 2020; Burchardt 2020; and Oliphant 2021). In contrast, beginning in France with its headscarf affair in 1989, and in Québec after 9/11, the visibility of symbols and rituals associated with Islam has been scrutinized. At the same time, we saw how promoting secular sensibilities through the curtailment of symbols associated with Islam—which now extends beyond hijabs, niqabs, and burkinis to bandanas, long skirts, abayas, and beards, and which come to bear the responsibility for their incompatibility with liberal secular sensibilities—has also meant that these same sensibilities' complex authorities are often left unquestioned (see Mahmood 2009; Amir-Moazami 2022).

With the regulation through symbols, "bad religion" is located on individual bodies. It remains untethered to long-standing politics and history. Its meanings are also radically reduced. We know that, in practice, the same religious symbol—the hijab—can be worn and interpreted in different ways and hold different meanings. But its biopower monitoring can also pivot. Amel, a central interlocutor in this book, who attended public school in northern France after the 2004 law was put into place at public schools, grew up habituated to removing and resetting her hijab throughout the course of a day. Passing in this way involved some subterfuge. Amel was proud that her employer outside of Paris was completely unaware of her religious life and had never seen her with a hijab. This strict separation for her was exemplified in her two social media accounts: two Instagram accounts (with separate friend lists) separated her religious from so-called secular self. Arguably, Amel's daily pivoting captures some implications when religion is reduced to symbols: it is located on individual bodies and expected to be externalized, and easily removed. In contrast, in Québec, my female hijab-wearing interlocutors possessed less ambidexterity regarding the compartmentalization of religious symbols. Zohra, who had migrated to Montréal with her family just prior to the passage of the 2019 secular law in Québec, experienced the state's regulation of her hijab there far more violently than Amel in France. Since the passage of Law 21, Zohra's transnational dream of becoming a high school math teacher in Québec has been jeopardized. Unlike Amel, Zohra could not imagine removing her hijab in the course of her daily life, completely privatizing her religiosity or hiding it from her employer. We can also take Zohra's case in Montréal to consider the politics undergirding the association of her religious symbol with an antiliberal position.

EMPHASIZING SEXUAL DIFFERENCE
I noted a contemporary shift in the regulation of religious symbols in France and Québec. Beginning with high-profile cases and legislation in 2008, nation-state governmentality has moved away from regulating religious symbols to emphasizing the centrality of sexual democracy for cishet women. Laws that targeted forced marriage, niqabs, burkinis, polygamy, abayas, and virginity certificates followed in France, with similar laws targeting niqabs, "bad faith" marriages, and polygamy in Québec and Canada. In both contexts, undesirable expressions of religiosity are associated with Islam and share concern for women's sexual freedom.

The larger overarching binary mechanism also encouraged sexual difference as an organizing principle in this post-2008 moment. Undesirable religious symbols are generally imagined in relation to men or women who are individualized. This logic, which began with the 2004 law against conspicuous religious symbols, continues to expand. The 2021 Antiseparatism Law in France further extends the surveillance of conspicuous religious symbols to girls under eighteen in the public sphere and to women who wear them in activities related to public schools.[2] The 2004 French law has thus expanded geographically beyond its initial foci on public schools and government offices to school trips, and to private businesses. It has also expanded sartorially to many other undesirable Islam-related garments, and ideologically to practices and beliefs imagined as sexually repressive, like virginity certificates.

With antiniqab legislative efforts—in France beginning with the Gerin Commission in 2010, and in Québec beginning with bills in 2010, and again in legislation passed in 2017 and 2019—restrictions became attuned to cisgender heterosexual women's rights and the promotion of specific forms of femininity and sexual emancipation above other forms, whether social, economic, or political. Together, this group of bills and laws share strikingly similar sensibilities that focus on religious symbols and promote a necessary visual access to female faces and bodies.[3] Women who wear religious symbols, and especially those few who wear niqab, are victims of sexual repression, coercion, and force. All of these laws emphasize a clear demarcation of sexualized women and men.

On Secular Romance

I first thought about romance when I read the 2006 laws in France against "love fraud" and in Canada against "bad faith" marriages and wondered why incursions against love and faith were deemed so injurious? Why so much time and ink on this issue and at this time? And why did romance come to act as a bastion against marriage fraud with a migratory aim?

Sociologist Eva Illouz (1997) has noted with reference to US-British culture that the location of romance in marriage is a twentieth-century phenomenon, which equates love and marriage as commensurate with attaining personal happiness.[4] Because it is imagined in popular culture as a universalist impulse and as spontaneous and uncalculated, romance bolsters a number of values. Indeed, romance is an unlikely location to map secular sensibilities, but its pervasiveness and desirability mask its politics. Following this thread, I have read the surveillance of love and romance in civil marriage and migration as a tool of citizenry, one that disciplines the parameters of normative citizenship and determines who can achieve legal and cultural forms of national belonging. Love is much more challenging to measure, while "romance," defined by the *Cambridge Dictionary* as to court or to woo or "the feelings and behaviour of two people who are in a loving and sexual relationship with each other," is far more performative. Signs of romance are especially read as proxies for women's free choice in the marital union: whether as an assurance of her individualism, as free from community and religious restraints, or as a sign of sexual consent. Alongside this critique of statecraft, in this last section, I also situate romance's desirability, namely as a marker of social class and consumerism, as an indicator of appropriate gender roles, particularly for women, and as a marker of proper sexuality and monogamous attraction. As my interlocutors' narratives capture, it is also a source of pleasure.[5]

ROMANCE AND CONSUMERISM

Romance sells. Gender studies scholar Catherine Roach (2016: 4) suggests that the attraction of these stories explains their enduring appeal in North Atlantic cultures: "The happily-in-love, pair-bonded (generally, although increasingly not exclusively, heterosexual) couple is made into a near mandatory norm by the media and popular culture." Readers are surely familiar with the fashions, experiences, cosmetics, perfumes, and objects that help shape the sights and sounds of romance.[6] These expressions also signal social class and sophistication. Once established, the modern wedding industry has fueled a robust capitalist consumerism that few in France, Canada, or elsewhere can escape.

My female interlocutors were especially attuned to trends in the larger wedding industry so as to purchase the right cosmetics, perfume, dresses, shoes, and so on. Rachida expressed frustration and disappointment that her elopement with Farid in the suburb next to Petit-Nanterre, celebrated with a paltry *grec* sandwich after their city-hall ceremony, had all the "wrong ingredients": no taste, no family, no sense of tradition. The Bled, Arabic for home country, was imagined as a key site of these cultural traditions. But so too were wedding shows. At a wedding show in Nanterre where I first met Amel, she purchased jewelry and personalized unity candles and planned dresses for her upcoming nuptials in Algeria. At the wedding party several months later, she insisted on having photos taken where she and Yacine stood in well-known romantic poses, not only for their future sponsorship file, but also because she really wanted to. She introduced a candle-lighting ritual, which she thought had never been done in her family before. Women typically have more at stake in these rituals. With exceptions, like Azdi and Khalil (see fig. 4.1), men were typically less invested in wedding-related rituals.

THE NIQAB AS ANTI-ROMANCE

If Marianne is a feminine ideal in France, the niqab counters notions of romance. The 2010 report that followed the six-month commission in France to assess the acceptability of the niqab is extremely long (658 pages, single-spaced). It develops multiple arguments against face-covering veils, ranging from the impediment of neighborliness (drawing on philosopher Emmanuel Levinas) to its theological unacceptability (drawing on testimony by the French Council of the Muslim Faith; see Selby 2011). The 2009 government resolution that led to the creation of the Gerin Commission depicts full-face veils as "an attack" on "a woman's dignity and on the assertion of her femininity" (Assemblée Nationale 2010: 4). This assertion gives a good sense of how the commission will conclude its report.

When I first read this document, its recurring argument that full-face veils exclude women from full sexuality and humiliate them struck me most. After reading the testimony by André Rossinot, then mayor of the city of Nancy, cited at length in the report, I should have not been surprised that there was no backlash to these comments in the French mainstream press or critique by Gerin in the report. Rossinot bemoans to the commission that the niqab means that women "are not free to show themselves, to exist on the outside, *even less to seduce*" (as cited in Assemblée Nationale 2010: 110; my emphasis). To be fair, Rossinot is but one of more than 200 individuals who testified before the commission. Still, this patriarchal-based fear of niqabs is also about women's responsibility to seduce men. Full-face veils impede this obligation.

NARROW GENDER ROLES

It is no accident that women enact these rituals of romance in civil weddings to a greater extent than men. From a psychological perspective, Roach (2016) argues that romance novels in contemporary North America are popular among cishet women because of how they recalibrate power differentials. The promised happy ending is appealing. "Romance," says Roach, "levels the playing field for women. . . . The romance story is a woman-centered fantasy about how to make this man's world work for her" (26). Beautiful flowers, diamonds, soft music, and candles may, following Roach's argument, serve to dull women's senses and mute the gendered power asymmetries to which they enter through cishet marriage. Moreover, cultural idealization of romance ensures cishet women's sexual availability to men in ways that parallel the Nancy mayor's concern that the niqab could inhibit men's ability to seduce (see also Illouz 1997).

Chivalry and seduction thus reinforce asymmetrical power relationships. Joan Wallach Scott (2011: 118) shows how the notion of seduction has been a long-standing pillar of French national identity. It has also been employed as a tool of differentiation. Seduction has been consistently positioned in contrast to an imagined retrograde sexual politics of racialized religious immigrants. Arranged marriage where immigration is at stake heightens these concerns. Scott argues that these mechanisms of French seduction are "governed not by law but by ritual" (120). In other words, even if forms of romance are implicitly required in the 2010 memorandum to marriage officiants I examined in chapter 3, the call for romance remains a *non-dit* or unspoken norm. These desirable performances of romance are clearer in the enforcement of these ideas. The 2011 amendment to the 2006 French law on "love fraud with a migratory aim" allowed state officials to surveil potentially suspicious unions for signs of marital intimacy—financial, emotional, and sexual—into the first *thirty years* of marriage.[7] Recall Fatima who, in chapter 3, had a sense of what the proper rituals and signs of intimacy in an unexpected police visit might be, even if these are not formally articulated by the state. She knew that her five-day-old baby was evidence of her and her French-born husband's sexual intimacy. "Romance" makes these violences appear desirable.

It is precisely the pleasure taken in the social, sexual, and consumerist sides of romance where politics are blurred and left unquestioned. For these reasons, I have sought to show how romance in this contact zone shields these gender politics. I hope that one takeaway for the reader will be to question the allure and benignness of romance. The premise that—thanks to secularism—women especially, have left backward, prudish religion behind and have become sexually liberated is worthy of our attention. Certainly in their celebration of sexual attraction, individualism, agency, and sexual liberalism, ideals of romance bolster secular values. But the idealized secular body as configured and promoted in contemporary France and Québec also masks other patriarchal violences, consumer cultures, and colonial entanglements worthy of our attention, if only to protect secularisms' promises of neutrality and freedom.

ACKNOWLEDGMENTS

One of the most thrilling and challenging moments in the writing of a monograph is the last lap, acknowledging those who have supported it. Apologies if I have missed you. First and foremost, I am forever grateful to my interlocutors. I have had the pleasure of knowing some of the folks featured in this book for more than twenty years through the joys and challenges of life. Others shared their stories with me over just a few hours. I sincerely thank everyone I interviewed in France, Québec, and Algeria for their generosity, time, and, often, hospitality. I acknowledge their trust in me with their stories, the greatest privilege. I hope I have done justice to the stories I heard. My ethics approval's anonymity requirements frustrate my desire to name people, but I will continue to honor these friends and interlocutors for all my days. شكرًا. *Tanmirt. Merci de tout cœur.*

Transnational fieldwork is time-consuming, and also expensive. Over the eight years of field research, travel costs rose as research supports dwindled. I gratefully acknowledge research support from the Social Science and Humanities Research Council of Canada for years-long support, as well as from my own institution, Memorial University, for its support of this project through start-up funds and a President's Award for Research. I extend special gratitude to the Centre for Studies in Religion and Society at the University of Victoria, especially to long-time mentor Paul Bramadat and esteemed colleague Rachel Brown, for accommodating a short research stay during which I completed a first draft. This book's arguments were further sharpened thanks to invited talks and conferences with the Nonreligious Beliefs and Practices in Turkey Research Group; the Departments of Philosophy and Gender Studies at Memorial University; the International Society for the Sociology of Religion (online and still fine!); for the Société Québécoise pour l'Étude de la Religion; for the American Academy of Religion and the American Anthropological Association; for the Society of the Anthropology of Religion; at Pamela Klassen and Monique Scheer's Making Promises Workshop; and, especially, the Secular Bodies, Affects, and Emotions workshop in Tübingen, Germany, in 2016. Thank you for engaging this work.

Much of the writing of this work took place amid the COVID-19 pandemic. Like those of many ethnographers, research stays in France in 2020 and 2021 were cancelled. Instead, I sought to write in the early morning in my basement. I am especially grateful to my "Bubble Family" for sharing the unexpected delights and burdens of home schooling and childcare on the remote island of Newfoundland. This book was significantly delayed, but unexpected joys happened too. Heartfelt thanks go to Maro Adjemian, Eric Biunno, Brian Feltham, and Natalie Slawinski, and to Myriam, Naïma, Luca, and Ela. Over a much longer period, numerous childcare workers have supported me as I have worked on this project. I note Xaiver Campbell, Katie Duff, Kenza Kara and staff at the P'tits Cerfs-Volants and the Crèche Nuages d'Ours, in particular. On the writing front, a special shout out to my formidable friend Amanda Bittner for inviting me to join the SMASH writing collective at a critical moment, and to the SMASHers for their unwavering commitment to show up and support of all things.

I am also grateful to have collaborated and have been in conversation with research assistants on this project. Graduate students have assisted with tasks as far ranging as transcribing interviews, locating statistical and opinion data, formatting the bibliography, conducting interviews, and driving in rural Algeria. Special thanks go to Kawtare Bihya and Julia Itel, who undertook very rich interviews in Montréal, and to Prudence Etkin, and Jessica Gibson, who assisted with bibliographical work. Shannon Fraser's unparalleled eye and indexing acuity are also acknowledged here. I thank administrative staff at Memorial University for their behind-the-scenes work to support this research, especially Matt Milner and Heather O'Brien in the Grants Office.

Many colleagues and friends have shaped my thinking in this book, and I thank them here: Melanie Adrian, Sadaf Ahmed, Schirin Amir-Moazami, Ellen Badone, Natasha Bakht, Ben Berger, Amanda Bittner, Jocelyne Cesari, Andrée-Anne Clermont, Carlos Colorado, Victor Collet, Dia Dabby, Carol-Lynne d'Arcangelis, Nadia Fadil, Nulifer Göle, Nacina Guénif-Souilamas, Nadia Hasan, Roshan Jahangeer, Hillary Kaell, Pamela Klassen, Anna Korteweg, David Koussens, Hélène Neveu Kringelbach, Bochra Manaï, Sarah Martin, Géraldine Mossière, Florence Rochefort, Celia Rothenberg, David Seljak, Monique Scheer, Sobia Shaikh, Saaz Taher, and Sarah Wilkins-Laflamme.

Special thanks go to Julia Martínez-Ariño for reading the manuscript in full and to the anonymous reviewers with UNC Press for their careful reading. I also take this opportunity to especially thank Lori G. Beaman for her unwavering intellect and humor, and Amélie Barras, *collaboratrice* extraordinaire, whose support and smarts are also unparalleled. The decades-long sharp critique and kindness of Martine Segalen (1940–2021) will be missed during my next *séjour* in Paris.

Kristy Nabhan-Warren's excitement for this project was infectious, and I thank her for shepherding it from our initial conversation through each stage. I am appreciative to share the company of other authors published in UNC's Where Religion Lives series. I particularly note my editor Mark Simpson-Vos's careful eye and sound advice over the years we have worked together on this monograph, and Thomas Bedenbaugh's organization of the many moving parts of publication. Alex Martin's copyediting care and meticulous work made this book better, and it was truly a pleasure to work with Val Burton, project editor at UNC Press.

Finally, I thank my families for supporting me on this decade-long journey. The advice of my grandmothers, Jacki and Peggy, are woven into these pages. Luísa and Dioni, Maria and Xavi, Wayne and Susan have all cared for me and my family at critical moments. Thanks to Brian, Jo, Kevin, and Laure-Anne for our adventures in France, Québec, and beyond. Alanna and Leah have been bright lights and reasons to keep plugging away. I thank them for joining me to Algeria, France, and Québec and, even as babies, asking for and listening to my stories. Lastly, Óscar makes everything possible. I dedicate this book to him.

NOTES

Introduction

1. All names have been anonymized. Translations from French to English are my own. Four interviews in Algeria were conducted with a translator present.

2. Nawal and Khalid's apartment was very small. Her goal was to become pregnant with a second child and apply for a coveted three-bedroom social housing apartment in the same neighborhood, moving out of their rent-unregulated junior one-bedroom apartment. Unlike Nawal, most of my French interlocutors lived in subsidized housing (*habitations à loyer modéré*, HLMs).

3. I mean "Oriental" as a reference not to East Asia but to Maghrebian or North African wedding styles, vendors, and colors. The mobilization of the Orient and Orientalism is not lost on me. I consider the coloniality expressed in these wedding fashions in chapter 4.

4. Maria (Nawel's mother) studied English in Canada and the United Kingdom, and, as her daughter Nawel proudly noted, once traveled solo to the United States. Nawel admitted that she questioned her mother's choice in marrying and migrating out of France, which she saw as a far more desirable place to live and love than Tlemcen: "When I asked her if it was forced, she said, 'Oh no, no. Not at all. It was my choice. . . . I decided. I chose. And I returned [to Algeria].'" This migration pattern of moving from France to Algeria was not common among my interlocutors. Only one other interlocutor's mother, Nadia's mother, whom we will meet in chapter 4, also migrated from France to Algeria for a transnational marriage.

5. I understand all of these concepts as changing social constructs that are sources of differentiation and discrimination (see Machery and Faucher 2005).

6. I thank Mayanthi Fernando for introducing me to Michel-Rolph Trouillot's framework as a way to consider how to delineate the political parameters of my work (see also Fernando 2014a).

7. Data from Québec suggest almost 50 percent of marriages end in divorce (https://statistique.quebec.ca/fr/document/divorces-le-quebec/tableau/nombre-de-divorces-et-indice-synthetique-de-divortialite-quebec-1969-2008). Percentages are similar in France (www.ined.fr/fr/tout-savoir-population/chiffres/france/mariages-divorces-pacs/divorces).

8. In *Dressing Constitutionally: Hierarchy, Sexuality, and Democracy from Our Hairstyles to Our Shoes*, Ruthann Robson argues that states support sexual hierarchies through the policing of attire. Not only do governments determine what is appropriate (as with nudity), but they can be specific in policing style, including "hair, jewelry, cosmetics, shoes, and bodily enhancements or markings" (Robson 2013: 60).

9. The conceptualization of the "Modern Girl" by Alys Eve Weinbaum and coauthors (2008) is helpful in further theorizing consumable femininity. As a heuristic device that emerged globally beginning in the 1920s, the Modern Girl captured an ideal womanhood centered on her use of specific commodities—provocative fashions and red lipstick, among others—and around explicit eroticism. The Modern Girl trope includes lipstick, nail polish, face creams and powders, skin lighteners, tanning lotions, perfumes, cigarettes, high heels, and fashionable,

sexy clothes (Weinbaum et al. 2008: 18). The Modern Girl's consumerist goals are clear. Her alignment with conceptions of progress and modernity echo how I conceptualize the idealized feminine secular body in France and Québec.

10. I became attuned to the performance of romance for the state when I sponsored my now-husband for Canadian permanent residency prior to our wedding in 2009 (after the laws on bad faith marriages had been imposed). In that application, I needed to prove the length and sincerity of our common-law relationship. I did so through photos and letters from family and friends, which attested to our financial, personal, and sexual intimacies. Our whiteness, his European country of origin, and other class privileges meant that our performance was not subject to the scrutiny experienced by many of my participants. He was granted permanent residency within nine months of our application.

11. I am not the only one to see this parallel. Politicians in Québec have also commented on shared secular politics with France. When the Charter of Values was debated in Québec in 2012–13, the then premier of Québec, Pauline Marois, noted that "the best example, in [my] opinion, was France . . . which has created a space to live well with individuals of all religious origins, and from other nation states" (Teisceira-Lessard 2013, cited in Koussens and Amiraux 2014: 55). Marois also stressed that "between Québec and France there are so many things in common that we learn from one another" (cited in Rioux 2013). Beyond the 2013 debates on the Charter of Values, Koussens and Amiraux (2014: 59) argue that the way French legislation is represented in Québec—especially in a focus on 2004 and 2010 laws of religious symbols—overemphasizes restriction and oversimplifies its goals related to the freedom of expression. The Québec representations also ignore France's Alsace-Moselle region, which in this respect differs historically and legally from the rest of France.

12. Fieldwork in Algeria took place over four weeks in April 2011 and July 2016 for two marriage trips. I have conducted fieldwork in Petit-Nanterre since 2004, and specifically on this project in May–July 2012, May–July 2014, and September 2015–July 2016. In Montréal, I conducted fieldwork in April and July–August 2017 and June–July 2018. A follow-up field trip to France in 2020 was canceled because of COVID-19-related travel restrictions.

13. In undertaking this France-Québec comparison, I have been inspired by other sociologists and anthropologists who have engaged uneven ethnographic data (cf. Marcus 1995 on the implications of multisited ethnography). Z. Fareen Parvez (2017), for one, compares Islamic revival movements in France and India through ethnographic fieldwork conducted in Lyon and Hyderabad. Her field sites and access to them differed substantially. The same is true in Elizabeth Bucar's (2017) exploration of the meanings and representations of Muslim women's dress, *Pious Fashion: How Muslim Women Dress*, for which Bucar visited Tehran, Yogyakarta, and Istanbul in person and remotely. Bucar spent unequal amounts of time in each location; her data are also not symmetrical. On the France/Québec comparison, Géraldine Mossière (2010, 2013) interviewed seventy-eight female converts to Islam in France and Québec who lived in urban centers, as well as "conversion agents" like imams and others who support converts. Rachel Brown (2016a; 2016b) has undertaken a rich comparative ethnography of Maghrebian life in Paris and Montréal comparing foodways, or engagements with their religiosity through discussion of food. Few other ethnographers have examined Muslims comparatively in France and Québec (one exception is Roshan Arah Jahangeer [2021], who

conducted interviews with hijab-wearing women in both locales). Many more have undertaken discourse analysis on legal projects related to Islam and secularism (see Lépinard 2014, 2020; Milot 2010; Milot and Koussens 2009; Koussens and Amiraux 2014; Baubérot and Milot 2011; Hachimi Alaoui 2007; Amiraux 2010; May 2016; and Koussens 2009, 2018, 2023).

14. On May 25, 2016, I held a focus group conversation at a local community association on the topic of marriage and migration that was open to all. The evening centered around a buffet meal and free babysitting, and more than thirty people attended (I do not include these individuals in my interview sample, however, because participants did not sign consent forms). Most striking were the differences between the experiences of racialized and nonracialized participants. White and white-passing participants, even when their marriage implied sponsoring a non-EU-origin spouse, did not share experiences of state surveillance.

15. Weinbaum et al. (2008) introduce the notion of a "connective comparison," which critiques the notion of discrete temporal or geographical locations and aims to capture how localities develop in conversation with one another. The connective element "highlights the inchoate manner in which things previously understood to be local come into being through complex global dynamics" (4). France and Québec are connected historically and contemporarily, including in the life trajectories of many participants, as well as on legislative and cultural planes.

16. Almost 90 percent of the seventy first-generation females I interviewed in this Parisian suburb between 2004 and 2006 had migrated through marriage. A 2011 study by the Institut national d'études démographiques (Hamel 2011) reported that 97 percent of marriages among citizens of Maghrebian origin in France are chosen marriages coordinated by family and friends. Data on these arrangements in Québec are similar. In her study of fifty Québécoise Muslim converts, Mossière (2010) found that many respondents were religiously but not civilly married, suggesting that common-law unions in Québec (where fewer than 30 percent of women legally marry) are replicating social norms. A qualitative study of Muslims in Ontario concluded that, in addition to their civil unions, more than 90 percent of Canadian Muslim youths seek a "halal marriage," regardless of their broader level of practice (Macfarlane 2012a, 2012b: 11). These examples suggest the importance of Islamic marriage contracts for Muslims in Montréal, including for those who are nonpracticing.

17. The fieldwork undergirding this book "began" when a friend I knew from a community association in Petit-Nanterre, Leila (chapter 4), who knew I was interested in pursuing a new project examining marriage migration, generously invited me to join her family for the transnational wedding of her cousin-in-law in Kabylia, Algeria, in April 2011. The bride and groom were both in their twenties and had both been born in Lyon. She noted lower costs, better food, and greater ambiance as reasons they chose a village destination wedding. Both of their fathers were of Kabylian origin. When I expressed reluctance to attend because I had neither received a formal invitation nor knew the couple, Leila's husband Mouloud reiterated that they would be insulted if I thought I should not attend. Hundreds of guests gathered in the bride's grandmother's village in the mountains above Tizi Ouzou to celebrate with food, a noisy car procession and a marching band. The bride's grandmother and aunts had coordinated and prepared all the food.

18. I would estimate that 85 percent of housing in Petit-Nanterre at the time of my fieldwork was social housing. This meant that with my partner and two children

in tow, I could no longer stay on Aisha's living room couch (see Selby 2012 on my previous year-long residency). Between 2004 and 2016, there were no rental properties available in the area.

19. Bochra Manaï (2015, 2018: 127) questions whether the lobbied-for Petit Maghreb neighborhood designation has made sense given that its visibility has also attracted more surveillance and negative attention.

20. Despite long-standing critiques of *communautarisme*, or the concentration of specific religious, ethnic, or racial groups in one area as a negative by-product of multiculturalism in France (see Schnapper 2007; Ryan 2010; and Bramadat and Koenig 2009), the Algerian population in Petit-Nanterre was more concentrated than in Montréal.

21. Julia Itel and Kawtare Bihya were graduate students at the Université de Montréal and Université du Québec à Montréal who had experience recruiting and undertaking qualitative interviews. We shared an interview schedule I developed. Katherine Pratt Ewing (2008) describes how her interlocutors engaged differently with her and her daughters as research assistants in Berlin. Data shifted when her daughters undertook interviews and when she did (109, 234).

22. In July 2020, President Macron commissioned historian Benjamin Stora to report on potential "reconciliation" between France and Algeria. Macron was more open to this narrative (he previously characterized French colonization in Algeria as a "crime against humanity") than his presidential processors, including Jacques Chirac, who pushed for a February 2005 law on colonialism that would have had public school teachers teach only the "positive" results of colonialism. Most significant among Stora's (2021) recommendations was his call for a "Memory and Truth" commission to examine colonial abuses in Algeria. It has yet to be funded.

23. On the reverberations of French colonialism for contemporary Algerians, see Silverstein 2002, 2004; Goodman 2009; Brahimi 2011; and Santelli and Collet 2012b.

24. The notion of a "lived" religion may seem to be an oxymoron (i.e., What would it mean to ethnographically capture "dead religion"?), but it generally aims to capture how, contrary to how they are often prescribed in texts or doctrine, people live their religious beliefs, practices, and doctrines in ways that are changing, multifaceted, and sometimes contradictory (see de Certeau 1984; Ammerman 2007, 2014; Orsi 2003, 2005; McGuire 2008; Woodhead 2014).

25. By the late twentieth century, Berbers constituted between 40 and 75 percent of Algerians in France (Silverstein 1996: 11). Yasser Boulmezaoud (2017: 15) found that approximately 19 percent of the North African Canadian population identifies as "Algerian," and 10.4 percent Berber (with 28 percent as Egyptian and 29.3 percent as Moroccan).

26. Anti-Muslimness is embedded within interlocking relations of oppression, which is why it is helpful to conceptualize anti-Muslimness as anti-Muslim racism (Allen 2010; Hage 2017; Beydoun 2019; Selby and Shaikh 2023). Islamophobia is one particular, historical articulation of anti-Muslimness, tied to histories of, and resistance to, colonialism, imperialism, Orientalism, and racialized othering (Thobani 2021).

27. Trouillot (1995: 26–27) reminds us that what we ignore has consequences. Silences, he says, occur in scholarship when sources are determined, when they are assembled, when they are analyzed, and when they are told as narratives. Silences are unequal. Certainly, my interest in how secular sensibilities shape gender frameworks in *marriage* amplifies a gap in my sample in its emphasis on monogamous, heterosexual, and cisgender interlocutors.

28. See Brettell 2017 for an overview of scholarly literature that shows how undocumented women are especially vulnerable to domestic abuse.

29. This *mariage blanc* situation changed unexpectedly and I was spared from having to decide whether to serve as witness. The day before the scheduled civil wedding at the Nanterre Préfecture, the groom, who was in his mid-seventies, was hit by a car at a pedestrian crosswalk and severely injured. He was admitted to hospital for surgery to repair his shattered leg. It was a terrible and surely avoidable accident. While supporting this interlocutor in this tragedy, I admit I was also relieved that the wedding was postponed indefinitely and that they no longer needed me as a witness. Because the bride-to-be had a pay-as-you-go mobile phone, could not read French, and did not have email access or computer literacy, I unfortunately lost touch with her following a 2012 field season. I do not know whether she married and/or secured legal status in France.

30. It is estimated that 80 percent of the world's population will marry by the age of thirty (see https://ourworldindata.org/marriages-and-divorces).

31. I recognize critiques of Foucault's undertheorization of race and colonization (see Mbembe 2003; and Bracke and Hernández Aguilar 2020). Achille Mbembe (2003: 11), for one, develops the notion of necropolitics to capture how these power plays dictate who lives and who dies. Stoler (2006) similarly critiques and extends Foucault's silence on colonialism and the "racisms of the state." Sarah Bracke and Luis Manuel Hernández Aguilar (2020: 17) show how governmentality is apparent in the "discourses, policies, and techniques to govern the 'integration' of Muslims," which, in turn, produce "a social and political reality where Muslims are deemed an inherent and dangerous problem."

32. Jumping to the twenty-first century, French people, owing to a number of transnational agreements that facilitate their arrival, are the most important immigration group to the province of Québec (Statistics Canada 2016). As primarily white secular elites, this group of immigrants has not disturbed prevalent secular sensibilities in Québec and thus has been largely invisible.

33. This transnational marriage circulation is not new and has been studied to a greater extent in other European contexts (see Foblets 1998; Lievens 1999; Hirsch 2003; Cole 2008, 2010, 2014b on mixed French-Malagasy unions; Williams 2010; Hense and Schorch 2013; and D'Aoust 2022), especially among British-Pakistani unions (Shaw and Charsley 2006; Charsley 2005, 2006, 2007, 2012). Caroline Brettell (2017: 82) shows that anthropological literature on marriage migration remains relatively limited, especially when compared to research on labor-market related mobility (see also Lee 2013).

34. Some scholars respond that love cannot be easily qualifiable. Cultural theorist Lauren Berlant asserts that "love always means non-sovereignty" (cited in D'Aoust 2014: 330), which I understand to mean that love cannot be contained by any singular reason or motivation. Drawing on Hannah Arendt's argument that love is an apolitical force, political scientist Anne-Marie D'Aoust (2015) argues that "technologies of love *carry excess that escapes intentionality*, which means that they cannot be reduced to technologies of government" (my emphasis). I agree, but I do not quantify its quotient among my interlocutors, given the way that the state and others already quantify sincerity through signs of intimacies and romance.

35. As a social scientist I do not quantify Allah's plans in these transnational relationships. In Amel's case, I focus on how her kinship ties were reinforced through this union.

36. While some of the scholarly literature on transnational marriage suggests that economics is a primary driver for these unions from the Global South to the Global North (see especially Cole 2010 and 2014b, 2014a on Malagasy women's migration to rural France), my interlocutors did not articulate their choices primarily in this way. Rather, status, adventure, and destiny were elements that recurred in these narratives.

37. *Blédard* refers to soldiers from Northern Africa, but with the exception of its use among those who claim it, it is usually an insult in popular parlance in France.

38. These attempts included Bill 94, *An Act to Establish Guidelines Governing Accommodation Requests within the Administration and Certain Institutions*, 1st Session, 39th Legislature, Québec, 2010 (not enacted); Bill 60, *Charter Affirming the Values of State Secularism and Religious Neutrality and of Equality between Women and Men, and Providing a Framework for Accommodation Requests*, 1st Session, 40th Legislature, Québec, 2013 (not enacted); *An Act to Foster Adherence to State Religious Neutrality and, in Particular, to Provide a Framework for Request for Accommodations on Religious Grounds in Certain Bodies*, SQ 2017, c 19 (enacted but stayed).

39. SQ 2019, c 12.

40. On racism and white supremacy, see Jugé and Perez 2006; Keaton 2010; J. Beaman 2019, 2021; and Hajjat and Mohammad 2013 on the French context, and Antonius 2008; Helly 2011; Bilge 2013; and Abedi 2019 on the Québécois context.

41. A number of agencies in Québec, including Justice femme, an organization providing legal support to women, have reported an escalation in both verbal and physical hate crimes at the time of debates on Law 21 prior to its passing in June 2019 among women who wear hijab (Abedi 2019; LeClair 2019; see also Bakali 2015a, 2016; Mekki-Berrada 2018; Wilkins-Laflamme 2018; Mugabo 2016; Selby, Barras, and Beaman 2018b; and Jahangeer 2020).

42. Statistics Canada (2023) data on hate crimes and Islamophobia show that children under eighteen were the most common perpetrators of these incidents.

43. This posture vis-à-vis the secular is not original. Joan Wallach Scott (2018: 7) makes this point, citing Saba Mahmood (2016: 21) on the care that encourages critique: "To critique a particular normative regime is not to reject or condemn it; rather, by analyzing its regulatory and productive dimensions, one only deprives it of innocence and neutrality so as to craft, perhaps, a different future" (see also Mahmood 2009, on critique as the investigation of the inherited self, and Burchardt 2020: 42).

Chapter 1

1. Ilias has dual French and Algerian nationality. That young people in this suburb are considered "third-generation" immigrants captures how immigration status remains with racialized individuals long past their grandparents' initial settlement. That Ilias's mother was a first-generation immigrant may also complicate these equations.

2. I purposefully do not use the term *secularization*. European sociologists including Durkheim and Weber circulated the concept in the early twentieth century. They argued that Western Europe underwent a gradual and progressive process of secularization. Both sociologically and demographically, this "progressive churn" has been disproved (Casanova 1994). "De-Christianization" better captures the waning public influence of the Christian church and its institutions in this period (on de-Christianization in Canada, see Gustafson and Selby 2016).

3. Attention to these multiple configurations has also been conceptualized as "multiple secularities" in four ideal types, as a nod to the inutility of a general theory of secularism (see Wohlrab-Sahr and Burchardt 2012), or, in nation-specific models, where France's institutionalized relationship between religion and politics is depicted as strictly separationalist.

4. Some scholars of secularism have found the "postsecular" a useful framework. Jürgen Habermas (2008), for one, uses the prefix to signal inequalities in the public sphere. Religious actors, for instance, must translate their arguments into a universal areligious language because theirs is not on equal footing in the shared secular sphere. Yet other scholars have used the "post-" prefix to call the stability of the noun into question (see Parmaksiz 2018: 111; see also Wilson 2014: 348; Mavelli and Wilson 2016: 251). Erin Wilson (2014: 348), for one, argues that the prefix usefully demarcates a progression beyond the secular but sees it as unhelpful beyond this obvious point. Following Wilson, I similarly do not employ a "postsecular" framework, seeing it as unnecessary to question the immutability of the secular.

5. My thanks to David Koussens for sharing Ferrari's distinction with me.

6. Initially hung in the Québec National Assembly in 1936 by then premier Maurice Duplessis, known for his support of institutional Catholicism, the cross, many argued, symbolized his government's deep ties with Catholicism. Yet the crucifix's presence invited no public debate or concern. Following Duplessis's death in 1959, the Quiet Revolution, and the beginnings of the de-Christianization of governmental institutions in the 1960s, critics began calling for the cross's removal from this visually significant location in the Blue Room. Prayer was abolished in the National Assembly in 1976. More than seventy years after the cross was hung, the 2008 Bouchard-Taylor Report, which stemmed from a government-appointed commission that sought to assess the acceptability of religion in the public sphere and outline parameters for "reasonable accommodation," formally recommended the crucifix's removal. Its presence, concluded Gérard Bouchard and Charles Taylor (2008: 152), "suggests that a very special closeness exists between legislative power and the religion of the majority." Despite these critiques, the cross remained untouched until after the passage of Law 21 in 2019. It was subsequently moved from its former prominent position to a display in a hallway between the Blue and Red Rooms (*CBC News* 2019).

7. Readers may be disappointed that I do not discuss actual sex (for more on this, see: Schrijvers and Wiering 2018).

8. Seeing *which* nonmonogamies in Canada have escaped legal censure, have gained limited legal sanction, or remain publicly and legally unaccepted illuminates webs of privilege and power. For example, Nathan Rambukkana (2015: 156) shows how, when practiced among white and economically privileged Canadians, adultery, swinging, and casual polyamory have been subject to much less state surveillance.

9. I saw the term's addition to the tripartite mantra on public school properties in Petit-Nanterre and Paris myself. The add-on followed the 2013 Charter of Secularism introduced to French public schools. The charter links it to *liberté, égalité, fraternité* in this way: "Secularism enables the exercise of citizenship, reconciling the freedom [*liberté*] of each individual with the equality [*égalité*] and fraternity [*fraternité*] of all, with a concern for the common good" (my translation).

10. Several scholars have noted the role of the media in provoking the debate. The cover of *Le Nouvel Observateur*, for example, featured the image of a hijab with the

headline, "Fanaticism: The Religious Threat" (Donadio 2021; see also Brulard 1997; Venel 1999; and Bowen 2004).

11. Lawmakers voted on the bill to ban conspicuous religious symbols (Law 2004-228) in public schools and government offices in February 2004. It received strong support and passed almost unanimously a month later (Assemblée Nationale 2004; Weil 2009).

12. The CCIF, headquartered in Saint-Ouen, had twenty regional branches. The emotional period following the *Charlie Hebdo* attacks inculcated the *esprit du 11 janvier* but also an unprecedented number of Islamophobic incidents (128 registered in the first three weeks) and an increased trivialization of anti-Muslim sentiment by politicians across the political spectrum. In its report from that year, the CCIF (2015: 16) argued that Muslims in France were represented by Ahmed Merabet, a police officer who died defending *Charlie Hebdo* journalists, and not by the Kouachi brothers who undertook the terrorist attacks. Women wearing visible religious symbols were the most targeted (81.5 percent of reported incidents).

13. The CCIF was one of fifty-one organizations listed by the French government as "separatist," and rumors circulated that it had offered legal counsel to the father of the terrorist found guilty of killing high school teacher Samuel Paty (Hizzir 2020).

14. Parts of the CCIF were reestablished in Brussels as the Collectif contre l'islamophobie en Europe (Collective against Islamophobia in Europe) (*France 24* 2020).

15. The 2021 law also aims to reshape a number of other social institutions in the interest of secularism, including public administration, education (i.e., limiting the parameters around home schooling), immigration, public safety, places of worship (seeking greater transparency on their funding arrangements), and the internet. Nevertheless, a central concern of the law is to "provide solutions to the problem of *identitarian withdrawal* and the development of *radical Islam*, an ideology hostile to the principles and values on which the Republic is founded" (my emphasis; www.vie-publique.fr/discours/277648-conseil-des-ministres-09122020-respect-des-principes-de-la-republique).

16. Bill 21 passed with a 73–35 margin in June 2019. Premier François Legault invoked a notwithstanding clause, allowing it to override sections of the Canadian Charter of Rights and Freedoms (namely Section 2, which explicitly entrenches rights related to freedom of religion and conscience) for a five-year period. In response to concern with Article 6 for already-employed public school teachers, the CAQ introduced a grandfather clause that allowed already-employed teachers to hold the same job, at the same institution. An appeal launched by the National Council of Canadian Muslims and the Canadian Civil Liberties Association in July 2019 failed. A second appeal in October 2020, including four groups, allowed for minor amendments to the bill in relation to the English school district (see more on the content of their appeals in Dabby 2020).

17. A second appeal in February 2024 was also unsuccessful (see *Mouvement laïque québécois c. English Montreal School Board*, 2021 QCCA 1675; *Organisation mondiale sikhe du Canada c. Procureur général du Québec*, 2024 QCCA 254). The English Montreal School Board may appeal to the Supreme Court of Canada.

18. Barras and Saris (2021) insightfully show how the conceptualization of conspicuous religious symbols that can be easily removed can be traced back to arguments heard in the midst of a 2006 Supreme Court of Canada (SCC) deliberation on religious freedom. The case involved a twelve-year-old boy whose metal kirpan fell out of its sheath as he played in a school playground; the

school called the symbol a weapon and called for its removal, while the World Sikh Organization called for its protection under religious freedom (*Multani v. Commission Scolaire Marguerite-Bourgeoys* 2006). Significantly, the school board argued that Multani should remove the kirpan while at school or replace it with a nonmetal replica. Here the SCC takes a different approach to religious symbols than those articulated in Québec's Bills 94, 60, 62, and 21. Notably, few Quebeckers agreed with the SCC decision (see Beaman 2012: 13).

19. The hip hop preferences of young men in my sample offers an interesting point of comparison. Young men in Petit-Nanterre often listened to and mentioned Black American hip hop artists, while Algerian origin youths I interviewed in Montréal referred to hip hop from the French banlieues as sources of meaning.

20. Notions of the importance of virginity were (predictably) gendered in my sample. Ilias's previous sexual past was not a barrier for him in this arrangement. While I note the unequal gender dynamics in concerns for Zara's virginity, I chose not to ask my interlocutors about their feelings on virginity. To do so would have been to mirror the surveillance of the state on questions of sexuality. Several interlocutors volunteered this information, but I made a conscious choice not to ask.

Chapter 2

1. First responders and health care professionals in Canada are responsible for screening for and reporting intimate partner and domestic violence, which could explain questions posed to Walid regarding the nature of his relationship with Fatima (Public Safety Canada 2020). However, as a racialized and religionized newcomer, scrutiny by the first responders was sharpened in relation to Farida's hijab and her perceived vulnerability because of her lesser French-language fluency.

2. Based on fourteen months of participant observation, and in the context of a 2008 amendment to Article 97a of the Swiss Code, which intended to limit fraudulent unions in ways similar to those in France and Canada, Anne Levanchy (2015: 282) offers analysis of the race-based politics and decisions made among registrars in Switzerland.

3. On average, weddings in France and Québec cost US$20,000 (Lee 2019).

4. Joan Wallach Scott (2018: 125) situates a social shift for women in France from the 1950s into the early 1960s, from the virtues of home and family toward women's sexual agency, within broader post–Cold War geopolitics. Women's sexual freedom in the so-called West became defined in contrast to Islam in the Middle East. By the 1980s, it was no accident that in so-called Western contexts hijabs became characterized as impediments to women's sexual freedoms.

5. After a firebomb attack in 2011, the cover of the weekly French satirical magazine *Charlie Hebdo* depicted undesirable Muslim masculinity as homophobic, with a cartoon of a bearded and presumably Muslim man awkwardly kissing cartoonist Charb, who was later killed in the 2015 terrorist attack on the magazine headquarters (see image in Davidson Sorkin 2015).

6. According to Penal Code Article 433-21, in effect as of January 2002, polygamy is punishable by one year in prison and/or a €45,000 fine (Légifrance 2002).

7. The police killing of seventeen-year-old Nahel Merzouk during a traffic check at 9 a.m. in Nanterre in June 2023 incited riots in neighboring Nanterre Préfecture, where Nahel lived with his mother, Mounia. Following Nahel's assassination, police doubled down on arresting young men, which further ignited conflict (Lemaignen and Lefief 2023). Nahel's death reflects continuing racial profiling and Islamophobia operating within policing in the suburbs (J. Beaman 2021; Esteves et al. 2023).

8. In the social scientific literature that focuses on France, the emphasis on Muslim women's head coverings is remarkable (see Jouili 2015; Bowen 2007; Winter 2008; Barras 2017; Fernando 2014b; Selby 2014a; Adrian 2016; and Jacobsen 2017). This emphasis also appears in the Québécois-focused work on secularism and female-identifying Muslims (see Milot 2009; Koussens and Amiraux 2014; Selby 2014a; Eid 2007, 2012, 2015; Barras 2018; Koussens 2018; Jahangeer 2020).

9. Mehammed Amadeus Mack's (2017) compelling analysis of contemporary French pornography captures a similar narrow version of religion and sexuality. Mack argues that French anxieties around race and Islam are reflected in how immigration and race relations are sexualized in mainstream pornography. Given its ubiquity and the visual importance of the performances of sexuality and gender roles, pornography is a significant site for these logics, both in the Algerian colonial period and today (Mack 2017: 222; see also Dorlin 2006; Alloula 1986; and Stoler [2002] 2010: 95).

10. The decision appeared in the Conseil d'État in February 2020 (n° 418299; see Gastrin 2020).

11. There is little data to substantiate fears of a meteoric rise of niqabs in France or in Québec. *Le Figaro* (Gabizon 2009) estimated 367 women, while a Minister of the Interior report counted 1,900 women who wear it, approximately one-quarter are French-born converts (cited in Assemblée Nationale 2010: 24–29). The Gerin Commission report suggests that approximately two-thirds of women who wear them are French citizens (Assemblée Nationale 2010: 161), so that proposed sanctions against citizenship or residency permits, and the requirement in the subsequent 2011 law for citizenship classes, are actually more symbolic than effective. In Québec, reports at the time of Bill 94 suggested that as few as twenty-five women wore niqab across the province (Bakht 2020).

12. In 2016, the French labor code was revised, allowing private companies to limit their employees' expressions of belief (Code du Travail, Article L 1321-2-1).

13. The impact of the 2004 sanctions against conspicuous religious symbols in public schools stretched beyond children and classrooms. Two years after the Gerin Commission, the September 2012 Chatel Memorandum extended the purview of the 2004 law to mothers (and presumably fathers) who wear conspicuous religious symbols, who enter the school area or attend school-related activities, regardless of whether they take place on school grounds (see *Libération* 2013; Koussens and Amiraux 2014; Karimi 2021). This law is symbolic in demanding that all aspects of children's education of on school grounds and in school-related excursions remain "neutral." The abaya "ban" in schools was introduced by the minister of education in the fall of 2023 (Ministère de l'Éducation nationale et de la jeunesse 2023; see also *Al Jazeera* 2023a, 2023b; Le Monde 2023). Opinion polls showed that more than 80 percent of the French population agreed with this new intervention (IFOP 2023).

14. *La journée de la jupe* enjoyed critical success in France. Isabel Adjani won a César, the French equivalent of an Academy Award, in 2010 for this role, and the film was nominated for best film and best original screenplay.

15. Anthropologist Miriam Ticktin (2008) stresses the political expediency of newfound attention to previously ignored violence against women and girls of North African origin who live in the banlieues.

16. On Bastille Day 2016 on the Promenade des Anglais in Nice, a terrorist truck attack, claimed by the Islamic State, took 86 lives and injured 458 others (Almeida 2018). Only a few days later a Catholic priest, Jacques Hamel, in the Archdiocese

of Rouen, was murdered by two terrorists, who also claimed affiliation with the Islamic State. As following the terrorist attacks in Paris in 2015, a state of emergency allowed for greater police presence, both responding to and heightening the fear of terrorism. This situation meant that signs associated with radicalism or Islamism engendered panic (Wieviorka 2016; Rosenblum 2020).

17. Two of these bills (Bills 62 and 21) have passed the province's legislature, of which one (Bill 62) was stayed in December 2017 on the grounds that it could be injurious to Muslim women. The primary contents of Bill 62 were folded into Article 8 of Law 21, so that its being stayed is no longer significantly relevant for discussion.

18. The ruling prohibiting Zunera Ishaq's oath taking was struck down in February 2015 when Federal Court judge Keith Boswell ruled that there was a conflict between the ministerial directive from Minister Kenney and current citizenship regulations that should allow for the greatest possible religious freedom (see *Ishaq v. Canada (Minister of Citizenship and Immigration*, para. 53; Alibhai 2023: 109). Significantly, Justice Boswell did not refer to Section 2a of the charter in his decision to protect the niqab in these ceremonies (see also Bakht 2022: 346 for insightful thinking on why Section 15 of the Charter on Freedom of Expression was not deployed in the appeal).

19. One of Rachida and Farid's children died of leukemia as a toddler.

20. Waël was interviewed by one of my research assistants in Montréal, Kawtare Bihya.

21. An Algerian tourist visa for a Canadian living in France (i.e., me) required a registered host. Given how challenging it would be for Amel's grandmother and aunt to get to the police station—Amel's grandmother was a full-time caregiver of her aunt and neither could read and write French—Yacine generously agreed to act as official host and gathered the necessary paperwork, which he mailed to me in France. I received a tourist visa in my first attempt at the Algerian embassy, unlike many of those I introduce in chapter 3 who seek French visas.

Chapter 3

1. Because my one-year-old had had a bad cold when I left France, and I didn't have a working phone or internet access in Ghazaouet, Boussad knew I hoped to check my messages. I eventually was able to connect at Amel's sister-in-law Sara's parents' home the next day.

2. Because this research project foregrounds France and Québec as points of reference and comparison, I do not include the testimonies I heard in Algeria from young women and men who said they had absolutely no desire to migrate to France or Québec or elsewhere. Not everyone dreams of moving abroad. Reasons for not doing so varied and included the importance of their families, a love for their native country, bad food and weather elsewhere, the lack of better employment opportunities, the likely rejection of their migration request, and what they had heard or seen regarding racism and Islamophobia.

3. I describe Québécois and not solely Canadian immigration policy because of the 1991 Canada-Québec Accord, which granted the province greater legislative power over its immigration. Owing to its distinct history and linguistic particularity, it is the sole Canadian province that retains control over immigration selection and settlement and gives priority to French-speaking immigrants. Criteria related to criminality, security, health and administrative processing, and physical port of entry remain in federal jurisdiction, but the accord delineates that Québec is responsible for the selection, reception, and "integration" of immigrants to its

province. Section 2 of the accord outlines the importance of preserving Québec's "demographic weight" and "integrat[ing] immigrants to the province in a manner that respects the distinct society of Quebec" (Canada-Québec Accord 1991: 2). Since this accord was established, different provincial parties in Québec have lobbied for greater autonomy in this process.

4. As I explained in the introduction, comparison of my French and Québécois samples on social class is complicated by the geography of these samples. My interviewees in Petit-Nanterre lived in a context that was more socioeconomically homogeneous than those I interviewed in Montréal.

5. Governmentality is a technology of power; its rationalities are orientated toward conduct (Foucault 2008) and markers of sexual differentiation, racialization and racism, in determining who is "acceptable" and who is not (see Weheliye 2014: 72).

6. I recognize that my sample of interlocutors has a selection bias in that, notwithstanding those I interviewed in Ghazaouet, Algiers, and Tizi Ouzou, Algeria, I largely interviewed Algerians who had successfully emigrated to France and Québec.

7. Data show clear discrimination against Algerians in the Québécois job market, where the unemployment rate of those of Algerian origin falls somewhere between 30 and 40 percent, three to four times higher than the average rate (of about 6.2 percent in January 2017; Belkaïd 2017). Notably, in 2011, 65 percent of Algerians in Montréal held a postsecondary degree (in comparison with the 36 percent average for all Montrealers) (see also Grenier and Nadeau 2011, 31; Hachimi Alaoui 2006; Brahimi 2011; Castels 2012). To be clear, underemployment and unemployment are not unique to Algerians and persist for many religionized and racialized newcomers.

8. The legacies of the conquest of Algeria have been characterized as a genocide, as there is evidence of 825,000 Indigenous Algerians killed initially between 1830 and 1875, and 1.5 million Algerians amid the War of Independence from 1954 to 1962 (Kiernan 2007: 374).

9. Halim explains that the consulate in Algeria pockets the application fee, even if it rejects the applicant. At the same time, I have interviewed individuals who gained illegal entry into France by purposefully overstaying their tourist visas, so the state concern has some legitimacy.

10. Since my interview with Halim, Chibanis have been allowed to spend up to six months in the Maghreb and maintain their French pensions. This was not the case at the time of our interviews.

11. The city of Nanterre has a long history of Communist Party leadership, which continues with Patrick Jarry, who at the time of writing is still the mayor, having been continuously reelected since 2004. He is white and non-Muslim, and grew up in an HLM in Petit-Nanterre.

12. The declaration of "national values" as a condition of French citizenship with the Contrat d'accueil et d'intégration (Reception and integration contract) in January 2007 shed further light on who was most vulnerable to these machinations. The obligatory contract aimed to ensure competency in French literacy and agreement with "Republican values" through a six-hour course followed by a formal interview to prove their support of the "values of French Republicanism" (see Hajjat 2012). Secularism and gender equality are listed as the first two of four values (the others being fundamental liberties and the educational system).

13. Civil and religious ceremonies are strictly separated in France, while they may be combined in Québec and Algeria. With the implementation of this 2003 law in

France, the fatiha (or Islamic or halal marriage) became surveilled by the state in ways it is not in Québec. Imams in France who officiate a religious marriage without the civil act in hand may be punished with six months' imprisonment and a €7,500 fine (Article 433-21) (Légifrance 2002). The law is meant to prevent couples from undertaking a solely religious union.

14. The marriage rate in France decreased 6 percent between 2006 and 2018, when it stood at 42.5 percent (Statista 2019).

15. If found guilty, a marriage certificate can be annulled for up to forty years and those guilty can be deported. Originally the 2006 law stipulated that a defendant found guilty faced one year of imprisonment or a €15,000 fine. These penalties increased substantially in 2011 with stricter penalties for men (and not women) and for organizations that profit from fraudulent matches: ten years in prison and a €750,000 fine.

16. There has been a significant decline in the number of family-class immigrants admitted to Canada: from 39 percent in 1994 to 22 percent in 2012 (Citizenship and Immigration Canada 2012a).

17. As for Yousra, a common narrative exists regarding Algerians in Québec that focuses on refugee settlement in the 1990s. Statistical data paint a slightly different picture. Most Algerian arrivals (75 percent) in this period through the 1990s settled through the skilled worker stream or on student visas (Boulmezaoud 2017: 10). The remaining immigrants entered under family reunification (18 percent), as refugees (6 percent), and "other" (1 percent).

18. Data for 2016 suggest that Algerians in Québec were relatively evenly distributed by gender, with slightly more women (54 percent) than men age twenty-five to forty-four. Before 1981, migration from Algeria was largely masculine (62 percent) (Boulmezaoud 2017: 17).

19. In addition to the Black Decade, other moments of unrest that impacted the migration of my interlocutors include the *Printemps berbère* (the Amazigh or Berber Spring) in 1980, the *Grève des cartables* (Schoolbag Strike) in 1994, and the *Printemps noir* (Black Spring) in 2001.

20. Randja described in salty and funny terms how she and her husband, Yousef, both atheists, agreed to a fatiha for their wedding to appease his family: "My husband comes from a Kabylian Sufi family for whom the fatiha was important. But we don't care about the fatiha. *Nous, on s'en câlisse de la fatiha* [we could give a fuck about the fatiha]. So, what we did [was] to please his family, because you still need their blessing a little bit." Using Québécois profanity, she expressed both her adaptation to the will of their families and her audaciousness. Her eldest son's desire to return to Kabylian tradition through marriage is made more notable by his parents' disavowal of Islam and associated traditions.

21. Approximately 3,450 Algerians settle annually; in 2016 there were approximately 105,000 individuals of Algerian origin recorded in Canada (Boulmezaoud 2017: 3), of whom 90 percent lived in the province of Québec and 80 percent on the island of Montréal.

22. When "conditional" permanent residency was first introduced in Canada—a hurdle not unlike the surprise follow-up visits in France to non-EU married couples—more than eighty immigrant- and women's rights-organizations across Canada opposed it because of potential domestic abuse (see Alaggia, Regehr, and Rishchynski 2009; and Merali 2009). In response to these critiques, the office of Citizenship and Immigration Canada created a clause ("Exception for Victims of Abuse and Neglect") that removed the requirement for constant cohabitation for

those able to provide proof of abuse (see also Bhuyan, Korteweg, and Baqi 2018: 363).

23. Algerians are not directly targeted by immigration policies in Canada then way that they have been in France (Hajjat 2012). Bhuyan, Korteweg, and Baqi (2018) show how applicants from the Philippines, India, and China (also countries with the highest overall volume of immigration to Canada) were the focus of scrutiny on a federal level.

24. *Dhaliwal, Jaswinder v. M.C.I.* (F.C. n° IMM-1314-07), de Montigny, October 15, 2007; 2007 FC 1051. A similar point was also decided in *Sharma v Canada (Minister of Citizenship and Immigration)*, 2009 FC 1131 (see https://irb-cisr.gc.ca/en/legal-policy/legal-concepts/Documents/SpoParo6_e.pdf).

25. To be clear, I do not necessarily disagree with Justice de Montigny's decision. The evidence presented suggests that Dr. Dhaliwal did not meet the threshold of "sincerity" as outlined in the Immigration Act. My point is to highlight *which* criteria flagged their arranged marriage as unacceptable for the state: the unreasonableness of an unmarried man marrying an older divorced mother of two, and the lack of romantic displays in their in-person interview.

26. A 2011 Supreme Court of British Columbia decision that ruled against decriminalizing polygamy in Canada through a change in the Criminal Code was based on a sect of Mormonism (see Reference re Section 293 of the Criminal Code of Canada, 2011 BCSC 1588).

27. Eight years after their migration to France, following a twenty-four-year marriage, Mouloud and Leila separated in 2012, spurred by Mouloud's extramarital relationship and departure from their family apartment.

28. I met Leila, Mouloud, and Yaseem in Algiers, having flown there separately from Canada. We stayed for a few nights at Mouloud's mother's small apartment outside the city. Hosting a foreign national took concerted effort on the part of my hosts, who had to fill out paperwork in the police station in Tizi Ouzou and send by mail for my travel visa application.

29. Since her separation from Mouloud in 2012, and once I was no longer a student, she accepted my restaurant invitations in the next half-dozen times we saw each other, in 2012, 2014, and 2015–16.

30. The adult children spoke French with complete fluency, having attended French schools in Kabylia run by Christian religious groups. Leila's mother and father preferred Tamazight but were at ease in French too. Before the trip I had successfully learned only a handful of words in Tamazight, so I was grateful for the family's linguistic abilities.

31. Having first met me in Tizi Ouzou in 2011 when I was expecting my first child, and having participated in family dinner conversations that had guessed the baby's sex, Hichem had also been keen to meet my children and partner during our stays in Montréal in 2018 and 2019.

32. Hichem stressed how generous this Tizi Ouzou–born, Montréal-living friend had been to him, showing the importance of small networks for his transnational migration. In February, when he first arrived in Montréal from Tizi Ouzou in February to visit Jeannette, "he [his friend] was the one waiting for me at the airport. He even lent me his shoes because I had bought new shoes and they hurt me. Seven hours of flight from Algiers to Montréal! *Tabarouette* [Shucks]. I was in pain! So he gave me his winter shoes. It was cold! The month of February, eh! I come from a warm country. So, for me, when I went outside, it was something."

Chapter 4

1. This interview was conducted by Julia Itel. Julia knew Maya (as well as her baby, Adam, and husband, Jean) well before interviewing her in her apartment in the Plateau neighborhood. Julia described Maya as sporty, with a prim and no-nonsense demeanor. At the time of the interview, she was on maternity leave from her job as an insurance adjuster.

2. I initially considered employing the term "intercolonial" to describe the interconnectedness of kinship, desire, and relationships with Algeria. I had hoped the "inter" prefix captured how people in diasporas exist between locations and within an inter-triangulation of Algeria-France-Québec. Nevertheless, I jettisoned the term "intercolonial" from this book given its historical usage to describe how colonies connect and as relating to trade and travel between two or more colonies (Akami 2017; Nguyễn-võ 2017). I sincerely thank Shannon Fraser for her thinking with me on this term.

3. *Lycées français* like Marie-de-France in Montréal powerfully promote the circulation of French culture and mores abroad (Fourny 2007).

4. Only one of my interlocutors in France, twenty-one-year-old Wassim, lived in a secret common-law arrangement in an apartment just outside of Petit-Nanterre while attending university in Paris. In our meeting at a restaurant where we shared Turkish brochettes, Wassim was cavalier about this living arrangement, noting *after* I gave assurances I would not tell his aunt (who had introduced me to him) that it was "no big deal." He was more interested in sharing his career aspirations. When I returned to Petit-Nanterre the next year, one of his cousins reported to me that, thanks to a lottery immigration system, Wassim had received a visa to the United States and was working for an engineering firm in Washington, DC. No one mentioned his previous girlfriend.

5. I thank Carol-Lynne D'Arcangelis (2022) for sharing her expertise and work on this topic with me.

6. A significant critique has emerged amid this scholarship, namely a decolonial *feminist* turn, that can be credited to María Lugones (2007, 2010), Gloria Anzaldúa, Emma Pérez, and Breny Mendoza (2020), among others. One of the most important insights to emerge out of this literature is Lugones's concept of "the coloniality of gender," which holds that gender, like race, is a colonial/modern imposition that has wreaked havoc on social relations.

7. While some quantitative studies have focused on immigrant youth and marriage in France (Rude-Antoine 1990; Santelli 2001; Moguérou and Santelli 2012; Santelli and Collet 2011, 2012a, 2012b), they have not explored the meanings and motivations behind transnational marriage preferences.

8. Scholars have long charted constructions of Algeria in France as proxies for normative and authoritative Muslimness (see Bourdieu 1979; Silverstein 2004; Hachimi Alaoui 2007; Selby 2014b; and Silverstein 2004).

9. In her fieldwork with teens in a nearby more ethnically diverse neighboring suburb to Petit-Nanterre, Chantal Tetreault (2015: 81) shows how *Le Bled* is used to reference not only home countries in North Africa but also Portugal and Cambodia.

10. There are parallels with these men's return to Algeria for potential wives with the "filles du roi" (king's daughters) migration phenomenon in New France (now Québec) between 1663 and 1673, when approximately 800 single women were sponsored by Louis IV to marry men in the Québécois colony (Wien and Gousse 2015).

11. I first encountered Gyps's work at an exhibit celebrating 100 years of Algerian immigration to France (1913–2013) in April 2014 at Paris's Musée de l'histoire de l'immigration (Museum of the History of Immigration).

12. This trip to Ghazaouet in July 2016 took place near the end of my twelve-month stay in France during a sabbatical year (August 2015–July 2016).

13. Thanks to social media, I have kept in touch with Sara in the years after our meeting in 2016. She has since given birth to two sons and has launched a social media- and home-based cake-making business.

14. As I describe in chapter 2, I got to know Amel well in the seven months leading up to her wedding. She generously shared her time and invited me to join her and her family on her wedding trip in the week beforehand in Ghazaouet.

15. Little research has been conducted on fatiha rituals in France and Canada (with exceptions of Al-Johar 2005 in France and Macfarlane 2012a, 2012b in Ontario).

16. In 2021, 42.7 percent of couples in Québec lived in common-law relationships, a figure that drops to 16.9 percent in the rest of Canada (cited in Battams and Mathieu 2024).

17. In 2021, Stora completed his report for President Emmanuel Macron on the legacy of the Algerian War and "questions of memory" (see Stora 2021). Now more than sixty years after the end of the war, components of the French national archives have been declassified, which should initiate new conversations about the meanings of the war (France Archives 2023).

18. I recognize that inclusion of "Indigenous issues" can sometime act as an erasure of Indigenous sovereignties.

19. The 2008–15 Truth and Reconciliation Commission of Canada subsequently released an executive summary of its work, as well as ninety-four calls to action (CTAs) to promote reconciliation between non-Indigenous and Indigenous Canadians. CTAs 48 and 49—which call on church groups to adopt the UN Declaration on the Rights of Indigenous People's framework for reconciliation, and to respect "Indigenous peoples' right to self-determination in spiritual matters," with relation to traditions and ceremonies (CTA 48.ii)—remain "in progress."

20. Some Indigenous leaders, like Ojibwe Manitoba premier Wab Kinew, deploy the term "religion" as a way to interrupt colonial tropes: "When I use 'religion' to describe Indigenous ways, part of it is to convey . . . that our worldviews are as complex, are as worthy of respect, as Christianity or Islam" (quoted in Colorado 2020: 79).

21. In a 2009 G20 summit speech, Prime Minister Harper publicly celebrated that Canada had "no history of colonialism." The statement was confusing given that fifteen months earlier Harper had officially apologized to Indigenous peoples for Canada's extensive residential school system. Jennifer Henderson and Pauline Wakeham (2009: 2) argue that Harper's previous apology isolates and contains residential schools "as a discrete historical problem of educational malpractice rather than one devastating prong of an overarching and multifaceted system of colonial oppression that persists in the present."

22. The death of a thirty-seven-year-old Indigenous woman, Joyce Echaquan, in a hospital emergency room in September 2020 laid bare these structures of endemic racism. Premier Legault formally condemned the medical staff's comments as "racist" but denied the existence of systemic racism in the province and that it contributed to her death (Feith 2020; Sioui 2021).

23. Díaz appears to be riffing on Aníbal Quijano's (2000, 2008) notion of the "coloniality of power." María Lugones (2010: 370; 2007: 186) later critiques Quijano's "coloniality of power" for its narrow take on gender and implicit heterosexism.

Conclusion

1. The dual logic between acceptable and unacceptable religious symbols was established in France in 1994 with the Bayrou Decree, named after the then-minister of education, François Bayrou. In the wake of the country's headscarf affairs, it more clearly delineated acceptable and unacceptable religious symbols in public schools. The 2004 law in France on conspicuous religious symbols anchored this dual regulation of the conspicuous and inconspicuous. This approach reappeared most prominently in the 2013 "Charter of Values," or Bill 60, proposed by the Parti Québécois, which distinguished overt and conspicuous from small and inconspicuous religious symbols (see fig. 1.4). Law 21 in Québec drew on four previous legislative projects, but especially Bill 60. While this binary was not officially invoked in Law 21 and religious symbols are presented in its legislative document more ambiguously than in Bill 60, the Bill 60 pictogram has remained lodged in conceptualizations of unacceptable religiosity in the public sphere in Québec.

2. The law also included new rules on how religious institutions are financed, which I do not examine here in my analysis on secular sensibilities. The Law Respecting the Principles of the Republic (n° 2021-1109) passed on August 24, 2021 (Légifrance 2021).

3. What if, following Natasha Bakht's (2014, 2021) brilliant thought experiment, we alternatively characterized the niqab as a bold statement against state intervention and counter to a patriarchal gaze? As a sign of freedom of expression rather than one of complete confinement? As a foil counter to a sexualized, bare-breasted Marianne?

4. Of course, these states' scrutiny of certain marital relations is not new (Segalen 2003). Establishing the acceptable contours of marriage and of sexuality have been long-standing concerns for colonial governments. Monogamous marriages were understood to support social stability and economic productivity, and therein formed the basis of modern capitalism.

5. The *Cambridge Dictionary*'s definition includes a note on the performativity of "romance" used as a verb: it may also mean "to describe an event in a way that makes it sound better than it was."

6. Illouz (1997: 38) shows the consumerism and consumption laden in modern romance, which requires disposable income and time. She argues that there are tremendous profits to be made if the requirements of romance extend beyond a couple's wedding (41; Ingraham 1999). This expectation is mirrored in the unexpected transnational marriage follow-up visits by French officials to transnational non-EU couples. The undergirding premise is that a surprise visit will engender a more genuine performance, and that signs of romance reflect a genuine relationship.

7. A 2011 amendment to the French law against love fraud with a migratory aim also included greater punishments for men found guilty of forced or fraudulent marriage, reinforcing the clear gendered hierarchy latent in these norms.

REFERENCES

Abedi, Maham. 2019. "Muslim Women in Quebec Facing Increased Hate amid Bill 21 Debate: Advocates." *Global News*, May 15, 2019. https://globalnews.ca/news/5274699/muslim-women-quebec-hate-incidents.

Abji, Salina, Anna C. Korteweg, and Lawrence H. Williams. 2019. "Culture Talk and the Politics of the New Right: Navigating Gendered Racism in Attempts to Address Violence against Women in Immigrant Communities." *Signs: Journal of Women in Culture and Society* 44 (3): 797–822.

Adrian, Melanie. 2016. *Religious Freedom at Risk: The EU, French Schools, and Why the Veil Was Banned*. Cham, Switzerland: Springer.

Agrama, Hussein Ali. 2012. *Questioning Secularism: Islam, Sovereignty, and the Rule of Law in Egypt*. Chicago: University of Chicago Press.

Ahmed, Sadaf. 2021. "Time for a 'Hijab Ban'? The Hypervisibility of Veiling in Scholarship on Islam in North America." In *Producing Islam(s) in Canada*, edited by Amélie Barras, Jennifer A. Selby, and Melanie Adrian, 137–54. Toronto: University of Toronto Press.

Ahmed, Sara. 2007. "A Phenomenology of Whiteness." *Feminist Theory* 8 (2): 149–68.

Akami, T. 2017. "Imperial Polities, Intercolonialism, and the Shaping of Global Governing Norms: Public Health Expert Networks in Asia and the League of Nations Health Organization, 1908–37." *Journal of Global History* 12 (1): 4–25.

Alaggia, R., C. Regehr, and G. Rishchynski. 2009. "Intimate Partner Violence and Immigration Laws in Canada: How Far Have We Come?" *International Journal of Psychiatry and the Law* 32 (6): 335–41.

Alibhai, Zaheeda P. 2023. "At Face Value? The Politics of Belief: The Refashioning of the Body in Law and Public Policy and on the Virtual Public Square in the Twenty-First Century." In *Corps in/visibles : genre, religion et politique / In/visible Bodies: Gender, Religion and Politics*, edited by Florence Pasche Guignard and Catherine Larouche, 103–24. Québec, QC: Presses de l'Université Laval.

Al Jazeera. 2023a. "Amid Abaya Ban, French School Sends Girl Home for Wearing Kimono." September 6, 2023. www.aljazeera.com/news/2023/9/6/french-school-expels-student-for-wearing-a-kimono-lawyer.

——. 2023b. "France's Top Court Rejects Appeal against Ban on Wearing Abaya in Schools." September 8, 2023. www.aljazeera.com/news/2023/9/8/frances-top-court-rejects-appeal-against-ban-on-wearing-abaya-in-schools.

Al-Johar, Denise. 2005. "Muslim Marriages in America: Reflecting New Identities." *Muslim World* 95 (4): 557–74.

Allen, Christopher. 2010. *Islamophobia*. Farnham, UK: Ashgate.

Alloula, Malek. 1986. *The Colonial Harem*. Translated by Myrna Godzich and Wlad Godzich. Minneapolis: University of Minnesota Press.

Almeida, Dimitri. 2018. "Marianne at the Beach: The French Burkini Controversy and the Shifting Meanings of Republican Secularism." *Journal of Intercultural Studies* 39 (1): 20–34.

Amiraux, Valérie. 2007. "The Headscarf Question: What Is Really the Issue?" In *European Islam: Challenges for Public Policy and Society*, edited by Samir

Amghar, Amel Boubekeur, and Michel Emerson, 124–43. Brussels: Centre for European Policy Studies.

———. 2010. "De l'Empire à la République : 'L'islam de France.'" In *Ruptures postcoloniales: Les nouveaux visages de la société française*, edited by Ahmed Boubeker, Françoise Vergès, Florence Bernault, Achille Mbembe, Nicolas Bancel, and Pascal Blanchard, 379–90. Paris: La Découverte.

———. 2014. "Le port de la 'burqa' en Europe : comment la religion des uns est devenue l'affaire publique des autres." In *Quand la burqa passe à l'Ouest : enjeux éthiques, politiques et juridiques*, edited by David Koussens and Olivier Roy, 15–37. Rennes: Presses Universitaires de Rennes.

———. 2016. "Visibility, Transparency and Gossip: How Did the Religion of Some (Muslims) Become the Public Concern of Others?" *Critical Research on Religion* 4 (1): 37–56.

Amiraux, Valérie, and Francis Desharnais. 2015. *Salomé et les hommes en noir*. Montréal: Bayard Canada.

Amiraux, Valérie, and David Koussens. 2013. "From Principle to Narratives: Unveiling French Secularism." RECODE Online Working Paper Series, no. 19. https://valerieamiraux.com/wp-content/uploads/2010/11/Amiraux-and-Koussens-From-Law-to-Narratives.pdf.

Amir-Moazami, Schirin. 2013. "The Secular Embodiments of Face-Veil Controversies across Europe." In *Islam and Public Controversy in Europe*, edited by Nulifer Göle, 83–98. London: Routledge.

———. 2016. "Investigating the Secular Body: The Politics of the Male Circumcision Debate in Germany." *ReOrient* 1 (2): 147–70.

———. 2022. *Interrogating Muslims: The Liberal-Secular Matrix of Integration*. London: Bloomsbury.

Ammerman, Nancy T. 2007. "Introduction." In *Everyday Religion: Observing Modern Religious Lives*, edited by Nancy T. Ammerman, 3–18. Oxford: Oxford University Press.

———. 2014. "Finding Religion in Everyday Life." *Sociology of Religion* 75, no. 2 (Summer): 189–207.

Anidjar, Gil. 2006. "Secularism." *Critical Inquiry* 33 (1): 52–77.

Antonius, Rachad. 2008. "L'islam au Québec : les complexités d'un processus de racisation." *Islam, Empire, and Modernity*, no. 48, 11–28.

Aranguren, Martin, Francesco Madrisotti, and Eser Durmaz-Martins. 2021. "Anti-Muslim Behaviour in Everyday Interaction: Evidence from a Field Experiment in Paris." *Journal of Ethnic and Migration Studies* 49 (3): 770–94.

Arnold, Martin. 2005. "French Minister Says Polygamy to Blame for Riots." *Financial Times*, November 15, 2005.

Asad, Talal. 1983. "Anthropological Conceptions of Religion: Reflections on Geertz." *Man* 18, no. 2 (June): 237–59.

———. 2003. *Formations of the Secular: Christianity, Islam, Modernity*. Stanford, CA: Stanford University Press.

———. 2011. "Thinking about the Secular Body, Pain, and Liberal Politics." *Cultural Anthropology* 26 (4): 657–75.

———. 2018. *Secular Translations: Nation-State, Modern Self and Calculative Reason*. New York: Columbia University Press.

Asal, Houda. 2014. "Islamophobie : la fabrique d'un nouveau concept." *Sociologie* 1 (51): 13–29.

Assemblée Nationale (France). 1905. "Projet de loi relative la séparation des églises et de l'État." www.assemblee-nationale.fr/histoire/eglise-etat/1905-projet.pdf.
———. 2003. "Rapport fait au nom de la mission d'information sur la question du port des signes religieux à l'école." Stasi Commission Report. www.assemblee-nationale.fr/12/pdf/rapports/r1275-t2.pdf.
———. 2004. "Loi n° 2004-228 du 15 mars 2004 encadrant, en application du principe de laïcité, le port de signes ou de tenues manifestant une appartenance religieuse dans les écoles, collèges et lycées publics." *Journal officiel de la République française*, March 17, 2004. Paris: Légifrance.
———. 2010. "Rapport d'information fait en application de l'article 145 du Règlement au nom de la mission d'information sur la pratique du port du voile intégral sur le territoire national." Gerin Commission report. www.assemblee-nationale.fr/13/pdf/rap-info/i2262.pdf.
———. 2011. "Loi n° 2011-672 du 16 juin 2011 relative à l'immigration, à l'intégration et à la nationalité." (1) Paris: Légifrance. www.legifrance.gouv.fr/jo_pdf.do?id=JORFTEXT000024191380.
Assemblée Nationale du Québec. 2010. "Projet de loi n° 94 : Loi établissant les balises encadrant les demandes d'accommodement dans l'Administration gouvernementale et dans certains établissements." www.assnat.qc.ca/fr/travaux-parlementaires/projets-loi/projet-loi-94-39-1.html?appelant=MC.
———. 2013. "Charter Affirming the Values of State Secularism and Religious Neutrality and Equality between Women and Men and Providing a Framework for Accommodation Requests." http://m.assnat.qc.ca/en/travaux-parlementaires/projets-loi/projet-loi-60-40-1.html.
———. 2017. "Projet de loi n° 62 : Loi favorisant le respect de la neutralité religieuse de l'État et visant notamment à encadrer les demandes d'accommodements pour un motif religieux dans certains organismes." www.publicationsduquebec.gouv.qc.ca/fileadmin/Fichiers_client/lois_et_reglements/LoisAnnuelles/fr/2017/2017C19F.PDF.
———. 2019. "Projet de loi n° 21 : Loi sur la laïcité de l'État." www.legisquebec.gouv.qc.ca/fr/document/lc/l-0.3.
Authier, Philip. 2019. "Religious Symbols: Quebec 'Convinced We Have Found the Right Balance.'" *Montreal Gazette*, March 29, 2019. https://montrealgazette.com/news/quebec/religious-symbols-quebec-to-table-secularism-bill-caq-will-propose-moving-crucifix.
Badinter, Élisabeth, Régine Deforges, Caroline Eliacheff, Claude Habib, and Nathalie Heinich. 2012. "L'interdiction de la prostitution est une chimère." *L'Obs*, August 23, 2012.
Bakali, Naved. 2015a. "Challenging Anti-Muslim Racism through a Critical Race Curriculum in Québec Secondary Schools." *Critical Intersections in Education* 3:19–24.
———. 2015b. "Contextualising the Québec Charter of Values: How the Muslim 'Other' Is Conceptualised in Québec." *Culture and Religion* 16 (4): 412–29.
———. 2016. *Islamophobia: Understanding Anti-Muslim Racism through the Lived Experiences of Muslim Youth*. Rotterdam: Sense.
Bakht, Natasha. 2014. "In Your Face: Piercing the Veil of Ignorance about Niqab-Wearing Women." *Social and Legal Studies* 24, no. 3 (October): https://doi.org/10.1177/0964663914552214.

———. 2020. *In Your Face: Law, Justice, and Niqab-Wearing Women in Canada*. Toronto: Irwin Law.

———. 2021. "2(b) or Not 2(b): The Expressive Value of the Niqab." In *Producing Islam(s) in Canada*, edited by Amélie Barras, Jennifer A. Selby, and Melanie Adrian, 341–58. Toronto: University of Toronto Press.

Barclay, Fiona, Charlotte Ann Chopin, and Martin Evans. 2018. "Introduction: Settler Colonialism and French Algeria." *Settler Colonial Studies* 8 (2): 115–30.

Barras, Amélie. 2013. "Sacred Laïcité and the Politics of Religious Resurgence in France: Wither Religious Freedom?" *Mediterranean Politics* 18 (2): 276–93.

———. 2016. "Exploring the Intricacies and Dissonances of Religious Governance: The Case of Quebec and the Discourse of Request." *Critical Research on Religion* 4 (1): 57–71.

———. 2017. "Secularism in France." In *The Oxford Handbook of Secularism*, edited by Phil Zuckerman and John R. Shook, 142–54. Oxford: Oxford University Press.

———. 2018. "Travelogue of Secularism: Longing to Find a Place to Call Home." *European Journal of Women's Studies* 29 (2): 1–16.

Barras, Amélie, and Anne Saris. 2021. "Gazing into the World of Tattoos: An Invitation to Reconsider How We Conceptualize Religious Practices." *Studies in Religion / Sciences religieuses* 50 (2): 167–88.

Battams, Nathan, and Sophie Mathieu. 2024. "Common-Law Unions Are Most Common in Quebec and Nunavut." In Vanier Institute of the Family, *Families Count 2024*. https://vanierinstitute.ca/families-count-2024/common-law-unions-are-most-common-in-Quebec-and-Nunavut.

Baubérot, Jean. 1998. "La laïcité française et ses mutations." *Social Compass* 45 (1): 175–87.

———. 2004. "La Commission Stasi vue par l'un de ses membres." *French Politics, Culture and Society* 22 (3): 135–41.

Baubérot, Jean, and Micheline Milot. 2011. *Laïcités sans frontières*. Paris: Seuil.

BBC News. 2016. "Paris Attacks: Who Were the Attackers?" April 27, 2016. www.bbc.com/news/world-europe-34832512.

———. 2018. "Canada Politician Says Crucifix 'Not Religious Symbol.'" October 12, 2018. www.bbc.com/news/world-us-canada-45842471.

Beaman, Jean. 2019. "Are French People White? Towards an Understanding of Whiteness in Republican France." *Identities* 26 (5): 546–62.

———. 2021. "France's Ahmeds and Muslim Others: The Entanglement of Racism and Islamophobia." *French Cultural Studies* 32 (3): 269–79.

Beaman, Lori G. 2011. "'It Was All Slightly Unreal': What's Wrong with Tolerance and Accommodation in the Adjudication of Religious Freedom?" *Canadian Journal of Women and the Law* 23 (2): 442–63.

———, ed. 2012. *Reasonable Accommodation: Managing Religious Diversity*. Vancouver: University of British Columbia Press.

———. 2013. "Is Polygamy Inherently Harmful?" In *Polygamy's Rights and Wrongs: Perspectives on Harm, Family, and Law*, edited by G. Calder and L. G. Beaman, 1–20. Vancouver: University of British Columbia Press.

———. 2017. *Deep Equality in an Era of Religious Diversity*. Oxford: Oxford University Press.

———. 2020. *The Transition of Religion to Culture in Law and Public Discourse*. New York: Routledge.
Beardsley, Eleanor. 2012. "In France, Politicians Make Halal Meat a Campaign Issue." National Public Radio, March 15, 2012. www.npr.org/sections/thesalt/2012/03/15/148521433/in-france-politicians-make-halal-meat-a-campaign-issue.
———. 2016. "Beach Season Winds Down, but Burkini Debate Rages on in France." National Public Radio, September 7, 2016. www.npr.org/sections/parallels/2016/09/07/492926635/beach-season-winds-down-but-burkini-debate-rages-on-in-france.
Beaud, Stéphane, and Michel Pialoux. 2003. *Violences urbaines, violence sociale : genèse des nouvelles classes dangereuses*. Paris: Fayard.
Belhassen-Maalaoui, Amel. 2008. *Au Canada entre rêve et tourmente : insertion professionnelle des immigrants*. Paris: L'Harmattan.
Belkaïd, Akram. 2017. "Little Maghreb, Welcome or Not?" *The Nation*, April 3, 2017. www.thenation.com/article/archive/little-maghreb-welcome-or-not.
Belmokhtar, Zakia. 2006. "Les annulations de mariage en 2004." Infostat Justice, 1–4. www.justice.gouv.fr/art_pix/infostat90.pdf.
Benaïcha, Brahim. 1992. *Vivre au Paradis : d'une oasis à un bidonville*. Paris: Desclée de Brouwer.
Benhadjoudja, Leïla. 2018. "Les femmes musulmanes peuvent-elles parler ?" *Anthropologie et sociétés* 42 (1): 113–33.
———. 2022. "Racial Secularism as Settler Colonial Sovereignty in Quebec." *Islamophobia Studies Journal* 7 (2): 183–99.
Bennhold, Katrin. 2008. "A Veil Closes France's Door to Citizenship." *New York Times*, July 19, 2008. www.nytimes.com/2008/07/19/world/europe/19france.html.
Berger, Benjamin. 2010. "Section 1, Constitutional Reasoning, and Cultural Difference: Assessing the Impacts of *Alberta v. Hutterian Brethren of Wilson Colony*." 51 *Supreme Court Law Review* 2d: 25–46.
———. Forthcoming. "Is State Neutrality Bad for Indigenous Religious Freedom?" In *Indigenous Spirituality and Religious Freedom*, edited by Jeffrey Hewitt, Beverly Jacobs, and Richard Moon. Toronto: University of Toronto Press. https://papers.ssrn.com/sol3/papers.cfm?abstract_id=3508967.
Beydoun, Khaled A. 2019. *American Islamophobia*. Berkeley: University of California Press.
BFMTV. 2020. "Le gouvernement envisage l'interdiction des tests de virginité en France." March 4, 2020. https://rmc.bfmtv.com/actualites/le-gouvernement-envisage-l-interdiction-des-tests-de-virginite-en-france_AV-202003040484.html.
Bhabha, Faisal. 2013. "*R v. NS*: What Is Fair in a Trial? The Supreme Court of Canada's Divided Decision on the Niqab in the Courtroom." *Alberta Law Review* 50 (4): 871–82.
Bhambra, Gurminder K. 2007. "Multiple Modernities or Global Interconnections: Understanding the Global post the Colonial." In *Varieties of World Making: Beyond Globalization*, edited by Nathalie Karagiannis and Peter Wagner, 59–73. Liverpool, UK: Liverpool University Press.
Bhopal, Kalwant. 2023. "Critical Race Theory: Confronting, Challenging, and Rethinking White Privilege." *Annual Review of Sociology* 49 (1): 11–28.

Bhuyan, Rupaleem, Anna C. Korteweg, and Karin Baqi. 2018. "Regulating Spousal Migration through Canada's Multiple Border Strategy: The Gendered and Racialized Effects of Structurally Embedded Borders." *Law and Policy* 40 (4): 346–70.

Bilge, Sirma. 2010. "« . . . Alors que nous, Québécois, nos femmes sont égales à nous et nous les aimons ainsi » : la patrouille des frontières au nom de l'égalité de genre dans une « nation » en quête de souveraineté." *Sociologie et sociétés* 42 (1): 197–226.

———. 2012. "Mapping Quebecois Sexual Nationalism in Times of 'Crisis of Reasonable Accommodations.'" *Journal of Intercultural Studies* 33 (3): 303–18.

———. 2013. "Reading the Racial Subtext of the Québécois Accommodation Controversy: An Analytics of Racialized Governmentality." *Politikon* 40 (1): 157–81.

Blankholm, Joseph. 2018. "Secularism and Secular People." *Public Culture* 30 (2): 245–68.

———. 2022. *The Secular Paradox: On the Religiosity of the Nonreligious*. New York: New York University Press.

Bouchard, Gérard. 2012. *L'interculturalisme : un point de vue québécois*. Montréal: Boréal.

Bouchard, Gérard, and Charles Taylor. 2008. *Building the Future: A Time for Reconciliation*. Report. Québec, QC: Gouvernement du Québec.

Boucher, Guillaume. 2021. "La recomposition du religieux post-Révolution tranquille : une modernité de responsabilité." In *Dits et non-dits : mémoires catholiques au Québec*, edited by Géraldine Mossière, 109–26. Montréal: Presses de l'Université de Montréal.

Boulmezaoud, Yasser. 2017. "Portrait de la population algérienne au Canada." Fondation Club Avenir. https://clubavenir.com/2017/01/19/portrait-de-la-population-algerienne-au-canada.

Bourdieu, Pierre. 1977. *Outline of a Theory of Practice*. Cambridge: Cambridge University Press.

———. 1979. *Algeria 1960*. Translated by Richard Nice. Cambridge: Cambridge University Press.

———. 1984. *Distinction: A Social Critique of the Judgment of Taste*. Translated by Richard Nice. Cambridge, MA: Harvard University Press.

Bowen, John R. 2004. "Does French Islam Have Borders? Dilemmas of Domestication in a Global Religious Field." *American Anthropologist* 106 (1): 43–55.

———. 2007. *Why the French Don't Like Headscarves: Islam, the State, and Public Space*. Princeton, NJ: Princeton University Press.

———. 2011. "How the French State Justifies Controlling Muslim Bodies: From Harm-Based to Values-Based Reasoning." *Social Research: An International Quarterly* 78 (2): 325–48.

Brabant, Annick. 2017. "Le Petit Maghreb, un projet ambitieux." MEM : Centre des mémoires montréalaises, June 2, 2017. https://ville.montreal.qc.ca/memoiresdesmontrealais/le-petit-maghreb-un-projet-ambitieux.

Bracke, Sarah, and Luis Manuel Hernández Aguilar. 2020. "Racial States-Gendered Nations: On Biopower, Race, and Sex." In *The Routledge International Handbook of Contemporary Racism*, edited by J. Solomos, 356–65. London: Routledge.

Bragg, Bronwyn, and Lloyd L. Wong. 2016. "'Cancelled Dreams': Family Reunification and Shifting Canadian Immigration Policy." *Journal of Immigrant and Refugee Studies* 14 (1): 46–65.

Brahimi, Hamida. 2011. "L'intégration économique des immigrants maghrébins du Québec : le cas des Algériens, Marocains et Tunisiens." Master's thesis, Université du Québec à Montréal. http://archipel.uqam.ca/id/eprint/13491.

Bramadat, Paul, and Matthias Koenig, eds. 2009. *International Migration and the Governance of Religious Diversity*. Montréal: McGill-Queen's University Press.

Bréchon, Pierre, and Subrata Kumar Mitra. 1992. "The National Front in France: The Emergence of an Extreme Right Protest Movement." *Comparative Politics* 25:63–82.

Brettell, Caroline B. 2017. "Marriage and Migration." *Annual Review of Anthropology* 46:81–97.

Brodeur, Patrice. 2008. "La commission Bouchard-Taylor et la perception des rapports entre « Québécois » et « musulmans » au Québec." *Cahiers de recherche sociologique* 46:95–107.

Brown, Callum G. 2012. *Religion and the Demographic Revolution: Women and Secularization in Canada, Ireland, UK and USA since the 1960s*. Woodbridge, UK: Boydell.

Brown, Rachel. 2016a. "How Gelatin Becomes an Essential Symbol of Muslim Identity: Food Practice as a Lens into the Study of Religion and Migration." *Religious Studies and Theology* 35 (2): 89–113.

———. 2016b. "Immigration, Integration and Ingestion: The Role of Food and Drink in Transnational Experience for North African Muslim Immigrants in Paris and Montréal." PhD diss., Wilfrid Laurier University.

Brulard, Inès. 1997. "Laïcité and Islam." In *Aspects of Contemporary France*, edited by S. Perry, 175–90. London: Routledge.

Bryant, L. 2020. "Macron to Outline France's Controversial Anti-separatism Bill." *Voice of America*, September 29, 2020. www.voanews.com/a/europe_macron-outline-frances-controversial-anti-separatism-bill/6196502.html.

Bucar, Elizabeth M. 2017. *Pious Fashion: How Muslim Women Dress*. Cambridge, MA: Harvard University Press.

Burchardt, Marian. 2020. *Regulating Difference: Religious Diversity and Nationhood in the Secular West*. New Brunswick, NJ: Rutgers University Press.

Burchardt, Marian, and Mar Griera. 2019. "To See or Not to See: Explaining Intolerance against the 'Burqa' in European Public Space." *Ethnic and Racial Studies* 42 (5): 726–44.

Cady, Linell E., and Tracey Fassenden, eds. 2013. *Religion, the Secular and the Politics of Sexual Difference*. New York: Columbia University Press.

Caeiro, Alexandre. 2005. "Religious Authorities or Political Actors? The Muslim Leaders of the French Representative Body of Islam." In *European Muslims and the Secular State*, edited by Jocelyne Cesari and Seán McLoughlin, 71. Aldershot, UK: Ashgate.

Canada-Québec Accord. 1991. "Immigration: The Canada-Quebec Accord." https://publications.gc.ca/Collection-R/LoPBdP/BP/bp252-e.htm#:~:text=In%20section%202%20of%20the,the%20distinct%20society%20of%20Quebec.

Carter, Sarah. 2008. *The Importance of Being Monogamous: The West Unbound*. Edmonton, AB: Athabasca University Press.

Carver, Peter J. 2016. "A Failed Discourse of Distrust amid Significant Procedural Change: The Harper Government's Legacy in Immigration and Refugee Law." *Review of Constitutional Studies* 21 (2): 209-34.

Casanova, José. 1994. *Public Religions in the Modern World*. Chicago: University of Chicago Press.

Castel, Frédéric. 2010. "La dynamique de l'équation ethnoconfessionnelle dans l'évolution récente de la structure du paysage religieux québécois : les cas du façonnement des communautés bouddhistes et musulmanes (1941-2001)." PhD diss., Université du Québec à Montréal. http://archipel.uqam.ca/id/eprint/3174.

———. 2012. "Un mariage qui aurait tout pour marcher : implantation et conditions de vie des Québécois d'origine algérienne." In *Le Québec après Bouchard-Taylor : les identités religieuses de l'immigration*, edited by Louis Rousseau, 197-239. Québec, QC: Presses de l'Université du Québec.

CBC News. 2011. "Marriage Fraud Targeted by Canada Border Agency." January 11, 2011. www.cbc.ca/news/politics/marriage-fraud-targeted-by-canada-borderagency-1.1003652.

———. 2019. "Crucifix Removed from National Assembly's Blue Room." July 9, 2019. www.cbc.ca/news/canada/montreal/crucifix-removed-national-assembly-from-blue-room-1.5205352.

CCIF (Collectif contre l'islamophobie en France). 2015. *Rapport sur l'islamophobie en France : six mois après les attentats de janvier 2015*. https://oumma.com/rapport-annuel-du-ccif-lislamophobie-progresse.

Cesari, Jocelyne. 2016. "Self, Islam and Secular Public Spaces." In *Islam and Public Controversy in Europe*, edited by N. Göle, 47-55. New York: Routledge.

Chapuis, Nicolas. 2015. "François Hollande compte sur 'l'esprit du 11 janvier' pour faire avancer les réformes." *Le Monde*, January 20, 2015. http://abonnes.lemonde.fr/politique/article/2015/01/20/francois-hollande-compte-sur-l-esprit-du-11-janvier-pour-faire-avancer-les-reformes_4559703_823448.html.

Charef, Mehdi. 2006. *À Bras-le-Coeur*. Paris: Mercure de France.

Charsley, Katherine. 2005. "Unhappy Husbands: Masculinity and Migration in Transnational Pakistani Marriages." *Royal Anthropological Institute* 11 (1): 85-105.

———. 2006. "Risk and Ritual: The Protection of British Pakistani Women in Transnational Marriage." *Journal of Ethnic and Migration Studies* 32 (7): 1169-87.

———. 2007. "Risk, Trust, Gender and Transnational Cousin Marriage among British Pakistanis." *Ethnic and Racial Studies* 30 (6): 1117-31.

———, ed. 2012. *Transnational Marriage: New Perspectives on Europe and Beyond*. New York: Routledge.

Chase, Steven. 2015. "Niqabs Rooted in a Culture That Is Anti-women." *Globe and Mail*, March 11, 2015. www.theglobeandmail.com/news/politics/niqabs-rooted-in-a-culture-that-is-anti-women-harper-says/2015/03/11.

Choquette, Robert. 2004. *Canada's Religions: An Historical Introduction*. Ottawa: University of Ottawa Press.

Chowdhury, Farrah Deeba. 2018. "Immigration through Marriage: A Case Study of Bangladeshis in Toronto." *Journal of Muslim Minority Affairs* 38 (2): 280-300.

Chrisafis, Angelique. 2018. "France Admits Systemic Torture during Algeria War for First Time." *The Guardian*, September 13, 2018. www.theguardian.com/world/2018/sep/13/france-state-responsible-for-1957-death-of-dissident-maurice-audin-in-algeria-says-macron.

Citizenship and Immigration Canada. 2011. *Consulting the Public on Marriages of Convenience*. Ottawa: Citizenship and Immigration Canada.

———. 2012a. "Conditional Permanent Residence Proposed to Deter Marriages of Convenience." http://news.gc.ca/web/article-en.do?nid=661969.

———. 2012b. "News Release: 'The Jig Is up on Marriage Fraud,' Says Minister Kenney." Ottawa: Government of Canada. www.canada.ca/en/news/archive/2012/10/jig-up-marriage-fraud-says-minister-kenney.html.

Clancy-Smith, Julia. 1998. "Islam, Gender, and Identities in the Making of French Algeria, 1830–1962." In *Domesticating the Empire: Race, Gender, and Family Life in French and Dutch Colonialism*, edited by Julia Clancy-Smith and Frances Gouda, 154–74. Charlottesville: University of Virginia Press.

Clarke, Lynda. 2013. "Women in Niqab Speak: A Study of the Niqab in Canada." Canadian Council of Muslim Women. www.ccmw.com/publications/2019/1/22/women-in-niqab-speak-a-study-of-the-niqab-in-canada.

Clifford, James. 1986. "Introduction: Partial Truths." In *Writing Culture: The Poetics and Politics of Ethnography*, 1–26. Berkeley: University of California Press.

Cole, Jennifer. 2008. "'Et plus si affinités': Malagasy Internet Marriage, Shifting Postcolonial Hierarchies, and Policing New Boundaries." *Historical Reflections / Réflexions historiques* 34 (1): 26–49.

———. 2010. *Sex and Salvation: Imagining the Future in Madagascar*. Chicago: University of Chicago Press.

———. 2014a. "Producing Value among Malagasy Marriage Migrants in France: Managing Horizons of Expectation." *Current Anthropology* 55 (9): 85–94.

———. 2014b. "Working Mis/understandings: The Tangled Relationship between Kinship, Franco-Malagasy Bi-national Marriage and the French State." *Cultural Anthropology* 29 (3): 527–51.

Collet, Victor. 2019. *Nanterre, du bidonville à la cité*. Marseille: Agone.

———. 2023. "La gangrène et l'oubli : Nanterre année 0." *Lundi Matin*, July 11, 2023. https://lundi.am/La-gangrene-de-l-oubli-Nanterre-Annee-0.

Colorado, Carlos. 2020. "Reconciliation and the Secular." *Social Compass* 67, no. 1 (April): 72–85.

Colorado, Carlos, and Jennifer A. Selby. 2020. "Introduction: 'Open Secularism' from the Margins / La « laïcité ouverte » vue des marges." *Social Compass* 67, no. 1 (April): 3–17.

Connolly, William E. 2011. *A World of Becoming*. Durham, NC: Duke University Press.

Cornelier, Bruno. 2016. "Interculturalism, Settler Colonialism, and the Contest over 'Nativeness.'" In *Biopolitics and Memory in Postcolonial Literature and Culture*, edited by Michael R. Griffiths, 77–102. Farnham, UK: Ashgate.

Côté-Boucher, Karine, and Ratiba Hadj-Moussa. 2008. "Malaise identitaire : islam, laïcité et logique préventive en France et au Québec." *Cahiers de recherche sociologique*, no. 46, 61–77.

Cott, Nancy F. 2000. *Public Vows a History of Marriage and the Nation*. Cambridge, MA: Harvard University Press.

Coviello, Peter. 2019. *Make Yourselves Gods: Mormons and the Unfinished Business of American Secularism*. Chicago: University of Chicago Press.

CSF (Conseil du statut de la femme, Québec). 2011. "Affirmer la laïcité, un pas de plus vers l'égalité réelle entre les femmes et les hommes." https://csf.gouv.qc.ca/article/2011/04/01/affirmer-la-laicite-un-pas-de-plus-vers-legalite.

CTV News. 2019. "National Assembly Votes to Remove the Crucifix." March 28, 2019. https://montreal.ctvnews.ca/national-assembly-votes-to-remove-crucifix-1.4355860?cache=yes%3FautoPlay%3Dtrue%3FautoPlay%3Dtrue%3Fot%3DAjaxLayout%3FautoPlay%3Dtrue%3FautoPlay%3Dtrue%3FautoPlay%3Dtrue.

Dabby, Dia. 2020. "Le western de la laïcité : regards juridiques sur la Loi sur la laïcité de l'État." In *Modération ou extrémisme ? Regards critiques sur la Loi 21*, edited by Leila Celis, Dia Dabby, Dominique Leydet, and Vincent Romani, 239–54. Québec, QC: Presses de l'Université Laval.

Daly, Eoin. 2016. "*Laïcité* in the Private Sphere? French Religious Liberty after the *Baby-Loup* Affair." *Oxford Journal of Law and Religion* 5, no. 2 (June): 211–29.

d'Aoust, Anne-Marie. 2013. "In the Name of Love: Marriage, Migration, Governmentality, and Technologies of Love." *International Political Sociology* 7:258–74.

———. 2014. "Love as Project of (Im)mobility: Love, Sovereignty and Governmentality in Marriage Migration Management Practices." *Global Society* 28 (3): 317–35.

———. 2015. "Moving Stories: Love at the Border." In *Mobile Desires: The Politics and Erotics of Mobility Justice*, edited by Liz Montegary and Melissa Autumn White, 94–107. London: Palgrave MacMillan.

———. 2022. "Negotiating Trust and Suspicion: Lawyers as Actors in the Moral Political Economy of Marriage Migration Management in Canada." In *Transnational Marriage and Partner Migration: Constellations of Security, Citizenship, and Rights*, edited by Anne-Marie D'Aoust, 153–70. New Brunswick, NJ: Rutgers University Press.

D'Arcangelis, Carol Lynne. 2022. *The Solidarity Encounter: Women, Activism, and Creating Non-colonizing Relations*. Vancouver: University of British Columbia Press.

Daro, Ishmael N. 2017. "How Many Quebec Women Wear the Niqab Anyway?" *BuzzFeed.News*, October 20, 2017. www.buzzfeed.com/ishmaeldaro/quebec-niqab-estimates.

Dauvergne, Catherine. 2020. "Gendering Islamophobia to Better Understand Immigration Laws." *Journal of Ethnic and Migration Studies* 46 (12): 2569–84.

Davidson Sorkin, Amy. 2015. "The Attack on *Charlie Hebdo*." *New Yorker*, January 7, 2015. www.newyorker.com/news/amy-davidson/attack-charlie-hebdo.

de Certeau, Michel. 1984. *The Practice of Everyday Life*. Translated by Steven Rendall. Oakland: University of California Press.

Deeb, Lara. 2010. "On Representational Paralysis, Or, Why I Don't Want to Write About Temporary Marriage." *Jadaliyya*, December 1, 2010. www.jadaliyya.com/Details/23588.

Deeb, Lara, and Mona Harb. 2013. *Leisurely Islam: Negotiating Geography and Morality in Shi'ite South Beirut*. Princeton, NJ: Princeton University Press.

de Lasa, Marguerite. 2022. "À son université d'été, la Grande Mosquée de Paris se pose en acteur fédérateur de l'islam de France." *La Croix*, September 19, 2022. www.la-croix.com/Religion/A-universite-dete-Grande-Mosquee-Paris-acteur-federateur-lislam-France-2022-09-19-1201233847.

Diallo, Rokhaya. 2020. "France's Ideological Wars Have Found a New Battleground: Universities." *Washington Post*, December 29, 2020. www.washingtonpost.com/opinions/2020/12/29/france-academic-freedom-universities-backlash.

Dickey Young, Pamela. 2006. "Same-Sex Marriage and Christian Churches in Canada." *Studies in Religion / Sciences religieuses* 35 (1): 3–23.

Dickinson, J., and B. Young. 2008. *A Short History of Québec*, 4th ed. Montréal: McGill-Queen's University Press.

Diffley, A. 2020. "Macron Denounces Islamists' Politico-religious Project in France." *Radio France Internationale*, October 2, 2020. www.rfi.fr/en/france/20201002-macron-condemns-radical-islamists-infiltrate-separatism.

Dobrowolsky, Alexandra. 2017. "Bad versus Big Canada: State Imaginaries of Immigration and Citizenship, Studies." *Political Economy* 98 (2): 197–222.

Donadio, Rachel. 2021. "Why Is France So Afraid of God?" *The Atlantic*, November 22, 2021. www.theatlantic.com/magazine/archive/2021/12/france-god-religion-secularism/620528.

Dorlin, Elsa. 2006. *La matrice de la race : généalogie sexuelle et coloniale de la nation française*. Paris: La Découverte.

Durin, Léo. 2022. "Pourquoi la France a-t-elle été une cible privilégiée de Daech ?" *La Croix*, May 9, 2022. www.la-croix.com/France/pourquoi-france-elle-ete-cible-daech-etat-islamique-terrorisme-attentats-2022-09-05-1201231679.

Durkheim, Émile. (1912) 1995. *The Elementary Forms of Religious Life*. Translated by Karen E. Fields. New York: Free Press.

Eid, Paul. 2007. *Being Arab: Ethnic and Religious Identity Building among Second Generation Youth in Montreal*, 2nd ed. Montréal: McGill-Queen's University Press.

——. 2012. "Les inégalités 'ethnoraciales' dans l'accès à l'emploi à Montréal : le poids de la discrimination." *Recherches sociographiques* 53 (2): 415–50.

——. 2015. "Balancing Agency, Gender and Race: How Do Muslim Female Teenagers in Québec Negotiate the Social Meanings Embedded in the Hijab?" *Ethnic and Racial Studies* 38 (11): 1–20.

Élysée française. 2022. "Marianne." www.elysee.fr/la-presidence/marianne.

Engelke, Matthew. 2015. "Secular Shadows: African, Immanent, Post-colonial." *Critical Research on Religion* 3 (1): 86–100.

Esau, Alvin. 2008. "Living by Different Law: Legal Pluralism, Freedom of Religion, and Illiberal Religious Groups." In *Law and Religious Pluralism in Canada*, edited by Richard Moon, 110–39. Vancouver: University of British Columbia Press.

Esteves, Olivier, Mayanthi Fernando, Farid Hafez, Alana Lentin, Shamim Miah, Tariq Mohood, Jennifer Selby, Paul A. Silverstein, and Jasmin Zine. 2023. "La mort de Nahel et l'interdiction faite aux hijabeuses sont les deux faces d'une même pièce." *Mediapart*, July 10, 2023. https://blogs.mediapart.fr/les-invites-de-mediapart/blog/100723/la-mort-de-nahel-et-linterdiction-faite-aux-hijabeuses-sont-les-deux-faces-dune-meme-p.

Etkin, Prudence. 2016. "French Law in the Baby Loup Case: *Laïcité* and the Ambiguous Margins of the Private-Public Binary." Master's thesis, Memorial University of Newfoundland.

Euronews. 2020. "Emmanuel Macron : 'Nous ne renoncerons pas aux caricatures, aux dessins.'" October 21, 2020. https://fr.euronews.com/2020/10/21/macron-nous-ne-renoncerons-pas-aux-caricatures-aux-dessins.

Europe 1. 2016. "Laurence Rossignol dénonce le burkini, « profondément archaïque »." August 15, 2016. www.europe1.fr/politique/laurence-rossignol-denonce-le-burkini-profondement-archaique-2820898.

Evans, Martin. 2012. *Algeria: France's Undeclared War*. Oxford: Oxford University Press.

Ewing, Katherine Pratt. 2008. *Stolen Honor: Stigmatizing Muslim Men in Berlin*. Stanford: Stanford University Press.

Fadil, Nadia. 2009. "Managing Affects and Sensibilities: The Case of Not-Handshaking and Not Fasting." *Social Anthropology* 17 (4): 439–54.

———. 2011. "On Not-/Unveiling as an Ethical Practice." *Feminist Review* 98:83–109.

Fanon, Frantz. 1967. *Black Skin, White Masks*. New York: Grove.

Farham, Abou. 2013. "Speculative Matter: Secular Bodies, Minds, and Persons." *Cultural Anthropology* 28 (4): 737–59.

Farris, Sara. 2017. *In the Name of Women's Rights: The Rise of Femonationalism*. Durham, NC: Duke University Press.

Fassin, Éric. 2006. "La démocratie sexuelle et le conflit des civilisations." *Multitudes* 3:123–31.

———. 2010. "National Identities and Transnational Intimacies: Sexual Democracy and the Politics of Immigration in Europe." *Public Culture* 22 (3): 507–29.

———. 2014. "Same-Sex Marriage, Nation, and Race: French Political Logics and Rhetorics." *Contemporary French Civilization* 39 (3): 281–301.

Feith, Jesse. 2020. "Indigenous Woman Records Slurs by Hospital Staff before Her Death." *Montreal Gazette*, September 30, 2020. https://montrealgazette.com/news/local-news/indigenous-woman-who-died-at-joliette-hospital-had-recorded-staffs-racist-comments.

Fernando, Mayanthi. 2014a. "Ethnography and the Politics of Silence." *Cultural Dynamics* 26 (2): 235–44.

———. 2014b. "Intimacy Surveilled: Religion, Sex, and Secular Cunning." *Signs: Journal of Women in Culture and Society* 39 (3): 685–708.

———. 2014c. *The Republic Unsettled: Muslim French and the Contradictions of Secularism*. Durham, NC: Duke University Press.

Ferran, Nicolas. 2009. "La politique d'immigration contre les couples mixtes." In *Douce France : rafles, rétention, expulsions*, edited by Olivier La Cour Grandmaison, 151–72. Paris: Seuil/RESF.

Ferrari, Alessandro. 2008. "De la politique à la technique : laïcité narrative et laïcité du droit. Pour une comparaison France/Italie." In *Le droit ecclésiastique de la fin du XVIIIe au milieu du XXe siècle en Europe*, edited by B. Basdevant Gaudemet and F. Jankowiak, 333–45. Leuven, Belgium: Peeters.

Fessenden, Tracy. 2016. "Afterword: Critical Intersections: Race, Secularism, Gender." In *Race and Secularism in America*, edited by Jonathan S. Kahn and Vincent W. Lloyd, 257–70. New York: Columbia University Press.

Foblets, Marie-Claire. 1998. "Family Reunification: Who Pays for Love in Europe?" *Love and Law in Europe*, edited by Hanne Petersen, 62–80. London: Routledge.

Foucault, Michel. (1966) 2005. *The Order of Things*. London: Taylor and Francis.

———. 2003. *The Essential Foucault: Selections from Essential Works of Foucault, 1954–1984*, edited by Paul Rabinow and Nikolas S. Rose. New York: New Press.

———. 2008. *The Birth of Biopolitics: Lectures at the Collège de France, 1978–1979*. Edited by Michel Senellart. Translated by Graham Burchell. New York: Picador.

Fourny, Jean-François. 2007. "Lycées et « grands établissements » français à l'étranger." *French Review* 80 (4): 822-32.
France 24. 2020. "Menacé de dissolution par le gouvernement, le Collectif contre l'islamophobie (CCIF) s'autodissout." November 11, 2020. www.france24.com/fr/france/20201127-menac%C3%A9-de-dissolution-par-le-gouvernement-le-collectif-contre-l-islamophobie-ccif-s-autodissout.
France Archives. 2023. "Les sources relatives aux rapatriés d'Algérie : les politiques sociales." Portail national des archives, October 9, 2023. https://francearchives.gouv.fr/fr/article/689586723.
Funk, Cory. 2017. "Hashtagging Islam: #JeSuisHijabi, Social Media, and Religious/Secular Identities in the Lives of Muslims in Winnipeg and St. John's, Canada." Master's thesis, Memorial University of Newfoundland.
Gabizon, Cécilia. 2009. "Deux mille femmes portent la burqa en France." *Le Figaro*, September 9, 2009. www.lefigaro.fr/actualite-france/2009/09/09/01016-20090909ARTFIG00040-deux-mille-femmes-portent-la-burqa-en-france-.php#:~:text=L'%C3%A9valuation%20est%20contenue%20dans,porteraient%20la%20oburqa%20en%20France.
Galonnier, Juliette. 2021a. "Barbes et foulards : les marqueurs genrés de l'islamophobie." In *Genre et islamophobie : discriminations, préjugés et représentations en Europe*, edited by Éléonore Lépinard, Oriane Sarrasin, and Lavinia Gianettoni, 157-79. Lyon: ENS Éditions.
———. 2021b. "Maneuvering Whiteness in France: Muslim Converts' Ambivalent Encounters with Race." *French Politics, Culture and Society* 39 (2): 69-94.
Gastrin, Émilie. 2020. "Laïcité et barbe longue en milieu hospitalier : le feuilleton continue !" *La revue des droits de l'homme*, May. https://journals.openedition.org/revdh/9349.
Gaucher, Megan. 2014. "Attack of the Marriage Fraudsters! An Examination of the Harper Government's Anti-Marriage Fraud Campaign." *International Journal of Canadian Studies* 50:187-205.
———. 2016. "Monogamous Canadian Citizenship, Constructing Foreignness and the Limits of Harm Discourse." *Canadian Journal of Political Science* 49 (3): 519-38.
———. 2018. *A Family Matter: Citizenship, Conjugal Relationships, and Canadian Immigration Policy*. Vancouver: University of British Columbia Press.
Gauvreau, M. 2015. *The Catholic Origins of Québec's Quiet Revolution*. Montréal: McGill-Queen's University Press.
Geertz, Clifford. 1973. *The Interpretation of Cultures: Selected Essays*. New York: Basic Books.
Goffman, Erving. 1956. *The Presentation of Self in Everyday Life*. Edinburgh: University of Edinburgh.
Göle, Nilüfer. 2007. "The Making and Unmaking of Europe in Its Encounter with Islam: Negotiating French Republicanism and European Islam." In *Varieties of World-Making beyond Globalization*, edited by Nathalie Karagiannis and Peter Wagner, 173-90. Liverpool, UK: Liverpool University Press.
———. 2015. *Islam and Secularity: The Future of Europe's Public Sphere*. Durham, NC: Duke University Press.
Goodman, Jane E. 2009. "Performing 'Laïcité': Gender, Agency and Neoliberalism among Algerians in France." In *Politics, Publics, Personhood: Ethnography at the Limits of Neoliberalism*, edited by Carol J. Greenhouse, 195-206. Philadelphia: University of Pennsylvania Press.

Government of Canada. 2008. "Bad Faith Family Relationships: The Legislative Framework." Immigration and Refugee Board of Canada. https://irb-cisr.gc.ca/en/legal-policy/legal-concepts/Documents/SpoParo6_e.pdf.

———. 2024. "Immigration and Refugee Protection Regulations (SOR/2002-227)." Justice Laws. https://laws-lois.justice.gc.ca/eng/regulations/sor-2002-227/section-4.html.

Grenier, Gilles, and Serge Nadeau. 2011. "Immigrant Access to Work in Montreal and Toronto." *Canadian Journal of Regional Science / Revue canadienne des sciences régionales* 1 (1): 19–33.

Griffin, C. 2021. "Why Has France's Islamist Separatism Bill Caused Such Controversy?" *Foreign Policy*, February 23, 2021. https://foreignpolicy.com/2021/02/23/why-france-islamist-separatism-bill-controversy-extremism.

Guénif-Souilamas, Nacira. 2006. "The Other French Exception: Virtuous Racism and the War of the Sexes in Postcolonial France." *French Politics, Culture and Society* 24 (3): 23–41.

Guénif-Souilamas, Nacira, and Éric Macé. 2004. *Les féministes et le garçon arabe*. Paris: L'Aube.

Gustafson, Diana L., and Jennifer A. Selby. 2016. "Theorizing De-Christianization in Women's Reproductive Lives in Newfoundland and Labrador, Canada." *Women's Studies International Forum* 59:17–25.

Gutiérrez Rodríguez, Encarnación. 2018. "The Coloniality of Migration and the 'Refugee Crisis': On the Asylum-Migration Nexus, the Transatlantic White European Settler Colonialism-Migration and Racial Capitalism." *Refuge* 34 (1): 16–28.

Gyps (Karim Mahfouf). (1998) 2009. *Algé-rien de France*. Paris: Dalimen.

Habermas, Jürgen. 2008. "Notes on a Post-secular Society." Signandsight.com, June 18, 2008. www.signandsight.com/features/1714.html.

Hachimi Alaoui, Myriam. 2006. "« Carrière brisée », « carrière de l'immigrant » : le cas des Algériens installés à Montréal." *Diversité urbaine* 1 (5): 111–23.

———. 2007. *Les chemins de l'exil : les Algériens installés en France et au Canada depuis les années 1990*. Paris: L'Harmattan.

Hage, Ghassan. 2017. *Is Racism an Environmental Threat?* Cambridge: Polity Press.

Hajjat, Abdellali. 2012. *Les frontières de l'« identité nationale » : l'injonction à l'assimilation en France métropolitaine et coloniale*. Paris: La Découverte.

———. 2014. "Rébellions urbaines et déviances policières : approche configurationnelle des relations entre les 'jeunes' des Minguettes et la police (1981–1983)." *Cultures et conflits*, no. 93, 11–34.

Hajjat, Abdellali, and Marwan Mohammad. 2013. *Islamophobie : comment les élites françaises fabriquent le problème musulman*. Paris: La Découverte.

Hall, R. Mark, and Mary Rosner. 2004. "Pratt and Pratfalls: Revisioning Contact Zones." In *Crossing Borderlands: Composition and Postcolonial Studies*, edited by A. Lunsdord and Lahoucine Ouzgane, 95–109. Pittsburgh: University of Pittsburgh Press.

Hamel, Christelle. 2011. "Immigrées et filles d'immigrés : le recul des mariages forcés." *Population et sociétés : bulletin mensuel d'information de l'Institut national d'études démographiques*, no. 479, 1–4.

Hancock, Claire. 2014. "'The Republic Is Lived with an Uncovered Face' (and a Skirt): (Un)dressing French Citizens." *Gender, Place and Culture* 22 (7): 1023–40.

Hargreaves, Alec G. 1998. "The Beurgeoisie: Mediation or Mirage?" *Journal of European Studies* 28:89–102.

———. 2007. "Muslims in France: The Quest for Social Justice." *Global Dialogue* 9 (3): 47–55.
Hart, William D. 2016. "Secular Coloniality: The Afterlife of Religious and Racial Tropes." In *Race and Secularism in America*, edited by Jonathon Kahn and Vincent W. Lloyd, 178–206. New York: Columbia University Press.
Hartigan, J. 2005. *Old Tribes: Toward a Cultural Analysis of White People*. Durham, NC: Duke University Press.
Hasan, Nadia Z., Lina El Bakir and Youmna Badawy. 2024. *Social Discord and Second-class Citizenship: A Study of the Impact of Bill 21 on Québec Muslim Women in Light of the COVID-19 Pandemic*. National Council of Canadian Muslims. www.nccm.ca/wp-content/uploads/2024/06/Bill-21-Report-ENGLISH.pdf.
Helly, Denise. 2011. "Les multiples visages de l'islamophobie au Canada." *Nouveaux cahiers du socialisme* 5:99–106.
Henderson, Jennifer, and Pauline Wakeham. 2009. "Colonial Reckoning, National Reconciliation? Aboriginal Peoples and the Culture of Redress in Canada." *English Studies in Canada* 35 (1): 1–26.
Hense, Andrea, and Maren Schorch. 2013. "Arranged Marriages as Support for Intra-ethnic Matchmaking? A Case Study on Muslim Migrants in Germany." *International Migration* 51 (2): 104–26.
Hirsch, Jennifer S. 2003. *Courtship after Marriage: Sexuality and Love in Mexican Transnational Families*. Berkeley: University of California Press.
Hirschkind, Charles. 2011. "Is There a Secular Body?" *Cultural Anthropology* 26 (4): 633–47.
Hizzir, Hamza. 2020. "Qu'est-ce que le CCIF, menacé de dissolution par le gouvernement, et que lui reproche-t-on ?" *TF1 info*, October 26, 2020. www.tf1info.fr/societe/video-qu-est-ce-que-le-ccif-menace-de-dissolution-par-le-gouvernement-et-que-lui-reproche-t-on-2168049.html.
hooks, bell. 1990. *Yearning: Race, Gender, and Cultural Politics*. Boston: South End.
Hunter-Henin, Myriam. 2015. "Living Together in an Age of Religious Diversity: Lessons from Baby Loup and SAS." *Oxford Journal of Law and Religion* 4 (1): 94–118.
Hurd, Elizabeth Shakman. 2012. "International Politics after Secularism." *Review of International Studies* 35 (5): 943–61.
IFOP (Institut français de l'opinion publique). 2023. "La position des Français sur l'interdiction du port de l'abaya et du qamis à l'école." www.ifop.com/wp-content/uploads/2023/09/120280_rapport_ifop_CH_2023.09.05.pdf.
Illouz, Eva. 1997. *Consuming the Romantic Utopia: Love and the Cultural Contradictions of Capitalism*. Berkeley: University of California Press.
Ingraham, Chrys. 1999. *White Weddings: Romancing Heterosexuality in Popular Culture*. New York: Routledge.
INSEE (Institut national de la statistique et des études économiques). 2015. "Fiche « Estimation de population par quartier »," Données sur les quartiers 2015 de la politique de la ville. www.insee.fr/fr/statistiques/5428762?sommaire=2500477.
———. 2018. "Dossier complet : Commune de Nanterre (92050)." www.insee.fr/fr/statistiques/2011101?geo=COM-92050#chiffre-cle-9.
Institut national d'études démographiques. 2011. "TeO: Enquête sur la diversité des populations en France." www.ined.fr/fichier/t_telechargement/35196/telechargement_fichier_fr_dt168.13janvier11.pdf.

Ishaq v. Canada (Minister of Citizenship and Immigration). 2015. 475 F.T.R. 94 (FC 156). www.canlii.org/en/ca/fct/doc/2015/2015fc156/2015fc156.html.

Jacob, Étienne. 2020. "Le Conseil d'État donne raison à un chirurgien stagiaire qui refusait de tailler sa barbe." *Le Figaro*, February 18, 2020. www.lefigaro.fr/actualite-france/le-conseil-d-etat-donne-raison-a-un-chirurgien-stagiaire-qui-refusait-de-tailler-sa-barbe-20200218.

Jacobsen, Christine M. 2017. "Veiled Nannies and Secular Futures in France." *Ethnos: Journal of Anthropology* 83 (3): 544–66.

Jahangeer, Roshan Arah. 2020. "Anti-veiling and the Charter of Québec Values: 'Native Testimonials,' Erasure, and Violence against Montreal's Muslim Women." *Canadian Journal of Women and the Law* 32 (1): 114–39.

———. 2021. "Fieldworking While Veiled: Autoethnography of a Brown + Muslim + Female Researcher in Québec." In *Producing Islam(s) in Canada: On Knowledge Production, Positionality and Politics*, edited by Amélie Barras, Jennifer A. Selby, and Melanie Adrian, 241–60. Toronto: University of Toronto Press.

Jeldtoft, Nadia. 2013. "The Hypervisibility of Islam." In *Everyday Lived Islam in Europe*, edited by Nadia Jeldtoft, Nathal M. Dessing, Jorgen S. Nielsen, and Linda Woodhead, 23–38. Farnham, UK: Ashgate.

Johnston, David. 2011. "The Speech from the Throne." *CBC News*, June 3, 2011. www.cbc.ca/news/canada/the-speech-from-the-throne-1.1057204.

Joly, Marie-Pier, and Jeffrey G. Reitz. 2018. "Emotional Stress and the Integration of Muslim Minorities in France and Canada." *International Migration Review* 52 (4): 1111–29.

Joppke, Christian. 2007. "State Neutrality and Islamic Headscarf Laws in France and Germany." *Theory and Society* 36 (4): 313–42.

Jouili, Jeanette S. 2009. "Negotiating Secular Boundaries: Pious Micro-practices of Muslim Women in French and German Public Spheres." *Social Anthropology* 17 (4): 445–70.

———. 2015. *Pious Practice and Secular Constraints: Women in the Islamic Revival in Europe*. Redwood City, CA: Stanford University Press.

Jugé, Tony, and Michael P. Perez. 2006. "The Modern Colonial Politics of Citizenship and Whiteness in France." *Social Identities* 12 (2): 187–212.

Kahn, Jonathan, and Vincent Lloyd, eds. 2016. *Race and Secularism in America*. New York: Columbia University Press.

Karimi, Hanane. 2021. "De l'application à l'extension de la nouvelle laïcité : le cas des mères accompagnatrices." *Mouvements* 107:104–12.

Kaufmann, Jean-Claude. 1995. *Corps de femmes, regards d'hommes : sociologie des seins nus*. Paris: Nathan.

Keaton, Trica Danielle. 2010. "The Politics of Race-Blindness: (Anti)blackness and Category Blindness in Contemporary France." *Du Bois Review: Social Science Research on Race* 7 (1): 103–31.

Kepel, Gilles. 1987. *Les banlieues de l'islam : naissance d'une religion en France*. Paris: Seuil.

———. 2012. *Banlieue de la République : société, politique et religion à Clichy-sous-Bois et Montfermeil*. Paris: Gallimard.

Khan, Arsalan. 2018. "Pious Masculinity, Ethical Reflexivity, and Moral Order in an Islamic Piety Movement in Pakistan." *Anthropology Quarterly* 91 (1): 53–77.

Kiernan, Ben. 2007. *Blood and Soil: A World History of Genocide and Extermination from Sparta to Darfur*. New Haven, CT: Yale University Press.

King, Rebekka. 2023. *The New Heretics: Skepticism, Secularism, and Progressive Christianity*. New York: New York University Press.

Klassen, Pamela E. 2018. "Treaty People and the Queen of Canada." In *Ekkesia: Three Inquiries in Church and State*, edited by Paul Christopher Johnson, Pamela Klassen, and Winnifred Fallers Sullivan, 107–74. Chicago: University of Chicago Press.

———. 2019. "Contraception and the Coming of Secularism: Reconsidering Reproductive Freedom as Religious Freedom." In *Secular Bodies, Affects, and Emotions: European Configurations*, edited by Monique Scheer, Birgitte Schepelern Johansen and Nadia Fadil, 17–30. London: Bloomsbury.

Koussens, David. 2009. "Neutrality of the State and Regulation of Religious Symbols in Schools in Quebec and France." *Social Compass* 56 (2): 202–13.

———. 2018. "Ce que la laïcité a de nouveau, ou pas : regards croisés France-Québec." *Revue des droits de l'homme* 14:1–18.

———. 2023. *Secularism(s) in Contemporary France: Law, Policy, and Religious Diversity*. Translated by Peter Feldstein. New York: Springer.

Koussens, David, and Valérie Amiraux. 2014. "Du mauvais usage de la laïcité française dans le débat public québécois." In *Penser la laïcité québécoise : fondements et défense d'une laïcité ouverte au Québec*, edited by Sébastien Lévesque, 55–75. Québec, QC: Presses de l'Université Laval.

Koven, Ronald. 1992. "Muslim Immigrants and French Nationalists." *Society* (New Brunswick) 29 (4): 25–33.

Laborde, Cécile. 2005. "Secular Philosophy and Muslim Headscarves in Schools." *Journal of Political Philosophy* 13 (3): 305–29.

Lapeyronne, Didier. 2005. "La banlieue comme théâtre colonial, ou la fracture coloniale dans les quartiers." In *La fracture coloniale : la société française au prisme de l'héritage colonial*, edited by P. Blanchard, N. Bancel, and S. LeMaire, 209–18. Paris: La Découverte.

Lau, Rachel. 2019. "'Quebec Will Always Be Open': Immigration Minister Defends Religious Symbols Bill." *Global News*, April 1, 2019. https://globalnews.ca/news/5118381/quebec-immigration-minister-defends-secularism-bill.

Laurence, Jonathan, and Justin Vaisse. 2006. *Integrating Islam: Political and Religious Challenges in Contemporary France*. Washington, DC: Brookings Institution.

Laxer, Emily. 2019. *Unveiling the Nation: The Politics of Secularism in France and Québec*. Montréal: McGill-Queen's University Press.

Laxer, Emily, Jeffrey G. Reitz, and Patrick Simon. 2019. "Muslims' Political and Civic Incorporation in France and Canada: Testing Models of Participation." *Journal of Ethnic and Migration Studies* 46 (17): 1–26.

Leblanc, Audrey. 2017. "Devenir la « Marianne de Mai 68 » : processus d'iconisation et histoire par le photojournalisme." In *La politique par l'image : iconographie politique et sciences sociales*, edited by Christine Pina and Erice Savarese, 145–67. Paris: L'Harmattan.

Lebner, Ashley B. 2015. "The Anthropology of Secularity beyond Secularism." *Religion and Society: Advances in Research* 6:62–74.

LeClair, Anne. 2019. "Teachers Removing Religious Symbols Proves Bill 21 Is a 'Good Law': Education Minister." *Global News*, September 18, 2019. https://globalnews.ca/news/5920646/teachers-religious-symbols-bill-21-education-minister.

Lee, Esther. 2019. "This Is How Much It Costs for Weddings around the World." *The Knot*, June 3, 2019. www.theknot.com/content/how-much-does-it-cost-to-get-married.

Lee, Lois. 2013. "Research Note: Talking about a Revolution: Terminology for the New Field of Non-religion Studies." In *Secularity and Non-Religion*, edited by Elisabeth Arweck, Stephen Bullivant, and Lois Lee, 111–22. New York: Routledge.

———. 2015. *Recognizing the Non-religions: Reimagining the Secular*. Oxford: Oxford University Press.

Lefebvre, Solange. 2008. "Between Law and Public Opinion: The Case of Québec." *Religion and Diversity in Canada*, edited by Lori G. Beaman and Peter Beyer, 175–98. Leiden, Netherlands: Brill.

Le Figaro. 2008. "L'annulation du mariage pour non-virginité rejetée en appel." November 17, 2008. www.lefigaro.fr/actualite-france/2008/11/17/01016-20081117ARTFIG00496-l-annulation-du-mariage-pour-non-virginite-rejetee-en-appel-.php.

———. 2020. "Le CCIF officiellement dissout par le Conseil des ministres." December 2, 1010. www.lefigaro.fr/flash-actu/dissolution-du-ccif-par-le-conseil-des-ministres-20201202.

Legault-Leclair, Jacob. 2023. "La migration interprovinciale chez les immigrants musulmans : la francophonie comme vecteur d'intégration ?" *Canadian Review of Sociology / Revue canadienne de sociologie* 60 (3): 385–408.

Légifrance. 2002. "Code pénal : Article 433-21, 1 janvier." January 1, 2002. www.legifrance.gouv.fr/codes/id/LEGIARTI000006418591/2002-01-01.

———. 2004. "Circulaire du 18 mai 2004 relative à la mise en oeuvre de la loi n° 2004-228 du 15 mars 2004 encadrant, en application du principe de laïcité, le port de signes ou de tenues manifestant une appartenance religieuse dans les écoles, collèges et lycées publics." May 22, 2004. www.legifrance.gouv.fr/jorf/id/JORFTEXT000000252465.

———. 2011. "Article L623-2. Loi n° 2011-672 du 16 juin 2011 relative à l'immigration, à l'intégration et à la nationalité." June 17, 2011. www.legifrance.gouv.fr/codes/id/LEGISCTA000006147815/2021-01-20.

———. 2021. "Law Respecting the Principles of the Republic." n° 2021-1109. January 20, 2021. www.legifrance.gouv.fr/jorf/id/JORFTEXT000043964778.

Lemaignen, Julien, and Jean-Philippe Lefief. 2023. "Le drame de Nanterre heure par heure, du contrôle routier de Nahel M. à la marche blanche pour l'adolescent tué." *Le Monde*, June 29, 2023. www.lemonde.fr/societe/article/2023/06/29/le-drame-de-nanterre-heure-par-heure-du-controle-routier-de-nahel-m-a-la-marche-blanche-pour-l-adolescent-tue_6179840_3224.html.

Lemke, Thomas. 2001. "'The Birth of Bio-politics': Michel Foucault's Lecture at the Collège de France on Neo-liberal Governmentality." *Economy and Society* 30 (2): 190–207.

———. 2007. "The Government of Living Beings: Michel Foucault." In *Biopolitics: An Advanced Introduction*, 33–52. New York: New York University Press.

Le Monde. 2023. "« Dès lundi », les élèves portant l'abaya ou le qamis n'entreront pas en classe, assure Gabriel Attal." August 31, 2023. www.lemonde.fr/education/article/2023/08/31/les-eleves-portant-l-abaya-ou-le-qamis-n-entreront-pas-en-classe-des-lundi_6187188_1473685.html.

Lemons, Katherine. 2019. *Divorcing Traditions: Islamic Marriage Law and the Making of Indian Secularism*. Ithaca, NY: Cornell University Press.

Lenoir-Achdjian, Annick, Sébastien Arcand, Denise Helly, Isabelle Drainville and Michèle Vatz Laaroussi. 2009. "Les difficultés d'insertion en emploi des immigrants du Maghreb au Québec : une question de perspective." *Choix IRPP* 15 (3): 1–44.

Le Nouvel Obs. 2008a. "Élisabeth Badinter « ulcérée »." May 29, 2008. www.nouvelobs.com/societe/20080529.OBS6164/elisabeth-badinter-ulceree.html.

———. 2008b. "Quand Gérald Larcher liait les émeutes urbaines à la polygamie." October 2, 2008. http://tempsreel.nouvelobs.com/actualite/politique/20080925.OBS2740/quand-gerard-larcher-liait-les-emeutes-urbaines-a-la-polygamie.html.

Lentin, Alana. 2019. "*Charlie Hebdo*: White Context and Black Analytics." *Public Culture* 31 (1): 45–67.

Lépinard, Éléonore. 2014. "Migrating Concepts: Immigration Integration and the Regulation of Religious Dress in France and Canada." *Ethnicities* 15 (5): 611–32.

———. 2020. *Feminist Trouble: Intersectional Politics in Postsecular Times.* Oxford: Oxford University Press.

Levanchy, Anne. 2015. "Glimpses into the Hearts of Whiteness: Institutions of Intimacy and the Desirable National." In *Colonial Switzerland: Rethinking Colonialism from the Margins*, edited by P. Purtschert and H. Fischer-Tiné, 278–95. Basingstoke, UK: Palgrave Macmillan.

Libération. 2011. "Un boulevard du 17-octobre-1961 à Nanterre." October 17, 2011. www.liberation.fr/societe/2011/10/17/un-boulevard-du-17-octobre-1961-a-nanterre_768397.

———. 2013. "La Circulaire Chatel sur les mères voilées « reste valable »." December 23, 2013. www.liberation.fr/societe/2013/12/23/les-meres-voilees-peuvent-participer-aux-sorties-scolaires_968600.

Lievens, John. 1999. "Family-Forming Migration from Turkey and Morocco to Belgium: The Demand for Marriage Partners from the Countries of Origin." *International Migration Review* 33 (3): 717–44.

Linke, Uli. 2006. "Contact Zones: Rethinking the Sensual Life of the State." *Anthropological Theory* 6:205–25.

Logit Research. 2024. "One-Third of Canadians Have Tattoos." March 22, 2024. https://logitgroup.com/one-third-of-canadians-have-tattoos.

Lugones, María. 2007. "Heterosexualism and the Colonial/Modern Gender System." *Hypatia* 22 (1): 186–209.

———. 2010. "The Coloniality of Gender." In *Globalization and the Decolonial Option*, edited by Walter D. Mignolo and Arturo Escobar, 369–90. London: Routledge.

Macfarlane, Julie. 2012a. *Islamic Divorce in North America.* Oxford: Oxford University Press.

———. 2012b. "Understanding Trends in American Muslim Divorce and Marriage: A Discussion Guide for Families and Communities." Institute for Social Policy and Understanding. www.ispu.org/wp-content/uploads/2016/08/ISPU-Report_Marriage-II_Macfarlane_WEB.pdf.

Machery, Édouard, and Luc Faucher. 2005. "Social Construction and the Concept of Race." *Philosophy of Science* 72 (5): 1208–19.

Macías, Teresa. 2022. "Postcolonialism and Decoloniality." In *Critical Social Work Praxis*, edited by Sobia Shaheen Shaikh, Brenda Anne-Marie LeFrançois and Teresa Macías, 331–45. Winnipeg: Fernwood Publishing.

Mack, Mehemmed Amadeus. 2017. *Sexagon: Muslims, France, and the Sexualization of National Culture.* New York: Fordham University Press.

MacMaster, Neil. 1997. *Colonial Migrants and Racism: Algerians in France, 1900-62.* London: Macmillan.
MacMaster, Neil, and Toni Lewis. 1998. "Orientalism: From Unveiling to Hyperveiling." *Journal of European Studies* 28:121-35.
Mahmood, Saba. 2008. "Feminism, Democracy, and Empire: Islam and the War of Terror." In *Women's Studies on the Edge*, edited by Joan Wallach Scott, 81-114. Durham: Duke University Press.
———. 2009. "Feminism, Democracy, and Empire: Islam and the War on Terror." In *Gendering Religion and Politics: Untangling Modernities*, edited by Hanna Herzog and Ann Braude, 193-216. New York: Palgrave Macmillan.
———. 2013. "Religious Reason and Secular Affect: An Incommensurable Divide?" In *Is Critique Secular? Blasphemy, Injury and Free Speech*, edited by Talal Asad, Wendy Brown, Judith Butler, and Saba Mahmood 65-100. New York: Fordham University Press.
———. 2015. *Religious Difference in a Secular Age: A Minority Report.* Princeton, NJ: Princeton University Press.
———. 2016. "Reflections on the Limits of Law." *International Journal of Middle East Studies* 48 (1): 157-63.
Maldonado-Torres, Nelson. 2007. "On the Coloniality of Being: Contributions to the Development of a Concept." *Cultural Studies* 21 (2): 240-70.
Mamdani, Mahmood. 2004. *Good Muslim, Bad Muslim: America, the Cold War, and the Roots of Terror.* New York: Three Leaves.
Manaï, Bochra. 2015. "Mise en visibilité de l'ethnicité maghrébine à Montréal : le cas du Petit-Maghreb." *Diversité urbaine* 15 (1): 109-24.
———. 2018. *Les Maghrébins de Montréal.* Montréal: Presses Universitaires de Montréal.
Marcus, George E. 1995. "Ethnography in/of the World System: The Emergence of Multi-sited Ethnography." *Annual Review of Anthropology* 24:95-117.
Marlière, Philippe. 2023. "The 'Islamo-gauchiste Threat' as Political Nudge." *French Cultural Studies* 34 (3): 234-49.
Martínez-Ariño, Julia. 2019. "Governing Islam in French Cities: Defining 'Acceptable' Public Religiosity through Municipal Consultative Bodies." *Religion, State & Society* 47, nos. 4-5 (August): 423-39.
———. 2021. *Urban Secularism: Negotiating Religious Diversity in Europe.* London: Routledge.
Massad, Joseph. 2008. *Desiring Arabs.* Chicago: University of Chicago Press.
Mavelli, Luca, and Erin Wilson. 2016. "Postsecularism and International Relations." In *Routledge Handbook of Religion and Politics*, 251-69. London: Routledge.
May, Paul. 2016. "Ideological Justification for Restrictive Immigration Policies: An Analysis of Parliamentary Discourses on Immigration in France and Canada (2006-2013)." *French Politics* 14 (3): 287-310.
Mbembe, Achille. 2003. *Necropolitics.* Durham, NC: Duke University Press.
McClintock, Anne. 1995. *Imperial Leather: Race, Gender, and Sexuality in the Colonial Contest.* New York: Routledge.
McCormack, Jo. 2010. *Collective Memory: France and the Algerian War (1954-1962).* Lanham, MD: Lexington.
McGranahan, Carole. 2016. "Theorizing Refusal: An Introduction." *Cultural Anthropology* 31 (3): 319-25.
McGuire, Meredith. 2008. *Lived Religion: Faith and Practice in Everyday Life.* New York: Oxford University Press.

Mekki-Berrada, Abedelwahed. 2018. "Présentation : femmes et subjectivations musulmanes : prolégomènes." *Anthropologie et sociétés* 42 (1): 9–33.

Mendoza, Breny. 2020. "Decolonial Theories in Comparison." *Journal of World Philosophies* 5:43–60.

Merali, Noorfarah. 2009. "Experiences of South Asian Brides Entering Canada after Recent Changes to Family Sponsorship Policies." *Violence against Women* 15 (3): 321–39.

Meunier, É.-Martin, and Jacob Legault-Leclair. 2022. "Religion, langue et génération : l'appui à la Loi 21 au prisme des variables sociodémographiques." In *La laïcité du Québec au miroir de sa religiosité*, edited by Jean-François Laniel and Jean-Philippe Perreault, 47–88. Québec, QC: Presses de l'Université Laval.

Mignolo, Walter D. 2007. "Delinking: The Rhetoric of Modernity, the Logic of Coloniality and the Grammar of De-coloniality." *Cultural Studies* 21, nos. 2–3 (May): 449–514.

Mignolo, Walter, and Catherine E. Walsh. 2018. *On Decoloniality: Concepts, Analytics, and Praxis*. Durham, NC: Duke University Press.

Milot, Micheline. 2009. "L'émergence de la notion de laïcité au Québec : résistances, polysémie et instrumentalisation." In *Appartenances religieuses, appartenance citoyenne : un équilibre en tension*, edited by P. Eid, P. Bosset, M. Milot, and S. Lebel-Grenier, 20–38. Québec, QC: Presses de l'Université Laval.

———. 2010. "Quand la religion dérange : la laïcité en débat au Québec." *Nos diverses cités* 7:90–95.

Milot, Micheline, and David Koussens, eds. 2009. "Reconnaissance de la diversité religieuse : débats actuels dans différentes sociétés." Special issue, *Diversité urbaine* 9 (1).

Ministère de la Justice (France). 2006. "Projet de loi relatif au contrôle de la validité des mariages. Discours de Pascal Clément, ministre de la Justice, garde des Sceaux, 22 mars." March 22, 2006. www.presse.justice.gouv.fr/discours-10093/archives-des-discours-de-2006-10094/projet-de-loi-relatif-au-controle-de-la-validite-des-mariages-11232.html.

———. 2010. "Circulaire relative à la lutte contre les mariages simulés." June 22, 2010. www.gisti.org/IMG/pdf/circ_civ0910_2010-06-22.pdf.

Ministère de l'Éducation nationale et de la jeunesse (France). 2023. "Le bulletin officiel de l'Éducation nationale, de la jeunesse et des sports." Official bulletin, no. 32, August 31, 2023. www.education.gouv.fr/bo/2023/Hebdo32/MENG2323654N.

Modood, Tariq. 2017. "Multiculturalizing Secularism." In *The Oxford Handbook of Secularism*, edited by Phil Zuckerman and John R. Shook, 354–68. Oxford: Oxford University Press.

Moguérou, Laure, and Emmanuelle Santelli. 2012. "Modes de (déco)habiter des jeunes descendants d'immigrés." *Agora débats/jeunesses* 61:79–92.

Monnin, Isabelle. 2008. "Une justice communautariste ? Scandale pour un hymen." *Le Nouvel Observateur*, June 5, 2008. http://archive.wikiwix.com/cache/index2.php?url=http%3A%2F%2Fhebdo.nouvelobs.com%2Fhebdo%2Fparution%2Fp2274%2Farticles%2Fa376444-.html.

Moore, Molly. 2005. "France Weighs Immigration Controls after Riots." *Washington Post*, November 30, 2005. www.washingtonpost.com/archive/politics/2005/11/30/france-weighs-immigration-controls-after-riots/4101acb8-8e8c-408e-beb4-3c142ac646b2.

Morgensen, Scott Lauria. 2011. "The Biopolitics of Settler Colonialism: Right Here, Right Now." *Settler Colonial Studies* 1 (1): 52–76.

Mossière, Géraldine. 2010. "Passer et retravailler la frontière. Des converties à l'islam en France et au Québec : jeux et enjeux de médiation et de différenciation." *Sociologie et sociétés* 42 (1): 245–70.

———. 2013. *Converties à l'islam : parcours de femmes au Québec et en France*. Montréal: Presses de l'Université de Montréal.

———, ed. 2021. *Dits et non-dits : mémoires catholiques au Québec*. Montréal: Presses de l'Université de Montréal.

Mugabo, Delice. 2016. "On Rocks and Hard Places: A Reflection on Antiblackness in Organizing against Islamophobia." *Critical Ethnic Studies* 2 (2): 159–83.

Nadi, Selim. 2021. "L'islamophobie comme modalité idéologique des contradictions raciales en France." *French Cultural Studies* 32 (3): 187–97.

Nagra, Baljit. 2018. "Cultural Explanations of Patriarchy, Race and Everyday Lives: Marginalizing and 'Othering' Muslim Women in Canada." *Journal of Muslim Minority Affairs* 38 (2): 263–79.

New York Times. 2018. "Don't Burn the Women: Warning to Immigrants Looms over a Quebec Village." April 12, 2018. www.nytimes.com/2018/04/12/world/canada/canada-herouxville-immigration.html.

Nguyễn-võ, Thu-hương. 2017. "Into Time." *South East Asia Research* 25 (1): 62–79.

Nilsson, Per-Erik. 2018. *French Populism and Discourses on Secularism*. London: Bloomsbury.

Noble, Brian. 2015. "Tripped Up by Coloniality: Anthropologists as Instruments or Agents in Indigenous-Settler Political Relations?" *Anthropologica* 57 (2): 427–43.

Norton, Anne. 2012. *On the Muslim Question*. Princeton, NJ: Princeton University Press.

Odasso, Laura. 2016. *Mixités conjugales : discrédits, résistances et créativités dans les familles avec un partenaire arabe*. Rennes: Presses Universitaires de Rennes.

Odasso, Laura, and Manuela Salcedo Robledo. 2022. "Intimacy Brokers: The Fragile Boundaries of Activism for Heterosexual and Same-Sex Binational Couples in France." In *Transnational Marriage and Partner Migration: Constellations of Security, Citizenship and Rights*, edited by Anne-Marie D'Aoust, 171–88. New Brunswick, NJ: Rutgers University Press.

Oliphant, Elayne. 2021. *The Privilege of Being Banal: Art, Secularism, and Catholicism in Paris*. Chicago: University of Chicago Press.

Orsi, Robert. 2003. "Is the Study of Lived Religion Irrelevant to the World We Live In? Special Presidential Plenary Address." *Journal for the Scientific Study of Religion* 42 (2): 169–74.

———. 2005. *Between Heaven and Earth: The Religious Worlds People Make and the Scholars Who Study Them*. Princeton, NJ: Princeton University Press.

Parliament of Canada. 2015. "Bill S-7: Zero Tolerance for Barbaric Cultural Practices Act: An Act to Amend the Immigration and Refugee Protection Act, the Civil Marriage Act and the Criminal Code and to Make Consequential Amendments to Other Acts, assented to June 18, 2015." 41st Parliament, 2nd sess. www.parl.ca/DocumentViewer/en/41-2/bill/S-7/royal-assent.

Parmaksiz, Umut. 2018. "Making Sense of the Postsecular." *European Journal of Social Theory* 21 (1): 98–116.

Parvez, Z. Fareen. 2017. *Politicizing Islam: The Islamic Revival in France and India*. Religion and Global Politics. Oxford: Oxford University Press.

Perreault, Jean-Philippe, and Jean-François Laniel. 2022. "La laïcité est (une question) religieuse." In *La laïcité du Québec au miroir de sa religiosité*, edited by Jean-François Laniel and Jean-Philippe Perreault, 1–14. Québec, QC: Presses de l'Université Laval.

Peter, Frank. 2021. *Islam and the Governing of Muslims in France: Secularism without Religion*. New York: Bloomsbury Academic.

Portier, Philippe. 2016. *L'État et les religions en France : une sociologie historique de la laïcité*. Rennes: Presses universitaires de Rennes.

Portier, Philippe, and Irène Théry. 2015. "Du mariage civil au 'mariage pour tous': Sécularisation du droit et mobilisations catholiques." *Sociologie* 6 (1). https://journals.openedition.org/sociologie/2528.

Prada-Bordenave, Emmanuelle. 2008. "Conclusions de la commissaire du gouvernement Emmanuelle Prada-Bordenave sous Conseil d'État." Decision no. 286798, June 27, 2008. www.conseil-etat.fr/fr/arianeweb/CE/decision/2008-06-27/286798.

Pratt, Mary Louise. (1992) 2008. *Imperial Eyes: Travel Writing and Transculturation*. New York: Routledge.

Pringle, Sarah. 2020. "The 'Threat' of Marriage Fraud: A Story of Precarity, Exclusion, and Belonging." *Canadian Journal of Family Law* 33 (1): 1–47.

Puar, Jasbir K. 2013. "Homonationalism as Assemblage: Viral Travels, Affective Sexualities." *Jindal Global Law Review* 4 (2): 23–43.

Public Safety Canada. 2020. "Clare's Law." www.publicsafety.gc.ca/cnt/trnsprnc/brfng-mtrls/prlmntry-bndrs/20200623/025/index-en.aspx.

Quack, Johannes. 2017. "Identifying (with) the Secular: Description and Genealogy." In *The Oxford Handbook of Secularism*, edited by Phil Zuckerman and John P. Shook, 21–39. Oxford: Oxford University Press.

Quijano, Aníbal. 2000. "Coloniality of Power and Eurocentrism in Latin America." *International Sociology* 15, no. 2 (June): 215–32.

———. 2008. "Coloniality of Power, Eurocentrism, and Latin America." In *Coloniality at Large: Latin America and the Postcolonial Debate*, edited by Mabel Moraña, Enrique Dussel, and Carols A. Jáuregui, 181–224. Durham, NC: Duke University Press.

Rambukkana, Nathan. 2015. *Fraught Intimacies: Non/monogamy in the Public Sphere*. Vancouver: University of British Columbia Press.

Razack, Sherene. 1998. *Looking White People in the Eye: Gender, Race, and Culture in Courtrooms and Classrooms*. Toronto: University of Toronto Press.

———. 2004. "Imperilled Muslim Women, Dangerous Muslim Men and Civilized Europeans: Legal and Social Responses to Forced Marriages." *Feminist Legal Studies* 12 (2): 129–74.

———. 2008. *Casting Out: The Eviction of Muslims from Western Law and Politics*. Toronto: University of Toronto Press.

République française. 2005. "Déclaration de M. Pascal Clément, ministre de la Justice, sur la prévention et la lutte contre les violences conjugales, à Paris, Assemblée nationale." http://discours.viepublique.fr/notices/053003958.html.

———. 2021. "Loi du 24 août 2021 confortant le respect des principes de la République." www.vie-publique.fr/loi/277621-loi-separatisme-respect-des-principes-de-la-republique-24-aout-2021.

RFI (Radio France Internationale). 2021. "France's Anti-separatism bill Deemed Constitutional with Only Minor Changes." August 14, 2021. www.rfi.fr/en

/france/20210814-france-s-anti-separatism-bill-deemed-constitutional-with-only-minor-changes-islamism-secularism.

Rioux, Christian. 2013. "Laïcité : Pauline Marois et Jean-Marc Ayrault sont sur la même longueur d'onde." *Le Devoir*, December 14, 2013. www.ledevoir.com/politique/quebec/395252/pauline-marois-et-jean-marc-ayrault-sont-sur-la-meme-longueur-d-onde.

Roach, Catherine M. 2016. *Happily Ever After: The Romance Story in Popular Culture*. Bloomington: Indiana University Press.

Robledo, M. S. 2011. "Bleu, blanc, gris . . . La couleur des mariages." *L'espace politique* 13. https://journals.openedition.org/espacepolitique/1869.

Robson, Ruthann. 2013. *Dressing Constitutionally: Hierarchy, Sexuality, and Democracy from Our Hairstyles to Our Shoes*. Cambridge: Cambridge University Press.

Rosen, Jean-Pierre. 2008. "Tempête artificielle autour de l'annulation d'un mariage." *Le Monde*, May 31, 2008. www.lemonde.fr/blog/jprosen/2008/05/31/annulation-dun-mariage-le-cri-des-ex-vierges-256.

Rosenblum, Darren. 2020. "Les quotas de femmes pour les entreprises et l'interdiction du burkini." *Revue générale de droit* 50:7–115.

Rousseau, Louis, ed. 2012. *Le Québec après Bouchard-Taylor : les identités religieuses de l'immigration*. Québec, QC: Presses de l'Université du Québec.

Roy, Olivier. 2005. *La laïcité face à l'islam*. Paris: Stock.

Rude-Antoine, Edwige. 1990. *Le mariage magrébin en France*. Paris: Karthala.

Ryan, Phil. 2010. *Multicultiphobia*. Toronto: University of Toronto Press.

Salvatore, Armando. 2009. "Tradition and Modernity within Islamic Civilization and the West." In *Islam and Modernity: Key Issues and Debates*, edited by M. Khahid Masud, A. Salvatore, and M. van Bruinessen, 3–35. Edinburgh: Edinburgh University Press.

Santelli, Emmanuelle. 2001. *La mobilité sociale dans l'immigration : itinéraires de réussite des enfants d'origine algérienne*. Toulouse: Presses Universitaires du Mirail.

Santelli, Emmanuelle, and Beate Collet. 2011. "De l'endogamie à l'homogamie socio-ethnique : réinterprétations normatives et réalités conjugales parmi les descendants d'immigrés." *Sociologie et sociétés* 43 (2): 327–52.

———. 2012a. "Le mariage « halal » : réinterprétation des rites du mariage arabo-musulman dans le contexte post-migratoire français." *Recherches familiales* 9:83–92.

———. 2012b. "The Choice of Mixed Marriage among the Second Generation in France: A Lifetime Approach." *Papers: Revista de sociologia* 1 (97): 93–112.

Sayad, Abdelmalek. 1980. "Le foyer des sans-famille." *Actes de la recherche en sciences sociales* 32 (1): 89–103.

———. 1995. *Un Nanterre algérien, terre de bidonvilles*. Paris: Autrement.

———. 1997. *L'immigration ou les paradoxes de l'altérité*. Paris and Bruxelles: De Boeck & Larcier.

———. 1999. *La double absence : des illusions aux souffrances de l'immigré*. Preface by Pierre Bourdieu. Paris: Seuil.

Schaefli, Laura, and Anne Godlewska. 2014. "Social Ignorance and Indigenous Exclusion: Public Voices in the Province of Québec, Canada." *Settler-Colonial Studies* 4 (3): 227–44.

Scheer, Monique, Nadia Fadil, and Birgitte Schepelern Johansen, eds. 2019. *Secular Bodies, Affects, and Emotions: European Configurations*. London: Bloomsbury.

Schepelern Johansen, Birgitte. 2022. "Chasing the Secular: Methodological Reflections on How to Make the Secular Tangible." *Religion and Society: Advances in Research* 13:126–39.

Schilbrack, Kevin. 2005. "Religion, Models of, and Reality: Are We Through with Geertz?" *Journal of the American Academy of Religion* 73 (2): 429–52.

Schnapper, Dominique. 2007. *Qu'est-ce que l'intégration ?* Paris: Gallimard.

Schrijvers, Lieke L., and Jelle Wiering. 2018. "Religious/Secular Discourses and Practices of Good Sex." *Culture and Religion* 19 (2): 139–59.

Sciolino, Elaine. 2005. "Immigrant Polygamy Is a Factor in French Unrest, a Gaullist Says." *New York Times*, November 18, 2005. www.nytimes.com/2005/11/18/international/europe/immigrant-polygamy-is-a-factor-in-french-unrest-a.html.

Scott, Corrie. 2016. "How French Canadians Became White Folks, or Doing Things with Race in Quebec." *Ethnic and Racial Studies* 39 (7): 1280–97.

Scott, James. 1990. *Domination and the Arts of Resistance: Hidden Transcripts*. New Haven, CT: Yale University Press.

Scott, Joan Wallach. 2005. *Parité: Sexual Equality and the Crisis of French Universalism*. Chicago: University of Chicago Press.

———. 2007. *The Politics of the Veil*. Princeton, NJ: Princeton University Press.

———. 2011. "Sexularism: On Secularism and Gender Equality." In *The Fantasy of Feminist History*, 91–116. Durham, NC: Duke University Press.

———. 2018. *Sex and Secularism*. Princeton, NJ: Princeton University Press.

Scott, Marian. 2010. "Majority Agree with Quebec's Veil Law, Poll Finds." *National Post*, May 20, 2010.

Segalen, Martine. 2003. *Éloge du mariage*. Paris: Découvertes Gallimard.

Selby, Jennifer A. 2009a. "Marriage-Partner Preference among Muslims in France: Reproducing Tradition in the Maghrebian Diaspora." *Journal of the Society for the Anthropology of Europe* 9 (2): 4–16.

———. 2009b. "When Distance Is Not Geographical: Paris and a Northeastern *Banlieue*." *Anthropology Now* 1, no. 2 (September): 88–93.

———. 2011a. "Islam in France Reconfigured: Republican Islam in the 2010 Gerin Report." *Journal of Muslim Minority Affairs* 31 (3): 383–98.

———. 2011b. "French secularism as a 'guarantor' of women's rights? Muslim women and gender politics in a Parisian banlieue." *Culture and Religion* 12 (4): 441–62.

———. 2012. *Questioning French Secularism: Gender Politics and Islam in a Parisian Suburb*. Anthropology of Religion Series. New York: Palgrave Macmillan.

———. 2013. "Polygamy in the Parisian *Banlieues*: Discourse and Debate on the 2005 French Urban Riots." In *Polygamy's Rights and Wrongs: Perspectives on Harm, Family and Law*, edited by Gillian Calder and L. G. Beaman, 89–103. Vancouver: University of British Columbia Press.

———. 2014a. "« C'est plus traditionnel ici qu'au bled »: analyse socio-spatiale du traditionalisme religieux dans une banlieue parisienne." *Ethnologie française* 44 (3): 515–26.

———. 2014b. "Islam in France." In *Handbook of European Islam*, edited by J. Cesari, 23–63, New York: Oxford University Press.

———. 2014c. "Un/veiling Women's Bodies: Secularism and Sexuality in Full-Face Veil Prohibitions in France and Québec." *Studies in Religion / Sciences religieuses* 43 (3): 439–66.

———. 2017. "Le *bled* en banlieue : le mariage musulman face à l'État français." *Ethnologie française* 167 (3): 693–705.

———. 2019. "Required Romance: On Secular Sensibilities in Recent French Marriage and Immigration Regulations." In *Secular Bodies, Affects, and Emotions: European Configurations*, edited by Monique Scheer, Nadia Fadil, and Birgitte Schepelern Johansen, 157–69. London: Bloomsbury.

———. 2022a. "Romance and the Male Secular Body: The Case of Algerian Men in France and Québec." *Journal of the American Academy of Religion* 90, no. 1 (March): 248–69.

———. 2022b. "'There Is No Place for the State in the Bedrooms of the Nation,' or The Case of Bill 21: A Response to Goodwin's Gender/Religion Lens." In *Key Categories in the Study of Religion: Contexts and Critiques*, edited by Rebekka King, 162–75. Sheffield, UK: Equinox.

Selby, Jennifer A., and Amélie Barras. Forthcoming. "Appels alternés entre la liberté d'expression et la liberté de la religion : mise en relation de moments politiques au Canada et au Québec contemporain." *Studies in Religion / Sciences religieuses*.

Selby, Jennifer A., and Kawtare Bihya. 2025. "La religiosité polarisée au Québec : le cas des femmes d'origine algérienne à Montréal." In *L'islam vécu au Québec*, edited by Géraldine Mossière and Roxanne Marcotte. Québec, QC: Presses de l'Université Laval.

Selby, Jennifer A., and M. L. Fernando. 2014. "Short Skirts and Niqab Bans: On Sexuality and the Secular Body." *The Immanent Frame: Secularism, Religion, and the Public Sphere*, September 4, 2014. http://blogs.ssrc.org/tif/2014/09/04/short-skirts-and-niqab-bans-on-sexuality-and-the-secular-body.

Selby, Jennifer A., and Sobia Shaikh. 2023. "Wait, What?! Islamophobia Exists in Newfoundland and Labrador?: Theorizing the Polite Dismissal of Anti-Islamophobia Public Engagement." In *Islamophobia as a Form of Radicalisation: Perspectives on Media, Academia and Socio-political Scapes from Europe and Canada*, edited by Abdelwahed Mekki-Berrada and Leen d'Haenens, 211–28. Leiden, the Netherlands: Brill.

Selby, Jennifer A., Amélie Barras, and Lori G. Beaman. 2018. *Beyond Accommodation: Everyday Narratives of Muslim Canadians*. Vancouver: University of British Columbia Press.

Shaw, Alison. 2001. "Kinship, Cultural Preference and Immigration: Consanguineous Marriage among British Pakistanis." *Journal of the Royal Anthropological Institute* 7 (2): 315–34.

Shaw, Alison, and Katherine Charsley. 2006. "Rishtas: Adding Emotion to Strategy in Understanding British Pakistani Transnational Marriages." *Global Networks* 6 (4): 405–21.

Shepard, Todd. 2012. "Something Notably Erotic: Politics, 'Arab Men' and Sexual Revolution in Post-decolonization France, 1962–1974." *Journal of Modern History* 84 (1): 80–115.

———. 2017. "The Global Erotics of the French Sexual Revolution: Politics and 'Arab Men' in Post-decolonization France, 1962–1974." In *The Global 1960s: Conventions, Contests, and Countercultures*, edited by Jadwiga Pieper-Mooney and Tamara Chaplin, 115–39. New York: Routledge.

———. 2018. *Sex, France, and Arab Men, 1962–1979*. Chicago: University of Chicago Press.

Shryock, Andrew. 2010. "Introduction: Islam as an Object of Fear and Affection." In *Islamophobia/Islamophilia: Beyond the Politics of Enemy and Friend*, edited by Andrew Shryock, 1–28. Bloomington and Indianapolis: Indiana University Press.

Silberman, Roxane, Richard Alba, and Irène Fournier. 2007. "Segmented Assimilation in France? Discrimination in the Labour Market against the Second Generation." *Ethnic and Racial Studies* 30 (1): 1–27.

Silverstein, Paul. 1996. "Realizing Myth: Berbers in France and Algeria." *Middle East Report* 200 (Fall): 11–15.

———. 2002. "The Kabyle Myth: Colonization and the Production of Ethnicity." In *From the Margins: Historical Anthropology and Its Futures*, 122–55. Durham, NC: Duke University Press.

———. 2004. *Algeria in France: Transpolitics, Race and Nation*. Bloomington: Indiana University Press.

———. 2018. *Postcolonial France: Race, Islam, and the Future of the Republic*. London: Pluto.

Simpson, Audra. 2007. "On Ethnographic Refusal: Indigeneity, 'Voice' and Colonial Citizenship." *Junctures: The Journal for Thematic Dialogue* 9:67–80.

———. 2014. *Mohawk Interruptus: Political Life across the Borders of Settler States*. Durham, NC: Duke University Press.

Simpson, Leanne Betasamosake. 2013. *Islands of Decolonial Love: Stories and Songs*. Winnipeg: ARP Books.

Sims, Alexandra. 2016. "French PM Manuel Valls Suggests Naked Breasts Represent France Better than Burkinis." *Independent*, August 30, 2016. www.independent.co.uk/news/world/europe/french-pm-manuel-valls-suggests-naked-breasts-represent-france-better-than-burkinis-a7217261.html.

Singh Judge, Rajbir. 2020. "Mind the Gap: Islam, Secularism, and the Law." *Qui Parle* 29 (1): 179–202.

Sioui, Marie-Michèle. 2021. "Legault reconnaît le racisme systémique . . . dans les pensionnats." *Le Devoir*, October 6, 2021. www.ledevoir.com/politique/quebec/638118/legaultreconnait-le-racisme-systemique-dans-les-pensionnats.

Six, Clémens. 2020. *The Transnationality of the Secular: Travelling Ideas and Shared Practices of Secularism in Decolonising South and Southeast Asia*. Leiden, the Netherlands: Brill.

Small, M. L., D. J. Harding, and M. Lamont. 2010. "Reconsidering Culture and Poverty." *Annals of the American Academy of Political and Social Science* 629 (1): 6–27.

Smith, Linda Tuhiwai. 1999. *Decolonizing Methodologies*. London: Zed.

Standing Committee on Citizenship and Immigration. 2014. "Evidence: Tuesday, March 4." Number 015, 2nd Session, 41st Parliament. Parliament of Canada. www.ourcommons.ca/documentviewer/en/41-2/CIMM/meeting-15/evidence.

Stasi, Bernard. 2003. "Commission de réflexion sur l'application du principe de laïcité dans la République : rapport au Président de la République." www.vie-publique.fr/rapport/26626-commission-de-reflexion-sur-application-du-principe-de-laicite.

Statista. 2019. Share of the Population in France from 2006 to 2018, by Marital Status. www.statista.com/statistics/459704/distribution-population-marital-status-france/#:~:text=The%20percentage%20of%20married%20persons,country%20was%20of%2047.8%20percent.

Statistics Canada. 2016. "Profil du recensement de 2016." www12.statcan.gc.ca/census-recensement/2016/dp-pd/prof/details/page.cfm?Lang=F&Geo1=POPC&Code1=0547&Geo2=PR&Code2=24&SearchText=Montreal&SearchType=Begins&SearchPR=01&B1=Immigration%20and%20citizenship&TABID=1&type=0.

———. 2023. "Police-Reported Hate Crime, 2021." March 22, 2023. www150.statcan.gc.ca/n1/daily-quotidien/230322/dq230322a-eng.htm.
Stephenson, Barry. 2015. *Ritual: A Very Short Introduction*. New York: Oxford University Press.
Stoler, Ann Laura. 1995. *Race and the Education of Desire: Foucault's "History of Sexuality" and the Colonial Order of Things*. Durham, NC: Duke University Press.
———. 2006. "Intimidations of Empire: Predicaments of the Tactile and Unseen." In *Haunted by Empire: Geographies of Intimacy in North American History*, edited by Ann L. Stoler, 1–22. Durham, NC: Duke University Press.
———. (2002) 2010. *Carnal Knowledge and Imperial Power: Race and the Intimate in Colonial Rule*. Berkeley: University of California Press.
Stolow, Jeremy, and Alexandra Boutros. 2015. "Visible/Invisible: Religion, Media, and the Public Sphere." *Canadian Journal of Communication* 40 (1): 3–10.
Stora, Benjamin. 1992. *Ils venaient d'Algérie : l'immigration algérienne en France (1912–1992)*. Paris: Fayard.
———. 2021. *Les questions mémorielles portant sur la colonisation et la guerre d'Algérie, rapport remis au président de la République*. www.elysee.fr/admin/upload/default/0001/09/0586b6b0ef1c2fc2540589c6d56a1ae63a65d97c.pdf.
Supreme Court of Canada. 2009. *Alberta v. Hutterian Brethren of Wilson Colony*. SCC 37, 2SCR 567, 32186. https://scc-csc.lexum.com/scc-csc/scc-csc/en/item/7808/index.do.
———. 2012. *R v. N.S.* SCC 72, 3 SCR 726, 33989. https://scc-csc.lexum.com/scc-csc/scc-csc/en/item/12779/index.do.
Surkis, Judith. 2010. "Hymenal Politics: Marriage, Secularism, and French Sovereignty." *Public Culture* 22 (3): 531–56.
———. 2019. *Sex, Law, and Sovereignty in French Algeria, 1830–1930*. Ithaca, NY: Cornell University Press.
Taher, Saaz. 2021. "Déni du racisme au Québec : post-racialisme, injustices épistémiques et actes de discours." PhD diss., Université de Montréal. https://papyrus.bib.umontreal.ca/xmlui/bitstream/handle/1866/27694/Taher_Saaz_2021_these.pdf?sequence=2&isAllowed=y.
Taylor, Charles. 2007. *A Secular Age*. Cambridge, MA: Belknap.
Teisceira-Lessard, Philippe. 2013. "Charte des valeurs québécoises : Marois vante l'intégration à la française." *La Presse*, September 12, 2013. www.lapresse.ca/actualites/politique/politique-quebecoise/201309/12/01-4688752-charte-des-valeurs-quebecoises-marois-vante-lintegration-a-la-francaise.php.
Tetrault, Chantal. 2013. "Cultural Citizenship in France and *le Bled* among Teens of Pan-southern Immigrant Heritage." *Language and Communication* 33 (4): 532–43.
———. 2015. *Transcultural Teens: Performing Youth Identifies in French Cités*. Hoboken, NJ: Wiley-Blackwell.
Tharoor, Ishaan. 2021. "France and the Spectral Menace of 'Islamo-leftism.'" *Washington Post*, February 22, 2021. www.washingtonpost.com/world/2021/02/22/france-macron-islamo-leftism.
Thobani, Sunera. 2021. *Contesting Islam, Constructing Race and Sexuality: The Inordinate Desire of the West*. London: Bloomsbury.
Ticktin, Miriam. 2008. "Sexual Violence as the Language of Border Control: Where French Feminist and Anti-immigrant Rhetoric Meet." *Signs: Journal of Women in Culture and Society* 33 (4): 863–89.

Tissot, Sylvie. 2011. "Excluding Muslim Women: From Hijab to Niqab, from School to Public Space." *Public Culture* 23 (1): 39–46.

Todd, Emmanuel. 2015. *Qui est Charlie ? : Sociologie d'une crise religieuse*. Paris : Éditions du Seuil.

Touzeil-Divina, Mathieu. 2020. "Au nez et à la barbe des juges du fond, le Conseil d'État rappelle (enfin) qu'en soi porter la barbe n'est ni illégal ni contraire au principe de laïcité." *La semaine juridique : administrations et collectivités territoriales* 8 (3). https://publications.ut-capitole.fr/id/eprint/42508.

Tremblay, Stéphanie. 2022. "La laïcité dans l'imaginaire des Québécois de culture catholique." In *La laïcité du Québec au miroir de sa religiosité*, edited by Jean-François Laniel and Jean-Philippe Perreault, 17–46. Québec, QC: Presses de l'Université Laval.

Triadafilopoulos, Triadafilos. 2013. "Dismantling White Canada: Race, Rights, and the Origins of the Points System." In *Wanted and Welcome? Policies for Highly Skilled Immigrants in Comparative Perspective*, edited by T. Triadafilopoulos, 15–38. New York: Springer.

Trouillot, Michel-Rolph. 1995. *Silencing the Past: Power and the Production of History*. Boston: Beacon.

TRTWorld. 2021. "French Lawmakers Approve Controversial 'Anti-separatism' Bill." February 16, 2021. www.trtworld.com/europe/french-lawmakers-approve-controversial-anti-separatism-bill-44228.

Truong, Fabien. 2013. *Des capuches et des hommes : trajectoires de jeunes de banlieue*. Paris: Buchet-Chastel.

———. 2017. *Loyautés radicales : l'islam et les mauvais garçons de la Nation*. Paris: La Découverte.

Truth and Reconciliation Commission of Canada. 2015. "Truth and Reconciliation Commission of Canada: Calls to Action." https://publications.gc.ca/collections/collection_2015/trc/IR4-8-2015-eng.pdf.

Tuck, Eve. 2009. "Suspending Damage: A Letter to Communities." *Harvard Educational Review* 79 (3): 409–27.

Tuck, Eve, and K. Wayne Yang. 2012. "Decolonization Is Not a Metaphor." *Decolonization: Indigeneity, Education and Society* 1 (1): 1–40.

———. 2014. "R-Words: Refusing Research." In *Humanizing Research: Decolonizing Qualitative Inquiry with Youth and Communities*, edited by Django Paris and Maisha T. Winn, 223–48. London: SAGE Publications.

TV5. 2020. "France : les certificats de virginité dans le viseur du gouvernement." September 14, 2020. https://information.tv5monde.com/terriennes/france-les-certificats-de-virginite-dans-le-viseur-du-gouvernement-37117.

Urquhart, Cathy. 2013. *Grounded Theory for Qualitative Research: A Practical Guide*. Thousand Oaks, CA: Sage.

Venel, Nancy. 1999. *Musulmanes françaises : des pratiquantes voilées à l'université*. Paris: L'Harmattan.

Verdier, Marie. 2018. "En Algérie, la Décennie noire a aussi frappé les religieux." *La Croix*, December 1, 2018. www.la-croix.com/Monde/Afrique/En-Algerie-decennie-noire-aussi-frappe-religieux-2018-11-30-1200986606.

Vertovec, Steven. 2009. *Transnationalism*. London: Routledge.

Wacquant, Loïc. 2005. *Parias urbains : ghetto, banlieues, État*. Paris: La Découverte.

Weheliye, Alexander G. 2014. *Habeas Viscus: Racializing Assemblages, Biopolitics, and Black Feminist Theories of the Human*. Durham, NC: Duke University Press.

Weil, Patrick. 2009. "Why the French Laïcité Is Liberal." *Cardozo Law Review* 30 (6): 2699–714.
Weinbaum, Alys Eve, Lynn M. Thomas, Priti Ramamurthy, Uta G. Poiger, Madeleine Y. Dong, and Tani E. Barlow. 2008. "The Modern Girl as Heuristic Device: Collaboration, Connective Comparison, Multidirectional Citation." In *The Modern Girl around the World: Consumption, Modernity, and Globalization*, edited by Alys Eve Weinbaum, Lynn M. Thomas, Priti Ramamurthy, Uta G. Poiger, Madeleine Yue Dong, and Tani E. Barlow, 1–24. Durham, NC: Duke University Press.
Wekker, Gloria. 2016. *White Innocence: Paradoxes of Colonialism and Race*. Durham, NC: Duke University Press.
Wesselhoeft, Kirsten. 2011. "Gendered Secularity: The Feminine Individual in the 2010 Gerin Report." *Journal of Muslim Minority Affairs* 31 (3): 399–411.
Wien, Tom, and Suzanne Gousse. 2015. "Filles du roi." In *L'encyclopédie canadienne*. www.thecanadianencyclopedia.ca/fr/article/filles-du-roi.
Wiering, Jelle. 2017. "There Is a Sexular Body: Introducing a Material Approach to the Secular." *Secularism and Nonreligion* 6:1–11.
Wieviorka, Michel. 1993. "Racism and Modernity in Present Day Europe." *Thesis Eleven* 35:51–61.
———. 2016. "Panique morale autour du 'burkini.'" *The Conversation*, August 26, 2016. https://theconversation.com/panique-morale-autour-du-burkini-64410.
Wilkins-Laflamme, Sarah. 2018. "Islamophobia in Canada: Measuring the Realities of Negative Attitudes toward Muslims and Religious Discrimination." *Canadian Review of Sociology* 55 (1): 86–110.
———. 2022. *Religion, Spirituality and Secularity among Millennials: The Generation Shaping American and Canadian Trends*. London: Routledge.
Williams, L. 2010. *Global Marriage: Cross-border Marriage Migration in Global Context*. New York: Palgrave Macmillan.
Willsher, K. 2020. "Macron Outlines New Law to Prevent 'Islamist Separatism' in France." *The Guardian*, October 2, 2020. www.theguardian.com/world/2020/oct/02/emmanuel-macron-outlines-law-islamic-separatism-france.
Wilson, Erin K. 2014. "Theorizing Religion as Politics in Postsecular International Relations." *Politics, Religion and Ideology* 15 (3): 347–65.
Winter, Bronwyn. 2008. *Hijab and the Republic: Uncovering the French Headscarf Debate*. Syracuse, NY: Syracuse University Press.
Woehrling, Jean-Marie. 2012. "Qu'est-ce qu'un signe religieux ?" *Société, droit et religion* 2:9–24.
Wohlrab-Sahr, Monika, and Marian Burchardt. 2012. "Multiple Secularities: Toward a Cultural Sociology of Secular Modernities." *Comparative Sociology* 11 (6): 875–909.
Woodhead, Linda. 2014. "Religious Other or Religious Inferior." In *Living with Religious Diversity*, edited by Sonia Sikka and Lori G. Beaman, 1–14. London: Routledge.
Zappi, Sylvia. 2015. "Le djihadiste, nouvel épouvantail des banlieues françaises." *Le Monde*, October 22, 2015. www.lemonde.fr/banlieues/article/2015/10/22/le-djihadiste-nouvel-epouvantail-des-banlieues-francaises_4794877_1653530.html#gyOTuk3mfeIczDkE.99.
Zia-Ebrahimi, Reza. 2020. "The French Origins of 'Islamophobia Denial.'" *Patterns of Prejudice* 54 (4): 315–46.

———. 2023. "The Islamogauchisme Discourse, or the Power to Create the Inner Enemy." *French Cultural Studies* 34 (3): 250-74.

Zine, Jasmin. 2022. *Under Siege: Islamophobia and the 9/11 Generation*. Montréal: McGill-Queen's University Press.

Zoghlami, Khaoula. 2020. "Qui peut témoigner ? Présences indésirables et paroles sous surveillance." In *Modération ou extrémisme ? Regards critiques sur la Loi 21*, edited by Leila Celis, Dia Dabby, Dominique Leydet, and Vincent Romani, 195-207. Québec, QC: Presses de l'Université Laval.

Zubrzycki, Geneviève. 2016a. *Beheading the Saint: Nationalism, Religion, and Secularism in Quebec*. Chicago: University of Chicago Press.

———. 2016b. "Laïcité et patrimonialisation du religieux au Québec." *Recherches sociographiques* 57, nos. 2-3 (May-December): 311-32.

INDEX

Page numbers in italics refer to illustrations.

abayas, 29, 47, *48*, 90, 93–94, 99–100, 208–9, 210–11, 230n13
acceptability, 10, 38–40, 102, 184, 205–10, 213, 227n6; of conspicuous religious symbols, 9, 58, 60, 67, 78, 156, 206, 237n1; of face coverings, 95, 105, 208; of gender performances, 5, 8–9, 29, 93, 204–5, 208; of migration marriages, 25, 32, 80, 152, 237n4; of niqabs, 50, 99, 107, 213; of the secular body, 31–32, 39, 58, 93, 99, 206–7; of sexuality, 89–90, 99, 117, 204
accommodations, 30, 49, 60, 66, 195, 199; as reasonable, 30, 66, 105, 197, 206, 227n6; religious, 30, 66, 78, 146; requests for, 59, 76, 78, 106, 226n38
activism, 6, 57, 91, 100, 165
Adjani, Isabel, 100–101, 230n14
adventure, 24, 27, 121, 124, 151, 166, 190
Affaire du foulard, 51
agency, 7–11, 74, 117, 135
Agrama, Hussein, 39, 41, 45
ahistoricity, 51, 195, 198–99, 200, 206–7
Ahmed, Sara, 24, 26, 42
Aïn Achache, Algeria, 127–28
Algeria, 1–3, 17, 51, 62, 119–24, 159–61, 210; civil war in, 18, 79, 159, 166, 205; colonial period in, 20, 26, 28, 84–88, 94, 125, 161–64, 196, 204, 206–7; as homeland, 28, 141, 161, 164–68, 170–72, 186–90, 194; independence of, 18, 125; as *ressourcement*, 80, 202; migration narratives from, 11–14, 23–24, 27–28, 63–73, 110–16, 174–81, 190–93; post-Independence period, 86, 89; regions of, 34, 175, 201, 205; as vacation destination, 70, 78, 109, 110, 147, 151, 152, 159, 168–70, 175, 180–81, 186, 190–91; as wedding location, 169, 172–73, 182–85. *See also names of Algerian cities*
Algerian Cultural Centre (Montréal, QC), 17, 76–7, 113, 123, 173–75, 190

algérianité, 19, 122, 152, 171
Algerian peoples, 1–13, 16–18, 28, 172; diaspora of, 20; diversity of, 19–21, 191; migration waves of, 47, 70, 124–46; racialization of, 4, 11, 21; as refugees, 18, 153, 201; relationship with France, 1–2, 18, 43, 84, 86, 88, 125, 133, 196, 224n23. *See also* Kabylians
Algerian War of Independence, 13, 86, 125, 127, 129, 197, 232n8
Algiers, Algeria, 77–78, 173, 190, 232n6, 234n28; in immigration stories, 63, 131–32, 234n32; refugees from, 132, 139, 141, 147–48, 152, 193; as vacation destination, 147–48, 156, 168
Amazigh (Berber) people, 19–20, 153–54, 224n25, 233n19; Tamazight (language), 19, 154, 175, 234n30
Amir-Moazami, Schirin, 28, 92–93
Annaba, Algeria, 65, 131
annulment, 4, 7, *48*, 58, 94–96, 116, 135–36, 138, 157, 202, 233n15
anticlericalism, 28, 94
anticolonialism, 21, 164
antiliberalism, 74, 211
antiniqabism, 101, 114, 117–18, 204, 212
antiracism, 21, 33
Antiseparatism Law (France), 57–58, 96, 211
Anvari, Fatemeh, 49
apoliticality, 158, 195, 198–200, 206–7, 225n34
Arabic language, 2, 19, 77, 109, 139, 167, 172, 181, 186, 193
Arab peoples, 19–21, 7f1, 85, 129, 158, 191, 201
areligiosity, 46–47, 98, 105–6, 136, 227n4
Armed Islamic Group, 153
Asad, Talal, 36, 38, 44
Atef, Naima, 106
atheism, 19–20, 44, 113, 192–94, 233n20

{ 271 }

Atif, Fatima, 98
Attal, Gabriel, *48*
attire, 79, 94, 107, 153, 159, 166, 170, 176, 180; as conspicuous religious symbols, 8, 46, 50, 60, 62, 100–101, 106, 117, 140, 212, 222n13; and modesty, 19, 44, 55, 93, 100, 209; as romantic, 135; as secular, 9, 44, 47, 55, 69, 101, 209; policing of, 52, 197, 221n8; restrictions on, 60, 90, 117, 207; wedding, 1, 3, 83, 110–11, 115, 123, 131, 161, 176, 182–83, 194–95, 203, 213

Baby Loup, *48*, 95, 98
Badinter, Élisabeth, 95, 100
baguettes, 15, 55–56, 209
bandanas, 19, 29, 47, 50, 52, 93, 210
banlieues, 14, 54–55, 71, 86, 88, 100, 108, 177, 230n15; Colombes, 13, 111; and coloniality, 197; as community spaces, 12, 16, 126, 130; culture in, 170–71, 229n19; Nanterre Préfecture, 1, 6, 9, 15, 131, 225n29, 229n7; Saint-Denis, 55, 93. *See also* Paris, France: suburbs of; Petit-Nanterre, France
banlieusards, 54, 87, 197
barbarism, 50, 125, 135. *See also* Bill S-7
Bardot, Brigitte, 207
Bataclan, Paris, 29, 55
Bayrou, François, 51, 237n1
Bayrou Decree, 51–52, 237n1
Beaman, Lori G., 41, 62
beards, 19, 29, 45, 47, 71, 90, 99, 115–16, 176, 209–10, 229n5; shaving of, 93, 106, 115
Belgium, 38, 55
Benna, Zyed, 87
Berbers. *See* Amazigh (Berber) people
Besson, Éric, 135
Bill 21 (Law 21), 31, 41, *49*, 50, 141, 162, 195–200, 206, 211, 227n6, 228n16, 231n17; and niqabs and hijabs, 30, 35, 105, 146, 162–63, 226n41; and religious symbols, 60–67, 78, 146, 237n1
Bill 60, *49*, 50–51, 58–60, *59*, 62, 116, 206, 212, 222n11, 226n38, 237n1; in public services, 30–31, 78–79
Bill 62, *49*, 231n17
Bill 94, *49*, 78, 105–6, 226n38, 230n11
Bill S-7, 122, 144–45

binaries, 4, 164; abnormal/normal, 130; colonial/Other, 37, 92, 165, 224n26; conservative/liberal, 25, 118; gender, 25, 33, 37, 90–91, 99, 118, 211; practicing/nonpracticing, 20; public/private, 25, 32, 37, 43, 90–91, 118; religious symbols and, 38, 51, 92–93, 117–18, 207, 211, 237n1; secular/religious, 37, 90–91
binationality, 5, 11, 128, 169
biopolitics, 9, 11, 21, 24–26, 84, 86–87, 90–91, 96, 122, 195
biopower, 25, 43, 81, 84, 116, 164, 210
Bled, 156, 163, 173, 176–77, 184, 186–87, 194, 225n9; and authenticity, 19, 167, 172; as *bled paumé*, 167; as cultural connection, 27, 31, 34, 69, 70, 111, 167, 169, 171–72, 187, 213; as imagined, 161, 165, 189, 200, 202, 204–5; and sociality, 69, 167; as transnational, 158, 164, 166–67, 189, 200
Blédard(e)s, 28, 110–11, 172, 177–78, 181, 226n37
borders, 2, 10–11, 139, 175, 181, 187, 200, 202
Bouchard-Taylor Commission Report, 30, *49*, 66, 78, 195–98, 227n6
Boumerdès, Algeria, 112, 159–60
Bourdieu, Pierre, 8–9, 13, 38, 81
boureks, 179
brides, 23, 72, 94–95, 136, 152, 154, 168, 179, 209, 223n17, 225n29; and fashion, 1, 7, 183
burkinis, 29, 46–47, *48*, 62, 90, 94, 102–4, 108, 117–18, 208–11

Canada, 7, 10, 20–21, 29, 96, 168–71, 213, 227n8, 233n21; citizenship in, 107, 143–44; and colonization, 26, 40, 88–90, 140, 164, 198, 206, 236n21; economic immigrants in, 139, 156; federal legal decisions in, 106–7, 228nn17–18, 231n18, 234n24; federal legislation in, 29–31, 43, 47, 50, 107–8, 121–22, 141–42; immigration policy of, 121–22, 125, 138–39, 141–43, 205, 231n3, 233n22, 234n23; immigration system of, 47, 77, 138, 233n16; Indigenous peoples in, 140, 197–99, 236n19; marriage migration and, 78, 119, 125, 143–45, 151, 203, 211–12, 229nn1–2; national values of,

272 } INDEX

121, 145, 198; realities of immigration to, 77, 112, 124, 141; religious regulation in, 29, 90, 99, 106, 205. *See also names of Canadian provinces and cities*
Canadian Citizenship Act, 107, 231n18
Canadiens de Montréal (hockey team), 151
Cannes, France, 103
capitalism, 9–10, 25, 83, 85, 88, 116–17, 158, 165, 195, 213, 237n4
Catholicism, 6, 26, 28–30, 37, 45–46, 84, 89, 210, 230n16; caricatures of, 208; and catholaïcité, 40; symbols of, 30, 41, 210
Cattan, Olivia, 100
Chanteloup-les-Vignes, France, 98
Charest, Jean, 41
Charlie Hebdo, 29, 53–54, 57, 228n12, 229n5
Charter of Québec Values. *See* Bill 60
Charter of Rights and Freedoms, Canadian, 29, 31, 107, 121, 228n16, 231n18
chedda, 3, 83, 183–85, *185*
Chibanis, 126–27, 129, 232n10
Chirac, Jacques, 52, 224n22
Christianity, 26, 39–42, 52, 88–89, 117, 206, 226n2, 234n30, 236n20; symbols of, 41, 61–62, 199, Christians, 37, 80, 89, 179
churchstateness, 40, 198
circumcision, 38, 90, 92, 99, 113, 179
cisgender, 4, 11, 32, 90–92, 118, 167, 203–4, 212, 224n27
cishet, 4, 82, 89, 92, 99, 118, 144, 211, 214
citizenry, 10, 89, 134, 138, 212
citizenship, 9–10, 23, 35, 38–39, 53, 188, 212, 227n9, 230n11; access to, 82, 122, 137–38, 143, 232n12; ceremonies of, 107; exclusions from, 25–26, 134, 234n24; and marriage partner selection, 72–73, 96–97, 122, 132, 134–35, 144, 186; and mutual monitoring, 31; rights of, 26, 95
Civil Marriage Act (Canada), 144
Clément, Pascal, 134
Coalition Avenir Québec, 30–31, 59–60, 64, 105, 198–99, 200, 228n16
Collectif contre islamophobia en France, *48*, 56–57, 228nn12–14

colonialism, 4, 12, 21, 25–27, 37; agents of, 25; Canadian, 40, 61, 205–6, 236n21; civilizing mission of, 26; French, 26, 29, 122, 195, 204–7, 235n10; legacies of, 205–6; silences on, 61, 122, 195, 197
coloniality, 24–28, 31–32, 35, 42, 134, 146, 162, 165, 203–4, 221n3; of being, 32, 162, 200, 205; and gender, 235n6; in interpersonal relations, 121, 158–59; in legislation, 158–59; marriage migration and, 5, 80, 82–83, 88, 121, 125, 158, 161; of power, 11, 25, 158, 165, 201, 237n23
colonization, 12, 26, 52, 94, 163, 165, 197–98, 207, 224n22, 225n31; counter movements against, 133; impacts of, 18; projects of, 205; and research, 21
color-blindness, 7, 42, 60, 121, 198, 200, 205
communalism, 51, 106
comportment, social, 19, 29, 44, 58, 81, 96, 123, 135, 204, 207
Conseil d'État (France), *48*, 96–97, 230n10
Conseil du statut de la femme (Québec), 105
Conseil français du culte musulman, 53, 214
Conservative Party of Canada, 107, 122, 142, 144–45
consumerism, 80, 83, 203, 213, 215, 222n9, 237n6; and capitalism, 10; cultures of, 3–4, 9, 44, 118, 136, 203, 205, 215; and Modern Girl trope, 221n9
contact zones, 39, 74; civil marriages as, 4–5, 8–10, 76, 80–83, 108, 116–18, 129, 157, 201–3, 209, 215; and coloniality, 158; definition of, 80–81, 83
cosmetics, 8–10, 105, 180, 183, 213, 221nn8–9
Cour de cassation (France), 51, 98
couscous, 108–9, 175
COVID-19, 58, 60, 105, 222n12
Coviello, Peter, 42, 44
Criminal Code of Canada, 43, 144–45, 234n26
culture talk, 145
curfews, 87–88

D'Aoust, Anne-Marie, 135, 225n34
Darmanin, Gérald, 58

Dati, Rachida, 96
dating, 34, 65, 69, 110, 152–54, 158, 179, 187, 190–94; online, 150, 152, 179
Décennie noire, 18, 79, 113, 139–40, 147, 152, 166, 170, 190
de-Christianization, 91, 106, 226n2, 227n6
decolonization, 52, 86, 88–89, 129, 164–65; decoloniality, 164–65, 200–201, 235n6
Défense, La, France, 13–14, 115, 136–37, 182, 187
Delacroix, Eugène, 46, 85, 94, 102, 207
Deneuve, Catherine, 207
deportation, 7, 157, 233n15
desirability, 5, 8–10, 27, 61, 161, 174, 221n4; feminine, 100, 207; masculine, 38, 92, 154; of romance, 33, 212–13, 215; and secularity, 46, 51, 89, 114, 158, 204, 206–7; and sexuality, 38, 46, 76, 92, 100, 114
desire, 24–27, 31–33, 83–84, 92, 99, 122, 161, 163, 184, 235n2; desire-based research, 21–22, 24, 31, 204; for an imagined past, 154, 165–67, 171–72, 178, 187, 201–5, 233n20; and migration, 121, 190, 231n2; and race, 158; religious, 155
de Villepin, Dominique, 88
Díaz, Junot, 200–201, 237n23
difference, 24, 30, 33, 47, 60, 121–22, 161, 167, 198–99, 206, 221n5; sexual, 84–85, 90–92, 100, 205, 207, 214
discipline, 21, 38, 42, 53, 94, 212
discrimination, 21, 51, 66, 77–78, 98, 133, 156, 167, 221n5, 232n7; and police, 13, 54
dispositions, 36, 38–39, 44, 81
divorce, 8, 27, 40, 65, 72, 105, 148, 155–56, 177, 181, 221n7
djellaba, 8
dress codes, 9, 19, 209

ear piercing, 92–93
Echaquan, Joyce, 236n22
Eid, 65, 192
Eiffel Tower, 180–81
emotional intimacy, 4, 7–10, 39, 71, 80, 82–83, 115, 215, 222n10, 225n34
employment, 15, 70, 77, 123, 129–30, 133–34, 151, 168, 175, 231n2; and conspicuous religious symbols, 64, 162; employability, 87, 133, 162
engagement, 62, 66, 136–37, 147, 150, 167–69, 171, 173, 194
eroticism, 89, 221n9
ethnicity, 19–21, 34, 89, 133–34, 154, 191, 204–5, 224n20; erasure of, 209
ethnography, 2, 5, 11–12, 21–22, 24, 82, 119, 164, 207, 222n13; as colonialist, 21; comparative, 5, 17; ethnographic refusal, 21–24, 114. *See also* practice of research
European epistemologies. *See* Western epistemologies
Évian Accords, 86, 129
exclusion, 25, 29–30, 54, 60–61, 94, 97, 99, 134, 163, 197, 214

Facebook, 69, 71, 120, 149, 171
faces, 30, 46, 50, 53, 60–62, 197, 204, 206, 208, 212–14; accessibility of, 11, 93, 99–103, 105–7, 114. *See also* niqabs; veils
Fadil, Nadia, 38
family, 17, 20, 37, 70–71, 80–83, 89, 111, 128, 147–48, 160–63; arrangements of, 25, 72, 87, 112–14, 135, 138, 144, 174; family law, 31, 36, 40, 85; nuclear, 84, 86, 88, 160; reunification, 2–3, 7, 13–15, 47, 86, 120–23, 129–31, 133–34, 138–39, 141, 233n17
family book, 4, 7, 9
family-class immigrants, 145, 233n16
Fanon, Franz, 12, 54, 102, 134
Fassin, Éric, 92, 94
fatiha. *See* marriage: contracts
femininity, 9, 93, 99–100, 102, 105, 212, 214; as consumable, 221n9; ideals of, 8, 117, 207–9, 213, 221n9
feminism, 33, 51, 57, 89, 92, 95, 100–101, 117, 235n6
Fernando, Mayanthi, 91, 94, 221n6
financial intimacy, 7, 10, 23, 36, 39
foreignness, 2, 4, 38, 46, 64, 123, 145, 161, 177, 209
Foucault, Michel, 11, 25, 37, 43, 81, 84, 162, 225n31
France, 1–30, 40–47, 76–77, 105–6, 146, 155–57, 158–70, 189, 208, 210–15, 227n3, 227n9; Alsace-Moselle, 222n11; beaches in, 104; Bordeaux, 6;

citizenship in, 2-3, 7, 18, 72, 96-101, 130-35, 138, 230n11, 232n12; colonial history of, 20, 26, 89, 125, 163, 197; coloniality of, 31, 80-88, 121, 164, 176, 195-97, 200, 205-6; connections to Québec, 11, 17-18, 26; employment issues in, 119, 140; immigration system in, 6, 32, 122, 125-38; legislation in, 5-8, 23-27, 29-33, 35, 37-39, 48, 52, 57-58, 61-62, 71-75, 90-93, 94, 99, 104-5, 116-18, 157, 200, 203-7, 210-12; marriage narratives in, 108-11; as metropole, 7, 18; migration narratives about, 23, 27, 34-35, 63, 67, 70-73, 114-16, 119-21, 123-38, 156-60, 176-89, 201-2; overseas departments of, 7, 196; Rennes, 6; sexual revolution in, 89, 103, 130; terrorism in, 29, 54; Toulouse, 6. *See also names of French cities and regions*
Francophone world, 4, 16, 122, 124, 139, 146, 160, 168, 192
French Communist Party, 97, 133, 232n11
French Council of the Muslim Faith, 53, 214
French language, 29, 54, 68, 106, 108, 133, 147, 177, 229n1; colonial influence of, 109, 139-40, 183, 234n30; fluency in, 2, 10, 77, 108-9, 120, 124, 128, 132, 136, 180, 232n12; and marriage migration, 172, 175, 187, 209; rights, 89
French officials, 6, 8, 39, 115, 237n6; consular, 1, 3, 7, 10; interpretative power of, 9, 134, 144; marriage officiants, 7, 80, 116, 122, 125, 134-36, 215; questioning by, 93, 136-38
French Republicanism, 7, 51-53, 57-58, 99, 103-4, 121, 135, 207-8; values of, 46, 94, 200, 228n15, 232n12, 237n2
French Revolution, 28, 46, 102, 207
French Riviera, France, 46, 48, 103
Front national. *See* National Front (now National Rally)

Gatineau, QC, 64, 163
gender, 4-6, 93, 97, 121, 158, 160, 192, 201, 203, 205, 237n23; and curtailment of religious symbols, 10, 90, 92, 102, 117, 204; equality, 7, 11, 96, 145, 232n12; and immigration processes, 122, 135-36, 237n7; performances of, 5, 9, 106, 230n9; politics, 27, 96, 101, 118, 152, 181, 189-90, 215; and religious practices, 19; and secularism, 18, 74, 99, 102, 105, 224n27; and sexual deviancy, 85, 87; as structure of inequality, 11, 33, 117, 138, 214, 229n20, 235n6; and transnational relationships, 151, 168, 172, 178, 181, 202, 229n20
genocide, 50, 232n8
Gerin Commission, 30, 53, 114, 195, 197, 212, 230n11, 230n13; niqab depictions in, 99-100, 214; participants in, 95, 97
Ghazaouet, Algeria, 11, 27-28, 109, 181, 191, 209, 231n1, 232n6, 236n12, 236n14; weddings in, 114-16, 119-21, 179-85
Giscard d'Estaing, Valéry, 130
Global North, 120, 226n36
governance, 5, 40, 123, 193
governmentality, 37, 42, 72, 76, 84, 123, 162, 211, 225n31, 232n5
Grande Mosquée de Paris, 58, 93
grooms, 7, 115, 165, 178, 189, 191, 223n17, 225n29
Groupe islamique armé, 133
Guénif-Souilamas, Nacira, 164

Habchi, Sihem, 95, 100-101
habitus, 8, 19, 42, 67, 97, 121, 195, 207; as dispositions, 9, 39; and lived religion, 19, 53; and marriage migration, 117; as secular, 9, 38, 44, 81, 203-4
hair, 108, 147, 156, 191, 208, 221n8; *chignon de cou*, 8-9, 209; ponytail, 8, 136
halal: food, 1, 15-16, 28, 55, 109; marriage, 186, 194, 223n16, 233n13
happiness, 9, 65, 82, 115, 118, 143, 212-14
harems, 85-86
Harper, Stephen, 107, 142, 236n21
hate, 21, 31, 226nn41-42
headscarves, 51-54, 62, 87, 94, 98, 206-7, 210, 237n1; as colonial, 140; as conspicuous religious symbols, 8, 76, 79; as imposition, 52. *See also* bandanas; hijabs; niqabs
heritage, 38-39, 41, 61, 101-2, 210
Hérouxville, QC, 30
heteronormativity, 43, 85, 90, 118
heterosexuality, 4, 44, 46, 55, 93, 204-5, 212-13, 224n27

hijabs, 47, 80, 85, 93–95, 98, 109, 115, 168, 172, 179, 187; as conspicuous religious symbols, 51–52, 65–67, 93, 116, 148, 177–78, 193, 209–10, 226n41, 229n1; legislation about, 28, 35, 48–49, 67, 162, 223n13; and modesty, 19, 28, 191; reasons to wear, 50, 66, 181, 183, 210; restrictions on, 12, 24, 90, 162, 210–11; and sexual agency, 90, 229n4; and stigmatizing research, 24, 92; as threat to social cohesion, 52, 114, 227n10; women's perspectives on, 62–64, 79, 146, 155–56
Hoffman-Rispal, Danièle, 100
Hollande, François, 64
homonationalism, 11
homosexuality, 43, 84–86, 113, 130
honor killing, 144
Hutterites, 49, 50, 106

iftars, 128
Île-de-France, France, 53
imams, 135, 153, 188, 205, 222n13, 233n13
immigration, 18, 51–52, 117–19, 188–89, 235n4, 236n11; experiences of, 3–4, 19–20, 63, 77, 141, 163; laws, 3, 10–11, 23, 32, 35, 58, 125, 134, 143–45, 154; motivations for, 23, 109, 124, 134, 141, 146, 171, 175, 190; narratives of, 6–7, 10–11, 13, 110; policies, 47, 76, 86, 121–26, 133, 138–39, 145–46, 156–57, 205, 233n23; research on, 6; status, 23–24, 71–73, 83, 133, 139, 142, 151, 186, 216n1, 225n29; waves of, 20, 125–26, 130, 139–41, 156–57. *See also* marriage; marriage, arranged; marriage, civil; migration
Immigration and Refugee Protection Act (Canada), 142, 144
imperialism, 21, 43, 81, 86, 123, 158, 162–64, 224n26
Indian Act (Canada), 29, 199
Indigeneities, 140; and coloniality, 201; legislation for, 85; politics of, 20, 197–200; and religion, 236n19
Indigenous peoples, 26, 88–89, 140, 163, 198, 232n8, 236n22; sovereignty of, 40, 138, 161, 165–66, 199, 236n18; spiritualities of, 29, 236n20
individualism, 10–11, 20, 51, 72–73, 92, 203, 212, 215

integration, 24, 40, 60, 121–23, 135, 147, 225n31, 231n3, 232n12
interculturalism, 121, 197–98
intersectionality, 63, 200
invisibilization, 26, 40–41, 44–45, 200, 206, 210
Ishaq, Zunera, 49, 107, 231n18
Islam, 6, 53, 58, 71–75, 77, 223n13, 229n4, 230n9, 233n20, 236n20; conversion to, 20, 155, 222n13, 223n16, 230n11; radicalism in, 29, 56, 57, 97, 103, 228n15; reduction to symbols, 66–67, 94, 133; reversion to, 20, 34, 70, 160, 181; partner preferences and, 71, 154, 167, 172, 192; relationship with the Bled, 19, 165–66, 172; stereotypes of, 78, 208–9; stigmatization of, 27, 30; visibility of, 9, 29, 66, 106, 141, 209–12; and women, 40, 66–67, 91, 95, 97, 107
Islamism, 97, 139, 210
islamo-gauchisme, 57
Islamophobia, 13, 74, 79, 163, 209, 224n26, 226n42, 231n2; in France, 27, 31, 48, 56–57, 228n14, 229n7; as legislative impact, 67, 78, 141, 200, 228n12; in Québec, 31, 200

jewelry, 1, 3, 7, 44, 59–61, 115, 135–38, 183, 194, 213–14
Jewish peoples, 38, 61, 92, 179, 196, 207
Johnston, David, 142
Jolin-Barrette, Simon, 60–61, 198, 200
ju'muah, 29. *See also* prayer

Kabylia, 34, 70, 146–47, 170–72, 175–76, 178, 223n17, 234n30
Kabylians, 20–21, 70–71, 141, 148, 153–54, 175–76, 191, 201, 223n17, 233n20
kabylité, 20
kebab, 111, 116
Kenney, Jason, 107, 142–43, 231n18
kinship, 19, 27–28, 123, 158, 161, 164, 166, 225n35; and coloniality, 168, 172, 178, 181, 188–89, 200, 202, 204–5, 235n2

labor market, 138, 142, 225n33
laïcité, 24, 36, 42, 58, 63, 123–24, 135, 146, 196–99, 208, 228n17; and conspicuous religious symbols, 30, 59, 60–61, 98; legislation on, 5, 11, 28, 33, 35, 49, 83,

105; in public schools, 52; and women, 28-29, 33, 45-46, 73, 89, 91
Laneyrie-Dagan, Nadeije, 101-2
Larcher, Gérard, 87
Laval, QC, 17, 155, 162, 177
Law 21. *See* Bill 21 (Law 21)
law enforcement, 54-55, 74, 87-88, 145, 177, 199, 228n12; discrimination by, 12-14; home visits by, 135-38, 215, 233n22, 237n6; violence by, 196, 229n7
Legault, François, 31, 41, 61-62, 65, 78, 105, 228n16, 236n22
legibility, 5, 10-11, 45, 66, 74, 114, 204
Le Pen, Jean-Marie, 133
Lépinard, Éléonore, 11, 198, 200
Lesage, Jean, 89
Levanchy, Anne, 82-83, 229n2
liberalism, 4, 9, 25, 80, 115, 118, 122, 145, 189, 206; and democracy, 36, 43; as racialized, 43; and secularity, 36, 38, 41-43, 114, 130, 210; and sexuality, 114, 130, 215
Liberal Party of Canada, 59, 89, 105
Lille, France, *48*, 58, 94-96, 100
lipstick, 8-9, 209, 221n9. *See also* cosmetics
livret de famille, 4, 7, 9
love, 5, 10, 39, 202, 212-13, 221n4, 225n34, 231n2; decolonial, 163, 200-201; ethnicization of, 173; experiences of, 83, 109-10; imagined, 73, 120, 201; legislative narratives of, 72, 123; performances of, 115-16, 188; social narratives of, 72, 82, 114; vs. rationalism, 69, 75, 82
love fraud, 75, 115, 126, 138, 154, 157; as border transgression, 10, 134-36, 203, 212; as emotional transgression, 10, 135, 203, 212; with migratory aim, 4, 7, 72, 122, 125, 134, 188, 215, 237n7
Lyon, France, 97, 147, 222n13, 223n17

Macron, Emmanuel, 57, 224n22, 236n17
Maghnia, Algeria, 187-89
Maghrebians, 34, 100-101, 126, 129, 174, 191, 221n3, 222n13, 223n16, 224n19
Mahmood, Saba, 38-39, 44, 226n43
Maldonado-Torres, Nelson, 162, 165, 200
Marches Républicaines, 53-54

Marianne (French symbol), 46, 94, 102, *103*, 104, 117-18, 207-8, 213, 237n3
marking, 8, 92, 102, 118, 134, 137, 183, 213; religious, 66, 91, 136, 154, 206; romance, 83; secular, 9, 11; for sexual difference, 85, 232n5
marriage, 24-26, 209, 214, 221n7, 224n27, 225n30, 233n14, 237n4; bad faith, 7, 10, 122, 125, 142-46, 152, 154, 157, 178, 202-3, 211-12, 222n10; certificates of, 135, 155, 182, 188, 205, 233n13; contracts, 127, 155, 182, 233n13, 233n16, 233n20, 236n15; forced, 7, 22, 58, 76, 94, 134, 142, 144, 175, 202, 211-12, 221n4, 237n7; fraudulent (*gris*), 7, 23, 72, 116, 134-36, 142, 145, 152, 188, 202, 225n9, 229n2, 233n15, 237n7; gay, 84; as gendered, 122, 157; love, 2-3, 32, 69, 109, 120, 137, 174, 179, 193, 213; marriageability, 136, 152, 167, 180; migration, 1-6, 12, 24, 78, 120, 147, 150, 154, 165, 181; research on, 6, 12, 223n17, 225n33; partner preferences and, 3, 21-23, 27-28, 31-33, 71, 77, 152, 204-5, 235n7; proposals, 3-4, 176; religious, 153, 161, 172, 174, 186, 192, 194; transnational, 4, 6-7, 11, 22, 27-28, 32, 39, 73, 122, 135-36, 144-45, 151, 167, 205, 210, 222n10, 225n34, 234n25. *See also* marriage, arranged; marriage, civil
marriage, arranged, 2-4, 8, 22, 71, 73, 80, 193; and gender, 77-78, 146, 152-53, 201-2; as generationally transnational, 27-28, 65, 70, 114-15, 183-84, 209; and marriage migration, 136-37, 142, 144, 152-53, 157, 177-78, 202, 205, 214, 234n25; and tradition, 9, 72, 75, 152-53, 165, 168, 205, 209-10. *See also* marriage; marriage, civil
marriage, civil, 5-7, 33, 84, 110, 116, 204, 209, 212; as contact zone, 32, 39, 76, 80-83, 108, 117-18, 122, 129, 201, 203; evidence of, 135, 155, 188-89; as oppositional encounter, 201. *See also* marriage; marriage, arranged
masculinity, 38, 92, 99, 101, 133, 154, 229n5, 233n18
Mayotte, 196
méchoui, 127

media, 51, 79, 87, 92, 96, 213–14; newspapers, 85–86, 149; debates, 39, 195, 204, 227n10; social, 55, 83, 211, 236n13; television, 58, 61, 109, 143, 227n6
mektoub, 27–28, 115, 144, 150, 166, 187
Merabet, Ahmed, 228n12
Merzouk, Nahel, 229n7
methodology. *See* practice of research
Mitterrand, François, 133
mixed couples, 82–3, 89, 161, 192, 225n33
mixité, 102
Mme H., 95–96, 100
Mme M., *48*, 94, 96–98
modernity, 81, 93, 96, 113, 161, 182, 213, 222n9, 237n4; and coloniality, 158, 162, 165, 235n6; and partner preference, 110, 177, 186; and romance, 115, 237n6; in relation to religion, 35–36, 38–39, 41, 73, 91
monogamy, 23, 37, 42–43, 82, 84, 203, 213; relationships in, 10, 25, 33, 75, 85, 87–89, 135, 145, 224n27, 237n4
Monsieur C., 95
Montréal, QC, 2, *18*, 23, 30–31, 35, 41, 61–67, 89, 106, 108, 112–13, 116, 119–24, 139–41, 146–57, 158–63, 188–95, 201–2, 205, 209–11; Ahuntsic, 17, 190; Cartierville, 17, 62, 162; Côte-des-Neiges, 140, 159; demographics of, 233n21; Hochelaga, 192; Mount Royal, 65; neighborhoods in, 11, 16–17, 77, 159, 166; Notre-Dame-de-Grâce, 159; Petit Maghreb, 16–17, 113, 174, 224n19; Plateau-Mont-Royal, 21, 235n1; Saint-Léonard, 16–17, 66; Snowdon, 152, 159; Vieux Montréal, 152; Villeray–Saint-Michel–Parc-Extension, 16
mores, 74, 82, 94, 117, 126, 209, 235n3
Mormonism, 42, 234n26; Mormons, 42–43
Morocco, 2, 88, 125, 131, 181; Moroccans, 38, 96, 224n25
mosques, 15–16, 19
Mouvement de libération des femmes, 47
Mouvement laïque, *49*, 228n17
multiculturalism, 29, 107, 121, 142, 198, 224n20
Multiculturalism Act (Canada), 29, 121
Muslims, 8–12, 38, 47, 55–58, 60, 62–66, 79, 85, 93, 191, 122, 222n13, 225n31, 228n12, 230n8, 231n17, 238n12; bodies of, 21, 30, 74, 92; nonpracticing, 19–20, 28, 34, 43, 78, 154, 165, 167, 174, 177, 210, 223n16; practicing, 15–20, 34, 43–45, 72, 80, 91–95, 107–10, 141, 150, 156, 168, 172–73, 176; sexuality of, 88, 91, 100

Nancy, France, 99, 214
National Front (now National Rally), 102, 104, *104*, 133, 208
neutrality critique, 21, 31, 33, 35–37, 40, 42, 58, 78, 91, 226n43; and dress codes, 98–99, 105, 230n13; of secularity, 44, 158, 198, 200, 204, 206, 215
newcomers, 11, 29, 63, 91, 106, 116, 162, 198, 229n1, 232n7
Nice, France, 29, 103, 230n16
nikah, 165, 188
Ni Putes ni Soumises, 95, 100–101
niqabs, 19, 47, 53, 80, 90, 94, 101, 230n11; as anti-romance, 213; as imposed, 97, 100, 135, 214; legislation about, 10, 29–30, 37, 50, 97, 99, 106–8, 117, 211; perspectives of women on, 96–97, 117; protections for, *49*, 231n18; restrictions on, 28–30, 35, 50, 97, 99, 106, 114, 117, 146, 208, 210; and sexuality, 99–100, 102, 208; as site of collusion, 201; as site of opposition, 96, 201, 237n3; as symbol of coloniality, 201
normativity, 5–6, 11, 25–26, 32, 203–5, 213, 215
North Africa, 16, 27, 235n9
North Africans, 1, 12, 16, 85–86, 100, 129–30, 133–34, 170, 221n3, 224n25, 230n15
North Atlantic region, 26, 40, 89–90, 203, 210, 213; as transatlantic, 5, 58, 144

Okba Mosque, France, 15–16
Ontario Superior Court of Justice, *49*
Oran, Algeria, 2–3, 7, 10, 110–11, 115, 119–21, 169, 209
Orientalism, 1, 8, 85, 92, 156, 191, 194–95, 221n3
Ottawa, ON, 64–65, 113, 146, 163

Paris, France, 34, 46, 133, 147, 169, 188, 197, 227n9, 236n11; arrondissements, 55, 100, 102, 170, 177, 208; Latin Quarter, 207; massacre in, 196; Montmartre, 69;

suburbs of, 1–3, 7, 11–13, 15–16, 27, 34, 51, 71, 112, 166, 177, 182, 223n16; terrorist attacks in, 29, 53, 231n16; transportation system in, 12–14, 55, 68, 71, 74, 93, 131–32; vs. Montréal, 16, 190, 222n13; vs. periphery, 12, 54

Parole de femmes, 100

Parti Québécois, 58–59, 78, 105–6, 206, 237n1

passing, 9, 93, 147, 211, 223n14

patriarchy, 22–23, 33, 99, 117–18, 159–60, 168, 203, 205, 214–15; gaze of, 37, 96, 237n3; relation to Islam, 54, 58, 74, 92, 94, 105; relation to secularism, 42–43, 46, 53

Paty, Samuel, 29, 56–57, 228n13

Penchard, Marie-Luce, 196

permanent residency, 17, 112, 159, 171, 174; in marriage migration, 63–64, 77–78, 116, 119, 136, 143, 150–51, 178, 189–90, 222n10, 233n22

Petit-Nanterre, France, 11–19, *15*, 155, 208, 210, 227n9, 232n11, 235n4; Canibouts section of, 34, *68*, 78; as *ceinture rouge*, 133; connections to Algeria, 156, 160, 166–67, 169, 172, 175, 201, 205, 223n17, 235n9; curfews in, 87–88; demographics of, 13–16, 224n20, 229n19; disenfranchisement of, 13, 15; history of, 62–63, 70, 76, 125, 196–97; homogeneity of, 15, 19, 161, 223n18, 232n4; geography of, 23, 27; migration narratives about, 70–72, 108–11, 120–22, 126–34, 136–38, 147–49, 151, 175–78, 182–84, 186–88, 191; as periphery, 12–13, 54; riots in, 14, 54, 87–88, 229n7

Plan Vigipirate, 54–55, 208

pleasure, 9, 38, 92, 101, 115–16, 118, 213, 215

politics, 13, 116, 172, 191, 200; of care, 22; colonial, 6, 21, 167, 197, 199; language, 29; racial, 5, 21; of research, 21–22; secular, 5, 10–11, 43, 50, 74, 92, 99, 122, 199, 222n11; sexual, 25, 29–32, 43, 46, 74, 80–81, 94–100, 122, 209, 214

polygamy, 42–43, 46, 50, 74, 85, 122, 221, 229n6, 234n26; relationships in, 25, 58, 88–89, 142, 145

popular culture, 27, 32, 82–83, 85–86, 212–13

postcolonialism, 21, 86, 89, 130, 164

postmigration, 12, 20, 63, 133, 141, 151, 160, 170, 179

poverty, 12, 15, 63, 163

practice of research, 2, 11, 16–17, 20–23, 96; as colonial, 12, 20–21; connective comparison in, 11, 17, 204–5; fieldwork in, 6, 11, 16–17, 22, 55, 67, 69, 224n21, 231n20 (chap. 2), 231n2 (chap. 3); and lived experiences, 6, 9–10, 16, 26, 119, 174; and object of observation/study, 6, 22; shadow approach in, 6, 69; as stigmatizing, 23–24

Pratt, Mary Louise, 81

prayer, 1, 28–29, 34, *49*, 175–76

privacy, 6, 159, 161, 201, 205–6; of marriage, 25, 40; of religion, 36, 40, 43, 66–67, 74, 90–91, 97, 193; of sexuality, 29, 43, *48*, 74, 90–91, 94–95, 97–98

private sphere, 37, *48*, 55, 95, 98, 118, 121, 168, 211, 230n12; as gendered, 32, 46; as imagined by secularism, 25, 32, 67, 90–91, 206–7

privatization, 8, 60–61, 207

problem spaces, 36, 45, 74

Prophet Muhammed, 57

propriety, 5, 8, 31–32, 78, 105, 111, 183, 205, 207; family, 84, 87; religious, 26; romantic, 83, 215; sexual, 29, 84, 94, 99, 138, 213; social, 25–26, 114, 192

Protestantism, 47, 72, 138, 155

public debates, 18, 28–29, 38, 46, 86, 90, 92, 113, 140, 226n41, 227n10; about accommodations, 66, 146, 195, 206; impacts of, 31, 81, 84, 156; legislative, 30, 39, 41, 58–60, 64, 79, 117, 204, 206–7; on religious symbols, 30, 62, 94, 104, 146, 156, 207, 209, 227n6

public housing. *See* social housing

public schools, 12, 14, 28, 31, 46, 95–96, 139–40, 150, 227n9, 228n11, 230n13, 237n1; restrictions in, 29, 47–50, 67, 94, 99, 195, 210–12; symbols in, 46, 50–54, 99, 208; teachers in, 29–30, 163, 196, 199, 224n22, 228n16

public sphere, 4–5, 50, 53–54, 67, 199, 206, 208, 211, 227n4, 227n6, 237n1; religion in, 29, 33, 43, 80, 97, 106, 114, 141, 168, 195

pure laine, 154

purity, 82, 110, 134, 165

qamis, 90
Québec (province), 2, 4, 10–11, 16, 200, 203; coloniality of, 121, 123, 138, 197–200, 202; comparisons with France, 17, 74–77, 80–81, 117–18, 121–22, 203–8, 210–15; cultural connections to France, 83–84, 123; distinctiveness of, 198; history of, 89–90; immigration policies in, 119, 121, 123; legislation in, 5, 7–8, 73, 78, 105, 117–18, 166, 212; migration narratives about, 123–25, 139, 146–64, 167–69, 171–74, 189–96; migratory circuits to, 17–18, 120, 138–41, 180–81, 189; professional opportunities in, 17, 77
Québec City, QC, 41, 61
Québec Court of Appeal, *48*
Quebeckers, 11, 22, 42, 45, 60–61, 65, 77–78, 146, 156, 158, 160, 173, 179, 193, 206, 223n16, 229n18; and laïcité, 29, 30, 37, 66
Québec National Assembly, 41, 61–62, 100, 227n6
Québécois(e)s. *See* Quebeckers
queer rights, 84, 91
Quiet Revolution, 30, 89, 195, 227n6
Quijano, Aníbal, 11, 165, 237n23
Qur'an, 85

race, 11, 61, 120–21, 161, 163, 200, 225n31, 229n2, 230n9; and nation-building, 90, 203, 205–6, 235n6; as proper, 5, 19, 21, 158, 203, 205–7, 209; and secular sensibilities, 35, 37, 41–42, 45, 74, 91, 116, 206, 209
racialization, 26, 42–43, 54, 60, 72, 85, 163, 224n26, 226n1; and employment, 12, 64, 133, 232n7; and gender, 12–14, 32, 35, 66, 70, 80, 204, 208–9, 214, 229n1; and marriage migration, 4–6, 33–35, 37, 82–83, 122, 143–45, 152, 167, 178, 206, 223n14, 232n5; and religion, 9–11, 20–21, 46, 50, 63, 74, 78–80, 87–88, 90, 98
racial profiling, 12–13
racial purity, 82, 154
racism, 22, 82, 86, 123, 138, 156, 198, 206, 226n40, 232n5; anti-Indigenous, 236n22; anti-Muslim, 12, 31, 56, 74, 163, 200, 202, 224n26, 231n2

radicalism, 29, 57, 96–97, 228n15, 231n16; radicalization, 55–56
Ramadan, 19, 34, 65, 127–28, 155, 172, 176
rationalism, 11, 37, 44, 46, 69, 73, 75, 92, 95, 204
reconciliation, 49, 198–200, 224n22, 236n19
refugees, 18, 124, 139, 141–42, 153, 159, 166, 192–94, 201, 210, 233n17
relationships, 23, 26, 31, 33, 38, 75, 128, 131, 161, 183; and coloniality, 158, 162–64, 195; common-law, 32, 152, 154–55, 192, 201, 223n16, 235n4, 236n16; evidence of, 3–4, 7, 76, 135, 137, 229n1; genesis of, 7, 150, 157, 173; as genuine, 122, 142–43, 145, 237n6; as halal, 193–94; as intimate, 4, 34, 203, 212; mixed, 89, 155–56, 192–93; normative, 113, 116, 158; as traditional, 160, 205, 210
religion, 5, 25, 37, 43, 167, 173, 179, 192, 198–99, 200, 215, 236n20; as bad, 39–40, 52, 62, 66, 195, 206; freedom of, 31, 36, 53, 228n16; as lived, 19, 193, 204, 224n24; regulation of, 29–30, 32, 36, 40, 93, 146, 196, 205–6, 210, 226n43, 227n6; as symbols, 61, 196, 207, 210–11, 230n9. *See also names of specific religions*
religionization, 4–6, 74, 90–91, 117, 145, 232n7; of men, 9, 85, 93; of women, 9, 32, 35, 80, 85, 98, 204, 208, 229n1
religiosity, 19, 46, 60, 69, 74, 90–91, 140, 156, 194, 222n13; acceptable expressions of, 5, 32, 98, 105–16, 205–6; normative, 5–6; partner preferences and, 71, 152, 155, 178, 181; privatization of, 8, 36, 66, 193, 198; unacceptable expressions of, 53, 65, 78, 94, 96–97, 117, 146, 152, 211, 237n1
religious bodies, 5, 10, 30, 55, 92, 136, 206, 208, 211
religious diversity, 6, 36, 121, 133
religious freedom, 11, 29, 59, 93, 98, 106–7, 228n18, 231n18
religious symbols, 5, 7–10, 20, 24, 60, 61, 130, 200, 228n12, 229n18; as acceptable, 39, 67, 78, 90, 156, 237n1; as antiliberal, 74; as antiwoman, 53, 212; as conspicuous, 24–25, 29–30, 35, 39, 45, 47, 50–52, 58–59, 59, 78, 93–95, 98,

195, 204, 228n18; as detachable, 207, 228n18; as gauges of integration, 24, 78; as heritage, 39, 41, 62; as inconspicuous, 25, 62; meanings of, 51, 53, 67; as patriarchal and political, 53; as polygamous, 74; as privatizable, 61, 207; as proselytizing, 39; protections for, 62; and secularization, 41, 105–6, 205; state regulation of, 28, 31–33, 35, 60–63, 78, 80, 87, 92, 94, 98, 105, 117, 140–41, 146, 195–97, 205–7, 211–12, 222n11, 228n11, 230n13, 237n1; as stigmatized, 27, 66, 117; visual assessment of, 5, 50, 53, 62, 66, 102, 106

remittances, 125–26, 128–29, 133, 151, 180, 182

retirement, 126, 129, 152, 169, 177

romance, 69, 71, 75, 111, 116, 118, 202–3, 205, 214; in entertainment, 82, 109–10, 214; expressions of, 4, 7, 33, 73, 116, 188, 213; narratives of, 108–10, 127, 174; performances of, 10, 83, 115, 138, 144, 215, 222n10, 237n5; as secular, 73, 80–81, 112–13, 203, 212–13; surveillance of, 4, 6, 10, 33, 83, 135, 138, 144, 203, 212, 225n34, 237n6; visibility of, 82, 135, 188, 209

Rossignol, Laurence, 47

Rossinot, André, 99–100, 214

Roxham Road, QC, 139

Royal Canadian Mounted Police, 145

sans papiers, 122. *See also* undocumented persons

Sarkozy, Nicolas, 54–55, 97, 104

Sayad, Abdelmalek, 13

Scott, Joan Wallach, 73, 91–92, 99, 214–15, 226n43, 229n4

secular bodies, 9, 50, 62, 81, 106–7, 203–4, 206; as acceptable, 11, 32, 39, 207; colonial, 26; as desirable, 5, 206–7, 209; as emancipated, 5, 10; expectations of, 55, 73; gendered, 92–94, 99, 101, 207; as idealized, 26, 29, 39, 47, 55, 65, 67, 80, 204, 215, 222n9; legibility of, 66, 83; as normative, 31, 35, 44–45, 72, 102; specters of, 120; symbols of, 46, 51, 201. *See also* faces

secular episteme, 19, 25, 36–37, 203

secularism, 4–7, 19, 38, 45, 227n4; and affective forces, 5, 27, 202–4; American, 42–43, 65; and body, 25, 37, 39, 203; as boundary-maker, 82; Canadian, 29, 40, 106–8; as civilizing, 145, 196; definitions of, 24–25, 32, 39, 44; discourses of, 32, 36, 116, 203, 210; dispositions of, 9, 36, 38, 44, 81; French, 27–29, 32, 40, 47, 50–57, 73–75, 80–88, 92–104, 158–59, 195–97, 227n9; and gender, 7, 25, 73, 91, 207, 215, 232n12; as grammar, 37, 82; immigration system and, 123–46, 158–59; as impartial, 40–41, 58, 78; legibility of, 11, 204; as liberatory, 33, 36, 215, 227n9; as lived, 19, 39, 203; as narrative, 38–39; as neutral, 31, 33, 35–37, 40, 42, 44, 91, 98–99, 105, 158, 198, 200, 204, 206, 215, 230n13; politics of, 11, 210; plurality of, 33, 35, 39, 227n3; Québécois, 32, 40, 47, 59–67, 76–80, 83, 88–92, 105–6, 158–59, 195, 197–200, 230n8; and race, 7, 42–44, 88–89, 215; and sexuality, 25, 37, 74; state, 10–11, 30–33, 35–38, 203, 223n13, 228n15; and white settler logics, 26, 195. *See also* secular sensibilities

Secularism Observatory, 48, 56

secular romance, 73, 113, 138, 203, 212

secular sensibilities, 11, 47, 50–51, 94, 98, 123, 204, 224n27, 225n32, 237n2; as colonial, 26, 32; definition of, 4–5, 32, 38–43, 206; dependence on binaries, 25; embodiment of, 4, 8–9, 35, 38–39, 61, 73, 102, 105, 117–18; as experiences, 5, 22, 31, 35, 69, 74, 76, 80, 209; and gender, 10, 32, 116; and habitus, 9, 81, 121; and marriage rituals, 22, 24, 35, 39, 76, 120; in public sphere, 4, 8–9, 33, 44, 67, 72, 81; and race, 21, 116; in relationships, 5, 22, 73, 76; and romance, 4, 9, 33, 39, 69, 80, 112, 135, 157, 202–3, 212; transmission of, 6, 9, 31, 62, 83, 98, 104, 116–18, 140, 207–10

seduction, 4, 99, 101, 214–15

separation, 137–38, 151, 160, 234n27, 234n29. *See also* divorce

settlement, 2, 4, 9–10, 12–13, 15, 20, 70, 130, 139–40, 173; Algerian patterns of, 129, 133, 141, 163, 168, 190, 194, 201, 226n1, 233n17, 233n21; in Canada, 63–65, 77, 106, 163, 231n3; in France, 108, 125, 129, 131, 148, 163

settler colonialism, 24–26, 42, 85, 88–89, 161–64, 168, 195, 198–99
settlers, 88, 161–63, 168, 198
sexual consent, 11, 80, 93, 203, 212
sexual democracy, 94, 211
sexual deviancy, 82, 85–87, 129, 209
sexual ethics, 76, 84–85, 97, 100, 114
sexual excess, 46, 154
sexual harassment, 86, 130
sexual intimacy, 3, 7–10, 23, 43, 80–81, 115, 136, 138, 215, 222n10; surveillance of, 4, 74, 76, 79, 91, 121, 123
sexuality, 21–29, 46, 80, 101, 117–18, 122, 130, 152, 207–8, 229n20, 230n9; Muslim, 21, 26–27, 38, 58, 62, 86, 91, 145; proper, 5, 9–10, 32, 37, 84–92, 99, 204, 213–14, 221n8, 237n4; religious, 73–74, 76; and repression, 91, 212; secular, 32, 35, 38, 83, 108, 120–21
sexualization, 46, 85–86, 92, 101–2, 212, 230n9, 237n3; and sexual availability, 89, 99, 204, 208
sexual liberation, 73, 103, 135, 208; of women, 28, 33, 44, 92, 99, 118, 211, 229n4
shantytowns, 13, 15, 34, 70, 86, 88, 125, 130, 186
Shepard, Todd, 84, 86, 89, 129, 164
Sikhism, 144, 228n17, 229n18
Simpson, Leanne Betasamosake, 163, 200
Skirt Day, 100–101
skirts, 29, 100–101, 210
Skype, 2, 149, 172, 179
slavery, 52, 196
social class, 8, 9, 19–21, 33, 61, 132, 222n10, 232n4; middle, 2, 100, 182, 189, 193; privileges of, 10, 232n4; as structure of inequality, 117, 120, 122, 129, 154, 167, 193, 198, 207, 213
social housing, 14–15, 34, 70, 88, 108, 115, 127, 132, 147, 186, 221n2, 223n18; conditions in, 13–16, 161
Socialists, 100, 103–4
social mobility, 27, 120, 161, 205
sponsorship, 120, 123, 145, 152, 154, 191, 223n14, 235n10; by men, 31, 72, 78, 115, 129–30, 143, 146, 168, 171–74, 178, 186, 188, 209–10; by women, 3, 23, 119, 161, 167, 181, 189, 201, 213, 222n10

Stasi Commission, 30, 52, 58, 94, 97, 100–101, 195–97, 207
state of emergency, 54–56, 208, 231n16
Stora, Benjamin, 197, 224n22, 236n17
Strasbourg, France, 126–29
Superior Court of Quebec, 49
Supreme Court of Canada, 49, 50, 106–7, 228nn17–18
Sunni, 15, 107
Surkis, Judith, 84–85, 202
surveillance, 9, 13–14, 21–25, 202–3, 205, 209–12; of marriage, 6, 23, 27–28, 33, 43, 71, 83, 104, 116, 122–26, 135; by the state, 47, 53, 57, 74–76, 83–84, 98, 135–37, 153–57; of women, 4, 29, 96, 98, 151, 159
suspicion, 8, 12, 36, 45, 74, 112, 135, 137, 143, 186, 215; of traditionalism, 138, 156; of transnational marriages, 71, 82, 145–46
swimming, 55, 112, 209

talaq, 40. *See also* divorce
Tamazight (Amazigh language), 19, 154, 175, 234n30
tattoos, 61, 207
Taubira Law, 196
tcherek m'saker, 180
temporary foreign workers, 126, 133
terra nullius, 195
terrorism, 29–30, 50, 54–55, 57, 86, 124, 139–40, 208, 231n16
theology, 42–43, 144, 214
Tizi Ouzou, Algeria, 11, 146–48, 150–51, 176, 223n17, 232n6, 234n28, 234nn31–32
Tlemcen, Algeria, 2–3, 179, 182, 190–92, 221n4
transnational bridging, 24, 28, 182, 191, 201
transnationalism, 28, 35, 166
transnational migration, 3, 6, 17, 32, 161, 204, 211
Traoré, Bouana, 87
tropes, 80, 87, 92, 165, 208; colonial, 8, 145, 236n20; Modern Girl, 221n9; romance, 9, 82, 110, 112, 114, 116, 203
Trouillot, Michel-Rolph, 6, 22, 221n6, 224n27
Trudeau, Justin, 145
Trudeau, Pierre Elliott, 43

Truth and Reconciliation Commission of Canada, 40, 49, 198–200, 236n19
Tuck, Eve, 21–22, 24, 165, 204
Tunisia, 125; Tunisians, 66, 161

underemployment, 64, 70, 77, 112–13, 124, 147, 166, 179, 189, 232n7
undocumented persons, 23, 122, 225n28
unemployment, 12–13, 15, 70, 87, 133, 140, 166, 232n7
Union pour un mouvement populaire, 87
United Kingdom, 44, 135, 221n4
United States, 39, 41–42, 112, 139, 212, 221n4, 235n4
unmarking, 26, 32, 40, 42

vacation, 70, 109, 147, 151–52, 159, 168–69, 170, 186
Valls, Manuel, 46, 54, 57, 103–4
values, 9, 80, 130, 166–67, 172, 195; Canadian, 145; French, 31, 46, 82, 94–95, 145, 198, 200, 228n15, 232n12; normative, 123, 203; Québec, 30–31, 46, 51, 58–59, 62, 78–79, 96, 98, 116, 222n11, 226n38, 237n1; and secular sensibilities, 5, 30, 36, 212, 215; and shared identity, 71, 73, 82, 113, 153–54
veils, 4, 38, 46, 66, 76, 79, 140, 196, 206; full-face, 60, 78, 117, 156–57, 195, 197, 206, 213; and femininity, 8, 62; as support to patriarchy, 53, 94–95, 99, 102, 104; as unacceptable, 10, 29–30, 86, 114, 214
violence, 14, 73, 78, 124, 132, 139, 152, 159, 166, 170, 190–91; colonial, 18, 26–27, 29, 86, 125, 165, 200–201, 205; extremist, 53, 55, 57, 60, 231n16; gender-based, 22–23, 50, 144–45, 175, 229n1, 230n15; legislative, 60, 63, 215; potential, 100, 145; religiously framed, 29, 38, 93, 100, 113, 140; sexual, 22, 26–27, 46, 85–86, 95, 97, 130, 134; systemic, 21–22, 33, 88, 156, 165, 206

virginity, 22, 70, 72, 94–95, 100–101, 110, 114, 207, 209, 229n20; certificates, 23, 58, 62, 74, 90, 96, 122, 186, 211–12
visas, 110, 128, 139, 235n4; interpretation of, 144; restrictions on, 169; student, 128, 188–89; tourist, 114, 128, 150, 190, 231n21, 234n28; visitor, 110–11
visual accessibility, 33, 44, 61, 95, 99–100, 114, 212
visual assessment, 5, 11, 66, 206–7
visual field, 207–9
visual materials, 5, 102, 206–9
vivre ensemble, 42, 51, 102, 206

wedding industry, 1, 9, 83, 183, 194, 203, 205, 213, 231n3
weddings, 1–3, 9, 123, 136–38, 144, 154, 164, 176, 192; in Algeria, 28, 111, 114–16, 119–20, 127, 131–32, *132*, 147–49, 167–69, 180–85, *184*, *185*, 232n13, 236n14; in Canada, 161, 169, 191, 222n10, 229n3, 232n13; civil, 6–7, 23, 80, 111, 116, 169, 188–89, 213–14; in France, 6–7, 23, 111, 135, 169, 187–88, 225n29, 229n3, 232n13; religious, 65, 188, 232n13; as rituals, 111, 116, 118, 153, 169–70, 195, 200–201, 203, 213–14; romance of, 116, 136, 205, 209, 214, 237n6; as state-sanctioned, 73, 83, 173; as traditional, 65, 131, 153, 173, 193, 233n20; transnational, 27–28, 150, 168, 183–84, 188, 202–3, 210, 223n17
Weshrak (website), 152
Western epistemologies, 25, 101, 130, 158, 165, 226n2
whiteness, 8, 11–12, 26, 32, 37, 40–42, 83, 89, 138, 187, 222n10
white supremacy, 31, 85, 226n40

xenophobia, 163, 198, 200

Yang, K. Wayne, 24, 165, 204
youth, 22, 69–70, 77, 91, 119, 138, 169, 175, 223n16, 229n19, 235n7; relations with authorities, 12–14, 54, 87

Zero Tolerance for Barbaric Cultural Practices Act. *See* Bill S-7

www.ingramcontent.com/pod-product-compliance
Lightning Source LLC
Chambersburg PA
CBHW020640230426

43665CB00008B/257